D1527988

THE UNREASONABLE SILENCE OF THE WORLD

The Unreasonable Silence of the World

Universal Reason and the Wreck of the Enlightenment Project

GARY SAUER-THOMPSON
Department of Philosophy
Flinders University South Australia

JOSEPH WAYNE SMITH
Department of Geography
The University of Adelaide

Ashgate

Aldershot • Brookfield USA • Singapore • Sydney

Published by
Ashgate Publishing Limited
Gower House
Croft Road
Aldershot
Hants GU11 3HR
Emgland

Ashgate Publishing Company
Old Post Road
Brookfield
Vermont 05036
USA

British Library Cataloguing in Publication Data

Sauer-Thompson, Gary
    The unreasonable silence of the world : universal reason
    and the wreck of the enlightenment project. - (Avebury
    series in philosophy)
    1. Reason
    I. Title II. Smith, Joseph Wayne, 1958-
    149.2

Library of Congress Catalog Card Number: 97-73876

ISBN 1 85972 580 5

Printed and bound by Athenaeum Press, Ltd.,
Gateshead, Tyne & Wear.

Contents

Acknowledgments

Our intellectual debts for this book have their roots in the hard-headed scientific Marxist culture of the 1970s and 1980s at Flinders University of South Australia, where we were both disciplined into the analytic style of working in the tough, rigorous philosophical manner. We have recoiled from the style of the analytic tradition, which a masculist Marxist culture defended as *the* way of working philosophically in a disenchanted universe. But we retain our passionate and strong convictions about justice, the injustice of inequality, and the oppressiveness of capitalist exploitation. We remain committed to historical materialism as a way of analyzing how the social order works, even as we reject its cavalier attitude to moral and political philosophy. We have recoiled from the ahistorical analytic tradition of abstract philosophical reflection about timeless entities, but we retain the anachronistic view that philosophy should be at the cutting edge of a radical culture helping to bring about a better future. We have recoiled from the failure of analytic philosophers to engage with economic rationalism; and from the failure of Marxists to realize that eventual equality through the development of productive forces transforming nature into use-value has run up against ecological limits. So our deepest thanks to the local Adelaide philosophical scene that "nurtured" us by teaching us how not to do philosophy in the 1990s. Philosophy has missed its cue to critically preserve the heritage of the radical Enlightenment in the dark times, and to confront the new cultural formation of *laissez-faire* economics, moral conservatism, and authoritarian populism. This is known in Australia as Howardism, but it looks remarkably like recycled Thatcherism, overlaid with American conservative concerns about the political correctness of the left.

The text was written without any financial support in the way of grants from either Flinders or Adelaide Universities—who receives ts grants for a critique of analytic philosophy these days? It was written in isolation from the challenging, incisive comments and searching Platonic dialogues that philosophers say they have with their colleagues. Instead of this Socratic spirit, we found that few were interested in helping with a project that critiques the Enlightenment tradition. Many were hostile to our thesis of the self-destructiveness of the Enlightenment tradition, or the need to rethink this tradition. Given the current hegemony of technocratic discourse in the decadent liberal university, non-conformism is penalized in the liberal university, which still sees itself as an autonomous sphere, where a self-enclosed community of scholars dispassionately work to realize the higher values of truth and justice. Illusions die hard in academe.

The "new" deal in academia is a quick comment in the corridor about the new book that has just been read, then a return to the deep shadows of a decaying intellectual culture, with its crude logic of friends and foes. Philosophers are being ground under by increasing their teaching loads to bring in the student numbers, so as to avoid being retrenched. The subject has gone bust. The future for research work does not look good, as the universities are currently downsizing their contract staff, proleterianizing academic labour, closing down research options, and laying off tenured staff. We face an uncertain future of short-term research contracts, ever-reduced piecemeal rates for teaching, and a growing divide between those who teach and those who do research. The centralization of research in the key research centres, which are being designed to fit the needs of corporate capitalism, represents a narrowing of research topics to those that will revitalize an export-orientated capitalism. Such is the way of economic Enlightenment at the end of history.

Gary would like to thank Trevor Maddock for his continual support for a melancholy philosophy that speaks against its own tradition. He realized that philosophy's deep silence about the depth and breadth of human suffering is the real scandal of philosophy. He saw that philosophy had stopped asking searching questions about the quality of life, and that it is progress in the development of an analytical philosophical culture, which is undermining philosophy as critical thinking. The initial impetus for this work came from his insights which showed that an education in philosophy is the transmission of tradition and that the crisis in education today is a conflict between technocratic and critical modes of thought. Thanks also to Ros Diprose. Her teaching sojourn in Adelaide, her work on Nietzsche and embodiment, and her willingness to share her views openly and engage in dialogue shaped the ideas in this book. These individuals are not responsible for the views and opinions expressed in this work.

It is our friends and families who provided the valuable encouragement, support and understanding that is needed to sustain left-orientated research work in these dark times. Gary would like to thank his friend Suzanne for her care, love and support, which kept him human in difficult times, and for her willingness to bankroll the project when the funds ran dry. This support was generously given whilst her mother Marjory was dying from cancer. In understanding the lived contradiction between philosophy and the everyday, she has been a precious and caring friend. Thanks to her sister Barbara and husband Malcolm. In spite of their wariness of the critical edge of a disembodied, onesided philosophical reason they accepted and understood the need to stealprecious family time to sit at a computer over Xmas in 1996. That is deeply appreciated. Deep gratitude to Marjory for providing space in her house down at Victor Harbour during Xmas of 1996, when the first rough draft was cut; and for the space during 1997. Her friendship, tolerance and acceptance of the strange, stoic habits of unemployed philosophers is sorely missed. Her gracious support and firm encouragement for philosophy to speak critically as part of an eco-cultural politics of a bad present is deeply remembered. Her suffering and dying from throat cancer during early 1997 highlighted the vast gap that exists between contemporary philosophy's indifference to the everyday world, and the intense human suffering in the world. She was firmly of the view that philosophers should reject the turn to the rarefied mountain tops of the ivory tower, in response to the technocratic reforming of higher education that reduces philosophy to technical concerns and depoliticized intellectual work. She supported philosophy, living amidst the common affairs of everyday life, critically talking about the issues that deeply concern ordinary people. She held that philosophy should do something to help resolve the ecological crisis that we are caught up within. Her death is deeply mourned. Her loss is sorrowfully remembered.

Gary thanks Suzanne and Barbara for providing the Victor Harbour house to rework the draft manuscript during the autumn and winter of 1997. He is very grateful to Fichte, for the breaks from the intellectual grind to take the necessary walks in the morning and evening. We both would like to thank Karen Gordon for laying out the manuscript at short notice over Easter, just prior to her holidays in New Zealand. We are forever indebted to Sally Fraser for her excellent editing of a very rough and ready manuscript in quick time. We both thank Roger Porter for his sterling, detailed proof-reading work. Joseph would like to thank Claire Smith. He acknowledges the assistance from the Australian Research Council for a Senior Fellowship at the University of Adelaide.

The book is dedicated to all those concerned human beings like Marjory Heath who are appalled at the destruction of the environment by those technocrats who speak in the name of the Enlightenment. It is also dedicated to those like Marjory who defend and affirm the caring values and practices of everyday life, and who are shocked by those academics who think like bureaucrats, act like experts, and speak like politicians.

1 Ragpicking amidst the wasteland's debris: the unreasonable silence of philosophy

Except among heretics, all Western metaphysics has been peephole metaphysics. The subject—a mere limited moment— was locked up in its own self by that metaphysics, imprisoned for all eternity to punish it for its deification. As through the crenels of a parapet, the subject gazes upon a black sky in which the star of the idea, or Being, is said to rise. And it is the very wall around the subject that casts its shadow on whatever the subject conjures: the shadow of reification, which a subjective philosophy will then fight against...There is no peeping out. What would lie in the beyond makes its appearance only in the materials and categories within.

Adorno, Negative Dialectics

The dominant tendency in analytic philosophy in Australia is affectionately known as Australian materialism. This home-grown form of a universal scientific reason, with its mechanistic materialist metaphysics grounded in the natural sciences, has been internationally successful. It has overcome the traditional cultural cringe of an ex-colony towards Europe and America, and has facilitated the development of a national philosophical culture. It has also enabled Australian philosophers to stride assuredly on the international Anglo-American stage, thereby putting Australian philosophy on the global map. Australian analytic philosophy is now internationally identified as a naturalistic, scientific realism, in which philosophy underlabourers for science to develop a physicalist metaphysics. This down-to-earth sparse materialism, which is held to reflect accurately the strong sunlight, harsh brown landscape and wide open spaces of Australia, is generally empiricist, typically physicalist, and resolutely reductionist. The mechanistic world picture that results from a universal scientific reason's self-validating knowledge of the pristine inner structure of the world, embodies the central values of the materialist Enlightenment. This tradition assumes that progress in scientific knowledge in seeking the Truth can be used to make the world a happier place for the majority. By using science and technology to control and master nature, we can ease our pain and increase our pleasure. Moral and political progress towards an enlightened and tolerant society then results. The role of philosophy in the public, liberal culture of late capitalism is to defend this materialist Enlightenment tradition, that has been successfully transplanted from Europe, and has grown up on Australian soil to philosophically underpin a secular liberal culture.

Yet Australian materialism's 15 minutes of fame may well have passed. The signs are there. The early work of the Australian materialists, with their physics-worship and utilitarian ethics has an unmistakably dated air, as French poststructuralism now seductively dances in the spotlight. Anglo-American philosophers have more or less appropriated what they found useful in the work of early Australian materialists of the 1960s and 70s, and they have rejected both its utilitarianism, and the strong reductionism of its unity of science programme.[1] The current adherents of the Australian materialist tradition now find themselves working on the edges of the work of the big names overseas, who are now making the running on the key issues.[2] It is the central American texts of physicalist materialism we currently read, not the Australian ones, as the production of philosophical texts has slowed in the Australian periphery. It remains unclear how Australian intellectuals will find a niche in the global market. The absence of an academic star system, coupled with the savage cuts to education, increased teaching and administrative loads, the centralization of research and the contraction of the broad postwar expansion of the universities, suggests that Australia will increasingly rely on overseas ideas rather than produce its own. Many who encountered reductive naturalism in the philosophy institution voted with their feet, as they left philosophy for politics, sociology, or cultural studies. The judgement they made was simple. Philosophy had lost its nerve and staying power, whilst its fetishizing of technique and dead totemic classics meant that it was no longer in tune with the advanced possibilities that history presented. The response to the increasing calcification of the Australian philosophical tradition has been to establish a special relationship with the American materialists in the metropolitan universities, and to provide a research home for those philosophers made homeless from the British universities by the economic logic of Thatcherism. These signs point to a slow painful death of analytic philosophy in Australia.

If the signs of the passing of Australian materialism from its moment in history's spotlight are evident, the effects of its increasing displacement by poststructuralism are not. We are just beginning to deal with the implications, and we do not yet have a picture of our condition within the late modern cultural landscape. Those of us who are not wandering postmodern cosmopolitan intellectuals, who are not firmly entrenched in the academic professoriate, or who are not able to become freelance intellectuals producing substantial bodies of work that sell millions, realize that we are forced to confront the politics of localism in the university during a period of economic contraction. We marginalized locals realize that we do not have the power to act at the global level, and so have to make do as best we can with a micro-politics of localism. As the philosophy discipline contracts, we increasingly find ourselves as unemployed philosophers, forced to survive on grants and part-time teaching, whilst confronting a closed, elitist academic world of philosophy that provides little opportunity for employing different philosophical voices. In trying to find our way in the world as philosophers, we continually crash into a universal reason that operates in terms of a restricted canon of philosophical problems. We continually collide into a philosophical discourse that constructs the readership of its books in terms of the narrow audience of one's immediate peers in the academy, has a deep suspicion of publicity and notoriety, and demands a certain kind of formal, scientific prose which alienates the philosophical text from a public readership.[3] We unemployed locals find ourselves increasingly marginalized and alienated from the self-assertive, self-confident philosophical tradition that it is full of strong, bold achievers who have done great things. We do not share its future hope, that in working on the hard problems at the cutting edge of neuroscience and philosophy, the analytic, materialist tradition will continue to do great things in the near future in terms of computational models of mind. Our future fear is an apocalyptic anxiety that this research programme will develop cyborgs for the war machine.

Unemployed, alienated philosophers have the free time for individual self-realization through philosophical labour, and they can achieve this by becoming critics of the analytic philosophical tradition. But such self-realization does not automatically entail recognition by other subjects. In reflecting on our experience of marginalization, we frame it as a rejection that forces an identity crisis. The rejection wounds, as it means living with resentment and pain, whilst continually putting up with being a negative object by the self-confident, established, tenured analytic philosophers. We rejected philosophers are not given recognition, as we are wrongly treated by others, in that our work is seen as the personal rumblings of discontent. It is not recognized as the philosophical continuation of a New Left linked to the rebellious and progressive nature of social protest of the new social movements, who hang onto a sense that the future should be better than the present and the past. We unemployed critics of academic philosophy are also seen as second rate, as never being as good as those overseas. We find our self-confidence being undermined, as we are continually being dismissed or ignored. These insulting and humiliating forms of disrespect represent the denial of recognition with regard to the positive understanding of ourselves that we had intersubjectively acquired.

The dual process of philosophical dissonance and radicalism underpins the need to give our resentment philosophical justification. This justification starts at the point where the analytic philosophical tradition represents our life experiences as mere appearance, a simulacra. The whole driving force of this tradition is the Platonic desire to get out of the cave of the everyday, and to aspire intelligibly to a transcendent world of scientific knowledge beyond the cave. Those left inside the cave with their discontents and prejudices are rejected by the mechanistic system, and discarded as rubbish. We unemployed locals experience this as living in the wasteland by the sewer outlets, where we are obliged to pick over the philosophical scraps and recycle them, if we desire to have a modest career as philosophers. We declassed, philosophical ragpickers are seen by our socially superior masters—the philosophical elite— as being not too bright, as impoverished, inhibited, dependent and rather weak. We are seen by our academic masters as pathetically huddled together in our paranoia, bitterly vindictive, plotting and scheming for part-time work; ambitious and self-seeking in terms of a career, yet continually frustrated by the obstacles not of our own making. Our sickly resentment at this disesteem is fuelled by the lack of help, support or encouragement for a questioning of, or departing from, the philosophical tradition. Resentment poisons us, even as it makes us think in terms of power. We seethe and fume, wishing to humiliate those who use their power to marginalize us.

The genuine disincentives within the academic system for those unemployed philosophers who desire to write for a general educated readership in civil society deepens the resentment and existential opposition to the philosophy establishment. The existence of a viable indigenous publishing industry, does not ease this smouldering resentment, as the print and media and publishing industry are not active in promoting and popularizing new directions in social, cultural and political thinking. Australia remains a large-scale importer of culture, and the small national market, which is dominated by multinationals, leaves little room to foster new and untested ideas, written, edited, published and marketed locally. Australian books still do not sell well overseas, even when Australian publishers have established co-publications with overseas publishers.[4] So Australia now produces only a few published thinkers who can function as public intellectuals in the public sphere in civil society. This impacts destructively on the cave-dwelling, unemployed, ragpicking philosophers, who exist between the rock of the philosophical establishment and a hard place of independent intellectuals. We become envious, rebellious and resentful, as we react against a world we did not make, and which we see as being ruled by people who do not deserve their advantages, tenure and privileges. Enduring the injustice of our existential situation stunts us, and we seethe with frustration, we struggle to figure out ways we can regain sovereign control over the conditions of our work from the well-fed, famous, academic philosophers in the pay of the state.

The emotional complex of bitterness, resentment and suffering can make one either long to side with the masters and their elitist values, or become sick or mad, or compensate for the humiliation by seeking revenge. When resentment is channelled into creativity it can provide the ground that pushes towards a critical distance from the philosophical world as a mad-house and a prison. We modest ragpickers can use our creativity to redefine the Socratic project: rather than leaving the cave for the world outside—Socrates never did leave the Athenian cave—we can do battle with the underlying assumptions of our own cave. There is no "outside the cave" of the philosophical tradition in modernity. The aspiration of Australian materialism to transcend the cave of the shared culture of the everyday world in late capitalist modernity, is based on a delusion that requires the intervention of a psychoanalytically informed philosophy. Resentment channelled into the creativity of a therapeutic philosophy becomes the self-reflexive rupture from the diseased master discourse of analytic philosophy. This rupture starts from defying philosophy's striving for a universality that transcends national custom and tradition, so that philosophy's project is deemed to be valid for all cultures, languages, peoples and histories. It is a defiance based on the existential focus on the here-and-now in this regional culture, with this particular philosophical practice, in this particular philosophical cave. Self-reflexive resentment is a tearing free from the canon of questions and modes of inquiry that have been handed down; and in its resistance and challenge to the reigning assumptions of professional philosophy and the academic establishment, it seeks a common front with those postmodernists who question the liberal assumptions of the culture of late capitalist modernity. The postmodern negative stance against the easy confidence and optimism of the Enlightenment starts with an expression of disappointment, expresses frustration and resentment, and speaks in terms of the collapse, ruin and death of tradition. It expresses the mood that it is a good time for taking stock and settling accounts, as many of the insular practices of Australian universities are being called into question with the increasing commodification of knowledge.[5]

This reactive questioning makes for a complex relation to the law of the philosophical tradition for the declassed, ragpicker philosophers. The rupture from tradition can only be made intelligible if it can demonstrate the points of continued contact with tradition; but it does so in terms of a project that speaks of something other than that of which the tradition speaks. It means the need to think within the context of the philosophical tradition determined by the demand for universality, whilst affirming the particularity of the existential situation we find ourselves within. These tensions can be initially resolved by brushing the particular Australian variant of the Enlightenment tradition in the wrong way, whilst remaining committed to the tradition's universal ideals of using reason to make a better world for all. This starts by breaking away the types of problems and modes of thinking associated with an abstract universal reason's conception of disembodied truth and rationality. Here Western intellectuals legislate for the good society in the name of a transhistorical mathematical science which gives us absolute truth of reality as it really is-in-itself. Such a modest beginning of "breaking away" can make no claim to capture or grasp the metaphysics of physicalist materialism as a whole, by pinning it down like a butterfly on the dissecting table, highlighting all its flaws with incisive cuts of a post mortem dissection. The initial work is more of an anti-text which possesses a fragmentary nature, as we do not have an overall picture of analytic discourse as philosophical system, nor do we possess a coherent narrative that enables and affirms our identity as ragpicking philosophers.

The anti-text endeavours to bring a physicalist, philosophical naturalism into visibility as a cultural object, and to highlight different aspects of it, and its neo-romantic oppositions. In bending our backs and recycling its philosophical wastes for a pittance, we place the recycled scraps of waste around the possibility of an alternative perspective in philosophy. This would explore the intertwining of social power, the domination of nature by science, and psychological repression in the poisoned well of the Enlightenment in late modernity. We philosophical ragpickers question this tradition in a melancholic mood, because in mixing with the ordinary folk rather than the technocratic elite, we see more clearly the fading charms and polluted dreams of the modernist Enlightenment tradition in the twilight of modernity in an ecological crisis. It is the decay and decadence of a tradition that provides us with our identity and our philosophical ethos.

This chapter gives a quick sketch of philosophy as a universal instrumental reason, the discontents of the ragpickers with technocratic discourse, and the philosophical need for an oppositional counter discourse. This preliminary sketch defines the terrain, and constructs a simple map of the conflict associated with the philosophical rupturing from the Enlightenment tradition. The aim is to create a space in the philosophy institution for the ragpickers to bring the issues associated with the collapse of the Enlightenment into a technocracy out into the open. This space can then be used by the dissident voices silenced by a hegemonic Enlightenment tradition to articulate their concerns about a badly wounded world, and to facilitate their desire to bring about a more ecologically sustainable world.[6]

That feeling of being "post-the-philosophical-tradition"

Philosophy in the liberal university is primarily a scientific and materialist analytic philosophy which holds that the universal reason of science gives us knowledge, which explains how the universe really works. Truth is the central value, and obtaining truth leads to a better culture, and a reformed society. Philosophy works within the bounds of science, and as a philosophical critique it is a clear, crisp analysis that exposes the obstacles that prejudice, religious dogma and erroneous belief place in the way of achieving scientific truth.

The narrative of the materialist warriors is that they fought the good fight against idealism and anti-naturalism, won the battles against religion, and handed on a better philosophical culture than the one they had inherited. They had succeeded in pushing their rivals aside, branding them as heretics, and ensuring that they were forced to live on the margins of philosophical culture as pariahs. The subjectivist idealism of Berkeley and Ayer within British empiricism was rejected, as it collapsed the external objective world into the subject's subjectivity. Post-Kantian idealist continental philosophy was rejected because it made philosophy the handmaiden of theology rather than science, and so it fell into an anti-naturalism where scientific reason was limited to make way for faith. The progress made by a rational and progressive materialist philosophy established philosophy as an autonomous academic discipline in the liberal university. Its success ensures that those who work there operate in terms of the codes, procedures, ethos and problems of a scientific culture with its materialist metaphysics.

This tradition is a continuation of the traditional core of the original Greek conception of philosophy as a universal reason and world-view. This idea, Husserl argued, is one that European culture bears within itself.[7] Hooker concurs with this reading of the Western philosophical tradition, and he says that the essential idea of Western intellectual culture is that:

> "man is a rational animal and that reason is what distinguishes men from other animals. The essential project of reason is transcendence, for example, transcendence of cognitive limitations and imperfection: ignorance, prejudice, bias, egocentrism, speciescentrism (anthropocentrism), and projection (anthropomorphism). In a large context, transcendence of moral and aesthetic limitation and imperfection are included. The application of reason brings about progress in objective understanding, cognitive, moral, and aesthetic, and is expressed in objective knowledge, ethics and aesthetics."[8]

The traditional bias of a universal reason towards a non-natural construal of reason was corrected by the naturalism of a scientific culture, and transformed into a mathematical physics which provides universal knowledge of the totality of what is, unfettered by myth and prejudice. Husserl identified this universal scientific rationality as a formal-logical form of a *mathesis universalis*, which he deemed to be a self-sufficient, pure, formal structure.[9] He held that 'a technization takes over all other methods belonging to the natural sciences', and there is 'the surreptitious substitution of the mathematically substructured world of idealities' for our everyday life world.'[10]

Universal mathematical reason in the Australian materialist Enlightenment tradition is part of a family of theories of science, realism and materialism that can be classified as a physicalist form of philosophical naturalism. This family of theories is commonly grouped under scientific realism, and it effectively aligns analytic philosophy with science and repudiates philosophy's heritage as one of the humanities. This self-image and self-definition of analytic philosophy is uncritically accepted, despite its institutional location in the liberal university within the humanities. Philosophical naturalism is defined by Arthur Danto in the *Encyclopedia of Philosophy* as:

> "a species of philosophical monism according to which whatever exists or happens is *natural* in the sense of being susceptible to explanation through methods, which although paradigmatically exemplified in the natural sciences, are continuous from domain to domain of objects and events. Hence naturalism is polemically defined as repudiating the view that there exists or could exist any entities or events which lie in principle, beyond the scope of scientific explanation."[11]

The central thesis of naturalism for modernist analytic philosophers like Smart, Armstrong and Quine is that there is a continuity of natural objects and events across the entire range of the special sciences. Armstrong defines naturalism as 'reality consisting of nothing but a single all-embracing spatio-temporal system in which nothing else exists except objects within this system involved in causal relationships.'[12] This naturalism amounts to a claim that a complete description of the spatio-temporal causal realm is a description of everything, and there is no place in it for non-natural objects or events. Supernatural entities like God or Cartesian mental substances are excluded on the grounds that they do not exist in the spatio-temporal system, and have no causal effect on the system. So Ockham's razor can be used to remove them from scientific theory. Abstract entities or universals, such as the sets of set-theory or abstract classes, are allowed into this austere ontology, even though they are not elements of the spatio-temporal system, and do not act physically upon it or any of its elements. Given their respect for science, which they see as telling us what there is, Australian materialists are placed in the position of having to countenance all the objects that physics countenances. They need to admit abstract entities, as science is the final arbiter on all matters, including philosophical matters. Routley describes the justifying argument as: 'classes are necessary for mathematics, which is necessary for physics, so classes are required to explain the workings of nature.'[13]

Australian materialism assumes a physicalist interpretation of philosophical naturalism. The justification is that this is given by science, by which is meant the natural sciences, which are then ultimately reduced to physics, or at least unified by the world-picture given by a fundamental physics.[14] The sciences are interpreted in terms of scientific realism, which is realist as to particles, atoms, molecules, and cells. As there are only these basic atomistic entities, so an account of a physical entity in terms of the laws of physics provides an adequate explanation and understanding of that entity and its interactions. The simplicity of the resultant world-picture is defended on the grounds that the ontology of the world consists of nothing more than the entities recognized by physics.[15] Physics is the empirical science *par excellence*, and the most fundamental science. The aim is to unify and systematize human knowledge through theoretical reduction to physics to achieve an intelligible and plausible world view.[16] The problem of the world appearing differently to humans in everyday life—it is solid, colourful, flux-like—from that represented by physics, is quickly resolved by reducing the appearances to the underlying microphysical entities of physics.[17] So human intentions are eliminated, the mind is identical to the brain, folk psychology becomes neurophysiology, socio-historical laws become physical laws, and persons become biological organisms theorized as machines. Though physicalist materialism is radically at odds with the way historical human beings see the ordinary everyday world, it deals with this difference by holding that common-sense is radically defective as a mode of knowledge.[18]

The single correct definition of philosophy today amongst scientific materialists is that it seeks the broad physicalist outlines of the whole system of the world.[19] The role for philosophy, as outlined by Jack Smart, is to develop a naturalist picture of the human being's place in the universe, as established by the natural sciences, and worked up into a world view by an optimistic synthetic philosophy.[20] Smart held that as science gets more general and abstract, it gets more metaphysical. Metaphysics is the search for the most plausible theory of the whole universe as it is considered in the light of science.[21] This conception of philosophy as a systematizing totalizer was recently reaffirmed by Hooker, who held that the 'business of philosophy is providing a general understanding of the nature of life and of how to live it.'[22] Philosophy is deemed to be continuous with science, and it works on the more abstract, theoretical or metaphysical end of science, to solve fundamental problems and puzzles. It does so through a serious and special sort of disinterested inquiry, which is value-free, disinterested and uncontaminated by politics. As the state of internal discord within the system of physicalist philosophical naturalism is deemed to be largely the result of family disputes over matters of detail, so the aim is to maximize the overall coherence, comprehensiveness and non-paradoxicalness of its systematic world-picture of modernity. The role of analytic philosophy as cultural criticism is directed at those critics outside the system, and it defends its world-picture from external criticism by using the adversarial method to disarm critics with knock-down arguments. Philosophy acts as a cultural overseer, whose surveillance over the whole field of knowledge ascertains what is true and false, rational and irrational to believe in terms of the conventions and criteria established by scientific reason as an ahistorical transcendent standard.

Such is the conception of philosophy as part of the hard sciences. The justification this materialist metaphysics provides for its existence derives from its grand narrative. This holds that a universal scientific reason breaks away from the religious tradition of medieval society with its fixed social hierarchies and ranks, and then facilitates the continuing process of Enlightenment, by protecting the claims of a self-legitimating, universal reason. Behind this conception of a universal philosophical reason sits the background ethos of philosophy in modernity defending the claim that a life conducted in a free-willed accordance with the dictates of reason—truth, justice and liberty—represents the highest ideals of civilised social existence, and so is the best form of life for human beings. Democracy, insofar as it respects these values, is the form of government best suited to the interests of reason and justice. Universal reason generates the harmony of nature and society from its own womb. The daily work of normal academic philosophy trades on this progressive narrative of the theoretical and practical discourse of the Enlightenment tradition. It operates within the secure confines of an already established tradition of progress and civilization in modernity, and sees itself as the embodiment of the Enlightenment ethos. Its modernist world-picture is marked by a denial of any fixed and rigid conception of the good life, and by the rejection of attempts to bind the principle of the good to any pre-existent or naturally occurring features of the world. It is self-evidently assumed that the current form of life of the modern liberal social order is the only rational or legitimate form of life, and that this has been established by reason, rather than by faith or theology.

This quick sketch of the scientific, materialist Enlightenment tradition is what we are thrown into as philosophers. Its hegemony in the philosophy institution has meant that there is little in the way of philosophizing as a living activity that directly undercuts this conception of philosophy by making it questionable. Even though reductive materialism does not recognize the specificity of human beings in the social world as it naturalizes history, there has been a virtual absence of debate about the satisfactory nature of the reductive materialist system as a whole. This system is assumed to be the truth of the way things are, as given by natural science, and so philosophy if it remains within the bounds of science, must accept this. But we resentful, declassed philosophers are intuitively uncomfortable and out of sorts with this materialist discourse. We find it hard to see the intrinsic links between the absolute truth of physics, the economic growth in capitalism that is required to change society for the better, and the increasing democratisation in the liberal polity. Theory and practice do not cohere. We suspect that a systematic universal reason that mathematizes the world—either physics or neo-classical economics—and so abstracts itself from the everyday world, is silent about the suffering in the historical everyday world that we experience as ordinary people. We suspect that this silence has to do with physicalist materialism's project of the mechanization of nature, which is also the naturalization of society. The naturalization of society is what analytic philosophy defends, and we sense that there is a gap here between what philosophy is—a systematic physicalist materialism—and what it professes to be—realizing the Enlightenment ideals by using scientific knowledge to make the world a happier place for human beings. These suspicions throw the modern project into question and raise doubts about its legitimacy.

These doubts are reinforced when we ragpickers see that what does not fit readily into the physicalist system must be either reducible to it—as with utilitarian ethics—or shown to be unnecessary "illusions" fit for the ontological rubbish dump—as with postmodernism. We note that the irrationality shown towards non-analytic philosophy—postmodernism's questioning of rationality provokes moral indignation, violent hostility, and the charge that it represents nothing less than the call for the return of the irrational—is linked to the repression of alternative ways of seeing the world. The processes of reduction and dumping seem to be inherent to the content of Australian materialism, as its self-understanding derives from the growth of modern natural sciences that currently constitute what it is to be rational. A universal knowledge of the universe, deriving from a fundamental physics which mirrors nature implicitly, denies differences between the theoretical sign of science and what these signify in reality. This sign-theory of presence, in which a fundamental physics pictures the deep structure of the universe, holds that the disinterested inquiry to improve our knowledge about the furniture of the world is, and should be, divorced from the broader social relations and our common culture. What is expelled from the universal mechanistic system is the rubbish and junk of particularity of culture and history. This is discharged as the non-philosophical, the non-scientific, the supernatural, and the irrational in the name of scientific progress. Hence the repression of alternative modes of inquiry to that of universal reason bounded by a modernist analytic tradition of mathematical science. Hence the disenchantment of we ragpickers with universal reason of the Enlightenment as embodied in Australian materialism. This places us in an awkward position. Even though we still cling to our belief that civilization is a process of enlightenment we are out of sorts with philosophy, because we distrust its unreasonable silence about the way it fails to live up to its ideals. We sense an inner incoherence of the Enlightenment tradition, even as we see that its ideology of progress mystifies the conflicts between different social groups.

We philosophical ragpickers endeavour to resolve our unease by taking our bearings from the problems and suffering in the everyday world. But we find that the analytic philosophical tradition bars access to the forgotten idea that philosophy is a critical Socratic voice within and a part of our common life. So our disillusionment with the philosophical tradition requires us to seek to negate the tradition, rather than affirm it. We have no choice. If the telos and unifying project of the Enlightenment tradition is deemed to be constitutive of an analytic philosophy alienated from everyday life, then what lies outside this tradition lies outside truth and reason. If we ragpickers speak in our own voice, then we do not speak truthfully or rationally, even though we speak within and about modern philosophy. The expulsion and marginalization of the ragpickers are deemed necessary because they undermine what is construed as scientific theory. They emphasize unique, individual items, work against the hierarchy of universal and particular, and are bound to a life of particularity and sensuousness. This threefold departure from universal theory is the reason for the ragpickers' expulsion from philosophy, and philosophy's attempt to suppress their protest to the reign of theory. We ragpickers are forced to affirm our marginalized being-in-the-everyday world that we live in as social beings; and to deny that our resistance to the scientific word picture of the natural sciences, is a replay of an irrational, nihilistic cult of existentialism, its poststructuralist successors and the mysticism of New Ageism. The ragpickers' resentment at their elitist, academic masters treating them with disdain and contempt is not just a turning against a universal enlightening reason because they resent their marginal role in society. We locate ourselves within the tradition of radical criticism that stems from Rousseau's resentful critique of the non-authenticity of the modern form of life; and we re-read Rousseau as being concerned with the problem of bourgeois civilization. He rebukes the Enlightenment project for its failure to live up to its ideals, and he highlights its resistance to opening up the option of a genuine alternative to modern life within capitalism. Following Rousseau, we ragpickers can creatively use our resentment to uncover the decay within the heart of the Enlightenment's discourse. This aims to re-fashion modern life rationally, by cleansing it of all those beliefs the adherents of this discourse hold to be extraneous to their project to create a rational social order.

Philosophy and crisis in liberal society

We can offer a snap-shot of the sickness within the Enlightenment tradition to indicate the philosophical origins of our disenchantment with scientific materialism. One frame is the way its naturalization of the social world points to technocracy. This can been most clearly seen in a biomedicine, as this straddles the social and the natural. Insofar as a physicalist materialism is limited to the biochemical level in terms of its explanations of social processes, it will have a systematic tendency to treat socio-political problems as reflections of biochemical disorders. To paraphrase Bentham, the question is not whether the aged reason nor whether they feel, but whether they are in pain because the body malfunctions. An illness like cancer is defined by bio-medicine as a biological disease of the body, and social disorders—depression and anxiety associated with cancer in old age for instance—are reduced to being disorders of the body. Biomedicine sees and treats the body as a functional machine that occasionally breaks down, and for whose dysfunctions a physical cause and remedy can be found by the scientist as repairman or engineer. These dysfunctions are then ordered and controlled by drugs prescribed by scientific experts who know the truth about the way diseases work in nature. Pain management of the body brackets out the quality of life of the whole person in relationships within a community as an illusion—and so the whole question of caring for the whole aged person in an unequal antagonistic society is sidelined. The reductive materialist Enlightenment tradition deepens this naturalization process inherent in bio-medicine because it reduces biochemistry to physics. It thereby makes social human beings into natural beings, who are then modelled as machines by scientific experts.

Another frame of the decay within Enlightenment discourse is the affirmative relationship between a theoretical reductive materialism and contemporary bourgeois society institutionalized as an objective mechanism for the self-expansion of economic production through constant technological change. Just as biomedicine and physics have become a part of big business and incorporated into the power relations of capitalism, so philosophy's universal reason is an integral part of the rationalization process in culture

12

that progressively disenchants myth and superstition within the self-reproducing socio-economic system of late capitalism. This system generates a need for greater regulation and closer control, because there is a continual dialectical conflict between the desire for freedom by modern subjects, and the need for social order.[23] To the extent that it does not protest the ideology of the naturalization of the social world, analytic philosophy as a part of scientific reason is tied up with, and integrated into, the technocratic regulation and control of freedom in a disordered society. So though universal reason in philosophy plays a progressive role in disenchanting modernity, it remains bounded by the disenchanted horizons of a liberal bureaucratic capitalism. It then takes on a regressive air, to the extent that it becomes involved in the social control needed to sustain the progress of a dynamic modernity.[24] The result is that universal reason is less genuinely concerned with lending a hand to the suffering of those who bear civilization on their backs, and more concerned with pledging trust in the rationality of a scientific elite whose expertise is used to play a vanguard role in shaping ordinary life.[25]

The third frame of the decay is the domination of nature. Despite its claim to be a progressive and rational shaping of a modern life, the rationalization process has transformed universal scientific rationality into an instrumental reason which dominates nature to further human desires through unlimited economic growth. This is exemplified in the state's management of Australia's tuna fish stocks. Here ecology is reduced to a set of managerial strategies aiming at resource efficiency and risk management which treats as a technical problem what is in fact an impasse—namely, the level of productive performance and resource use already achieved is not ecologically sustainable. The natural world of the sea is a standing reserve from which a high industrial apparatus expects a return on its investment, and it results in a roller coaster of bigger and bigger tuna ships, greater investment, bigger catches and bigger profits. This massive high-tech fishing for profit realized within the circuits of the Japanese market ends up with the collapse of fish stocks because the resource has been destroyed. Conservation management then becomes crisis management which continually prioritizes the Japanese demands for more fish over human communities and natural ecosystems. This rationalization process in a post-Fordist flexible mode of accumulation is one which currently empties out the non-instrumental rationality of those areas of everyday life in civil society still outside the capitalist market and the state. Capitalism's productive capacity is celebrated as generating sufficient economic resources for meeting most of the nation's social and economic needs; yet economic reform today is a code word for deregulation, capital mobility, deskilling, union rollback, the feminization of poverty, and overt class war from above.

In the model of society articulated by neo-classical economics, utility machines are pictured as being required to adapt to the economic reshaping of society undertaken according to guidelines deduced from the Platonic blueprint or form of a perfectly competitive, harmonious market that mirrors the order of nature. The assumptions of the way of life pictured in this model ground modernity self-justification as a form of life. These assumptions are:

> "that nature exists for human use; the unwillingness to begin initiating conservation measures until imminent depletion of natural communities threaten human prosperity; the assumption that public regulators can and do "referee" private economic interests; the assumption that science model the interactions of natural communities so as to come up with a magic number which defines sustainable exploitation of natural communities; and the assumption that an external authority can manage human and natural communities so as to promote economic and ecological stability."[26]

The consequences of instrumental reason seeing nature as a large resource for producing economic wealth are that a modern form of life is a wounded world.[27] Instrumental reason is a functional rationality in the service of system-preservation of the economic machine. This machine is rationally guided by experts within a technocratic model of decision-making. Their research and planning shape a liberal capitalist future to help those in power know what they must do to keep holding onto their power in the future.

The ragpickers' alienation from analytic philosophy is the local expression of a broad disenchantment with reason, and the loss of meaning, that reason suffers when it represents nature, society and human beings as a causal mechanism. There is big trouble brewing in the house of reason, as reason is losing its authority in the world. Philosophy, for instance, is currently in the dock. It is being required to answer questions about its credentials, according to its own rule of law of having to give a full and detailed account for all its claims. This includes the claim that post-Kantian philosophy's critique of reason is irrational. Rodolphe Gasché puts it situation succinctly. He says:

> "Even if it is granted (but are things that easy?) that some of the criticism of reason has turned irrational, it must still be said that it is also an attempt to bring reason—especially in its modern techno-scientific form—before the tribunal of reason itself. What has been called "postmodernity", that is, philosophical thought after Kant, demands of reason that reason be rendered...By asking for reason's credentials, this critique inaugurates another phase in the history of reason."[28]

The questions being asked of philosophy in the trial are simple ones: is philosophy a rational and progressive enterprise? Is the physicalist materialist research programme or research tradition a progressive or a degenerating one? Is the spread of Enlightenment also the increasing irrationality of the human relationship to nature, and the increasing death of the bio-diversity of species and life-enhancing ecosystems? Is instrumental reason rational and progressive? Those ragpickers watching the trial observe that analytic philosophy's dogmatic responses about science do not fully comply with the demands of reason. They also note that the academic mandarins, who come as witnesses to defend the Enlightenment, are having difficulty in reactivating the positive side of Enlightenment progress:—as a critical thinking that questions an instrumental reason, and its modernist, mechanist picture of modernity. There is too much pomp and too little self-examination.

Outside of the courtroom the journalists covering the trial, which has turned to questioning universal reason's picture of modernity, interview one of the ragpickers leaving the trial. He had spoken on behalf of the limitationist environmental critique of macro-technological development defended by those neo-classical economics everyone loves to hate. He offered a snap-shot of his disenchantment with reason. The green understanding of nature, he says, no longer corresponds to nature as represented by a mathematical physics continually appealed to by scientistic philosophers. The representation of nature by a fundamental physics fails to consider the way an independent nature has been altered by human beings and their technology, in such a way that we are now concerned with policies to maintain a habitable planet that has become a fabricated greenhouse. The world of nature is being destroyed by the new global pollution of carbon dioxide and the CFCs, which are produced through the pursuit of a better life by the mechanism of unlimited economic growth. Economic progress through a deregulated market is causing global warming and ozone depletion, as human beings in capitalist societies have changed the atmosphere and the weather as a consequence of driving our cars, building our factories, cutting down our forests and turning on our air-conditioners. Yet mechanistic materialism is slow to incorporate the knowledge produced by the natural sciences about climate warming, or consider the implications. Its assumptions about nature are challenged by "the end-of-nature thesis", as this means that a world entirely independent of us, and which was there before we arrived and which encircled and supported human society, has been radically transformed by science and technology's brute domination over the Earth. It is now a fabricated machine that is in need of being redesigned and managed more effectively, if the species is to survive. As a machine is a human fabrication, so nature is no longer just a simple realm of scientific law in which human beings are physical objects in nature. Nature is a historical self-sustaining ecological system, and it is so overheating from gung-ho economic growth, that we live in a greenhouse.[29] A critical eco-reason indicates the need for a genuine alternative to the modern form of life of liberal capitalism.

Inside the courtroom a defence of the Enlightenment's form of life is mounted by the academic, analytic mandarins. They state that the indications of an ecological crisis shown by the hard research of the natural sciences justifies the need for more enlightenment, as we are not sufficiently enlightened in conserving nature. It is therefore necessary to oppose those Rousseauean eco-romantics who hold that we can live in harmony with nature, that decentralization and local autarchy are necessary for social and ecological health, that scientific progress is inherently harmful and dehumanizing, and that the capitalist system is inescapably destructive and wasteful.[30] But the ragpickers outside the courtroom are not convinced by this defence. They tell the media journalist, who is seeking fame and glory with the big story for the six o'clock news, that analytic philosophy stands condemned on its own terms. It is more concerned with developing a connectivist architecture of the mind than developing an ecological understanding of nature; more preoccupied with developing a plausible mechanistic account of intentional systems than working out a better decentralist ecological future in a steady state world. It shows little sign of connecting up to our everyday hopes and fears about the changing the conditions of our collective lives in the face of the painful prospect of ecological collapse. It shows little interest in considering what could count as a genuine alternative to the modern form of life, and more concerned with sustaining a closed shop around science and scientism. Rigor is prized ahead of relevance, and the philosopher has become, and is valorized, as a value-free technician working on problems like a pure mathematician, or thinking up research hypotheses like a value-free scientist. What has been lost is any concern with the truth or goodness of the social system as a whole in relation to an environmental crisis that is causing substantial ill-health. It has little conception that there is a crisis of civilization that will endanger the basic sustainablity of the life-support systems of Earth.

The media journalist asks: "What about the analytic defence of reason which holds that the present crisis in late modernity is due to the limitation of the authority of science?" The eco-ragpicker appears taken back. Sensing blood she presses her case; "should not any attempt to limit the authority of science by the ragpickers be seen as a malicious and irrational threat to human society, civilization and material progress? Is it not the case that science and technology will solve our problems?" She smiles. She knows she is looking good on camera. "That line of defence does not convince as it once did," the green ragpicker responds. He warms to his theme. The gist of this holds that the core of modern science and technology is an instrumental, technical reason that converts and organizes being into a secure, verified and manipulated object. Instrumental reason accepts its allotted role in techno-capitalism of which it is a part. Philosophers become minor specialists in the highly developed division of labour within the unified field of knowledge and technology of techno-science. Like technocrats, they perform their functions as efficient experts within a definite ordering of reality, in which the world is transformed practically and theoretically into an object, which is then subject to exact investigation and control. Nature and society are organized into a system that can be grasped, perfected and objectified, as part of an attempt to turn the planet into a gigantic inexhaustible storehouse of energy and raw materials to achieve capital accummulation through ever increasing levels of production and consumption. The self-destructive tendency of the Enlightenment project turns modern society into a modern perpetual-motion machine, that takes the form of a gigantic technocratic mechanism for production and consumption, via the free market. Philosophy needs to question the authority of techno-science, since the natural and social sciences are intertwined in the technocratic domination of nature for human benefit.

The journalist looks uncomfortable. It is all too highbrow for the evening news. A slogan for popular entertainment is needed. The ragpicker responds. The historical background to technocracy's self-understanding is Americanism plus Fordism, in which the utility of technological progress as applied science is the primary legitimation for economic growth.[31] The technocratic future can be glimpsed in the megaprojects of a high-tech Japanese capitalism. This envisions the ecosphere as a technosphere where everything—the sky and weather included—has become a mediated second nature, and our bodies durable and efficient cyborg bodies. The political discourse of technocracy excludes politics. The representation of things through the intermediary of science in the laboratory is disassociated from the representation of citizens through the intermediary of the state. The autonomy and independence of science are then sustained by institutionalizing a distinct and authoritative domain outside the changing, fragile, human world. However this early modern separation of an independent nature represented by science, and the politics of citizens constructing a free republic, is undercut by science being harnessed by corporate industry. Industry increasingly controls science, whilst the capitalist state is impotent without science and technology booming. The result is the technocratic streamlining of society, the administration of capitalism by the state to further the ruthless struggle for power over nature and human beings, and science becoming locked into the efficiency and profitability of a high-tech modernizing capitalism. The journalist is pleased. She has her news grab: "Science attacked by greens. The future is cyborg." She gives a big personality smile for the camera. She knows that the defining characteristic of TV news is popularity, not information.

Inside the courtroom an expert in Critical Theory elaborates an argument about the crisis of modernity. "Horkheimer," he said, "had observed in the 1940s, a situation where the physical sciences were endowed with universal objectivity but emptied of human content, whilst the humanities preserved the human content, but only as ideology at the expense of truth."[32] He quotes Horkheimer, who said:

> "The collapse of a large part of the intellectual foundation of our civilization is to a certain extent the result of technical and scientific progress. Yet this progress is itself an outcome of the fight for the principles which are now in jeopardy, for instance, those of the individual and his happiness. Progress has a tendency to destroy the very ideas which it is supposed to realize and unfold. Endangered by the progress of technical civilization is the ability of independent thinking itself."[33]

The critical theorist said that the implication of this was that though the old emancipatory Enlightenment structures in civil society are still in place, universal reason's critical potential of doing away with myth and prejudice is increasingly being hollowed out from within. Economics, philosophy, science and technology and capitalism, which used to exist independently and alongside of one another, are increasingly coalescing into a managed symbiotic whole. This managed coordination of science, technology and capitalism, which can be tentatively designated as techno-capitalism, behaves with lordly superiority towards nature and human communities, and in its search to transcend all boundaries and all limits, it does away with all difference. Its accelerating transformation of converting reality into a calculable and controllable reality by a perfectible efficient cybernetic system produces golden commodities, permanent unemployment, and the destruction of nature.[34] A self-certifying techno-science, caught up in the search for and perpetuation of economic growth, has gained in effectiveness and power, but lost its wisdom. It does not reflect upon the meaning of its activity of transforming nature into matter in the service of capital accumulation in the name of utility.

We ragpickers, as experiencing subjects living after the victorious materialist enlightenment, are disenchanted with analytic reason. We intensely feel its obsolescence, decay, and decadence. At the same time we try to articulate the way this old philosophy is experienced within the horizons opened up by post-analytic philosophy. In living in the aftermath of mechanical materialism, we ragpickers find that we think within the context of the Enlightenment tradition. Yet we speak differently from those who accept the language of the materialist tradition, and who function in the academy as the defenders of science. In questioning this tradition of scientific realism without abandoning its emancipatory ethos, we become entangled in its complications, as the unity of the tradition disintegrates. History dislodges the contents from its Enlightenment form, and as the contents come to the surface, the unity of form and content becomes illusory. The contents become external and fragmented, and the different layers of content appear at different historical points. This tradition is no longer seen as a safe, secure house in which we live and work. The knowledge acquired through natural science does not provide guidance as to the ethical principles we should follow, nor does it lead to the construction of a just or good social system.

So we move outside the house we once lived in to the *sensus communus* of everyday life. The philosophical form of universal reason then becomes Shrunken, fragmented and enigmatic, as it increasingly becomes a technical domain. It becomes a dead and mute form of lines and contours as its progressive content is emptied, and its progressive ideals become ghostly after-images, recycled by the culture industry. This decay of a once-noble Enlightenment tradition signifies a crisis of meaning within a capitalist civilization with its permanent class of unemployed, and its severe environmental problems such as soil erosion, declining bio-diversity, the degradation of water resources, the rupture of Earth's ozone shield and the enhanced greenhouse effect. It is a crisis of meaning as consumerism, the

18

hedonism of self-gratification, and a will to dominate, masquerade as healthy ethical values in contemporary capitalism.

A Marxist objection

Those analytic Marxist philosophers who came into the universities in the 1960s and 1970s would, if they were called as witnesses to defend an analytic philosophy, challenge the above sketch of the problematical relationship between universal reason and the world. Their objection holds that this sketch fails to provide a fair evaluation of the rational emancipatory content of the Enlightenment tradition. The ragpickers' impressionist depiction of this tradition is that it exhibits consensual agreement within a physicalist materialist system, closes down debate about the overall plausibility of that system, and defines it as a degenerating research tradition whose contents are departing. So we are left with an empty form of a universal scientific-techno rationality, and the demonization of technology as a runaway dark force that controls human freedom. The analytic Marxist philosophers would hold that most of this is assertion, as little in the way of rigorous argument is offered by a tacit humanist philosophy linked into cultural studies. Its paranoia is derived from reading too many mass cultural sci-fi texts and B grade movies, and as an aesthetic reason, it fails to deal with the political intervention by Marxism into the Enlightenment tradition.

They hold that a modern enlightening critique has moved into the newly formed social sciences to destroy the excesses of the naturalization of society by a physicalist materialism. In reaffirming the second Enlightenment, that of the nineteenth century which was concerned with the knowledge of society, Marxism in the 1970s injected the contents of radical social science into an analytic form. This rupture with an academic philosophy represents progress, as it sorted out the kernels of the rationality of science from the chaff of ideology. Philosophy's practical character made it different from an elitist analytic philosophy, engaged in reproducing a hidden set of liberal moral and political values within the limits of capitalism. A radicalized analytic philosophy continues as a politically-informed, self-conscious, rational and progressive enterprise, and Marxism, as a universal scientific reason, should be respected as the most developed and clear defence of the radicalized Enlightenment. It retained the portion of truth belonging to the natural and social sciences, and carefully finished off their condemned ideological portion.

Things are not as rosy, as this narrative makes out. History has moved on since the 1970s. The Marxist beach-head against bourgeois class power was blocked in the early 1980s. The fusion of an aesthetic postmodernism and French poststructuralism in the 1980s into a critical and marginal tendency of cultural criticism displaced Marxism as a critical force, along with the working class as a revolutionary historical subject. The disenchantment with the scientific reason of Marxism was justified on the grounds that Marxism seen to be too dogmatic in terms of justifying its metaphysical presuppositions about its traditional theory of epistemological representation. Thus Paul Patton and Judith Allen, in calling for papers dealing with contemporary social theory and the crisis in Marxism in the early 80s, observed that:

> "With few exceptions, marxists did not submit copy dealing with debates or problems within marxism. We were offered several defences of marxist orthodoxy. Regrettably, those which materialised were more often attempts to deny that there was a problem, or to propose imaginary solutions, rather than serious attempts to deal with the criticisms addressed to fundamental principles of historical materialism in recent years."[35]

They read this as a refusal by Marxists to defend the presuppositions of their realist science rationally; both in terms of acknowledging that these existed, and that their metaphysical presuppositions about reason, the subject, and totality were seriously flawed. Poststructuralist feminists argued that the attempts by Marxist-feminists to develop historical materialism's universal theory of capitalism into a theory of patriarchal and capitalist social relations was premised on a contradiction. It could only give an account of gender relations through the suppression of feminism and sexual difference as its ontological assumptions were phallocentric. Jan Flax puts the case. The most:

> "basic categories of Marxist analysis, no matter how radically extended or reworked by feminists, replicate the devaluation and invisibility of important aspects of women's experience so prevalent in male-dominated cultures and discourses. As feminist discourse has matured, the extent to which these notions are intrinsically gender-bound and biased becomes increasingly evident. It is difficult to avoid the question of whether a feminist appropriation of Marxism would not require such a radical transformation of the entire system that it would become simply unrecognizable to its founder. Feminist theorists may inadvertently find themselves in the position that Marx imagined the proletariat would eventually assume *vis-à-vis* capitalism—"seizing" its means of production would overthrow an entire historical structure and replace it with a new one."[36]

This disenchantment with scientific reason effectively denied that historical materialism can be the basis for a universal critical social science, as Marxists had claimed. Historical materialism, as a realist social science which aims to further the freedom of the oppressed, is implicated in capitalism as its opposition, and so is a part of the cultural practices of modernity. It is subject to postmodernist criticism because it represents only a half-hearted break with the Enlightenment.[37] There was also the complimentary claim that the analytic philosophical style of reasoning—abstract and deductive with purely logical forms of demonstration and proof—was seen as "boy's own games" whose ultimate aim was control and domination over others.[38]

20

Analytic reason began losing its authority in late modernity, as it was being put into question by postmodernists, whose form of critique was primarily directed at decentring the autonomous modernist subject. This was seen as a nexus of psychic and social forces, rather than an egoistic master of these forces.[39] In moving on from the mute form of scientific Marxism, some of the most innovative, vibrant and productive theoretical work in social theory was increasingly being centred around the cross-over between feminism and poststructuralism.[40] This postmodern theory wanders amongst the fragments, stitching them together, without drawing them back into the Enlightenment tradition. It negotiates the interpretation of modernist texts in relation to history, by closely scrutinizing the contents which were previously hidden behind the muted contours, but now lie scattered about on the surface. The implications of this emptying-out of the radical content from the Enlightenment form resulted in an analytic, Marxist philosophy degenerating into intellectual isolation and stasis.

It foundered in Australia on its deep suspicion of philosophical idealism, and continental philosophy in particular. This isolation was reinforced by Marxists generally avoiding poststructuralist criticisms, in the hope that they would fade away like all Parisian fashion and fog. Thus Bob Connell held that the promotion of difference theory with its:

> "new technical jargon to be expounded and learnt, its Parisian theorists to be admired and applied, its classic texts to be translated, pondered, and quoted, its denunciations of past error, and its forays into this and that area to show how the new concepts reveal its hidden truth—is eerily like the promotion of Althusserian marxism, by the same techniques and indeed in much the same places, eight or ten years ago."[41]

Marxists either blocked poststructuralism by denouncing the philosophy of difference as more flip-flop French fashion, or it claimed that from these prophets intellectual deserts come. Poststructuralism was seen as a new decadent linguistic idealism that collapsed into a cultural and a cognitive relativism, in which there can be no such thing as universal principles of validity, truth or rationality.[42] It was necessary to turn away from an affirmative populist culturism that functions as the cultural expression of late capitalism, and return to political economy.[43] The conflict then became increasingly bitter between those in a scientific culture, who adhered to the modern scientific narrative of a progressive scientific reason, and the disenchanted left-wing, perspectivalist, postmodernists working in the broad field of cultural studies, who became increasingly disenchanted with science.

What was not taken up by Marxist philosophers in the analytic tradition, in response to a radical critique of reason, was the option of a general philosophical response that would affirm philosophy as a practically-oriented collaboration with the empirical social sciences. This would retain systematicity and universalism whilst abandoning non-falliblism. It would reject the doctrine of scientific neutrality, consider the ethical implications of science, and work on the problems of everyday life. This is a viable option for Marxism, as it does allow us to think of history as progress and catastrophe simultaneously. It provides us with an analysis of the transformation of society by the imperatives of capital in terms of disembedding of both economic forces from social institutions and the concept of value from the embedded relations of things themselves. It indicates the way that previous aboriginal and feudal forms of social relations have been all but absorbed by globalizing capital relations; and it identifies the difficulty in recognizing the presence of social relationships between human communities and the non-human world outside of the commodified world, with its modern categories of economics and abstract value. The tragedy was that academic Marxism was co-opted by a scientistic philosophical culture that was hostile to everyday life and commonsense. The materialism in Marxist materialism was deemed to be compatible, if not identical, with the materialism of physicalist reductionism. To all intents and purposes Marxist philosophy became a variant of philosophy within the physicalist research tradition, working away on a sub-theme of the systematicity and coherence of historical materialism, and so foregrounding a realist social science, rather than natural sciences like physics.[44] An incoherence ran through this amalgam. From the side of reductive materialism science is an intermediary that gives access to a transcendent nature in which human beings are physical mechanisms. But from the Marxist side, nature is a world constructed by human hands. What passes in the space between the two is mediation. But this space does not exist in the amalgamed theory. Either society is naturalized, or society and nature are deemed to be two separate realms, or the natural is absorbed into the social. There was little place for mediation between nature and society in the unconscious of these late moderns.

Marxism continued to loose its radical edge as the disenchantment with this scientistic reason grew. Its mirror of production spoke the system-language of the dialectic of the forces and relations of production, rather than the language of population health, and animal and human suffering because of damage to the planet's natural systems.[45] Whilst it is true that there is no single Marxist story about social growth governed by a science aiming to make the world a better place, one did dominate. This was the progressivism and rationality of analytic Marxism, with its roots in the Enlightenment's faith in scientific progress through technical mastery of the natural world's resources. It meant that it functioned in the public culture as a left technocratic radicalism associated with a progressive futurism. Its productivism has meant that it has been slow to engage with the challenge of the environmental crisis, the new methods of dominating the earth through biotechnology and genetic engineering, and the health risks from damaged life support systems. It has been slow in questioning the assumptions and values that neo-classical economists have brought the debate over sustainable development.[46] Most strands of Marxism work with the dualism of use-value and exchange-value, and they have been reluctant to question the way they viewed the domination of nature as a humanization of the world for human wellbeing.

22

Marxism's mirror of production thesis did not allow it to tackle the increasing automatization of the signifier in all aspects of social exchange. As first nature becomes historicized into second nature, the qualities of life, that were once grounded in nature, are now taken over by the reified cultural categories of development as economic progress. As meaning is displaced from nature and community into an ever-expanding system of consumer signs, these signs increasingly become trapped within the operation of a logic of a conservative 'baroque' postmodern culture. Here the fantastic images, spectacles, colour and music, emphasize deception, complexity, decadence, artificiality; and the socially constructive nature of reality becomes one in which the sirens of instant paradise in the culture industry promise an entertaining spectacle of a cornucopia. Cashed out, the classic ideology/science distinction becomes an opposition between what I feel, desire and am attracted to in a commodified world (ideology) and what we know because of knowledge (science).[47] So we readers of mass cultural texts are caught up the dark pleasurable feelings of the conspiratorial messages of *Dallas, Blue Heelers* and *X-Files* whilst the Marxist critic, operating in the light of knowledge, supposedly stands outside and apart from these texts. Marxism becomes caught up in a political "holier than thou" moralism; an "us and them", with the critic (us) feeling bad and guilty about consuming images and commodities. Its tacit ambivalence about everyday life and the working class is then resolved by authentic folkways counterpoised to a decadent commercialized mass culture that ideologically manipulates the masses. The high moral ground of communitarian socialist-humanism as a realm beyond economic value becomes a besieged stronghold of heroic resistance to the commercialization of culture. This is a hopeless way of exploring the questions of politics, culture and value. Hence the postmodernist turn to cultural populism.[48]

The consequence of the poststructuralist critique is that historical materialism, as a hegemonic critical voice within left culture has been undermined, its vocabulary has gone out of style, and socialist-feminism has declined. Though a Hegelian-Marxism still survives, its current existence is so marginal that it would be dismissed by all as a decayed historical philosophy, if sighted at all.[49] The conclusion Rorty draws, and most would follow him here, is that Marxism is finished.[50] It has died as a research culture in Australian philosophy. Liberalism lost its whipping boy, Analytic Marxism embraced the left-liberal moral principles of Rawls and Dworkin, and Marxists turned to dissecting the corpse.[51] After Marxism's collapse we confront the hegemony of the scientistic Enlightenment tradition grounded in the natural sciences. The mechanistic form of the refined representations of human beings as computational survival mechanisms, driven by their genetic base to adjust and conform, makes human emotion meaningless, and bars access to bodily subjectivity. The traces of humanism in the analytic tradition are undercut and overtaken by the promise of self-replicating mechanisms, in which the contents of human brains are downloaded into robotic bodies. Humanism has been hijacked and displaced into a technoscience, which holds that there is more potential for the rapid evolution of the species with machines than with humans.[52] Humanism's collapse, and the long and sorry history of an Eurocentric scientific Enlightenment justifying the conquest of the physical world, and its human and non-human inhabitants, leaves us disenchanted with scientific, analytic reason.[53] Analytic reason reduces modernity to its Enlightenment inheritance, and its tacit humanist defence of the social mission of science is increasingly undercut, as science is used as an instrument of domination. This tradition becomes a problem, when we realize that the horror of history is progress, which is also a catastrophe. The human species faces threats to its survival due to its disruption of Earth's life support system. Humans have so transformed the natural world that we are 'exceeding the biosphere's carrying capacity—i.e, we are overloading the planet's "metabolic" capacity to absorb, replenish, and restore.'[54] Scientism's repression of the romantic critique of the Enlightenment as the subjugation of nature and society to the power of science, leaves us with our disenchantment with a shrivelled up analytic reason, which constructs romanticism as the other of reason. What is left is progress reduced to technical, economic and administrative progress, which is then confused with progress towards a better state of being of a human life well lived. A scientistic analytic Enlightenment, in which reason is an instrument, becomes incapable of rationally determining the ends of life. The appropriate ends of reason cannot be derived from instrumental reason itself, as it is essentially an effective system for achieving known ends. So it undermines our capacity to give authoritative reasons for living a meaningful life in late modernity. The ragpickers disenchantment with analytic reason leads them to take a post-philosophical turn, to escape from analytic philosophy at the end of tradition, in order to be able to defend a genuine alternative to the destructive modern of life in capitalism.

After Marxism we ragpickers are marginalized voices outside the paradigm of cognition provided by mathematical physics, yet we still continue to work within the Enlightenment tradition. This still provides the pre-established public language for making something coherent from the contingency of the fragments at the edge of the human-machine interface. We are caught up in the demands and difficulties entailed by Enlightenment, the increasing need for freedom from its conventions of the past, and the temptation to regress and retreat into the apparent security of its humanist cultural form of the philosophy of the subject. We quickly come up against the limits of the language of the scientific Enlightenment, when we use the embodied subjective experience of our damaged lives as the starting point for cultural analysis. Whilst recognizing that this experience, in both its content and form, is already culturally formed and inscribed, and subject to historical transformation, we find ourselves philosophically speechless in the face of our own experience. This "ineffable" is locked in the muteness of individual experience, and the speechlessness in the face of one's own experience is also speechlessness in the face of reality. Instrumental reason continues to impact on our daily lives, as embodied in a neo-classical economics that is currently being used by the state to globalize Australian capitalism. This re-engineering of Australian society to construct a competitive and efficient capitalist economy modelled on textbook capitalism is deemed to be unavoidable, necessary and desirable.[55] Yet our suffering cannot be expressed in the formal language of a *sub specie aeternitatis* science mirroring the real. This language blocks our suffering, truncates it, and turns this particularity into a pathology, which can only be understood in the language of the scientific Enlightenment as untruth. Our suffering is the non-identical, and it becomes the other of reason. The metaphysical realist language of a *sub specie aeternitatis* mathematical science is hopelessly inadequate for a philosophy in the city committed to socialism.

The two cultures revisited

How are we to avoid this speechlessness associated with running up against the limits of language, with the critique of analytic reason at the end of tradition? We search for those resources within philosophical language upon which we can draw to name the suffering, and to allow the particular to come into its own. At this point we enter into a tension field between the Enlightenment and romanticism. The classic way that this conflict in our intellectual culture has been historically mapped by scientific analytic philosophy is in terms of anti-naturalism and naturalism. In this narrative our intellectual culture was seen to be torn by a long and bitter conflict between the two cultural formations of religion and the secular Enlightenment. Analytic materialist philosophers were resolutely for the tough materialist Enlightenment, and resolutely against all forms of religion and theism which they defined as anti-naturalism. Mechanism developed in opposition to religious obscurantism and mystification, and its grand Enlightenment narrative of a progressive, demystifying, mechanistic materialism overcoming theism and all forms of idealism, holds that victory has gone to science. We live in an enlightened culture as scientific reason has only to engage in a few clean-up operations against oddities like religious myth posing as creationist science and madness. Post-tradition is post-enlightenment. It is anti-Enlightenment.

This old map of the conflict in modernity is commonly marked by positivism and romanticism, whose theories are almost the reverse images of each other.[56] It is overlaid by a new map of the agonistic struggle within modernity, which splits liberal culture into the two antagonistic traditions of a technocratic scientific elite and an expressive literary one. C. P. Snow argued that this divide between a techno-science and the humanities has gradually widened, that the scientists held the future in their bones, whilst the humanist intellectuals, whom he cast as Luddites, spent their time wishing the future did not exist.[57] Though Snow's two cultures are becoming increasingly interlocked, as we can see from the Gulf war over non-renewable resources and precision co-ordination of military and media presentation, his thesis is affirmed by the scientific materialist philosophers. They see Enlightenment culture arising from the hard sciences of artificial intelligence and cognitive science, with their technically-defined domain and engineering culture as the future.[58] Their roots are in the French Enlightenment that had declared with Descartes that nature was mechanistic, and, with Baron d'Holbach, who held that man was a machine. This culture is aligned with Bacon, who held that science and technology dominate nature to ensure utility to man's estate. It speaks in the voice of English utilitarianism, which assumes that society was a machine, and holds that the required social control needed to deal with private interest, speaks in the name of scientific reason from a central tower. This research field is concerned with an artificial language as a universal language, with cognitive psychology which takes the computer to be the model of the mind, and a politics which holds that human beings are sub-systems in a larger machine controlled by scientific experts. It had been prefigured in the cybernetics movement which had attempted to show that self-organizing systems, such as living things, could be explained on the basis of the same principles of feedback, homeostasis, and control that applied to machines.[59]

This places the humanities in a difficult position of being bypassed by the scientistic utilitarian spirit of the age, which defines the natural sciences as the progressive enterprise *par excellence.* The marginalized humanist's position has been aptly characterised by Adorno:

> "Anyone who is defending something that the spirit of an age rejects as out of date and obsolete is in an awkward position. The arguments put forward sound lame and overdone. He addresses his audience as though he is trying to talk them into buying something they don't want. This drawback has to be reckoned with by those who are not prepared to be dissuaded from philosophy."[60]

The out-of-date is an obsolete ethical/political humanist philosophy that articulates our suffering, and is concerned with the self-realization of human potential and citizenship in a free republic. The defenders of the Enlightenment fortress say they are defending the realm of reason, truth, knowledge, science against its many enemies, who have drunk too deeply from the poetic and embraced the Dostoevskian revolt against reason and science. These ragpicking greenies seek refugee in pre-industrial fantasies, pre-technocratic values and organic communes filled with a communal nostalgia of the golden age of an Aboriginal yesteryear. This is the violent dimension of the identity thesis of science mirroring the objectively real. What is non-identical is the untrue, the irrational, and the mythical.

The debate is more complex than this scenario allows. There are several considerations. First a humanist philosophy sees a reductive materialist tradition working with a dualism in which the enlightened few, who are not swayed by their emotions, are superior to the ignorant vulgar who are caught up in myth and emotion. This tradition gives cultural expression to the way we currently see ourselves as machines in a mechanized world, and so provides the social habitus for the way we act in the world and our identity as philosophers. Politicians pull levers, administrative managers control the machine, scientist/philosophers design the machine, whilst ordinary folk press each other's buttons and think in computational terms. The classic, autonomous individual is liquidated, to be replaced by the fad-like cult of the television personality, created by the objective processes of mass cultural industry. The popularity of these machine images is disturbing, as these images imply that mechanistic systems are closed systems, in which human beings are more or less a working part which can be bio-engineered to become more efficient. Bentham's Panopticon is the early iron-cage image of instrumental reason in a modern enlightened capitalist society. It captures the dream of a virtually seamless, closed system articulated by organizations and institutions of domination that have a life of their own, tied to a logic of functioning that shapes, controls and directs every aspect of life, even of those who apparently direct, control and benefit from the system.[61] Enlightened reason as an instrumental reason is a means/end rationality that claims to represent the whole of reason, and it needs particular enclaves of irrationality to justify the seemingly rational world that capitalism has created, and neo-classical economics ideologically reflects.

A second consideration is that the ragpickers in the humanities, who have experienced a form of life living in the scientistic fortress on the hill of knowledge overlooking the plains of everyday life in civil society, realize that the scientific defenders of the Enlightenment practise peephole metaphysics. Through the peephole inside the castle, 'as through the crenels of a parapet, the subject gazes upon a black sky in which the star of the idea or being, is said to rise.'[62] The irrational star that is seen these days is the postmodern current in the humanities. Through the crenel of the black glass skyscraper of instrumental reason, the growing numbers of postmodern literary intellectuals are seen to be causing chaos and disorder in the land, as they spread the false doctrines of relativism, irrealism, idealism and nihilism. Philosophy defines itself through negation, as the philosophical creates its other, engenders its opposite, which then is put into play as a hostile principle. The resentful, melancholic, declassed ragpickers must conform to the hierarchy of reason, as they stand for the return of an outmoded romanticism that a modernist philosophical reason spurns. In revolting against this violent repression, the ragpickers see the scientific philosophers as seeking refuge in their own scientific language for the sake of their protection and security against the pain and suffering caused by the Enlightenment project. The compulsion of conceptual thought to systematize makes everything non-identical that does not fit; this non-identical then appears as threatening. Rage and fear are the typical forms of reaction to the experience of the non-identical in the philosophy institution. Yet the map of the agonistic conflict signifies that it is the traditional moral discourse of the humanities that provides the pre-given public language for the expression of the ragpicker's mute experience of suffering.

The third consideration is the irrationality within a scientific culture's rational claim that the defence of reason and science against the emergence of error and illusion is our best hope in a liberal civilization. Science's sovereign claim to be the guardian of reason is undercut by the undesirable characteristic of reason hunting down the enemies of reason. The defence mechanisms that have been erected against the non-identical functions to repress the other, as in the socialization of the philosopher, denied as in forms of dogmatism, or even physically eliminated by hunting it down. One instance of this tendency is Plato who says:

> "if we meet with the Sophist at bay, we should arrest him on the royal warrant of reason, report the capture and hand him over to the sovereign. But if we should find some lurking place among the subdivisions of this art of imitation, we must follow hard upon him, constantly dividing the part that gives him shelter, until he is caught."[63]

Platonic philosophy polices the boundaries of reason to seek out the dark side of non-reason. Its method is one of arrest and discipline. Running through the language of the republic of Platonic theory and universal philosophy in a just society is the sub-text of the expulsion of the artists. Art was deemed to be both alienated from truth and belonging to the world of opinion (*doxa*), appearance, (political life), and non-being (communal ethical life). If we view this hunting down from the perspective of an autonomous art, then scientific philosophy's suppression of political life, its liquidation of everyday life, and the suppression of art and aesthetics converges into an implicit unity of art and politics becoming one.

Another instance of the irrationality buried in the scientistic solution Jacques Monod offered to resolve the radical disjunction between science and the humanities, in terms of a reconstruction which eliminates the latter. According to Monod the:

> "traditional concepts which provided the ethical foundations of human societies from time immemorial, all consisted of imaginary ontogenes, none of which remains tenable in the face of scientific inquiry....This contradiction creates intolerable tensions under which (modern) societies will collapse unless radically new foundations for their value systems can be found."[64]

Monod's solution is simple. The rational reconstruction of our value system is one that embraces the findings and attitudes of science. We abandon the sources of cultural tension in bourgeois culture to ensure social stability by keeping science, and eliminating the mythical and religious resources of the competing values of the humanities.[65] The irrationality of scientific reason is the repressed desire to eliminate the humanities. We find this buried in the way analytic philosophers currently repudiate the dubious continental poet-philosophers, such as Nietzsche, Heidegger, Rorty and Derrida, all of whom are associated with the return of repressed aesthetic/literary tradition in the humanities. The hunting down of these Sophist aesthetic philosophers is best seen in the attacks on Derrida's writings, as he is deemed most likely to lead us into the abyss of nihilism and madness.[66] Derrida is currently singled out because he probably goes further than any philosopher since Nietzsche and Heidegger to break with the unconscious assumptions of logocentrism of analytic philosophy. His anti-theory (analogous to the anti-art in high modernism?) offers a style of writing that provides a greater awareness of the ways in which certain theories of language constrain our view of objects, texts, art, reality, science, philosophy and experience. Postmodernism, as the other of reason, upsets the normal workings of philosophy. It is pinned down by the searchlight of universal reason because it threatens the analytic philosophical edifice of a universal science. A law and order game of hunting down ideologies, imposters and clowns in the value spheres of ethics and aesthetics is institutionalized. This is one where resistance on the fringes is tolerated if it stabilises the reign of law of a universal science. What remains unthought in Anglo-American philosophy is the critical enlightening role that art and aesthetic reason can play in opposition to techno-science. This is what can be salvaged by oppositional, humanist intellectuals in the face of a formalist neo-Kantian aesthetics, which alienates art from truth and ethics.

What is notable about the hunting metaphor is that the ultimate wielders of hermeneutic power are those who have the cultural clout to decide such matters, and they then interpret others in terms of their own preferential terms. This implies that those who do not hold to the basic principles and metaphysics of reductive materialism are in error, if they are not ignorant or have deficient ability as reasoning beings. This conceptual framework polarizes and splits apart two orders of being into a hierarchical relationship, to ensure that the subordinate order is systematically and pervasively construed and depicted as inferior. Scientific philosophy dominates as it orders the moral and aesthetic spheres into their place by offering the choices to the postmodern Sophists to assimilate or be hunted down as quarry.[67] In hunting down the new postmodern Sophists the prestige of the scientific tradition is used to tell us continually what reason is and what it isn't, what is allowed and what is not. That it is able to do this indicates that a theoretical scientific reason which puts a practical utilitarian ethics in a subordinate place, rules the roost as an arrogant scientism. In the form of economism it has reduced liberalism to economic rationalism's revival of the free market with its principles of efficiency and negative liberty. It has pushed a cultural liberalism to the periphery as outmoded, where it now survives in a decadent form of privatized self-expression and self-fulfillment.[68]

The fifth consideration is that the rational core of the humanities lies in aesthetics, which was hatched and nurtured in the Enlightenment as the implacable enemy of instrumental reason. It was the cultural refugee of self-determining autonomy, creativity and the sensuous particularity of the body for the bourgeoisie from its own actual values of competitiveness, exploitation and material possessiveness that found expression in civil society.[69] Scientism tries to resolve this contradiction between scientific and aesthetic culture within bourgeois civilization by repressively disavowing the very history which constitutes the Enlightenment. But what is disavowed as Sophist irrationality returns to haunt an elitist technocratic culture as a radicalized aesthetic reason. Art may well be an increasingly marginal pursuit compared to science. But as Eagleton observes, aesthetics is not. It deals with the mess made by scientific reason, with its marginalization of pleasure and the body, reification of reason and the emptying of morality.[70] The different value spheres of science, ethics and aesthetics are not radically incommensurable, as they have developed out of the Enlightenment tradition, and so have a shared history in attaining an enlightened community of thought and judgement, wherein philosophical disputes are open to constructive dialogical exchange. The aesthetic returns after its banishment with postmodernism as the politics of nature, because nature— including the body—is the medium for linking biopolitics to the large-scale forces of the physical and social worlds. It returns innocuously enough in the early 1980s, as an exploration of the relationship between the body, sexual difference and social inequality.[71] It develops into an account of how power, domination and difference intersect in the lived experiences of men and women, and in the body politic.

These considerations indicate that Snow's map of hard science versus the soft humanities needs reworking. Science's hunting down of an aesthetic culture shows the Enlightenment devouring its own, at a time when we need aesthetics to explore capitalism's creation of a baroque consumer culture as spectacle in leisure, tourism and consumption which manipulates our pleasure and desires.[72] In *America* Baudrillard argues that the US., as the leading edge of hyper-reality, transforms the social universe into a system of simulated cultures. Even political reality can no longer be distinguished from TV reality, since the majority consume news reports of political violence, street warfare and gangsterism in the same way they consume fictions and fantasies about simulated violence.[73] This indicates that the humanities are not of antiquarian interest, as they have an engaging sense of relevance.[74] The humanities can give a different understanding of the historical relationships between the value spheres of science, ethics and aesthetics to that offered by the master perspective of scientism in a scientific culture. If the hunting metaphor implies the adoption of authoritarian principles of mastery, control and domination, then a step to a non-dominating way of dealing with philosophical conflict is suggested by the philosophical metaphor of debate/dialogue in philosophy between the different spheres of reason.

Aristotle is suggestive here, as he argued in his *Metaphysics* that one way of dealing with someone who disagrees with the basic principles or presuppositions of a tradition is not to accuse them of stupidity, absurdity, logical error and wrong-headedness. We should, he argued, give them the *paideia* they lack. *Paideia* is a kind of initiation into the way things are done in a community, a sort of acculturation into the tradition of philosophy, a moral education. Aristotle then adds ominously: 'Some need persuasion, others need compulsion.'[75] Sometimes this can be done gently, other times it is done with violence, other times not at all. Aristotle's model suggests that the basic principles of reason are relative to a certain body of knowledge—a contextual *a priori*—which offers an opening into a dogmatic science that assumes its basic principles and axioms represent the truth. Aristotle's model suggests that we can be educated into the different value spheres with their metaphysics, bodies of knowledge and styles of reasoning. Its advantage is that it allows us to acknowledge that the universality of Australian materialism is grounded on the particularity of modernity, and that the Enlightenment is a cultural tradition of rational inquiry, with its own set of prejudices that reason suggests can be discarded, because they are untenable. Because reason has fractured in modernity, philosophy can operate from the ethical or aesthetic sphere as well as the scientific, and so acknowledge that there have historically been many different philosophical styles.

Philosophy operating from an ethical or aesthetic sphere can pose questions like: Why take Australian materialism as the final vocabulary? Why not a bit more liberal tolerance in the contest between the rival discursive regimes of the different value spheres? Why not a bit more dialectical give and take, that would enable us to resist the lure of scientistic closure by bringing the competing intellectual discourses into dialogue? Once we begin to explore the complex criss-crossing of the problems that lie between the value spheres, we could then define the resistance to the scientific Enlightenment's universal project as an oppositional criticism, that rejects the privileging of a universal theoretical scientific reason over the other value spheres. It is oppositional because the naturalization of society by a scientistic economic science makes the social institution of the market natural, and so denies the way that human beings give determinate social meaning to non-economic activities. Such a humanist philosophy sees the market as a social institution, which embodies a set of norms, values and relationships, and socializes us into a certain kind of possessive, embodied individual with particular kinds of virtues. This is a critical stance of an ethical reason, not that of unreason that needs to be eliminated.

Re-establishing bridges

We unemployed ragpickers have the free time to deal philosophically with our resentment at being dispossessed by the servants of capital, and at not being recognized by the gatekeepers of a scientific culture. We can employ our creativity to think what our resentment about modernity means when philosophically expressed in the language of the humanities. We are in a position to do so, because in being rejected from the elite professional academic world, we enter into the everyday life-world. We realize that our embodied experiences in this life-world are at odds with the instrumental rationality of the work-world, formalized into calculation procedures, rules and formulae. Our suffering makes contact with the sensuous particularity of the everyday, which is also the realm of the aesthetic, currently full of mourning, grief and remembrance at its banishment from philosophy.

A philosophy aligned with the humanities starts with being mindful of what has been forgotten. In standing at the critical vantage point an aesthetic reason permits, we can begin our rethinking by rejecting the scientific conception of human beings as desiring machines; as operators putting a set of mathematical procedures to work; or of thinking as technique in terms of rational decision-making. We realize that what has been left out of academic philosophy is a critique about the meaning and value of technocracy, and that the lived experience of the life-world is virtually forbidden to speak in its different voice within a technical and quantifying culture. Here the mind, which has been disciplined by the work culture to become capable of functioning like a machine, recognizes itself in the machine which is capable of functioning like itself. This calculative decision-making form of thinking dispenses the subject from giving meaning to the decisions and from making value judgements by accepting ethical responsibility for them. It is just a question of whether or not they were following correct procedure laid down in the manual which codifies the conventions. In accepting this picture of the subject representing the world-in-itself as authoritative, trust or faith is placed in the instrumental rationality of the detached unbiased subject. In assuming its account is pure insight, (the unbiased detached look at the world, that is freed from all tradition and irrational authority), it fails to understand its own activity as historical social practice. Instead it posits a metaphysical support for itself by holding that its representations match up with the world as atomistic physical matter. So its authoritative reasons really are authoritative.

It is at this point that the ragpickers, in getting their socialist bearings after Marxism, make contact with the artist-philosopher Nietzsche. He is the philosopher *par excellence* of the body, who links sickness from suffering to the need for a future philosophy. Nietzsche, as the physician-philosopher, declares war on a philosophical reason that embraces atomism which 'leads a dangerous afterlife in physics'; and a God's-Eye-View which culminates in a formal propositional logic, employing abstract signs to describe a reality which exists independently of the act of description. He counterpoises perspectivism and the diversity of the things of this world to a disembodied, transcendental, universal reason which holds that as there is only one reality, there will ultimately be only one adequate description of it. Nietzsche observes that he has often asked himself 'whether taking the large view, philosophy has not been merely an interpretation of the body and a *misunderstanding of the body*.'[76] He says that he is 'still waiting for a philosopher *physician* in the exceptional sense of that word—one who has to pursue the total health of a people, time, race or of humanity' and that 'what is at stake in all philosophizing hitherto was not at all "truth" but something else—let us say, health, future, growth, power, life.'[77] Nietzsche's conception of art as the countermovement to a decadent, nihilistic science, avoids an art which responds to nihilism by seeking refuge in the beauty of form, because value is attributed to the body as a work of art. He refunctions Greek humanism as an aesthetics of self-formation which aims to achieve a full and flourishing life predicated on relationships to others.[78] Embodied self-creation of the body as

32

cultural artefact works against the normalizing effects of declining moral codes like Christianity and utilitarianism which, as systems of rules to regulate behaviour, hold that the body is alien material which reason masters and regulates. It is the health and vitality of the body, coupled with an aristocratic Stoic ethics of virtue of noble and excellent character, that is offered as an alternative to moral values.[79]

It is a left-Nietzschean poststructuralist feminism that has placed an emphasis on our sexed and embodied place in the world, and so taught us to read the semiotic mark of violence of reason on the body in terms of the effects of politics on the sexed body.[80] This feminist philosophy grapples with the universalistic ideals of modern humanism, and the particularist masculine viewpoint from which they have been articulated. It makes visible the masculine perspective from which philosophy has been constructed, and has shown that philosophy's mask of neutrality is illusory, as it has been prejudicial to women. It equates woman's exclusion in and from philosophy with silence, so that she has little voice in a universe of rationality that represses what refuses to speak this specifically masculine discourse. What is repressed by a formal reason is emotionality, the body, animality, particularity and a poetic, emotive reason.[81] So the question is what to accept or reject from the analytic tradition, and on what basis such acceptances or rejections rest.[82] It suggests that women opt for transforming philosophical discourse beyond its self-enclosure, by adopting non-hegemonic forms of reason.[83] The strategy is to read the old texts that do not give the answers by immersing ourselves in them, extracting what is needed to develop our positions, by looking at the unconscious of texts. Even though Merleau-Ponty, for instance, says virtually nothing about women, he is read because he has written a great deal on the body, subjectivity and perception.[84] This engages in a productive and constructing critique rather than just discarding the past.

This critique of philosophy by philosophy could result in a critical reason remaining within philosophy's institutional boundaries, thereby ignoring the challenges philosophy does not want to meet by discounting them as non-philosophical. We ragpickers can counter this strategy by rupturing the boundaries of the philosophical, by linking up with the humanist tradition in sociology. This is concerned to preserve and recover an embodied subjectivity that is able to articulate itself in a meaningful way against the depersonalized world of modern capitalism, so that subjectivity does not go under.[85] This is not the pained resignation stance standing out from the mass expressly marked by the pathos of distance, nor a romantic retreatism in the face of mechanism. It is a stance of an ethic of responsibility to face up to one's times as a minimalist answer to the instrumental rationality that ends in Enlightenment nihilism.[86] This sociology holds rationalization to involve a set of ascetic practices based on the subordination of the desires of the body and the control of emotion. It actively seeks a substantive rationality that is concerned with the goals of human beings within a self-defeating rationalization process. This process robs industrial capitalism of the moral legitimacy which makes rational inquiry purposeful with respect to values in a world of value conflict. The requirement is for a non-instrumental conception of reason that has the resources to reverse Weber's diagnosis of rationalization as engendering the loss of meaning and value in modernity.

This rupturing of philosophy's narrow institutional boundaries allows a humanist ethical philosophy with more resources to engage critically with the expansion of a formal instrumental reason in the guise of a hegemonic utilitarian economic rationality. This has expanded its sphere of operations, as a result of economic restructuring by the economic planners, who have achieved dominance in the Federal Treasury. The technocratic power elite works with a model of society as an abstract cybernetic system, that can be regulated by pulling the right economic levers to ensure that the machine keeps ticking along, by extending the possibilities for the human utilization of the environment. The bureaucratization and increasing technological transformation of society endeavours to make society into a single cybernetic machine, in which human beings are cogs, and efficiency, profit and technically superior administration are the ultimate and sole values in the ordering of affairs. Economic planning works with a conception of planning and decision-making that is remote, hierarchical and undemocratic, and its hegemony means that all arguments must be couched in neo-classical economic technical terms of solving problems within the utilitarian ethos, the parameters of the free market, with all political questions bracketed. Social problems are reduced to problems of technical control and manipulation, and this is seen as the only model for reflecting on practical questions. Economic liberalism provides the ideological vehicle for the vast transformations ushered in by corporate capitalism's current economic, social and cultural restructuring of society. Economics achieves this by holding that the free market is an efficient resource allocation machine that generates growth. Neo-classical economics holds that the economy, as a free play of the market, resembles the great machine of nature as it is governed by strict mathematical laws, with the economic laws viewed as the counterparts of those laws of physics that regulate the configurations and movements of the universe. Nature and society mirror each other.[87] It maintains that society must bow to the market, and that politics must abdicate in favour of the market. Both society and politics should conform to the logic of economic rationality, and that no goals which run counter to the free market economy should be granted legitimacy.[88]

A humanist, sociologically informed, ethical philosophy engages with this arrogant scientific culture, by holding that as a formal instrumental reason has expanded into more and more dimensions of social life, cultural modernity has produced a diremption of universal and particular, generalized and concrete other, morality and ethics The result of the broadened market is that it now creates its own culture, as a civilizing impulse, and has its own habitual modes of conduct, and a legal and administrative system whose functioning can be rationally predicted by an instrumental reason as if it were a machine.[89] The market has a particular kind of politics, based on the trickle-down effect of wealth, created from the efforts of the industrious entrepreneurs and the need to create wealth by freeing up the market.[90] The tendency is for the growing control of nature to be also the subjugation of human subjectivity and freedom, is countered by the technological image the media offers. The image is one of a self-sustaining system of rules and lifestyle, a form of governance and subjectivity, and a set of strategies by which the self comes to make itself over in the market image of the new liberal social order. The utilitarian self as utility machine manages its personal identity as human capital seeking a good return on its investment. In the new order of the free market and strong state in a high-tech global economy, the Protestant asceticism of the work-ethic is counterbalanced by an emotionalist pleasure at home, where pleasure-seeking and self-expressive people can consume media images, and turn themselves into images of the body beautiful.[91] Though the economic machine does protect some from insecurity and anguish, by making us comfortable with rising standards of living, it does so at the cost of the deprivation of meaning and freedom, and a general dehumanization. Life at head office in the modern bureaucracy is still dull, meaningless, and empty.[92] With economic rationalism it is more pressured and controlled.

Social pessimism can be avoided by opening up the possibility of reading modernist culture in terms of the contradiction between the principles of abstract universalism, instrumental rationality and formal coherence of a scientific culture and state administration, and the principles of otherness, contradiction, ambivalence, and catastrophe of an aesthetic culture. The latter holds that instrumental reason functions within the coordinated control of surveillance systems over the violence of the passions and suffering of socially-inscribed gendered bodies within the territory of a nation-state. It opens up a space to rethink the ends of human action so that we can live a different way of life from that offered to us by the ethos of utilitarianism. Here the negation of suffering is overcome by the happiness of individual desire satisfaction of consumers joyously shopping in the postmodern global market. This is the compensation for the senselessness of suffering wrought by the unemployed bearing the weight of civilization upon our backs. Yet our sufferings are not appeased by the market's false offers of the happiness of self-realization in the form of holidays to exotic places. It is also a question of identity as the linguistic forms of systematic production of knowledge in the institutionalized discourse of neo-classical economics provides the cognitive frame for reifying practices. The reifying practices of the economists are inextricably linked to the reification of people by economics which, in deriving its language and methodology from the natural sciences, sees people as utility machines surviving in the competitive jungle of the marketplace. In contrast this ahistorical science, that now functions as orthodoxy that speaks in terms of timeless truth, our identity as social beings is linked to a practical ethical reason that gives voice to suffering, includes a cognition of human ends, grants a space to the recognition of others, and is sensitive to the issue of who gets to define what counts as knowledge. The production of knowledge is a political enterprise that involves a contest among conflicting ideas and interests. Reason is now part of the everday world rather than squatting outside it.

Blocking the expansion of instrumental reason

An alternative language to that of neo-classical economics can be found in a decayed humanist culture. This once contended that modern self-identity, as authentic self-fulfilment is perfectly reasonable and worthy of aspiration. Its relevance today lies in its rational antagonism to technocracy's conception of human beings as mechanisms or computer-controlled biological robots.[93] In movies like *Blue Thunder, Robocop*, and *Terminator* the machine culturally functions as part of what Freya Mathews calls the 'cosmology of modernity.'

Cosmologies, she says, depict the large-scale structure, origin and evolution of the concrete world. She says that Marxists have lumped cosmologies 'together with religions and mythologies as outmoded instruments for the ideological legitimation of social orders', and that analytic philosophers in the empiricist tradition of Hume, Russell, Carnap and Ayer have rejected cosmologies as being beyond the scope of verification procedures. However, she says, cosmologies satisfy the need that we have to form a conception of the place in the entire scheme of things. To be viable they must be in accord with the knowledge of the time. She adds that 'science itself has seen a renaissance of cosmological speculation in the second half of the twentieth century, a renaissance the implications of which social critics and philosophers alike have underrated.'[94] As it is science which now gives us this knowledge so it is the source of our cosmology of the world as a machine, whose symbols are rockets, space stations, and computers. The cultural function of Australian materialism was to elaborate the root metaphor of the machine into a sophisticated picture of ourselves in modernity, thereby giving philosophical intelligibility to a conception of the world as a collection of physical particles, inert, insensate, devoid of telos of value, purpose and meaning.[95]

A philosophical humanism can contest this metaphysics of machines within commodified social relations in the shiny new network world of cyberspace, with its prosthesis, genetic tinkering and computer augmentation of the brain. Its contention that modern self-identity is authentic self-fulfilment represents a non-acceptance of the universalization of the mechanistic framework in which all things have been drawn into the vortex of commodities, and whose dynamic requires that each subject as a machine adapts to the functioning of industrial economy. The technocratic picture is viewed as one of happy slaves within cybernetic systems dominated by artificial intelligence, where our pleasures are obtained from the world of mass carnage in computer war-games, or watching the Gulf War on television. Humanism contests the implicit conception of the subject in televised Gulf War, where the bodies of the abstract other as the barbaric enemy disappear from the actual scene and from memory, as fast as virtual reality corpses disappear from the screen. It does so by highlighting the way that any conception of real concrete human bodies with needs and desires mutilated by violence is suppressed. It then articulates the inferno of concrete human suffering and degradation.

A humanist philosophy can also contest a capitalist economic system which continually promises, and then postpones, a technocultural utopia. It can do so because the promised modernist industrial utopia, with its development of productive forces, the triumph of reason, the scientific domination of nature, and the expansion of the economy, is unable to deliver a humanist conception of a full and flourishing life. Guy Rundle observes that the Australian economy has now become regressive. It has:

> "ceased to be an economy capable of producing the bulk of the fundamental needs of the population, of employing the population in useful or interesting work, and ensuring a framework in which competing political projects for achieving social justice the good life can be pursued. Instead we have an economy which has been hollowed out by the debilitating effects of an increasingly globalized production system, and by a range of government policies which have facilitated that process, allowing it to occur far more rapidly. People recognize in their everyday lives, in the altered landscape of recession and depression that society is changing."[96]

The humanist protest against this economic system can bite, because this system promises to liberate us from scarcity, injustice and misery, but actually delivers a retreat of prosperity. It can develop the protest into ethical interpretation of the process of de-industralization. This results, it is held, from the technological advance of robotics and computerization, characterized by the desire to use the factors of production as efficiently as possible. The process of freeing up the market through deregulation is not creating a whole new series of new full time jobs. The part time and causal jobs it does create, leave the unemployed stranded between vanished old jobs, and the yet to be created new fulltime jobs. The new economic order is giving us a privileged stratum of permanent workers managing the running of the increasingly automated machine as part of a multi-skilled team won over to capital. But these are unable to find personal fulfilment. On the other hand there is a growing mass of unemployed, casuals and odd-jobbers with free time, serving as a reserve army for institutions adjusting their workforce rapidly according to fluctuations in demand. Though the unemployed now have free time in those spaces where economic rationality ceases to govern fully, the resultant dual-economy does not create the conditions for a flourishing human life in a community of needs and solidarity. Its path which leads to a goal of a better world, is one strewn with ruins. It is a path to a world in which a large section of the population will continue to be expelled or else marginalized from the sphere of economic activities, whilst a well-paid working section of the population will buy leisure time by getting their own personal tasks done for them at low cost, by other people who constitute the servant class of low-paid workers.[97] The late modernist culturalscape signifies the departure of subjectivity, and has as its counterpart, an economic landscape strewn with ruins, vast fissure and holes. The soundscape is one of the cries of anxious terror of the suffering, whose bleeding eyes and organs turn to mush from being infected by a rapidly spreading doomsday Ebola style virus. The fiery subtropical flashes of lightning illuminate the ruined present of silent shuffling of the hungry, poor and homeless bodies alienated from a society obsessed with mastery over nature. It also reveals an uncertain future in which old resurgent diseases, such as tuberculosis, cholera, malaria, dengue fever, and pneumonia, reappear in newly virulent and resistant strains.

The ragpickers contemplate this tragedy with melancholy, and their gaze discloses that scientific-technological practice can no longer be considered ethically neutral, as its goal is the perpetuation of its own form of life, even as it becomes progressively less able to deal with the problems it has engendered. In uncovering the repression of ethics by technocratic discourse, they can provide an ethical form for the content of the resentful mood of deep and bitter cynicism that recoils from the grand narrative of economic progress through globalization. It counters the economic liberal way of life of consumerism and possessive individualism with a model of community formed through needs and solidarity, with human flourishing based on concrete individuality, and identity formed through reciprocal interactions with others. This new ethic with its humanist conception of a flourishing life is more responsible, and cares more about the effects of exercising the power used to dominate and lay waste to the non-human world.[98] The violent and deep reaction to the intrusion of the commodity relation and form into more and more areas of everyday life, is also a desire to defend the traditional social democratic way of life as one well worth living. It is one where the norms of our interactions with others are those of solidarity, friendship, love and care.

This humanist ethics sees the struggle for recognition arising from the resentment at being hurt by rejection and unemployment as an ethical struggle for the restitution of social conditions that provide for the full recognition of an individual with a concrete history, identity and affective-emotional character. It is an ethical/political struggle for a community in which human beings relate to, are recognized by, and confirmed by others, as a concrete individual with specific needs, talents, and capacities. This recognition-based struggle is forming because the new work ideology of the deregulated market represses and silences a community of need and solidarity. Consider the way the intellectual mandarins of high modernist philosophical culture, who see themselves with superior skills and abilities, hold that as there are not enough permanent jobs to go round, so they should have the best paid jobs. The best succeed, they say. Those ragpicking, declassed postmodernist and continental philosophers, who are aligned with and have their roots in the humanities, have only themselves to blame for being out of work. They are just not good enough. They are not a part of a high-tech scientific culture, and they have embraced pseudo-philosophy which is full of the errors of irrealism, relativism, skepticism, and nihilism. As these errors need to be corrected by the managerial, analytic custodians of scientific reason, so the entrepreneurial managers should not subsidize the unemployed, the poor, and marginalized philosophers. Casual and unemployed philosophers are not serious about looking for teaching, and do not possess the adequate research skills to carry philosophical culture forward. Departments cannot afford to encourage the ragpickers' idleness by over-generous wage rates, grants, or subsidies, since the whole economy is groaning under the weight of an excessive welfare burden, and it is no longer strong enough to create a growing number of jobs. What is eliminated in the new discourse of the multiversity is the recognition and confirmation of concrete others, with specific needs and talents in a community of need and solidarity. This standpoint is suppressed by the economic and liberal political tradition, whose categories of preferences, utility, rights and entitlements cover up the destruction of community by the fragmentation of jobs in a dual economy.

A humanist philosophy has relevance because the cultural mood of suffering, anxiety and resentment cannot be crammed into the categorical system of neo-classical economics. This views human beings as utility machines seeking satisfaction in the global market through unconstrained consumption. The identity of the human being as a machine, fixed by a set of physical properties which uniquely individuates the object through processes of change, fails to account for the way that the cultural mood of suffering and resentment is tied up with the identity of being a person. This identity is internally linked to a cultural background, whose qualitative distinctions concern those desires that matter more to us than utility, because they involve alternative courses of action and ways of living in a destructive present. So we ragpickers, who have been marginalized as fulltime academic philosophers, suffer an identity crisis. We have lost contact with the framework of distinctions of being a universal intellectual that provides the sense of discernment between the more and less worthwhile. The identity crisis results in a kind of vertigo before the question "Who am I?" The ragpicker has no resource by which to answer it. She/he says "I am unemployed, and I am no longer a part of the small professional circle of academic philosophers furthering the Enlightenment, even though the money still comes in from the dole." The question of identity demands an answer, even if we are not in a position to give one, because it involves a different way of doing philosophy. As our identity defines the space of distinctions within which we live and choose in orientation to the good, so things matter for us over and above being a desiring utility machine. We are self-interpreting social animals who consider it important that one lives as a concrete human being, who engages in meaningful activity, and whose needs and courses of action can be recognized and judged in terms of a cultural background of strong evaluation.[99] The ragpicker's identity is tied up with being a philosopher carrying on the Socratic tradition in the common life, of becoming public intellectuals in the nation-state. Though this is contingent upon a historically specific cultural horizon and social conditions, a cultural background of strong evaluations is indispensable for public intellectuals to live a flourishing life within a community.[100] But the new economic liberalism just gives us the regulation of the desires and preferences by the unfettered market in terms of ego-utility maximization. So it subsequently reduces the strong qualitative distinctions that matter for identity to the weak subjective preferences of choosing consumer goods. It denies the conditions for recognition based on self-realization within the communal ethos of a particular form of good life, as it reduces ethics to desires and economic interests of the abstract, isolated subject alone in the disenchanted universe.

The critical edge of this humanist ethical philosophy within everyday life provides the ground from which a criticism of technocracy can be launched. It blocks the expansion of instrumental reason in terms of an inter-human struggle over identity, meaning and value. It counters the spread of instrumental reason in a scientific culture by making practical reason primary, and then challenges the reduction of practical reason to a universal utilitarian moral reason. A humanist ethical conception of being in the everyday world that Hegel called *Sittlichkeit* provides the refuge and vital space for autonomy and opposition to a hegemonic scientism.[101] It roots are practical reason as phronesis, with its particular vision of the virtuous person and the good life, and its conception of politics as changing the conditions of social life to enable the formation of citizens capable of virtuous action in a free republic. This is what Heidegger calls an unthought in the scientistic part of our culture: it is a non-utilitarian practical reason concerned with the good life within ecological sustainable development.

Articulating this unthought involves both stepping beyond the modernist tradition, and being against it. The utilitarian subject's self-assertion over an intrinsically valueless nature works with a formal instrumental reason, that stands mute as to the ends of social action, and is powerless to make meaningful distinctions among values. In the end we are offered nothing but expressions of personal preferences within a global economy. The utilitarian self is at sea amongst its various competing desires, not knowing how to choose appropriate ends, and so is continually being seduced by the siren consumption songs spun by the aesthetized commodity in a disenchanted world. This shows that the reliance on the assumption of people's "natural" inclinations to self-interest would, if structured by "reason", lead to harmony is ill-founded. Reason and nature, morality and happiness may be in natural harmony in the perfectly, competitive market, with its model of reason as a form of quasi-mathematical representation. But in the real world of Australian capitalism the subject as citizen is in populist revolt at the economic destruction of his/her way of life. This revolt by citizens talking about people power highlights the way the utilitarian Enlightenment produces a set of self authenticating principles of knowledge and evaluation, by putting an abstraction called reason in place; and then taking it on faith that from this "reason" we can logically deduce the social institutions, that will unify the impersonal view from nowhere, and the personal view of individuals as autonomous subjects within a historical social order. The full union of the two points of view in the Platonic form of the perfectly competitive market fails to take fully into account the destruction of community, and the ecological limitations of the destruction of nature that endangers the survival of life on earth. The collapse of capitalist civilization from self-destruction is a real possibility.

Conclusion

This sketch of the scientific Enlightenment is constructed from the perspective of those resentful, unemployed ragpickers, situated on the border of analytic philosophy, sociology and cultural studies. The story they tell is one about observing reason in early modernity, which used science to force nature to reveal its secrets, then gave rise to a view of people as independent agents, which in turn gave rise to the modern idea that its form of life can be completely self-justifying.[102] It affirmed its social and political institutions for itself without appeal to anything other than what is demanded by human reason. But the unfolding of the Enlightenment project within capitalism has resulted in its being turned inside out, and becoming its opposite. Human beings have become enslaved by the very technical apparatus that gave them mastery over nature. The situation is one of self-destruction under the guise of self-preservation, with catastrophe being things continuing as they are in the disorientating labyrinth of high consumption in the global market. Though this form of life has become authoritative in late modernity, there is an awakening up from the fetishistic dream of progress sung by the commodity sirens of advertising, with their eternal recurrence of the new, where social relations have decayed into relations between things.[103] There is a political recoil from the Treasury model of the economically educated, state administrator, guided by instrumental rationality, and a rejection of his aim to scientistically redesign society on behalf of global capital.

These offer a critical diagnosis of the techno-economists recycling the discredited early Enlightenment idea of simply "reading off" the so-called rational economic laws from observation of the existing set of social practices. The naive trick being performed by the Treasury mandarins is to take a particular social and historically formed set of desires and beliefs, and then posit them as "universal human nature". Then they use a universal formal reason to deduce a form of life of the free market, and conclude that reason and reality are one. The ragpickers, in responding to human suffering caused by this redesign of society, have worked out a conception of academics in the humanities as public intellectuals.[104] The oppositional humanist culture, which has been misunderstood, isolated and discriminated against, has historically provided the basis for a philosophical criticism tentatively linked to a morally-informed sociological critique of modernity. Conservatives such as T S. Eliot and Heidegger reacted against progressive industralization, mass democracy and universalism, and worked up a conservatism that developed the romantic critique of technological capitalism in the name of an anti-capitalist utopia.[105] A Left-humanism in the 1990s has questioned the value of unimpeded industrialization, by developing green alternatives of ecological sustainablity, and questioned the desirability of universalism and globalism by defending localism.[106] This political left operates within the Weberian thesis of the social world as a well oiled machine, which has been accepted and developed by Marcuse and Ellul into the technocratic thesis.[107] This sees scientific rationality as thoroughly integrated into a modern industrial capitalism which threatens to absorb all opposition. Though there is an absence of an organized radical humanist intelligentsia, such a thesis erodes the grounds from which any criticism of technological discourse could be launched.[108]

The ragpickers resolved this by claiming that the crisis of modernity involves the emancipatory ideals of the authoritative Enlightenment tradition not being realized. They developed fragmentary grounds for critique through the hermeneutical recovery of concrete persons entering in dialogue with another in everyday life. Here understanding another involves an understanding of social meanings that always commences from the background of a meaningful world. Dialogic practical reason functions to block the encroachment of instrumental reason the latter into the everyday domain of the former, and to resist its colonization of ethical reason in everyday life.[109] This violent rupturing from the analytic tradition, then turns to speaks critically about the sciences. So the ragpickers become part of the "academic left" who have crashed the gates of the academy, are now camped in the low rent suburbs of the academy, and suffer from the disease of German philosophy. It is these squatters, who are trying to place a limit on science, who are currently being policed by the defenders of the natural sciences, who present themselves as the guarantor of the Enlightenment and the measure of reason.

Notes and References

1   John Rawls, *A Theory of Justice,* (Oxford University Press, Oxford, 1971); John Dupré, *The Disorder of Things. Metaphysical Foundations of the Disunity of Science,* (Harvard University Press, Cambridge, Massachusetts, 1993).
2   As for instance Daniel Dennett, *The Intentional Stance,* (MIT Press, Camb., Mass, 1987).
3   Judith Brett, "The Bureaucratization of Writing", *Meanjin,* no. 4, (1991), pp. 513-522.
4   M. Dever and R. Black, "Chasing Popularity: On the difficulty of publishing ideas in Australia", *Arena Magazine,* no. 2, (December-January 1993), pp. 40-41.
5   Postmodernism as an expression of frustration and resentment is developed in Robert C. Solomon, "Nietzsche, Postmodernism, and Resentment", in C. Koeb, (ed.), *Nietzsche as Postmodernist. Essays Pro and Con,* (State University of New York Press, Albany, 1990), pp. 267-293.
6   See Joseph Wayne Smith, G. Lyons, G. Sauer-Thompson, *Healing a Wounded World. Economics, Ecology and Health for a Sustainable Life,* (Praeger, Westport, 1997).
7   E. Husserl held that philosophy as universal science was the core of philosophy. This is spelt out in *The Crisis of the European Sciences and Transcendental Phenomenology,* trs. D. Carr, (Northwestern University Press, Evanston, 1970), Part 1, pp. 3-18.
8   C. A. Hooker, *Reason, Regulation and Realism,* (State University of New York Press, Albany, 1995), p. 291.
9   E. Husserl, *The Crisis of the European Sciences,* op. cit. part 11, section 9g, pp. 45-46.
10 Ibid, section 9g & 9h, pp. 48-9.
11 A. Danto, "Naturalism", *Encyclopedia of Philosophy,* (ed.), P. Edwards, (MacMillian, London, 1967), vol. 5, pp. 448-50, citation p. 448.

12   D. M. Armstrong, "Naturalism, Materialism, and First Philosophy" *Philosophia*, vol. No. 2-3, (Nov. 1978), pp. 261-178, citation p. 261.

13   Richard Routley, *Exploring Meinong's Jungle and Beyond,* (Research School of the Social Sciences, Australian National University , Canberra, 1980), p. 761.

14   For the logical empiricist account of reduction, see, E. Nagel, *The Structure of Science: Problems in the Logic of Scientific Explanation,* (Routledge and Kegan Paul, London, 1961).

15   J. C. C. Smart, "Materialism", *Journal of Philosophy*, vol. lx, (1983), pp. 651-622; D. M. Armstrong, "Naturalism, Materialism and First Philosophy", op cit.

16   For the background to scientific realism, refer to, C. A. Hooker, "Towards a General Theory of Reduction", in *Dialogue,* vol. 20. Part 1, "Historical and Scientific Setting", (March 1981), pp. 38-60; part 2, "Identity in Reduction", (June 18 981), pp. 201-236; part 3, "Cross-Categorical Reduction", (September 1981), pp. 496-529.

17   The reference here is to Eddington's two table problem. A. S. Eddington, *The Nature of the Physical World,* (University of Michigan Press, Ann Arbour, 1958).

18   For a general review of the difficulties faced by theoretical reduction to micro-entities, refer to J. W. Smith, *Reductionism and Cultural Being,* (Martinus Nijofff, The Hague, 1984), ch. 3, pp. 39-76.

19   So it has has affinities with the work of Quine. See "Dialogue with W. V. Quine" in Brain Magee, (ed.), *Men of Ideas,* (Oxford University Press, Oxford, 1982), pp. 143-44.

20   J. C. C. Smart, *Between Science and Philosophy,* (Random House, New York, 1968).

21   J. C. Smart, *Ethics, Persuasion, Truth,* (Routledge and Kegan Paul, London, 1984), p. 138.

22   C. A. Hooker, *Reason, Regulation and Realism,* op. cit., p. 1.

23   The attempts to explain this by left culture have generally been in terms of conflicts in modernity being between different social groups, in which some have more power than other with no group being entitled to dominate the rest.

24   This does not deny the regressive, conservative critiques of modernity by conservative thinkers like Leo Strauss, Stanley Rosen and Alasdair MacIntyre.

25   This is not to deny the progressive side, as illustrated in Peter Singer's levelling of the traditional hierarchal speciest distinction between inferior animals and superior human beings. Singer argues that the similar interests of animals and humans in avoiding suffering from pain means that the pain of animals is important, and that we have no ethical basis for the appaling treatment of lethal experiments in scientific research on animals. Peter Singer, *Practical Ethics,* (Cambridge University Press, Cambridge, 1979), and P. Singer, (ed.), *In Defence of Animals,* (Blackwell, Oxford, 1985). For a critical response refer to, Mary Warnock, *The Uses of Philosophy,* (Blackwell, Oxford, 1992).

26   Raymond A. Rogers, *Nature and the Crisis of Modernity. A Critique of Contemporary Discourse on Managing the Earth,* (Black Rose Books, Montreal, 1994), pp. 7-8.

27   See Smith, Lyons, Sauer-Thompson, *A Wounded World,* op. cit., ch. 1.

28   Rodolphe Gashé, *The Invention of Difference. On Jacques Derrida,* (Harvard University Press, Cambridge, Massachusetts, 1994), pp. 108-9.

29   Bill McKibben, *The End of Nature,* (Viking, London, 1990). McKibben argues that nature is no longer separate from human society as there are no pristine places outside of the destruction of nature from global pollution. Nature is now man-made and artificial.

30   Martin Lewis, *Green Delusions: An Environmentalist Critique of Radical Environmentalism,* (Duke University Press, Durham 1992), p. 3. This defence of enlightened modernity continues to divorce or decouple society from the natural world, and to acknowledge the profound division between human kind and the rest of nature in order to preserve nature. (p. 26). It is a moderate environmentalism allied with an emergent globalization of the world economy. This defence is based on a familar

analytic dualism: on the one side rational, logical, realistic, and pragmatic cost/benefit analysis; on the other shamanism/animism, fantasy, idealism, and wild enthusiasm.

31 For an exploration of the switch in popular culture from streamlined technocratic utopian futures to fears, anxieties and suspicion of a 'futureless' future of dystopian thinking, refer to Andrew Ross, *Strange Weather. Culture, Science and Technology in the Age of Limits,* (Verso, London, 1991), especially ch. 4, 'Cyberpunk in Boystown.'

32 Max Horkheimer, *The Eclipse of Reason,* (Continuum, New York, 1974),p. 75.

33 M. Horkheimer, "Reason against Itself: Some Remarks on Enlightenment", in *Theory, Culture and Society,* vol. 10, no. 2. (May 1993), pp. 79-88, citation, p. 79.

34 For an attempt to explore the dimensions of the crisis of modernity from a post-Heideggerian perspective as refracted through state socialism in Czechoslavakia, refer to Karel Kosik, *The Crisis of Modernity. Essays And Observations From The 1968 Era,* (ed.), James H. Satterwhite, (Rowman & Littlefield, London, 1995).

35 Paul Patton and Judith Allen, "Introduction", *Intervention,* vol. 17, (1983), Beyond Marxism?, Interventions after Marx, pp. 4-7 citation pp. 4-5.

36 Jan Flax, *Thinking Fragments Psychoanalysis, Feminism, & Postmodernism in the Contemporary West,* (University of California Press, Berkeley, 1990), pp. 155-6.

37 A central text which pulls the scattergun poststructuralist criticisms together on behalf of an altenative perspective is Michelle Barrett, *The Politics of Truth: From Marx to Foucault,* (Polity, Cambridge, 1991). She argued that reductionism, functionalism, essentialism and universalism are the ways that historical materialism has failed to break with the untenable assumptions of the enlightenment tradition.

38 M. Halibury, "Feminist Epistemology: An impossible project?", *Radical Philosophy,* no. 53, (Autumn 1989), pp. 3-7.

39 E. Grosz, *Jacques Lacan. A Feminist Introduction,* (Allen and Unwin, Sydney, 1990).

40 E. Grosz, *Sexual Subversions,* (Allen and Unwin, Sydney, 1989).

41 Bob Connell, "Marxists and Anti-Marxists: Reflections on Similarity and Difference", *Intervention,* No. 18, (1984), pp. 76-83, p. 79.

42 For an account on these lines re the Nietzschean influenced structuralized relativism, refer to, P. Dews, "Introduction", *Habermas: Autonomy, and Solidarity,* (Verso, London, 1986), pp. 22-7. For a similar Marxist response to Rorty's postmodernism, refer to, N. Geras, "Language, Truth, and Justice", *New Left Review,* vol. 209, (1995), pp. 110-135.

43 Postmodernism as the expression of late capitalism is argued by Frederic Jameson, "Post-Modernism, or the Cultural Logic of Late Capitalism", *New Left Review,* vol. 146, (1984), pp. 79-146. The antagonism to poststructuralist culturalism can be found in Boris Frankel, *From The Prophets Deserts Come,* (Arena Publications, North Carlton, 1992).

44 Ian Hunt, *Analytical and Dialectical Marxism,* (Avebury, Aldershot, 1993).

45 G. A. Cohen, *Karl Marx's Theory of History: A Defence,* (Oxford University Press, Oxford, 1978).

46 But see Ted Benton, *Natural Relations: Ecology, Animal Rights, and Social Justice,* (Verso, London, 1993).

47 The tension between false pleasure and true knowledge was recognized by Judith Williams, *Decoding Advertisements: Ideology and Meaning in Advertising,* (Marion Boyers, London, 1978), p. 9.

48 John Fiske, *Reading the Popular,* (Unwin Hyman, London, 1989); John Docker, *Postmodernism and Popular Culture,* (Cambridge University Press, Cambridge, 1994).

49 G. Markus, *Marxism and Anthropology,* (Van Gorcum, Assen, 1978), & *Language and Production, A Critique of Paradigms,* (D. Reidel Publishing, Dordrecht, 1986); Agnes Heller, *A Theory of History,* (Routledge and Kegan Paul, London, 1982), *For a Radical Philosophy,* (Basil Blackwell, 1983); Agnes Heller and Ferenc Feher, *The Postmodern Political Condition,* (Blackwell, Oxford, 1988); Pauline Johnson, *Marxist Aesthetics: The Foundations Within Everyday Life for an Enlightened Consciousness,* (Routledge

and Kegan Paul, London, 1984); John E. Grumley, *History and Totality. Radical Historicism from Hegel to Foucault*, (Routledge, London, 1989).

50   R. Rorty, "We Anti-Representationalists", in *Radical Philosophy*, no. 60, (Spring, 1992), pp. 3-14, citation p. 42.

51   R. Aronson, *After Marxism*, (Guildford Press, New York, 1995); J. Townsend, *The Politics of Marxism: The Critical Debates*, (Leicester University Press, London, 1996). See also M. Roberts, *Analytic Marxism-A Critique*, (Verso, London, 1996).

52   For a look into the future of MIT whizkids, refer to Stewart Brand, *The Media Lab: Inventing the Future at MIT*, (Penguin, Harmondsworth, 1986); Grant Fjermedal, *The Tomorrow Makers: A Brave New World of Livng-Brain Machines*, (MacMillian, New York, 1986).

53   See the essays in Sandra Harding, (ed.), *The 'Racial' Economy of Science: Towards a Democratic Future*, (Indiana University Press, Bloomington, 1993).

54   A. J. McMichael, *Planetary Overload*, (Cambridge University Press, Cambridge, 1993), p. 1.

55   The argument is that it has to be done to prevent the long term decline of Australia in a globalized world. It can be found clearly stated in Bob Catley, *Globalizing Australian Capitalism*, (Cambridge University Pess, Cambridge, 1996).

56   For one mapping, refer to Richard Harvey Brown, "Symbolic Realism and the Dualism of the Human Sciences: A Rhetorical Reformulation of the Debate between Positivism and Romanticism", in H. W. Simons, (ed.), *The Rhetorical Turn*, (The University of Chicago Press, Chicago, 1990), pp. 320-340.

57   C. P. Snow, *The Two Cultures and the Scientific Revolution*, (Cambridge University Press, Cambridge, 1959), p. 11.

58   For early views in this field refer to, John Haugeland, (ed.), *Mind Design: Philosophy, Psychology, Artificial Intelligence*, (MIT Press, Cambridge Massachussetts, 1980).

59   See M. Yovitts and S. Cameron, (eds.), *Self Organizing Systems*, (Peragmon, Oxford, 1960).

60   Theodore Adorno, "Why Philosophy?", in *Critical Theory, The Essential Readings*, (ed.) David Ingram and Julia Simon-Ingram, (Paragon House, New York, 1992), pp. 20-30, citation p. 20.

61   It is articulated by Foucault as the 'carceral society' and by Adorno and Horkheimer as the 'totally administered society.' Both share the idea of society as a negative totality that was already anticipated in Weber's 'iron cage'. Foucault can be read as providing the detailed analysis of the precise mechanism and techniques of control missing from the more general abstract account of Adorno and Horkheimer.

62   Theodore W. Adorno, *Negative Dialectics*, trs. H. B. Ashton, (Continuum, New York, 1987), pp. 139-40.

63   Plato, *Sophist* in *Collected Dialogues*, (ed.), Edith Hamilton and Huntington Cairns, (Princeton University Press, Princeton, 1961), 235c, p. 978.

64   J. Monod, "On Values in an Age of Science", in *The Place of Values in a World of Facts: The Fourteenth Nobel Symposium*, (Swedish Academy of Sciences, Stockholm, 1964).

65   Ibid. Refer also to J. Monod, *Chance and Necessity*, (Knopf, New York, 1971).

66   Brian Medlin, "Objectivity and Ideology in the Physical and Natural Sciences," in John Heil, (ed.), *Cause, Mind and Reality Essays in Honour of C. B. Martin*, (Kluwer Academic Publishers, Dordrecht, 1989), pp. 201-220.

67   This hunting down mentality is clearly seen in the 'science wars.' See P. Goss and N. Levitt, *HigherSuperstition: The Academic Left and Its Quarrels with Science*, (John Hopkins University Press, Baltimore, 1995).

68   A description of the birth, flowering and decay of cultural liberalism is outlined by G. Melleuish, *Cultural Liberalism in Australia*, (Cambridge University Press, Cambridge, 1995).

69   Those who parade their ignorance in automatic contemptuous dismissals of the aesthetic would do well to glance through Terry Eagleton, *The Ideology of the Aesthetic,* (Blackwell, Oxford, 1990).

70   Ibid, p. 368.

71   Moira Gatens, "A Critique of the Sex/Gender Distinction", in Gatens, *Imaginary Bodies: Ethics, Power and Corporeality,* (Routledge, London, 1996).

72   For an early theorist of this spectacle thesis refer to, Guy Debord, *The Society of the Spectacle,* (Black and Red, Detroit, 1977). A latter account is J. Baudrillard, *In the Shadow of the Silent Majorities,* (Semiotexte, New York, 1983).

73   J. Baudrillard, *America,* (Verso, London, 1988).

74   This is where a more revisionist Marxism is making an appearance, American style. A. Calleri, S. Cullenberg, C. Biewener, (ed.), *Marxism in the Postmodern Age: Confronting the New World Order,* (The Guildford Press, New York, 1995).

75   Aristotle, *Metaphysics,* Bk IV, Chap 5, 1009a17 in *The Basic Works of Aristotle,* (ed.), Richard McKeon, (Random House, New York, 1941), p. 743.

76   Friedrich Nietzsche, "Preface for the Second Edition", *The Gay Science,* trs. Walter J Kaufmann, (Vintage, New York, 1974), pp. 34-35.

77   Ibid, p. 35.

78   F. Nietzsche, *The Will To Power,* trs. W. J Kaufmann, (Vintage, New York, 1968), Bk. 111, section 1V, pp. 419ff.

79   F. Nietzsche, *Beyond Good and Evil,* trs. W. J. Kaufmann, (Vintage, New York, 1989), Part Seven, pp. 145-170.

80   R. Diprose, *The Bodies of Women,* (Routledge, London, 1994).

81   Val Plumwood, "The Politics of Reason: Towards a Feminist Logic", *Australasian Journal of Philosophy,* vol. 71, no. 4, (1993),pp. 436-462.

82   M. Gatens, *Feminism and Philosophy,* (Polity Press, Cambridge, 1991), p. 5.

83   Michelle Walker, "Silence & Reason: Woman's Voice in Philosophy", *Australasian Journal of Philosophy,* vol. 71, no. 4, (1993), pp. 400-24.

84   E. Grosz, "Theorizing Corporeality: Bodies, Sexuality and the Feminist Academy: An Interview", *Melbourne Journal of Politics,* vol. 22, (1994), pp. 3-29

85   For this reading of Weber, refer to Wilhelm Hennis, *Max Weber, Essays in Reconstruction,* trs. Keith Tribe, (Allen and Unwin, London, 1988). See Byran S. Turner, *The Body and Sociology,* (Blackwell, Oxford, 1984).

86   For this conflict between the two spheres in relation to the Weberian defence of sociology as a value-free science refer to, Wolf Lepinies, *Between Literature and Science. The Rise of Sociology,* trs. R. J. Hollingdale, (Cambridge University Press, Cambridge, 1988). For Weber's explorations of rationality in capitalism, refer to R. Brubaker, *The Limits of Rationality: An Essay on the Moral and Social Thought of Max Weber,* (Allen and Unwin, London, 1984); and S. Whimster and S. Lash, *Max Weber, Rationality and Modernity,* (Allen and Unwin, London, 1987).

87   For one attempt to explore this correspondence of society and nature, refer to, Philip Mirowski, *More Heat than Light: Economics as Social Physics, Physics as Nature's Economics,* (Cambridge University Press, Cambridge, 1989).

88   For this view, as articulated by the Treasury economic mandarins, refer to M. Pusey, *Economic Rationalism in Canberra,* (Cambridge University Press, Cambridge, 1991).

89   Max Weber, *Economy and Society: An Outline of An Interpretative Sociology,* vol 3. (ed.), G. Roth & C. Wittich, (New York, 1968), p. 1394.

90   K. Lee, *Social Philosophy and Ecological Scarcity,* (Routledge, London, 1989), pp. 285-6

91   The complex road to modern capitalism is explored by Colin Campbell, *The Romantic Ethic and the Spirit of Modern Consumerism,* (Blackwell, Oxford, 1987).

92   As held by Max Weber, *The Protestant Ethic and the Spirit of Capitalism*, (Unwin Hyman, London, 1985), pp. 181-2.

93   Charles Taylor, *The Souces of Self: The Making of the Modern Identity*, (Harvard University Press, Cambridge Massachussets, 1989); & *The Ethics of Authenticity*, (Harvard University Press, Cambridge, Massachussets, 1992).

94   Freya Mathews, *The Ecological Self*, (Routledge, London, 1991), p. 11.

95   See Sandra Harding, *Whose Science? Whose Knowledge?*, (Cornell University Press, New York, 1991), pp. 77-101. She argues that the metaphor of nature as a machine, whose content is derived from society in modernity, becomes a crucial part of the metaphysics of natural science which provide the dominant standpopint in modernity. Given the efforts made by Australian materialists in interpreting the natural sciences in terms of a mechanistic metaphysics, it is a suprise tofind, an adherent of that school, namely G. Couvalis, arguing that the connection of classical physics to this ideological understanding of the world is very tenuous. See G. Couvalis, *The Philosophy of Science: Science and Objectivity*, (Sage, London, 1997), p. 166.

96   G. Rundle, "Editorial: politics and meaning", *Arena Magazine*, no. 3, (Feburary-March, 1993), pp. 2-3, citation, p. 2.

97   A. Gorz, *Critique of Economic Reason*, trs. G. Handyside et.el, (Verso, London, 1989).

98   Hans Jonas, *The Imperative of Responsibility: In Search of an Ethics for the Technological Age*, (University of Chicago Press, Chicago, 1984).

99   Charles Taylor, *Sources of the Self*, op. cit, pp. 27-30.

100   This would be rejected by a physicalist philosophical naturalism on the grounds that normative orientations are an optional-extra to basic desires and preferences. But the life of a utiltity mechanisms would be seen as an impoverished, incomprehensible and pathological one in relation to the romantic cultural background of self-fulfilment that forms an intregral part of modernity.

101   This reworks the argument of Marcuse that the humanities offer a refuge and space for critique of technocracy. *One Dimensional Man*, (Beacon Press, Boston, 1964), pp 158-9.

102   This conception of observing reason comes from G. W. F. Hegel, *The Phenomenology of Spirit*, trs. A. V. Miller, (Oxford University Press, Oxford, 1977), section c, para 240ff, pp. 145ff.

103   It is Walter Benjamin in *Charles Baudelaire: A Lyric Poet in the Era of High Capitalism*, trs. Harry Zola, (Verso, London, 1983), who explores these baroque themes in relation to the decay of the Enlightenment.

104   For an argument that the public intellectual died during the university boom of the post-war period, refer to Russell Jacoby, *The Last Intellectuals: American Culture in the Age of Academe*, (Noonday Press, New York, 1987).

105   For an insight into reactionary conservativism refer to, J. Herf, *Reactionary Modernism, Technology, Culture and Politics in Weimar and the Third Reich*, (Cambridge University Press, Cambridge, 1984). The conservative reaction to industrial capitalism in Australia was A. B. Santamaria, who was part of the legacy of Catholic conservatism in Mebourne.

106   See Graham Lyons, Evonne Moore, and Joseph Wayne Smith, *Is the End Nigh*, (Avebury, Aldershot, 1995).

107   Joseph Wayne Smith, *The High Tech Fix*, (Avebury, Aldershot, 1991).

108   Herbert Marcuse, *One Dimensional Man*, op. cit; Jacques Ellul, *The Technological Society*, (Vintage Books, New York, 1964).

109   For the distinction between instrumental and communicative action see J. Habermas, *The Theory of Communicative Action*, vol. 1. (trs. T. McCarthy, (Beacon Press, Boston, 1984).

2 Reason in and out of history

> It is part of the cowardice of abstract thought that it shuns the sensuous present in a monkish fashion; modern abstraction takes up this attitude of fastidious gentility towards the moment of the sensuous present.
>
> Hegel, *Philosophy of Religion.*

> Hegel felt the sterility of all so-called intellectual work that takes place in the general sphere without dirtying itself with the specific; but rather than lament it he gave it a critical and productive turn.
>
> Adorno, *Hegel: Three Studies.*

One way to come to grips with, and dig our way out of, the modernist analytic tradition that we ragpickers have been thrown into is to utilize Heidegger's hermeneutical notion of truth as disclosure or uncovering of what is previously hidden. Heidegger expresses truth as disclosure in terms of the metaphors of light and darkness, in the sense that bringing something into the light entails a background of shadows and darkness.[1] Heidegger's truth as disclosure is a form of 'root-digging' at the decaying trunk of philosophy, to expose what is hidden and to recognize the way reason works in the philosophical tradition. He held that a hermeneutical conception of truth as disclosure is partial, as it is conditioned by time and place.

This conception of truth as disclosure can be used by the ragpickers to lighten up, disclose or make manifest the deep metaphysical commitments in the analytic Enlightenment tradition we have been thrown into. This gives us a perspective on a tradition by lightening up the way that analytic philosophy and science have strenuously strived for metahistorical knowledge via a fundamental physics. It also highlights the way that a historicist conception of reason—one which bears the stamp of the period of its origin, incorporates history within itself, and is a product of the culture of the twentieth century—has been repressed within analytic philosophy. Since its inception at the beginning of the twentieth century, analytic philosophy has displayed a deep hostility to tradition. It can be connected to and seen as late expression of the world view of modernity, which, as we saw in the previous chapter, held that the development of science and technology would permanently improve the condition of mankind. But this world view since Descartes has also acted to condemn and overthrow tradition.[2] There is a general acceptance that modernity represents a break with an intellectual past in which reason 'slept' and people were 'slaves' to tradition. A heavy-handed moralism surrounds this discourse with its play of reason and prejudice, and its narrative of the storms the Enlightenment encountered with Romanticism and Hegelianism in the nineteenth century. When expressed by analytic philosophy, not only did it mean that it turned its back on philosophical tradition, but that its hostility to tradition was so deep that it lacked the resources to understand itself as a particular cultural tradition in late modernity.

The issue of the relationship between philosophy and its history has not been a prominent problem in analytic philosophy.[3] It remains hidden in the shadows of the backwaters of philosophical culture, and the debate over the historicity of reason has being couched in terms of a simple opposition of reason versus unreason, of reason versus relativism. Philosophy is ahistorical in character, and doing philosophy has nothing to do with the history of philosophy. Analytic philosophy is assumed to be an unambiguous step forward, as it is the replacement of delusion and error by a reliable method. In rejecting historical modes of understanding, the approach to reason has been primarily epistemologically orientated, with Armstrong for instance, holding that Kuhn's historicist account of science is irrationalist.[4] The scientific Enlightenment has succeeded in placing reason in opposition to tradition, and it currently manifests itself in the philosophy institution with philosophy's dogmatic security guards requiring those on the fringes of the analytic tradition to affirm their faith in reason continually, to avoid being branded as heretics. The content that is sneaked into "affirming reason" is the abstract universal reason coded as a universal, transcendent and ahistorical reason which grounds scientific and philosophical truth. Obedience is required from the ragpickers to this conception of reason if they want to be accepted and recognized as philosophers. Yet in spite of the commitment to "timeless validity", there is a disturbing quietism of analytic philosophers in their acceptance of the authority of the analytic tradition as tradition. It is therefore difficult to identify the structurally invisible assumptions which are operating, to scrutinize them in such a way that they are bought to light so they can be seen clearly, and to identify the level of the conceptual framework at which one is working. The debates about the fundamental assumptions of Enlightenment reason are messy and confusing at the 'edges where the great tectonic plates of theory meet and shift.'[5]

This chapter defends the historical nature of reason by initially recovering the excluded historicist thesis of reason in history, initially given voice by Richard Sylvan in his diagnosis of the wretched state of Australian philosophy in a neo-colonial culture.[6] Though the historicist tradition is marginalized in our philosophical culture, it remains an underground current, which is contained by a censorious, analytic, scientific Enlightenment tradition. We defend Sylvan's historicist 'situatedness' of philosophy from criticism by showing that the modernist analytic conception that philosophy is like a free-floating mathematics or science is untenable. Reason is historically impure, a part of tradition like literature, and it is caught up in institutional power relations. We then defend Hegel's historicist conception of philosophy as an expression of its times by suggesting that this can be interpreted in terms of Heidegger's world-picture of modernity, as exemplified in Australian materialism's picture of our place in nature as mechanisms in a mechanistic world. This scientific picture of the world is the way that modernity is aware of its historicity—the way it comprehends itself in relation to the pre-modern ancient 'world picture'—and this picture provides the criteria and conventions that determine the truth or falsity of the answers to philosophical problems. Historicism provides us with a way to break through the unconscious figures of thought associated with a certain habitual picture of philosophy.

An underground historicism

Historicism has the negative connotations of the counter-Enlightenment, and it is unconsciously linked to hermeneutics, anti-naturalism, German idealism and the romantic reaction to the Enlightenment. It signifies the imposition of the textual model on the whole of reality, the quasi-theological orientation of a humanistic philosophy, and the denunciation of the concept of method of modern science and philosophy. It is the continuation of theology by other means, exemplified by Hegel and Heidegger, who are held to see philosophy as still serving as the handmaiden of theology. It is also an anti-Platonic cultural constructivism, exemplified by Nietzsche, Derrida and Rorty, which denies the existence of universals and essences and supposedly insists that words are merely conventions that in no way touch the intelligible structure of reality itself. As human beings construct their world, and there are no fixed inherently intelligible referents for human thought, so it makes little sense to talk about truth.[7] Philosophy's traditional quest for truth is displaced in favour of a concern with the generation of meaning and rhetorical questions about belief formation. In this broad analytic response to continental philosophy we have rejoined old battles about the objectivity of knowledge, realism and truth. The different strands in this new battle circulate around two central issues: the recent concern in post-analytic philosophy that our linguistically mediated grasp of the world recognizes that only in understanding language do we participate in the recognition of truth; and the claim that linguistic meaning cannot be reduced to the subject's intentions and experiences.

The complex links between history, philosophy, politics and culture that arise from these considerations were originally opened up in the Australian philosophy institution by the self-justifying narrative constructed by the heretic philosopher Richard Sylvan. This narrative construed the past in terms of a privileged present, which appeals beyond the orthodox analytic canon to account for the conditions which have shaped the character of the philosophical present. His reflection on the neo-colonial heritage and Australia's contemporary semi-peripheral position in a world culture and global economic system was based on putting a question to our philosophical tradition: in what sense is philosophy produced in Australia a philosophy of Australia? Sylvan answered this question in relation to the entire philosophical tradition in Australia, and in terms of the destructive effects of a neo-colonial discourse on Australasian philosophical culture. Sylvan's diagnosis of the sickness of Antipodean philosophy was the overwhelming Anglo-American dominance of Australasian philosophy and the shoddy intellectual goods imported from the North. He put forward a historicist argument that analytic discourse was constituted by a cultural cringe towards northern Anglo-American analytic philosophy, which then set the agenda for the work being produced in the periphery of the metropolitan centres in Britain, and then the USA.

The cultural background that informs Sylvan's approach is the big question of national identity. This has its roots in Herder, who held that nations have diverse cultural characteristics, which develop over time into a national individual culture. Such a historicism seeks to understand particular cultures in their own terms; and the radical historicist tradition in Australia has generally argued that our national culture is constituted by an unthinking admiration for everything foreign, which precludes regard for any excellence that exists in Australia.[8] It argued that value and worth came from metropolitan imperial Britain, and that everything colonial or Australian is inferior to the British equivalent; and that authentic Australian culture and self-expression has been thwarted by an apathetic acceptance of a metropolitan culture.[9] It holds that Australian intellectual work is thought to be necessarily derivative or awkwardly provincial; that a regional inferiority permeated the cultural and educational establishment until the end of the Menzies era; that Australians meekly accept the reminders of critics that they occupy a subordinate cultural place on the periphery; and that the intellectual standards are set, and the innovations occur elsewhere.[10] Historicism holds that if there is to be a basic equality of worth among all nations as contributors to the richness of human life, then the nation-building process in Australia needed to develop a unique individual culture. Its narrative involves manipulation of a cast of characters in such an manner as to demonstrate how we come to ask those philosophical questions we now believe to be important. Sylvan related these background themes to Australian philosophy in terms of a critical regionalism concerned with the creation of place, rootedness, the renewal of a regional tradition and the conscious cultivation of a critical philosophical culture which belongs to a particular place.

His thesis was that regionalism in philosophy in the latter part of the twentieth century was a strategy of resistance to the universal model of a hegemonic centre surrounded by dependent intellectual satellites. He held that this has historically been the condition of Australian philosophy, as it was part of a neo-colonial society with a pervasive inferiority about its cultural and intellectual life. Analytic philosophy in Australia has been mediated by its relationships with the past, through colonial moulds of thought:

> "when local people have been appointed to positions in Australasia they have been bought up on a solid diet of Anglo-American material, and they have often been reforged or finished in the North as well. In particular, the requirements of Australasian universities in the major period of post World War Two expansion were conveniently seen to in the case of philosophy by the Oxford B. Phil. degree. Many departments of philosophy remain full of the products of this cultural mill; indeed until the mid 70s candidates finished in Oxford were hard to beat when they applied for positions, such was the (unwarranted) prestige of Oxford and the regrettable, but still continuing, 'cultural cringe.'"[11]

Philosophy in Australia, Sylvan held, has been dominated, indeed swamped, by Northern philosophy, initially from Britain, and now increasingly from America and France. This historically resulted in the overwhelming Anglo-American dominance of Australasian philosophy based on the intellectual goods being imported from the North. Much of these imported intellectual goods, despite their attractive packaging, are shoddy, with built-in obsolescence and a limited range of application. He observed:

> "Yet buying this material is encouraged by hard sell cultural ambassadors from the North, who are often paid to visit. This is part of the philosophical imperialism from the North—the successor to Northern colonialism—that the Antipodes too willingly suffers, or, more remarkably, encourages."[12]

So our philosophical education has traditionally been a solid diet of Anglo-American material taught by philosophers forged or finished in the North, whose research interests and teaching have bent to Northern concerns. The result was that Australian philosophy came from a large component of both those academics defining their research and teaching within the boundaries of Northern concerns, and the middle-men who make a living and career importing the Northern stuff. The universities were full of villains—those fellow travellers and the middle-men who defined their research and teaching within the boundaries of Northern concerns. The content of philosophy was primarily that practised by the large component of Northern trained academics who made a living and reputation as professional philosophers importing the Northern stuff. Most of the British philosophy that was imported, he held, was very supportive of the status quo—especially the ordinary language philosophy from Oxford and the Popperian philosophy of science.

The effects of the economic power relations of a dependent nation state was that its philosophical culture was British to its 'bootstraps'. The violence of the neo-colonial phase of the process of nation-building meant that the indigenous intellectual elites in the universities were mediocre Northerners with inflated references, or fellow travellers who made a living as philosophical middle-men importing Northern philosophy. Local Australian intellectuals became subaltern subjects in their own local institutions, constructed as inferior philosophers, and obliged to teach the Northern analytic stuff to suffering, bored students. Sylvan argued that the way out of this tragic situation was not to beaver away on the footnotes of the research work set by the big overseas names, but to resist the North by obtaining a critical distance from them.[13] Philosophers in Australia needed to extract themselves from neo-colonial moulds of thought, examine their own intellectual resources, and develop a home-grown regional philosophy in opposition to the cultural imperialism from the North.[14]

Sylvan's narrative can be interpreted as a nativist tradition which protects itself against the global waves of Northern philosophy by producing a narrow localism, with its local products and local cult heroes replacing the Northern ones. As part of the decolonizing process, postcolonial philosophers in the periphery should stop importing foreign ideas, and do our own thing in our own distinctive way in the form of self-reliance. But this is not a simple-minded defence of the local, unique, provincial tradition, seen as a resistant enclave against a global Anglo-American analytic philosophy.[15] Sylvan's narrative holds that slowly, ever so slowly, heroes—regional Australian philosophers—worked out their own research projects by appropriating the ideas from Britain, America, France and Germany, and then reworking them into their own projects. The emphasis is on the regional projects. We can do our own thing in our own way by developing our own research paradigm, rather than working with pale northern reflections of Northern paradigms.[16] Sylvan mentions Australian materialism, relevant/para-consistent logics, and environmentalism as flourishing regional programmes, and picks the sunrise projects of Australian feminism, and social and political philosophy. It is a viable strategy, he concludes, because the regional resistances to the power relations which form the cultural cringe represent niches in the market which have not been satisfactorily filled by a universalistic Northern philosophy.

This historicist regionalist narrative of the knowledge/power regime in philosophy points to the professionalization and institutionalisation of philosophy in the university; increasingly marked by a tendency towards centralisation, organisation in terms of a hierarchical bureaucracy. Here the control over rewards and progress favours some lines of research and investigation at the expense of others, and structures what is taught, published and promoted. It explicitly shows philosophy to be immanent in history and how certain conditions will ensure the development of philosophy, whilst others will deform it. It highlights the way that Australian social thought and cultural studies have acted as a conduit whereby limited selections of Marxism and post-Marxism from European texts produced in Paris and Frankfurt have been imported, along with the migration of English academics themselves to Brisbane and Adelaide during the 1980s. Australian intellectual life in this social sphere has remained parasitic on continental European thought, mediated through English social philosophy and sociology. It has grown out of the Marxist legacy of Althusser, Gramsci and Poulantzas and the French attacks on that legacy by Foucault, Barthes and Baudrillard.[17] From Sylvan's regionalist perspective, this radical current remains deeply neo-colonial, and beholden to the North.

Sylvan's narrative, as an attempt to hold our time in thought through the device of 'self-assertion' of the locals, is schematic. It does not explore the conflicts amongst the 'we' who are regional Australian philosophers; it lacks any account of how the local narrative fits into the broad concerns of a grand narrative of modernity; it fails to explore the split between scientifically-orientated Enlightenment thinkers and Romantically-orientated humanistic disciplines; and it ignores any account of philosophy's turn away from the social sciences after John Anderson, and its disengagement from highbrow cultural criticism. It presupposes philosophy's shift to scientific rationality, the natural sciences as the dominant discipline, the deep-seated disdain for a literary culture ushered into philosophy by Hegel, and subsequently shaped by romanticism, and the legitimacy of modernist philosophy.[18] It also lacks a conception of hegemony of the analytic school, and the way that new critical philosophy can only be produced on the margin, as an emergent form of resistance in the philosophy institution. Despite these shortcomings, Sylvan's thesis that Australian philosophers ought to be intellectuals doing independent research work within the university as professional academics, was picked up by the new stratum of university-trained social critics, who were drawn from the middle and working classes, and educated at provincial universities in disciplines like sociology and politics. Their intellectual adoption of Marxism signified their political separation from the traditional academic establishment. This social group of "up-starts" had little political or social influence in the academic system, remained detached from the university elite, and with the collapse of Marxism, became self-defined outsiders in the system. But the crisis conditions in capitalism, and the success of economic rationalism and authoritarian populism, provides an opportunity and place for these marginalized outsiders to become a politically committed, self-conscious, radical intelligentsia.[19] This turn to philosophers becoming intellectuals initiates a rupture from the tradition of analytic philosophy. It represents the continual deepening of a historical reflection upon that tradition, and a rejection of analytic philosophy living in its own world, closed off from contact with non-analytic philosophy.[20]

Ahistorical reason in the analytic tradition

Sylvan's historicism foregrounds the way an ahistorical scientific reason has been a central assumption of a hegemonic modernist, analytic philosophy, and it uncovers the conflict between the different conceptions of reason in modernity. Ernest Gellner identifies this conflict in terms of the different conceptions of reason between the early modern philosophy of Descartes and the subsequent response of Hegelian historicism. He says:

> "The essence of the Cartesian tradition was the supposition that a cognitive *procedure* existed which stood outside the world and any one culture, and was capable of independent judgement of cognitive claims about the world. This transcendent faculty alone was sovereign. The Hegelo-Marxist tradition by contrast absolutizes a process within the world (and thereby, affirmations about it), elevating it above mere procedural rules."[21]

Descartes' dream of discovering a secure method for establishing unassailable truth through absolute certainty by a transcendent reason took the form of modern mathematical science, which saw culture as the domain of ignorance, bigotry, prejudice and superstition. It deemed that knowledge is gained through the emancipation of scientific reason from the distortions and parochial perspectives of our historically embodied subjectivity and culture. This dream has been relayed to us through the positivist's conception of objectivity and method in the natural sciences. This understood method and language as an instrument which needed to be polished by philosophy to gain objective knowledge by picturing the world in itself. Only when language is viewed this way can it be adequate to the enterprise of the natural sciences. Objectivity in the analytic tradition historically exhibits a modernist flight from culture, social interest and society, as it is generally understood to involve cutting reason away from historical particularity, and abstracting a universal reason from social practices. The emphasis is on the formal scientific and the mathematical forms of rationality with their ahistorical mode of understanding. This results in analytic philosophy stressing formal method, decision-making procedures as unchanging canons or principles, philosophical problems being universal, timeless and pure, and an analysis of meaning based on logical form. Its ahistoricism was so evident in the project of the analytic Marxists to reconstruct historical materialism by importing into the marxist heritage the tradition of the analytic philosophical method.[22]

One consequence of this dream of objectivity that is widespread in analytic philosophy is the way it defines the autonomy of its own perennial problems as being divorced from history. From this it follows that we study classical philosophers like Locke to help us find solutions to these timeless problems.

John Mackie says in his book on Locke that the main aim 'is not to expound Locke's views, or to study their relations with those of their contemporaries or near contemporaries, but to work towards solutions of the problems themselves.'[23] The emphasis is on solving given problems, with philosophy seen a co-operative activity like science. The validity or invalidity of the arguments to justify particular solutions to problems are considered to be independent of historical context. The historical aspects of philosophical texts—when they were written and from what social interest—becomes irrelevant. Philosophy is an autonomous sphere of intellectual life independent of society, in which ideas are understood solely in terms of other ideas. In doing philosophy, according to the canons of analytic philosophy, we identify, interpret and evaluate timeless and culturally disembodied philosophical arguments, which are located in a history of isolated talking heads. It is assumed that master thinkers like Descartes, Hume or Russell have isolated the central, deep and defining problems of the discipline, which demarcate an autonomous philosophy from other signifying practices like sociology or literature.[24]

As philosophy is outside history, philosophy talks about morality as such, rather than specific moralities such as the morality of fourth-century Athens, or knowledge as such, rather than the principles and presuppositions of knowledge specific to Newtonian physics in seventeenth-century England, or society as such rather than twentieth-century Australian society. So we approach Descartes' *Meditations* as a series of philosophical arguments concerning the ultimate foundations of knowledge, and then proceed to evaluate the ahistorical formal structure of the ideas in this text in terms of the validity of Descartes' arguments, according to the best rational methods. There is no need to engage with history or consider that the best rational standards are socially determined. Analytic philosophy conceives itself as taking place within timeless space, in which contemporary writers attempt to refute the views of past philosophers. Its history of philosophy is not really history, as analytic philosophers see the past existing in a state of potential rivalry to the present; and they approach past philosophers like Hegel to refute him, rather than understand the Hegelian system through interpretation or its continuing influence on us.

A further consequence of Descartes' dream of objectivity is the way it has played itself out in variations on the attempt to reduce all philosophical problems state in ordinary language to propositions of the language of formal logic. Gadamer says that this dream:

"believes that the whole secret and sole task of all philosophy consists in forming the proposition so exactly that it really is in a position to state what is meant univocally. Philosophy should develop a system of signs that is not dependent on the metaphorical ambiguity of natural language, and also not dependent in general on the linguistic multiplicity of modern culture out of which flow misleading and erroneous claims, but rather one that attains the univocity and precision of mathematics. Mathematical logic is seen here as the way to solve all problems that science up to now has left to philosophy."[25]

The analytic tradition has generally held it has found a method to resolve its problems, and that this logical method will enable philosophy to establish itself on a scientific basis. Thus Russell says the study:

"of logic becomes the central study in philosophy: it gives a method of research in philosophy, just as mathematics gives the method of research in physics. And as physics...became a science through Galileo's fresh observation of facts and subsequent mathematical manipulation, so philosophy, in our day, is becoming scientific through the simultaneous acquisition of new facts and logical methods."[26]

The method is the logic of Frege and more particularly of *Principia Mathematica,* and it advocates that philosophical problems can be split up, tackled little by little until definite and non-controversial results are reached. It hopes that the logic of Frege and Russell would enable us to find an agreed neutral framework that would enable analytic philosophers to solve problems and so achieve something like the status of science. The focus is on meaning of the logical form of a pure universal language grounded on the analysis of the real form of propositions. These are objective entities that exist outside of their apparent form in ordinary language. The aim of philosophical logic is to achieve clarity and rigor by focusing on the form of discourse, analyzing the structure of the language used to describe the furniture of the universe, so that language can mirror the furniture without distortion. The starting point of the analytic tradition is the Platonic atomism of Russell, and it evolves into Dummett's concern with meaning, or with the relation between words and the world, which endeavours to give a general formal account of the nature of all word-world semantic connections. But it comes out as implying that a theoretical language, which radically reconstructs everyday experience, must begin with precisely defined axioms, terms and principles of transformation. The analysis of propositions by mathematical logic as a philosophical tool, the ideal of clarity and rigor, and the use of elementary logic may be as definitive of analytic philosophy as any other feature. As Russell said, 'That all sound philosophy should begin with an analysis of propositions, is a truth too evident, perhaps to demand a proof.'[27]

Another result of Descartes' dream is the way that analytic rationality is defined by a set of unchanging canons or principles, or an ahistorical organon which defines what it is to be rational. This organon provides for an objective foundation for philosophical arguments, and so distinguishes philosophers from those in the literary institution who may be studying the same text. This organon separates form and content, since logic is concerned with the study of the formal relations between sentences in order to establish their validity, and not concerned with the content. Form and content belong to different realms and thus, because of this they can be investigated quite separately. Formal logic is an *apriori* discipline which is a self-contained formal activity, whilst the content is the realm of the empirical sciences. Logic has to do with propositions, which are entities in the world which we can study. Meanings reside in propositions, not in sentences of everyday languages, which are imperfect formulations of propositions residing outside natural language as entities in their own right. These propositions have a structure when linked as an argument. Propositions are not the result of the synthesis of the mind, as Kant held, but are independent self-subsistent entities. We can be in direct and unmediated contact with them, but in no sense do we make them by a synthesizing mind in nature. An extreme form of this Platonism can be found in the early Russell, who held that among the independent objects with which we may be acquainted are propositions, objective entities, capable of truth or falsehood, which may be very roughly identified with the content or meaning of a declarative sentence. Hence the idea of philosophy consists in giving an analysis of propositions, of saying what their real form is, as opposed to their apparent form, what entities are really about, as opposed to what their appear to be about, and explaining why they have the implications that they have in terms of the logical structure of the world.[28]

It is formal logic which is implicit in the analytic practice of considering arguments in Plato's dialogues in abstraction from their historical context and from the context of the text; and to rewrite them in a formal language to mirror the formal structure of the argument in terms of the premises, the inference and the conclusion. This practice is underpinned by a general presupposition that each of our utterances and beliefs has a perfectly definite content or meaning which may be abstracted from its context and analysed. In practice it amounts to the very familiar activity of bringing philosophers into the present as conversation partners, engaging the arguments of past thinkers with the issues of the present, re-formulating a sentence using logical constants; together with the claim that this sentence is a more precise and more correct version, or a better and more truthful representation of the content or meaning of the original. Philosophy becomes an autonomous disciplinary matrix defined by an essentially unchanging set of questions, rules and methods.[29]

The dream of philosophy as a series of absolutely clear propositions has been largely played out in analytic philosophy, with Wittgenstein's talk about the relativity of meaning to language games and the holism of philosophers such as Quine and Davidson. Here we have the break from an empiricist-behaviourist metaphysics with its language-neutral sensory impressions and a convergence with the continental critique of the common Cartesian heritage by hermeneutical interpretation. It is Rorty who currently represents the historicizing shift within analytical philosophy, and the attempt to mediate between the conflicting analytical and continental traditions. But what is still not accepted is the radical historicist thesis of the politicization of philosophy. This is generally resisted by analytic philosophers, who replay the image of a pure philosophy—pure reason—proclaimed in opposition to politics.

Analytic philosophy remains pure by appealing to the free and unhampered pursuit of knowledge, by proclaiming that any attempt to turn science or philosophy towards the common good of the nation state is to politicize these disciplines illegitimately. As philosophy and science are neutral, politics and morality should be excluded, as they represent bias which compromises objectivity and the neutral impartial ground. Science and philosophy do not serve political interests, as they explore the timelessly true. Neutrality in the form of method, logical form and analytic precision represents a shield against the radical critique of philosophy and science serving certain economic and political interests in capitalist patriarchal society. Neutrality proclaims that both are autonomous, inherently progressive and stand apart from other forms of culture, and from society. So the general Anglo-American modernist response to Sylvan's implicit political narrative about philosophy has been to hold that it represents an external sociological point of view; one which is unrelated to the internal, purely philosophical and scientific investigation of the nature of the things detached from politically-based class interests.

Robert Brown, in his survey of recent Australian philosophical work, defends an international Anglo-American philosophy from Sylvan's historicism, by divorcing it from its historical and cultural context in which it is produced. He says that philosophy has its own specific field of problems which is held to be universal, and that like science and mathematics, it is not affected by its situatedness in culture and society.[30] The historicist thesis, he says, just adds a bit of local colour and contextual background to philosophers working on the universal problems. He states the case bluntly: philosophy should not be treated differently from physics and mathematics. In these fields the cultural background is not relevant in any obvious way to the matters at issue. Brown acknowledges that philosophy does not emerge in a vacuum, but he pushes the broad neo-colonial national culture and cultural cringe into the background as 'historical setting'. He argues that we do not judge good work in terms of its national origins, and even if certain cultural backgrounds do contribute recognizable assumptions, arguments or forms of error, it is unlikely that Australian philosophers will make an intellectual contribution that is uniquely Australian. This is because the internationalization of Anglo-American philosophy in the analytic mode is both a barrier to local differentiation in the future and evidence of its weakness in the past. There is not much that Australian regionalism can contribute, except in the way the various elements of overseas philosophy are combined, and the directness in which they are expressed. He concludes by suggesting that the marginal position of Australian philosophers in the international market place should be countered by focusing on improving the quality of the product exported and increasing the share of trade.[31]

If the core of philosophy is understood to be an axiomatic system with unchanging categories of understanding, then historicists are concerned with the surface and ephemerality of the historical context, and fail to grasp that the core of philosophy is the problems of philosophy which require solution. As historical knowledge of past theories does not have any relevance to the scientific work of physicists and economists, so the knowledge of philosophy's past does not have any relevance to solving philosophical problems with the logical method. So historicists do not do philosophy. They do sociology.

Clearing away some misunderstandings

There is some misinterpretation of the historicist claim in Brown's negation of Sylvan's thesis. Sylvan contests the claim that philosophy stands outside the cultural and social spheres of a social formation to obtain a view from nowhere, as he tries to show the way analytic philosophy has been socially constructed as part of the nation-building process since 1945. So it has been formed by the historical conditions of the neo-colonial form of life. Sylvan's renegade historicist story of how we got this way offers us an interpretation of our philosophical tradition, and his insight into the historicity of all knowledge is an implicit recognition that the Cartesian dream is over. The historicist aim is not to discredit philosophy by revealing its reprehensible neo-colonial origins. The target of the criticism is the analytic claim about the ahistorical nature of reason. It is Brown's claim that philosophy is like science, and so not affected by its being historically situated, that is the object of critique. Brown's claim can only get off the ground if it is assumed that science is a God's eye perspective rather than a partial historical one. The former is one which Nagel describes as being:

> "The attempt is made to view the world not from a place within it, or from the vantage point of a special kind of life or awareness, but from nowhere in particular and no form of life in particular at all. The object is to discount for the features of our pre-reflective outlook that make things appear as they do, and thereby reach an understanding of things as they really are."[32]

Here we abstract ourselves from the partisanship, our social relationships and the particularities of our culture and history so that we can arrive at a neutral, impartial and universal point of view according to ahistorical methods of rational justification. The modernist sentiment in analytic philosophy holds that reason is not a suitable object for historicization, as it is only unreason—magic, myth and religion—that is historical. This sentiment implies metaphysical realism, in that physics as the language of nature pictures how things hang together in themselves outside the appearances of history.

The second misunderstanding in Brown's response to Sylvan arises from his overlooking Sylvan's narrative with its story about past events creating the present situation, with its plot of heroes and villains and mixture of philosophy, history and myth. This narrative is less concerned with the truth of a particular philosophical claim than the meaning that analytic discourse, as embodied in the universities, has for us as philosophers in the historical present. We are thrown into this way of doing philosophy, encounter experiences, undergo sufferings, and often feel that the point of significance of the whole analytic project in which we find ourselves caught up is not obvious. We need to make sense of it in the light of our interests and goals, and the meanings of our activities within a particular form of life, as distinct from evaluating the truth claims of individual arguments. Human institutions like that of philosophy do not carry their meanings on their faces as it were, and so it is legitimate to ask: "Does this form of philosophy deserve our approval or disapproval?" "Is it worth doing?" "Is it is a waste of time?' It is also necessary to ask: "What significance does it have for us today at a time of cultural and economic crisis for ragpickers or public intellectuals?" Answering these questions requires a retrospective placing of philosophy in a context, or series of social actions which detail the way in which these actions are interrelated.[33] This narrative can only be from a particular historical perspective, with the meaning of these events changing with changes in historical perspective. If the interpretation of their meaning is contingent upon the vantage point and social interests of the interpreter, then historical understanding of a social formation is perspectival and partial. To this extent historical knowledge, is a form of practical knowledge, as it reflects the social actions of historically classed and gendered agents with their own projects.

The problem with the suprahistorical God-like objectivity of the Platonic view from nowhere is that it implies a complete knowledge of history. But as history is open—we do not know the future of philosophy in Australia in the twenty-first century—then philosophy is continually changing in a changing social formation. As our historical experience changes the meaning that historical events have for us, we can never represent the whole. As the object history is not closed and complete, we cannot give a complete account from where we stand in 1997, and so our explanations and understanding can only be partial: better and broader than those offered in 1984 but not as good as those in 2024—perhaps. The only way to obtain the God-like stance is to assume knowledge of the end point of history, and hence attain a historical understanding that is not contingent upon our place in it. If we deny the knowledge of the end of history thesis we need to acknowledge that historical understanding and explanation will reflect, as Gadamer puts it, a specific historical horizon.

Brown's ahistorical conception of philosophy as akin to mathematics is not a straightforward exclusion of the historical. He preserves and downgrades the historical by reconstructing it within the universal system of Anglo-American philosophy as local colour and national origin. But the margins of Brown's text can be read as a celebration of the continuity, flourishing and power of a regional tradition in philosophy.[34] His marginalia say that it is worthwhile to remember rather than forget the deeds, hopes, work and suffering of the past generation of Australian philosophers. In doing so, Brown implicitly affirms that philosophical works oppose the market's central principle of exchange. He affirms their social character which recalls the human purposes of production. He affirms that these works deny that everything is simple exchange value. We can revalorize this insight in Brown's marginalia to make the point that we cannot erase our historicity when we do philosophy.

So it is no longer a simple case of either sociology or philosophy. Sylvan's historicism offers a viable alternative to an autonomous philosophy, as a discipline defined by an essentially, unchanging timeless set of questions, problems and methods. It broadens the analytic canon of philosophy, and to cancel any strict disciplinary criteria for membership in the canon.

Beyond philosophy as mathematical science

In assuming that philosophy is like mathematics or science, Brown overlooks the missing term of literature. What is missing from his argument is the implied premise that philosophy is not like literature. There are two reasons why we should question Brown's assumption that philosophy is like science or mathematics rather than literature. The first is that philosophers do not do experiments in the laboratory like scientists, for all their talk about putting their hypotheses to the test. They are like literary critics, to the extent that they read texts, pose questions to texts, make interpretations of texts within specific intellectual traditions, and they do so from particular perspectives. They deal with highly contextualized knowledge claims whose truth is never beyond dispute, and the interpretation of texts makes truth in philosophy—unlike truth in mathematics—a highly allusive and ambiguous phenomena. The answers they provide of a text 'have their truth' but the contextualized, relative nature of such answers precludes them from being univocally true as such. The second reason for questioning Brown's likening philosophy to physics and mathematics is that philosophy is unlike mathematical physics and economics, to the extent that the nature of philosophy is something that arises in the course of a philosophical argument. Philosophy is a subject in which the nature of the problems, the procedures and the purpose of the enterprise is an issue in a way that it is not for physics.

Brown's late modernist replay of philosophy as being like a mathematical physics/economics is misleading, because philosophy has affinities with literature. Though the perimeters of the analytic canon change, its core of Hume, Russell, Frege, Quine, Davidson, Smart and Armstrong remains unchanged. Their texts are read with a certain kind of attention that identifies what we know in advance as the philosophical—the arguments in the text which we dig out by exercising our philosophical competencies. Such a reading of a text is constituted by the interpretative communities, whose shared intersubjective protocols establish the philosophical as distinct from the literary value of a text. These protocols, competencies, and value are institutionally constructed, whilst the current objects and methods of philosophy are different from what they were in Greek or mediaeval philosophy. So the category of the philosophical text is distinguished by the distinctive uses to which the canonical texts are put by the analytic philosophical community, as distinct from that of literary critics.

Philosophy is also like literature in that it involves some notion of readership, which implies a tacit background knowledge about the conventions of analytic philosophy. We understand that the problems of philosophy are the problems of philosophy in modernity, rather than those of ancient Greece or mediaeval Europe. We understand the strange conventions of a philosophical paper in which the speaker is talking about Plato or Descartes as if they were alive and well, and we appreciate the points about how the dead philosophers went wrong on solving this particular problem. This odd relationship of philosophy to its dead history assumes a certain form of education into a form of professional life in terms of reading and writing papers as the canonical literary form. It requires an awareness that the philosopher is resolving the problem from a particular position, rather than being the vehicle for an utterly impersonal philosophical truth that speaks through him; a recognition of a specific historical canon of philosophers that one can legitimately make reference to; and an understanding of the debate about the problems in philosophy. The canon of analytic philosophy is sustained so that analytic philosophy can continue to identify itself with mathematics and logic and embrace propositions as the foundation of a formal system whose goal is to disambiguate natural language. A seminar implies an acceptance of a humanist conception of philosophy as an exchange of viewpoints or dialogue within everyday language within a historical human world.

From this humanities perspective, in doing philosophy we actually work within our historical philosophical tradition, engage in a dialogue with the past and present, and do so within a community of regional philosophers to whom one has a variety of attachments and ties. If we find the character of the particular philosophical community uncongenial because of its power relations, we don't just choose not to live in it, as Nozick claims.[35] This liberal conception of community, as an association in which we are free to join or opt out at will, ignores that our shared membership of our philosophical community with its incumbent moral obligations is not a stage to be transcended. This community is constitutive of our self-esteem and well-being, as we share our philosophy, are affirmed or negated by others, and in doing so we develop mutual responsibility and antagonisms towards one another. The philosophical community is established largely upon a set of shared cultural inherited social practices, with their intersubjectively constituted values which establish the deep agreement amongst subjects about what it is to do philosophy. In doing philosophy we go beyond the present, not in the sense of an abolition of our present historical situation, because the horizon of the present cannot be formed without the past. We, as Gadamer argues, encounter the past, understand the tradition from which we have come, even as we interpret it to forget, erase or write off those bits that are no longer needed.[36] This educational formation or *Bildung* is a process of negation and affirmation of the past within a regional philosophical community, which is carried on through dialogue with others in which the hegemonic meanings of philosophical texts are contested by insurgent philosophers with subjugated knowledges.

These considerations suggest that analytic philosophy's image of itself as a stand-alone entity assumes itself to be discontinuous with what has gone before—from tradition. Analytic philosophy sees itself as a liberation from the dogma of the tradition of neo-Hegelian idealism of Bradley and McTaggart which was the darkness, vagueness and obscurantism of philosophical tradition that the slum-clearing revolution of analysis was designed to eradicate.[37] So we have the imagery of creative destruction, of carting away the rubbish of the nineteenth century to reveal the right way of doing things; that is has grasped the real task of philosophy and its true problems. Hence the pre-analytic is really the pre-philosophical. There can only be the history of almost philosophy with the past figures being interpreted as only having done poorly those things which contemporary analytic philosophers now do well. Russell's break with idealism is commonly seen as a decisive point in the development of revolutionary discourse which liberates itself from the past. The general lack of mediation between philosophy and history means that analytic philosophers see themselves as being at the beginning of genuine philosophy because of their method. The revolutionary analytic school stands at the beginning of philosophical history, because its adherents are finally in possession of the true problems, and the correct method of resolving problems. This can be seen from the way that Michael Dummett expresses the revolutionary analytic spirit. He says:

"Only with Frege was the proper goal of philosophy finally established: namely, first, that the goal of philosophy is the analysis of the structure of *thought*; secondly, that the study of *thought* is to be sharply distinguished from the study of the psychological processes of *thinking;* and, finally, that the only proper method for analysing thought consists in the analysis of *language*...The acceptance of these three central tenets is common to the entire analytical school...(but) it has taken nearly a half-century since his death for us to apprehend clearly what the real task of philosophy, as conceived by him, involves."[38]

Dummett holds that the real foundation of all other philosophy is the philosophy of language, because it is only through language that we can analyze thought.[39] He takes the principal functions of language to be an instrument of communication and a vehicle of thought.[40] Analytic philosophers eschew a continuous narrative about philosophical practices, because they have taken themselves to have been the first to understand what philosophy is, and what questions are genuinely philosophical questions.

However, this modernist *avante garde* narrative, with its heroes and villains and simple story about breaking free from an oppressive tradition, works with a flawed philosophy of history. Its thesis of pure discontinuity presupposes that analytic discourse is a stand-alone entity, with its whole being contained within itself. So analytic discourse is self-grounding, immediately given and has no presuppositions. But this is highly misleading, because being discontinuous with the past means denying that we need to comprehend what Russell was fundamentally reacting against, in order to understand and make sense of analytic discourse. But as Gadamer observes, 'philosophizing does not begin at some zero point, but must think and speak with the language we already possess.'[41] Analytic philosophy's explicit rejection of neo-Hegelian and Kantian philosophy was mediated through Russell and Moore returning to the empiricism of Hume by initially standing within the idealist discourse of British philosophy, which formed a horizon of interpretations in which they were already involved. Russell's general philosophical project in 1898 was entitled *On the Idea of a Dialectic of the Sciences*, and in his *Foundations of Geometry* he argued that not only was this or that formulation of geometry contradictory, but that the subject was inherently and irredeemably contradictory.[42] So the historical context of our shared philosophical culture mediates our relation to reality by pre-shaping our outlook, values and ways of thinking and links the present to the past in such a way that the old becomes a part of the new.

Russell's break with idealism featured an emphasis on absolute truth—what is true absolutely and completely independently of us—and was opposed to the idealist notion that truth could be a matter of degree, and thus conditioned, as seen from the standpoint of the whole or absolute truth. Russell, in contrast, held there was only Absolute Truth, and his logicism in *The Principles of Mathematics*, in which mathematics was reduced to logic, was designed to refute Kant, by showing that both logic and mathematics were wholly independent of space and time. Modern logic and mathematics could be used to refute Kant's notion of our reliance on spatio-temporal notion, and thus his thesis our knowledge is conditioned by the nature of our cognitive faculties. Mathematics and logic were true, absolutely and unconditionally, with no distinctions of standpoint accepted.[43] The absoluteness of truth requires the objectivity and independence of propositions, and Russell argued that propositions are abstract objective non-linguistic and non-mental entities, they have their truth-values independently of our language, and our acts of synthesis and any interpretation. So the rejection of idealism shaped Russell's philosophy to the extent of making the analysis of propositions of crucial and central importance in the defence of realism, which stood opposed to the view which makes the entities which are the bearers of truth or falsehood mind-dependent. This makes the analytic tradition defined by its relations to the previous idealist tradition, and not just a stand-alone self-sufficient entity discontinuous with what has gone before.

The second way that analytic philosophy's conception of itself as a stand-alone entity with a predefined identity is flawed, is indicated by the way analytic philosophers continually define their identity in relation to opposing philosophical traditions. When they come into contact with an alien continental philosophy they spell out the significance of the analytic project with its distinctive philosophical concerns, vocabulary and methodological procedures. Isaiah Berlin, for instance, when he gazed into the deep abyss between philosophers on the continent of Europe and those in the Anglo-American world in the 1950s, observed that the chasm was so deep that 'philosophers on one side can scarcely bring themselves to think of those on the other as being occupied with the same subject as themselves.'[44] The reason for the difference was clear. Continental philosophers 'had lived through the great logico-philosophical revolution of the last half-century, initiated by Frege and Russell—perhaps the most complete transformation of thought in this field since the seventeenth century—without being noticeably affected by it.'[45] The most complete transformation of thought in this field since the seventeenth century boiled down to the analytic method. The significance of this method was expressed by Russell in relation to denouncing non-analytic continental philosophy as irrational. He says:

> "I respect Descartes, Leibniz, Locke, Berkeley and Hume, all of whom employed the analytic method. I do not believe that Kant or Hegel or Nietzsche or the more modern anti-rationalists have contributed anything that deserves to be remembered."[46]

This led Russell to hold that the whole romantic movement, beginning with Rousseau and Kant and culminating in pragmatism and futurism, was a regrettable aberration. This strategy of defining identity in relation to the other tradition is continued with the postmodern critics of the current conventions and metaphysics of modernist philosophy. They are often dismissed as non-philosophy because they do not adhere to analytic philosophy's own standards and protocols of logic, open debate, appeals to evidence and arguments. The analytic narrative then works with a simple story in which philosophical progress is made by an analytic scientific philosophy in opposition to the regression of continental philosophy aligned with literature.

The modernist philosophy of history, which posits the analytic tradition as a stand-alone entity discontinuous from pre-philosophical tradition, implies that analytic philosophers are not able to recognize the discontinuities in what constitutes philosophical procedures, or how these have radically changed in philosophy's history. In order to make their narrative of the one true philosophy stick, they eliminate from philosophical discussion those texts which cannot fit the specific standard and criteria of the analytic tradition. Analytic discourse operates with a history of philosophy in which philosophy, prior to the analytic revolution, is prehistory or pre-philosophical on the one hand; and that one's contemporary continental opponents are in error on the other. The distorted view of the history of philosophy in terms of philosophy/non-philosophy produced by Russell, Ayer, Popper, and Gellner is an apt illustration of this. Their interpretation of continental philosophy fails to understand how continental philosophy has been a form of intervention in a pre-existing dialogue or debate, how its claims are a move in an argument, or why it seemed appropriate to make just that move, and why it possesses its distinctive shape and character. To hold that only analytic philosophy is sound philosophy, in the face of the recognition of a plurality of philosophical traditions, and our philosophical and scientific justifications being social and historically determinate, is merely to privilege one philosophical system. It is to operate within the pre-reflective cultural prejudices of the analytic tradition, and merely to generalise from its own standards of what constitutes sound philosophy. This reduces a complex cultural process of interpretation to a simple one of opposing good to bad, of posing philosophical problems in order to eliminate the bad.

A marginalized historicist philosophy has a more coherent notion of the way the analytic tradition operates than that of analytic philosophy. The latter's universalism endeavours to free its analysis of the tradition-bound philosophy and to excoriate tradition-bound thinking by adopting a standpoint independent of tradition, from which one can question and consider the philosophical tradition. Here the subject is independent of tradition and not formed by it, as he does not see himself as a tradition of inquiry. This is plainly false, as analytic philosophy is a particular modernist tradition of inquiry, as can be seen from the internal history mapped by Rorty. In drawing attention to analytic philosophy as a tradition, his narrative centres on the disintegration of the neo-positivist programme of the Vienna Circle and its logical empiricist allies.[47] In building on Wittgenstein's philosophical critique of philosophy in *Philosophical Investigations,* Rorty gives a plausible narrative about the undermining of the epistemological foundationalism of philosophy, conceived as a distinct foundational discipline, with a distinct disciplinary technique. Rorty's historical genealogy, with its stress on the historicity of philosophy, is also philosophy's self-knowledge. After Rorty we can see that the cultural form of knowledge that is analytic philosophy was caught in a web of its own institutionalization, and the institution 'philosophy' was not defined historically enough to be able to come into the view of the analytic philosophers who practised it. With Rorty's rewriting of the history of philosophy, we can see a different set of problems arising. As the questions that philosophers ask change, so questions once considered philosophical fall away, to be replaced by new ones, even those once considered sociological. We can now see that analytic philosophers work on texts which are thoroughly embedded in a particular philosophical tradition within the broad tradition of Western philosophy. There was no total escape from the latter, as the analytic tradition revised some part of the broad tradition—the empiricist—by relying on other parts. A hermeneutical philosophy breaks out of the analytic binary divide of reason and tradition, because of its concept of a tradition of rational inquiry that goes through various stages, due to a series of disputes within its historical horizons.[48]

Sylvan's underground historicism can be used to open a window onto a historicist philosophical hermeneutics, which sees reason as historical, and so cannot wholly free itself from prejudice, tradition, and the historical conditions from which it operates.[49] Beyond the window is Rorty's narrative of analytic rationality evolving in history and the historically situated philosophical subject. This makes for a mediated relationship to the philosophical tradition, one which Gadamer calls *Bildung,* by which he meant cultivation or education through the reflective appropriation of one's own tradition that develops as a positive or negative reaction to the views and events of one's own times. This appropriation of our tradition becomes a second nature, as *Bildung* actualizes some of the potentialities we are born with and so is 'an element in the normal coming to maturity of the kind of animals that we are.'[50]   It highlights that, in being situated within particular traditions, we make particular assumptions, and have particular standards, expectations, and aspirations. As these are influenced by a particular history, we are not neutral observers of our history and tradition; but, rather, the inheritors and producers of their meaning. Gadamer's conception of language is one in which is the repository of tradition, and a store of accumulated practical wisdom, that is subject to reflective modification by each generation that inherits it. *Bildung* as cultivation, holds that in order to mature to be the sort of social animals that we are, it is necessary to engage in critical reflection of the tradition we have inherited. This is part of our inheritance of our human mode of life in which we endeavour to be at home.[51] This takes us a long way from an ahistorical analytical philosophy, which, as part of a scientific culture, develops our awareness to a tradition, only in order to consign it to the scrap heap without major loss. It junks the philosophical theories of the past, as unfortunate errors from which we have nothing to learn.[52]   Hermeneutics, therefore, stands for the repressed historical dimension of an analytic philosophy that is unable to grasp itself as tradition.

Is historicism a mere sociology?

There is a defensive, bunkered reaction to the appearance of philosophical hermeneutics from a scientistic, analytic philosophy, which defines itself as a purely technical discipline. One objection that is sometimes levelled at Sylvan's historicist narrative of analytic philosophy in Australia is that this grandstanding is a mere sociology of the philosophy institution, and so does not deal with the autonomy of philosophy. Historicists like Sylvan or Gadamer are seen to commit the genetic fallacy which confuses the historical origin of a discourse with its truth or falsity, and the appraisal of the truth of a representation with an assessment of its genesis and context.[53] The general line of defence followed by analytic philosophers like Brown, is to concede that values and culture might affect the choice of questions the philosopher brings to the inquiry. It is granted that this inquiry takes place within a cultural tradition located within the social institution of the liberal university. But these sociological considerations do not affect the truth or falsity of the solutions philosophers give to such problems. The criteria which determine the truth or falsity of such solutions are independent of the specific perspective of philosophers and their social context. Such an argument employs the distinction between the contexts of justification and of discovery, and it means that when and where philosophical or scientific claims were or are made is not relevant to whether they are true.

Historicists need to hold that sociological considerations do affect the truth or falsity of the solutions philosophers give to such problems. The first point that needs to be established in countering this objection is that historicity of philosophy thesis, of reason evolving in history within cultural traditions, does not necessarily deny the autonomy of philosophy. Philosophy is autonomous and socially conditioned. Hegel expresses the relationship thus:

> "Philosophy is identical with the spirit of the era in which it makes its appearance; it is not superior to its era but simply the consciousness of what is substantial in it—or, it is thinking knowledge of what belongs to that era....No one can escape from what is substantial in his era—any more that he can get out of his own skin. Thus, from the substantial point of view, philosophy cannot leap beyond its own times."[54]

This does not mean that analytic discourse is merely the contingency of a particular historical and socially conditioned understanding of modernity, which functions as the modern commonsense ontology of a scientistic culture. Philosophy is, Hegel continues, a rational attempt to grasp or understand our place within modernity:

> "Nevertheless philosophy does stand over and above its own era, which is to say, from the point of view of form, since it consists in the thinking of what is substantial, i.e., makes it an object over against itself, it has the same content but as a knowledge of it goes beyond. The difference, however, is simply formal; there is no difference in content."[55]

But as this knowledge, Hegel goes onto say, is the actuality of spirit, spirit's self-knowledge which was formerly not present, then:

> "this formal difference is also a real, actual one. This knowledge produces a new form in the development of spirit. In this context developments are simply ways of knowing. By self knowledge spirit posits itself for itself (as independent), develops in itself. This involves a new difference between what it is in itself and what its actuality is; and, thus, a new manifestation appears."[56]

Philosophy is the process of thought thinking thought, as distinct from the description of thoughts, or outlining the stages of their development. It produces it own object, from something else—religion, art or science—thereby negating the other in the movement. This process has a history, whatever its meandering may have been, in the sense that philosophy develops, rather than merely changes.[57] It develops into a system, the meaning of which is totality.

Sociology intervenes to assert that the autonomy of philosophy as an analytic system of concepts which are divorced from society and culture is idealism— ideas live in an autonomous realm and philosophy works by generating ideas from ideas. From a materialist perspective philosophical texts do appear to have a life of their own, do hide the social labour that has gone into them, and appear to be superior cultural entities somehow detached from conditions of economic, political and cultural production. The social position of philosophical texts is that they appear as detached autonomous cultural entities, but the position is illusory. They are produced and consumed in a society in which exchange has become the dominant principle of social relationships. In so covering up the problematic division of labour that makes them possible in a capitalist society, and the way they are socially mediated in terms of their production and reception, philosophical works or texts are fetishes. A Weberian/Marxist sociology informs us that philosophy's autonomy from other institutions is conditioned by society as a whole, and that this makes that autonomy increasingly problematic, even though that autonomy remains crucial for philosophy's social contribution and function with advanced capitalist society. The special and privileged enclave called philosophy is marooned from our common activities in civil society; and the values that it represents—disinterested inquiry into truth in order to realise the ideals of the Enlightenment—are increasingly under threat from the crass economic rationalism, with its utilitarian values of making a fast buck, getting to the top of the ant-heap, and lording it over the minions below as an executive manager. Philosophy as a form of critical thinking is part of the cultural discursive space in bourgeois society, which represents the highest values of bourgeois culture—inquiry, truth, freedom, beauty, justice—which are differentiated from the crude instrumentalism of Rupert Murdoch or Kerry Packer in the market place or the state. But under capitalism the use-value of philosophy as critical thinking is replaced by the exchange-value of a degree which destroys use-value, and then presents exchange-value as use-value. This particular historical way of understanding philosophy within modernity has become institutionally embodied, and this institution frames, conditions and largely determines the function of philosophical texts in our culture and society.

That autonomous works of philosophy are socially mediated by exchange relations in the market place does not mean that we have to deny an internal history of the development of the analytic tradition, like that advanced by Rorty in *Philosophy and the Mirror of Nature.* We can accept Rorty's narrative as an internal history, but as materialists, set it in a wider cultural context of modernity, by linking it to the dynamics of a capitalist market society, located within the wider concerns of modernity. So analytic philosophy is a typical product of early twentieth-century modernist culture that had developed with the rise of industrial capitalism. This form of cultural modernism represents the linking of logic and empiricism in the form of positivism, which was a resurgence of Enlightenment beliefs in the form of science, being linked to social hope and capitalist forms of urban industrial growth, as part of the need and plan to rebuild the war-torn capitalist economies of Europe. The motor of the development of analytic philosophy was logical positivism embodied in the work of the Vienna Circle. This produced a counter-movement with Wittgenstein, then another with scientific realism, with its physicalist ontology and language mirroring the inner structure of the independently real. The content of the cultural form of the philosophical is Australian materialism, which is a systematic theoretical discourse about the shape and nature of mechanism of nature, society and human beings combined into a coherent totality.

The historicist thesis that an autonomous philosophy is socially mediated is a viable one. Philosophy springs from what Husserl called the life world, as distinct from the marketplace. He says that the life world:

> "for us who live wakefully in it, is always already there, existing in advance for us, the "ground" of all praxis whether theoretical or extratheoretical. The world is pregiven to us, the waking, always somehow practically interested subjects, not occasionally but always and necessarily as the universal field of all actual and possible praxis, as horizon."[58]

Philosophy and the sciences are located in the everyday world, which grounds the interests and purposes that orientate research in them. It is the everyday world in which all of us consciously have our existence, and this gives philosophy and science their historically and culturally situated character. It is this surrounding world of everyday life world that analytic discourse takes for granted, but does not adequately theorize its relation to. Though philosophy abstracts itself from history to be autonomous from society, it has its roots in civil society, with its forms of knowledge which reflect the concerns of specific communities and serve their needs. A materialist account can hold philosophy to be autonomous with its own problems, methods and conventions, for though philosophy is a part of history, its form stands outside it. We can cash this out by distinguishing between the historical and transhistorical dimension of our concepts. The conceptual apparatus of analytic philosophy has historical and transhistorical referents. Science does genuinely apprehend specific social practices in different forms of society; but the social content of science today is science within modernity. The physicalist naturalist's appeal to science as an abstraction constantly smudges over these differences, and systematically conflates the historical and transhistorical dimension of their objects. The result is that the specific quality of science in capitalism—say self-standing natural sciences like chemistry or physics—is falsely identified with science *per se.*; and the specifically historical roots of science in capitalism are obscured—the way the social sciences have become progressively disconnected from human emancipation.

Analytic philosophy's failure to provide a social and historical analysis of science and philosophy means that it remains unreflexive about the way the prestige of scientific progress is used to legitimate existing social reality as the irreversible achievements of progress. The Hegelian account of philosophy, expressing its own time in thought, takes us beyond this form, as it suggests that philosophy develops by working up an internally consistent coherent world view of modernity. Hegel's thesis of philosophy's form, expressing its own age in concepts as a system or totality, is developed by Heidegger into a concept of a world picture. In his text "The Age of the World-Picture" Heidegger is concerned to establish the defining features of modernity relative to the ancient Greeks. The reconstructive project of Australian materialism, based on the unity of science, and the synthesis of physicalism, metaphysical atomism (or methodological individualism), and the universal covering law model, can be interpreted as establishing the world picture of modernity. The modernist picture of Australian materialist philosophy, in David Armstrong's words, aims 'to give an account of the most general nature of things and of man.'[59] This systematizes the underlying values, beliefs which form our social formation's characteristic manner of thinking. Derived from the natural sciences this world-picture has been worked up through centuries of effort, and is the product of past achievement. As a handed down legacy the subject matter of this materialist tradition has been built on, modified and transformed, and so has undergone constant development, refinement, and transformation within modernity. This world-picture is the way that modernity is aware of its own historicity, *vis-à-vis* the classical Greeks. Heidegger holds that it is possible to talk about this picture as a unity. Physics has been the prototype of modern knowledge which presents itself expressly as mathematical knowledge, and it provides the framework through which we view the world in modernity. The perimeters of the scientific framework are set by the following: movement signifies change of place, no movement or direction of movement is privileged over another, all places are equal to each other, and no point in time is privileged before others. This framework has been posited by humans as subjects who view objects in nature in terms of the realm of natural law which is held as the truth.[60] The distinctiveness and superiority of this modern world-picture is highlighted by the Greek view of a teleological nature or the mediaeval one as a world full of meaning.[61] Heidegger stresses the mathematical nature of the world-picture of natural science, the way it functions as the pregiven, unquestioned axiomatic metaphysical framework, and the way the epistemic representation of an object stands under a logic in which propositions are understood as either true or false. If the mathematical representation of nature, in the form of laws of nature, is understood as knowledge that is methodically on the true path to the truth about nature, then what is divergent or different is excluded as false—romanticism—or as not yet sufficiently clear—ethical values about being at home in the world.

Having established the historicized autonomy of the analytic picture of modernity we can now return to the objection against historicism. This, we recall, concedes that values and culture affect the choice of questions philosophers bring to the inquiry; but then goes onto deny that these do not affect the truth or falsity of the solutions philosophers give to such problems. The problem with this objection is that it overlooks the way that the content, sedimented in the form of the world picture, provides not only the problems, particular approach, canonical philosophical texts, but also the very criteria used to demarcate the true from the false. These criteria are internal to modernity, and cannot be established or legitimated outside the philosophical traditions of modernity. This means that the very conventions that we use in order to do philosophy, as distinct from literature and science, are conventions internal to modern discourse. We have a set of rules/procedures which we follow, if we want to be accepted within the institution of philosophy. What is regarded as an authoritative set of procedures and set of practices depends on some background set of criteria in modernity, which are implicitly held. These hold that we rely on an autonomous reason to justify our claims, not dogma, that reason is self-legislating, that science is self-grounding and self-reflexive. Thus the background knowledge about modernity implies that the context in which philosophy takes place cannot be discounted, since the very particular way of doing philosophy is historically formed. The approach, the way the inquiry is conducted, the concepts used, the criteria adopted for evaluating the solution and even the solution itself are dependent on a historical perspective within the conventions of modernity.

Thus progress in knowledge is working towards the goal of more complete knowledge of the world in itself, rather than the seeking of wisdom as it was with the Greeks. Physicalism, which aims at reducing our commonsense image of human beings with intentions and goals to the physical and chemical processes of a mechanistic body, holds this.[62] Richard Bernstein argues that the basic thrust of physicalism is that as scientific inquiry proceeds:

> "we are becoming clearer and clearer about the basic microphysical regularities exhibited by these basic elements and processes. Furthermore, scientific inquiry is leading to a unity of science resulting from the convergence of the independent investigations of physicists, chemists, biologists, psychologists etc. There is an overall unity in this inquiry, for although there is a proliferation of subsciences and we are becoming increasingly aware of the complexity of the universe, the general outline of a scientific image of man and the universe is emerging whereby all the manifest phenomena can be explained in terms of more basic elements and laws, and ultimately in terms of physical elements and laws. When this view is applied to the study of man the mechanistic materialist tells us that man is *nothing but* a complex physical mechanism."[63]

Physicalism has an *a priori* commitment to the reduction of the complex phenomena of nature and society to more basic physical simples as *the* method to achieve clarity. The reduction can be assessed as successful if the reduction theory gives us all the explanatory power of the theory being reduced, and the explanations are of the same object.[64] From these basic simples for human praxis they would be colourless movement and mere receptor impulses and we can reconstruct step by step a more complex conception of the human beings as self-maintaining servo-mechanisms.[65] This is held to be the truth, and what cannot be so reduced is bracketed out as unimportant, or identified as illegitimate, nonsensical or mystical.

The world picture of modernity therefore is the one analytic philosophers and scientists work within, and it is this modernist world picture which provides the justification in terms of truth, and the way we view truth in relation to the basic furniture of the world. So the justification and criteria of knowledge within analytic philosophical practice are internal to this modernist picture. So are the central concerns of a systematic analytic philosophy—its investigation of the foundations of the sciences by setting universal standards of rationality and objectivity, its doctrine concerning truth and knowledge where truth is correspondent to nature, and knowledge being a matter of possessing accurate representations. These concerns work to keep analytic philosophy within the historical bounds of traditional ahistorical limits of modernity. Its role of classifying, comprehending and criticizing the rest of culture implies an acceptance of a set of categories that would, in some non-arbitrary way, serve to order and assess the reality of various cultural and philosophical practices. Such a set of categories arises from the metaphors of probing deeply and seeing things through to the end via a scientific inquiry into the nature of things, based on rising above the prejudices, superstitions and ordinary beliefs of our culture. The whole notion of scientific objectivity then turns out to be a historical one, with the standards suited to certain kinds of knowledge with certain purposes and goals formed within a plurality of different cultural lifeworlds. This world picture enframes the way we see things in modernity—as objects as standing reserves mathematically represented and controlled—and we operate within the boundaries of the implicit conventions sedimented within this world picture of modernity.

Going beyond analytic philosophy. Power/knowledge

The problem with analytic philosophy's identity between its world picture and reality is that it has an impoverished conception of development. Analytic philosophy in a scientistic culture represses the particular philosophical voices by filtering out, dominating or dismissing the non-identical as not being genuine or sound philosophy. The world picture of a mathematical universe of material objects interpreted as geometric bodies, has no place for meaning and value. It influences our praxis. We come to conceive of ourselves in terms of our power to think objectively by raising ourselves above the prejudice imposed by the constraints of embodiment, ordinary language and history. Yet the universe, as modern natural science presents it, is a reduced version of how the world is from the perspective of our pragmatic, moral and aesthetic interests. What does not fit the space as conceptualized by a mathematical physics is not relevant. Yet this space is the place wherein we dwell. The mode of knowledge of natural science and its style of defence by Australian materialists closes off the social dimension of human life, our ethos or dwelling place is outside the framework of natural science; and it is either dismissed as nonsense, superstition, mysticism, or as full of errors which need to be eliminated, or its content is translated into the natural science picture of modernity by being reduced to the language of physics. Development in philosophy would be reworking the materialist picture to incorporate the social dimension of human life.

One way to do this is once again to take up Brown's thesis that philosophy is like science. The deep presupposition here is Brown's assumption that science is both ahistorical and so unaffected by power relations in society. This provided the justification for Brown's autonomous realm of the philosophical which denies its own social mediation in civil society, and the way those particular social relations determine its being. It holds that philosophy and science operate in internalist terms, according to which the progress of science or philosophy is driven by its internal theoretical structure, which is independent of larger historical processes. This assumption that science is independent of power and political interests is common. Brian Ellis says:

> "the practice of science, and the body of knowledge it has yielded, are the products of a long history of inquiry by many thousands of dedicated men and women, operating with a code of honesty and objectivity, or reporting designed precisely to yield objective knowledge of the world, ie knowledge that which is independent of creed, political interest and authority."[66]

This reaffirms one of the most sacred principles in standard Anglo-American analytic philosophy: that science is a disinterested and dislocated view from nowhere. So philosophy is also unaffected by creed, power relations and political authority. But to assume that science constitutes a socially and historically independent account of reality in the face of the social constitution of science, is to claim that science is a privileged institution which is not constituted by the social relations of society, and over which society has no responsibility or control. It is to claim that science alone is objective and capable of representing reality, for it is a perfect disinterested knowledge, and so unaffected by political expediency, history, social relations of gender and class, myth, bias and prejudice. Philosophy then hides behind science.

The assumption of there being an entity called science cannot be accepted as a given after Kuhn and Feyerabend. Let us grant the realist theses that the world is structured and stratified; that concrete reality is a union of many determinations; that abstraction and analysis are appropriate methods of developing knowledge of human beings; and that there is an ontological similarity of natural and social science in that both analyse concrete structured wholes, and explain them in terms of the abstractions arrived at.[67] Rather than there being just "science", we have different sciences with a plurality of different research programmes, with their own set of general assumptions about the entities and processes in a domain of study, and the appropriate methods to be used in investigating the problems and constructing the theories in that domain.[68] Secondly, the sciences are social practices embedded within social relations of class and gender, and these social relations shape the basic role of the sciences in our society. The natural and social sciences have become an integral part of the state and industrial capital. Witness the militarization of physics in which a large proportion of scientists work within the secrecy of the state to design weapons for a particular use, with their work not being open to public scrutiny. Or biotechnology firms doing research in areas of anticipated applicability, subsidized by the state, on the grounds that ignoring research and development means that Australia will be doomed to languish in the backwater of economic uncompetitiveness. The sciences have become caught up in the process of its commodification, and are controlled as part of the national interest with the state pushing industrial firms to fund basic research in the universities, which are becoming a place for capital to invest. The interests of the sciences are now those of industry and the state. In replaying the image of a pure science, and so implicitly deny that the sciences are social human practices inextricably connected to capitalism in modernity, analytic philosophy remains blind to the historical actuality of science in capitalism. The claim by Ellis that "science" is 'independent of creed political interest and authority' does scant justice to actual science. The post-empiricist philosophy of science of Kuhn and Feyerabend has shown that scientific decision-making is a political affair, in which prestige, power and polemic decisively influence the outcome between competing theories and theorists. They also indicated the way that irrational/ideological elements are contained within science.[69]

The position held by Ellis presupposes a modernist relationship between knowledge and power. This is an external relationship in that it holds that pure knowledge can be applied to manipulate and control nature in order to achieve power; that in an unfree society like Nazi Germany, Stalinist Russia, or medieval Christendom political power can be used to impede or distort the acquisition of knowledge; that its power problem lies with the commercial application of science. The condemnation of Galileo by the Catholic Church and the suppression of Mendelian genetics in the Soviet Union are classic examples. Power and knowledge remain extrinsic to one another, in the sense that the realm of epistemological justification is a space of conflicting reasons set off from the struggles of competing groups.[70] Joseph Rouse argues that on this account the intrusion of ideology, politics and economics is circumscribed by philosophy, which emphasizes:

> "a *conceptual* separation between science viewed as a field of knowledge and science viewed as a field of power. Various attempts to distinguish between internal and external history of science, or between philosophy and sociology of science, reflect this desire to sustain a conceptual separation between science and the way power operates within or upon it. What is "internal" to science are the cognitive, rational, intellectual, and epistemological concerns and activities that account for the development of knowledge. The effects of political, sociological and individual psychological factors upon the development of science are external to knowledge and can be compartmentalized in separate inquiries."[71]

This theme of the influence of external interests and values on scientific findings runs through the strong programme of the sociology of knowledge of Barnes and Bloor, and through the feminist criticism of science by Helen

Longino.[72] These are then held to undermine the objective justification of scientific theories. The debate then centres around how these external values and interests can be excluded or modified to protect the claim that science give us objectively justified knowledge.[73]

Adorno and Horkheimer show how the external thesis of the relation between knowledge and power is misleading. They argued that the process of rationalization in modernity meant that a new form of reason has evolved in capitalism, one which they identified as an instrumental reason concerned with the efficiency of means towards pregiven ends of the domination of nature and human beings. Instrumental reason, they argued, casts myths and veils over what is, it collapses into a form of deception and social control, and operates through mechanisms of repression and domination. So it becomes an obstacle to the process of enlightenment. Power is the content inside the form of science, as it resulted scientific reason turning into a mere concern for means and ends, a reason focused on the adequacy of procedures for social purposes that are taken for granted.[74]

This is not the voice of romantic irrationalism saying that reason, upon which the domination of nature is based, is in itself repressive, as some, like Seyla Benhabib, claim.[75] Adorno holds that it is the use of scientific instrumental reason in capitalism that makes it repressive: repression results from both the domination of nature in conditions of scarcity and the class rule of the capitalists. But as material scarcity has been overcome in capitalism, and poverty exists because of the unequal class distribution of wealth, so a positivist or instrumental scientific reason is used to sustain class repression.[76] Adorno also argues that capitalism's recommodification of culture has crippled an autonomous philosophy. Philosophy has its roots in society. from which it distinguishes itself, but it has, along with the rest of culture, become incorporated into the dynamics of capitalism, which has little time for philosophy. Philosophy, in becoming subject to the same economic processes as any other commodity, loses much of its ability to act as a public Socratic conscience in society.[77] It becomes a purely technical discipline.

There is no point in responding to this politicization of reason by regretting this situation, and yearning for the golden days of a pure scientific reason divorced from politics, economics and history. Pure science or philosophy is an academic myth, perpetuated by ideologues. The central issue about power is not the way that scientific claims can be distorted or suppressed by polemic, propaganda or ideology, because power is neither essentially repressively censorious nor external to knowledge. Foucault argued that power is a constructive power that shapes the world and the way it is represented. So it is internal to knowledge, in the sense that knowledge arises out of the exercise of this sort of power. Power relationships permeate the most ordinary activities in science and philosophy, because knowledge is embedded in our research practices within the laboratory and the philosophy institution, and the capillary power relationships in these hierarchical institutions constitute the social world in which we act as particular agents with interests.[78] Writing a

PhD, for instance, is a form of subjection in which an apprentice is disciplined through norms and regulations to produce certain forms of expression. The apprentices are bureaucratically classified in terms of the acquisition of skill, and can be differentiated according to their diligence, efficiency and obedience to the norms of instrumental reason within the analytic tradition. But they are also formed as subjects by the power relations internal to the discipline, as these shape the body of student subjects into particular kinds of philosophers: that is, one who operates in the masculine mode, thinks that philosophy is non-political, is piecemeal problem solving, and is like science.

The power relations operating in the institution of philosophy do not merely impinge on philosophy from without. They permeate the most ordinary activities in philosophical research to the extent that philosophical knowledge arises out of these power relations as well as in opposition to them. Foucault holds that power is best understood as relational, rather than as a possession of an instrument, that can be held and used, or not used, at the will of those in authority. Power is an aspect of the relations between individual philosophers in which our actions are incited, guided or constrained, and this structures the possible field of action. Foucault remarks:

> "Power must be analyzed as something which circulates, or rather as something which only functions in the form of a chain. It is never localized here or there, never in anyone's hands, never appropriated as a commodity or piece of wealth. Power is employed and exercised through a net-like organization."[79]

This can best analysed at a micro level within networks or systems and can be located in the capillaries that run throughout the philosophy institution.[80] These networks have not been set up by someone outside the power network, as we always find ourselves within these networks that have evolved of their own accord. We cannot escape them but only shift to other power relations, and so we are inscribed within power relationships. This does not necessarily mean that we are reduced to the status of victims, forever trapped in mechanisms of power, and unable to extricate ourselves. Relational resistance is inscribed within power relationships in sites of resistance, which give rise to subjugated discourses, such as feminism and environmentalism which challenge hegemonic ones like Australian materialism. These modify particular power structures by turning network against network in terms of local or regional forms of resistance in the micro-practices of daily life. The stark dichotomy between truth and power is undermined when power is no longer seen as just a social instrument,

Foucault's diagnosis of modernity details the way the process of the development of reason into a legislative, modernist instrumental reason is a part of a complex set of disciplinary technologies for the control, subjugation and production of the population of human beings. The social space is littered with bodies, and the social institutions which had been designed to control them, required, after the disenchantment of morality and religion, new forms of surveillance and supervision. The spread of scientific and techno-rational procedures provided this new form; and these having gained a foothold in technology and consciousness, hooked onto the new terrain of the body and the body of populations. The result was an institutionalization of the body—what Foucault calls panoptics. The detailed political policing of the bodies in society was, on Foucault's account, a condition for the expansion of capitalism. He remarks that these regulatory controls of the bodies of population was:

> "an indispensable element in the development of capitalism; the latter would not have been possible without the controlled insertion of bodies into the machinery of production and the adjustment of the phenomena of population to economic processes. But this was not all it required; it also needed the growth of both these factors, their reinforcement as well as their availability and docility; it had to have methods of power capable of optimizing forces, aptitudes, and life in general without at the same time making them more difficult to govern."[81]

Capital could profit from the resources of the population of human beings and the enlargement of markets only when the health and docility of the population had been made possible by a network of regulations and controls.

The rationalization of the body by new techniques of power and knowledge turns the desire of bodies to philosophize into modernist philosophers. These utilize the techniques of the logical method, systematic scientific theory, rigorous analysis, and mathematical deductive reasoning. These techniques then become part of a way of supervising and containing philosophical practices by keeping them enclosed in its own institutional space. Consider the analytic tool of clarity, which is employed in the supervising, site management, and disciplinary system of the philosophical. This is used to clear away the conceptual log jams, tortuous syntax, elliptical exposition, enigmatic hints, woolly metaphors and rhetorical paradoxes.[82] The analytic stress on clarity involves a strategy of semantic ascent to practise a sort of intellectual hygiene against the clotted pap of a dense and obscure philosophy. As a mode of self-policing it makes an organized space in which individuals are placed as philosophers. It transforms them into analytic philosophers, who are observed in terms of an objective gaze to see whether they perform their function in terms of its own normalizing standard and norms. The controlling of the philosophical by techniques like clarity, functions to produce philosophy's legitimacy by dividing and partitioning it from literature, and the social sciences like sociology and geography. The clarity of reason is used by analytic philosophers to preserve and defend the conventions of the analytic tradition in the face of the postmodernist challenge. They labour to tidy up the mess on the borders, repair the boundary fences and lock the gate. They aim to preserve the conventional modernist ways of thinking, writing and arguing from the chaos and disorder resulting from postmodernists' breaking of the boundaries. This underlabouring is deemed to be a reasonable task for philosophy, as postmodernism is a kind of thinking that escapes conventional disciplinary boundaries, since it is not exactly philosophy, literary criticism or social theory. Reason's shadow—everything that is not reason—threatens to erupt as monstrous unreason and uncontrollable chaos, and so these demons must be controlled, repressed, contained and put in their place, because submission to a modernist reason is the means to freedom.

So it is plausible to hold that knowledge and power are internally related, rather than being externally connected, as assumed by Brown and Ellis. Philosophy cannot be partitioned off from political criticism, as it is a political practice and politically engaged. To think otherwise is self-deception. This incorporation of the social dissolves the coherence of the analytic tradition, and it may well mean its disintegration. The incorporation of the historical into philosophy negates a modernist formalism, but it also opens up new possibilities for philosophy, as it brings it out of its self-enclosed sphere into the historically formed social world.

Conclusion

The underground historicist current in Australian philosophy has been recovered and the plausibility of its constructivist conception of knowledge defended. Russell's notion of mathematical logic as the essence of philosophy is limited, because its conception of autonomy isolates and severs philosophy from its intrinsic links to society, politics and social praxis. A historicist philosophy has something fruitful to offer after this negation of modernist philosophy, as its conception of philosophical reason as a tradition of rational inquiry within institutional power relationships suggests that philosophy has affinities with literature. This indicates that the questions are changing rather than the questions being the same, and the answers changing. This opens up a philosophical space to ask new questions. Philosophy becomes a series of texts whose meanings are changed by historical context. This opens up a linguistic turn towards language, introduces questions about the way that representations in language mirror the world, and the constitutive role of language in the cultural and social worlds that people make for themselves. Questions about how we understand the world through language now become crucial.

The historicist tradition takes an hermeneutical turn, with interpretation as the point of departure. We ragpicker critics of the analytic enterprise do not dump the analytic tradition in the name of breaking free from metaphysics, nor do we attempt to situate ourselves outside the mechanistic metaphysics and institutional power relations of the analytic tradition, as does the new growing postmodern orthodoxy, in the name of Nietzschean overcoming. Hermeneutics leads to the notion of rational conversation which has to trade on the notion of truth, if the conversation is to have any point, other than uttering a series of sounds which we hope will affect the behaviour of the other for our advantage. The questioning of the legitimacy of the structurally invisible assumption of the conceptual framework of the analytic world-picture involves doing an alternative kind of philosophy, from within the modernist analytic power-knowledge regime. So the ragpickers hold that though intellectual clarification is an important objective for philosophers, it is not the object of philosophy, nor will it solve the substantive philosophical disputes between us. Clarity is a necessary part of the means to an end, but it is not a sufficient end in itself. The maps provided by good analytic philosophy should enable us to come to grips with the content of substantive issues involved with postmodernism's challenge to the assumptions of the analytic philosophy. Complex strategies of reading, writing and arguing operate here, and this involves going about the job of questioning differently from that operative from those strands in analytic philosophy, which hold that science gives us true pictures of the world, and go on to discuss the issues around theory laden observation in experience without ever mentioning language. Here language primarily represents objects.[83]

Notes and References

1   Martin Heidegger, *Being and Time,* trs. John Macquarie and Edward Robinson, (Blackwell, Oxford, 1962), Division 1, section 44, pp. 256-273; Martin Heidegger, "On the Essence of Truth", in *Basic Writings,* (ed.) David Krell, (Routledge and Kegan Paul, London), pp. 113-141. For a commentary see Hans-Georg Gadamer, "What is Truth?", in Brice R. Wachterhauser, (ed.)*Hermeneutics and Truth,* (Northwestern University Press, Evanston, 1994), pp 33-46, especially pp. 35-36.

2   For the revisionist connection between analytic philosophy and the world picture of modernity, see Hilary Putnam, *Realism and Reason: Philosophical Papers Volume 3,* (Cambridge University Press, Cambridge, 1989).

3   For a review of the new reflective openness by analytic philosophers to their own tradition, refer to Peter Dews, "The Historicization of Analytical Philosophy" in Dews, *The Limits of Disenchantment,* (Verso, London, 1995), pp. 59-76.

4   D. M. Armstrong, "The Nature of Mind" in *The Nature of Mind and Other Essays,* (University of Queensland Press, St. Lucia, 1980), pp. 1-15, citation footnote 1, p. 4.

5   Val Plumwood, *Feminism and the Mastery of Nature,* (Routledge, London, 1993), p. 1.

6   R. Sylvan, "Prospects for Regional Philosophers in Australasia", in *Australasian Journal of Philosophy,* vol. 63, no. 2, (June 1985). pp: 188–204.

7   Nowhere is this more apparent than Nietzsche. He writes: 'when, then, is truth? A mobile army of metaphors, metonyms and anthropomorphisms—in short, a sum of human relations, which have been enhanced, transposed, and embellished poetically and rhetorically, and which long after use seem firm, canonical and obligatory to a people: truths are illusions about which one has forgotten that this is what they are: metaphors which are worn out and without serious power; coins which have lost their pictures and now matter only as metal, no longer as coins.' F. Nietzsche, "On Truth and Lie in an Extra-Moral Sense", in W. Kaufmann, (ed.), *The Portable Nietzsche,* (Penguin, Harmondsworth, 1976), pp. 42–7, citation pp. 46–7.

8   H. P. Heseltine, "Introduction" to A. A. Philipps, *The Australian Tradition,* 2nd edition, (Longman Cheshire, Melbourne, 1980), p. viii.

9   Stephen Alomes, *A Nation at Last? The Changing Character of Australian Nationalism, 1880-1988,* (Angus and Robertson, Sydney, 1988), pp. 56, 215 & 217.

10   Brian Head and James Walter (eds.), *Intellectual Movements and Australian Society,* (Oxford University Press, Melbourne, 1988), pp. viii, 8 & 10.

11   Richard Sylvan, "Prospects for Regional Philosophers in Australasia", op. cit., p. 189.

12   Ibid, pp. 201-202.

13   Ibid, p.197.

14   Ibid, p. 189.

15   The model of global or universal culture beating against resistant enclaves can be found in Kenneth Frampton, "Towards a Critical Regionalism: Six Points for an Architecture of Resistance", in Hal Foster, (ed.), *The Anti-Aesthetic: Essays on Postmodern Culture*, (Port Townsend, Washington, 1983, pp. 16-30.

16   Sylvan, op. cit., pp. 197-198.

17   For an account of the very influential British cultural studies refer to, G. Turner, *British Cultural Studies. An Introduction,* (Unwin Hyman, London, 1990).

18   For recent broad attempts at a comprehensive investigation of modernity, refer to, David Kolb, *The Critique of Pure Modernity-Hegel, Heidgger and After*, (The University of Chicago Press, Chicago, 1986); J. Habermas, *The Philosophical Discourse of Modernity*, trs, F. Lawrence, (MIT Press, Cambridge, Massachusetts, 1987); S. Toumlin, *Cosmopolis-The Hidden Agenda of Modernity*, (The Free Press, Glencoe, 1991).

19   For instance, Graham Lyons, Evonne Moore and Joseph Wayne Smith, *Is the End Nigh?*, (Avebury, Aldershot, 1995).

20   G. Sauer-Thompson and J. W. Smith, *Beyond Economics,* (Avebury, Aldershot, 1997).

21   Ernest Gellner, *Reason and Culture,* (Blackwell, Oxford, 1992), p. 82.

22   For a general response see S. Sayers, "Marxism and Dialectic Method: A Critique of G. A. Cohen", in S. Sayers & P. Osborne, (eds.), *Socialism, Feminism, and Philosophy,* (Routledge and Kegan Paul, London, 1990).

23   J. L. Mackie, *Problems From Locke*, (Oxford University Press, Oxford, 1976), p. 2.

24   Bertrand Russell maintained this in *A Critical Exposition of the Philosophy of Leibniz*, (George Allen and Unwin, revised edition, 1926). A recent defence in response to Rorty's *Philosophy and the Mirror of Nature* is given by W. Charlton, *The Analytic Ambition: An Introduction to Philosophy,* (Blackwell, Oxford, 1991), pp. 10-11.

25   Hans-Georg Gadamer, "What is Truth?", in Brice R. Wachterhauser, *Hermeneutics and Truth,* op. cit, p. 39.

26   B. Russell, *Our Knowledge of the External World as a Field for Scientific Method in Philosophy,op. cit.* , pp. 233-4.

27   B. Russell, *A Critical Exposition of the Philosophy of Leibniz*, op. cit., p. 8.

28   See Peter Hylton, *Russell, Idealism and the Origins of Analytical Philosophy*, (Clarendon Press, Oxford, 1990).

29   It is a form of historiographical genre which Rorty terms a doxography, and which he rejects as an attempt to envision philosophy as a 'natural kind'. R. Rorty, "The Historiography of Philosophy: Four Genres", in R. Rorty et el, (ed.), *Philosophy in History*, (Cambridge University Press, Cambridge, 1984).

30   Robert Brown, "Recent Australian Work in Philosophy", *Canadian Journal of Philosophy,* vol. 18, no. 3, (Sept 1988), pp. 545-578.

31   Ibid, p. 546.

32   Thomas Nagel, *Mortal Questions*, (Cambridge University Press, Cambridge, 1979), p. 208.

33   This is the argument advanced by Arthur Danto, *Analytic Philosophy of History*, (Cambridge University Press, Cambridge, 1965), p. 168.

34   Robert Brown, "Recent Australian Work in Philosophy", op. cit., p. 573.

35   Robert Nozick, *Anarchy, State and Utopia*, (Basic Books, New York, 1974), pp. 323-324.

36   Hans-Georg Gadamer, *Truth and Method*, (Sheed and Ward, London, 1975), p. 273.

37   G. Ryle, *The Revolution in Philosophy*, (MacMillian, London, 1956).

38   M. Dummett, "Can Analytical Philosophy be Systematic, and Ought It to Be?" in *Truth and Other Enigmas*, (Gerald Duckworth, London, 1978), pp. 437-58, citation, p. 458.

39   Ibid, p. 442

40   M. Dummett, "Language and Communication", in Alexander George, (ed.), *Reflections on Chomsky,* (Blackwell, Oxford, 1989), pp. 192-212.

41   Hans-Georg Gadamer, "On the Origins of Philosophical Hermeneutics," in *Philosophical Apprenticeships,* trs. Frederick G. Lawrence, (MIT Press, Cambridge, Massachusetts, 1985), p. 181.

42   B. Russell, *An Essay on the Foundations of Geometry,* (Cambridge University Press, Cambridge, 1897). P. Hylton, *Russell, Idealism and the Emergence of Analytic Philosophy,* op. cit.

43   P. Hylton, "The nature of the proposition and the revolt against idealism", in R. Rorty et el, (ed.), *Philosophy in History,* op. cit., pp. 375-397.

44   Isaiah Berlin quoted in Jonathen Ree, "English Philosophy in the Fifties," *Radical Philosophy,* vol. 65, (Autumn, 1993), pp. 3-21, citation p. 14.

45   Ibid, p. 14.

46   B. Russell, quoted in Frederich Will, "The Concern about Truth," in G. W. Roberts, (ed.), *The Bertrand Russell Memorial Volume,* (Allen and Unwin, London, 1979), pp. 264-284, p. 283, note 5.

47   A. MacIntyre, "Philosophy and Its History", in *Analyse and Kritik,* vol. 1, no.1, (October 1982), pp. 101-105.

48   The phrase 'a tradition of rational inquiry' comes from Alasdair MacIntyre, *Whose Justice? Whose Rationality?,* (University of Notre Dame Press, Notre Dame, 1988).

49   For the distinction between historicism and hermeneutics refer to Gadamer, *Truth and Method,* op. cit. pp. 460-490.

50   John McDowell, *Mind and World,* (Harvard University Press, Cambridge, Massachusetts, 1994), p. 88

51   Hans-Georg Gadamer, *Truth and Method,* op, cit, pp. 10-19.

52   This is the position of Rorty in "The Historiography of Philosophy: Four Genries", in R. Rorty et el, (ed.), *Philosophy in History,* op. cit., p. 49. It shows how deeply Rorty still is embedded within the analytic tradition.

53   H. B. Acton, *The Illusion of the Epoch,* (Cohen and West, London, 1955), pp. 108-9.

54   G. W. F. Hegel, "Introduction" to *Lectures on the History of Philosophy,* in Q. Lauer, (ed.), *Hegel's Idea of Philosophy,* (Fordham University Press, New York, 1983), p. 95.

55   Ibid, p. 96.

56   Ibid.

57   Ibid, p. 78-9.

58   E. Husserl, *The Crisis of European Sciences and Transcendental Phenomemology,* (Northwestern University Press, Evanston, 1970), p. 142.

59   David Armstrong, "The Causal Theory of the Mind", in *The Nature of Mind and Other Essays,* op. cit., p. 17.

60   M. Heidegger, "The Age of the World Picture", in *The Question Concerning Technology and Other Essays,* trs. William Lovitt, (Harper and Row, New York, 1954), pp. 69-104.

61   This is spelt out in chapter 1 of Charles Taylor, *Hegel,* (Cambridge University Press, Cambridge, 1975).

62   David Armstrong, *A Materialist Theory of the Mind,* Revised edition, (Routledge, London, 1993).

63   R. J. Bernstein, *Praxis and Action,* (Duckworth, London, 1972), p. 252.

64   Alan Garfinkel, *Forms of Explanation,* (Yale University Press, New Haven, 1981).

65   For a classic manifesto of reductionism, refer to, Paul Oppenheim and Hilary Putnam "Unity of Science as a Working Hypothesis", in Richard Boyd et el, (ed.),*The Philosophy of Science,* (MIT Press, Cambridge, Massachusetts, 1991), pp. 405-28.

66   Brian Ellis, *Truth and Objectivity,* (Basil Blackwell, Oxford, 1990), p. 27.

67   R. Bhaskar, *A Realist Theory of Science*, (Harvester Wheatsheaf, Hemel Hempstead, 1978).

68   L. Laudan, *Progress and its Problems: Towards a Theory of Scientific Growth*, (University of California Press, Berkeley, 1977), p. 81.

69   This is acknowledged by L. Ludan, *Progress and Its Problems*, op. cit., p. 4.

70   It is held by David L. Hull, *Science as a Process*, (The University of Chicago Press, Chicago, 1988).

71   Joseph Rouse, *Knowledge and Power, Toward a Political Philosophy of Science*, (Cornell University Press, Ithaca, 1987), p. 17.

72   B. Barnes and D. Bloor, "Relativism, rationalism and the sociology of knowledge, in M. Hollis and S. Lukes, (ed.), *Rationality and Relativism*, (Oxford University Press, 1982), pp. 21-44; H. Longino, *Science as Social Knowledge*, (Princeton University Press, Princeton, 1990).

73   This is how the debate is structured by G. Couvalis, *Philosophy of Science*, (Sage, London, 1997).The implication of Longino's arguments, he says, is that the choice of background assumptions and, hence, the choice of theories which are justified , must depend on the prejudices of individuals or communities. He then argues that her argument from history is both paradoxical and not plausible. (pp. 160-161).

74   M. Horkheimer, *The Eclipse of Reason*, (Seabury Press, New York, 1974); T. W. Adorno and M. Horkheimer, *Dialectic of Enlightenment*, trs. J. Cumming, (Verso, London, 1979).

75   Benhabib is quite explicit. She says 'Adorno...views reason to be inherently an instrument of domination.' Seyla Benhabib, *Critique, Norm, Utopia: A Study of the Foundations of Critiaal Theory*, (Columbia University Press, New York, 1986), p. 167.

76   K. J. Heller, "Adorno Against the Grain: Re-Reading Theodore Adorno's Philosophy of History", *Praxis International* , Vol 11, No. 3, (October 1991), pp. 354-376.

77   T. Adorno, "Cultural Criticism and Society", in Adorno, *Prisms*, trs. Samuel and Shierry Weber, (MIT Press, Cambridge, Massachusetts, 1983), pp. 17-34.

78   Refer M. Foucault, *Power/Knowledge*, (ed.) Colin Gordon, (Harvester Wheatsheaf, Hertfordshire, 1980).

79   Ibid, p. 98.

80   M. Foucault, "The Subject and Power", in H. L. Dreyfus and P. Rabinow, *Michel Foucault: Beyond Structuralism and Hermeneutics*, 2nd ed. (University of Chicago Press, Chicago, 1983), p. 221.

81   Michel Foucault, *The History of Sexuality*, vol. 1, An Introduction, (Vintage, New York, 1980), p. 141.

82   This is the way David Stove defends the borders in "A Farewell to Arts" in *Cricket Versus Republicanism and Other Essays*, (Quakers Hill Press, Quakers Hill, 1994).

83   See George Couvalis, *The Philosophy of Science*, op. cit.,chapter. 1. He acknowledges that our experience is not totally unstructured, and that our understanding of it uses conceptual categories. But he operates on the assumption that abstract subjects, who he defines as the products of millions of years of evolution, perceive items in the world without discussing the way something is understood as something also involves a public language. He assumes that our perceptual world is systematically related to the actual characteristics of the real world without the mediation of language. The question to be asked of this realism is: from what location is one to judge what is within and what is outside the public language game?

3 Cruising with pastiche on the dialectical highway

> The central nerve of the dialectic as a method is determinate negation. It is based on the experience of the impotence of a criticism that keeps to the general and polishes off the object being criticized by subsuming it from above under a concept as its representative. Only the critical idea that unleashes the force stored up in its own object is fruitful; fruitful both for the object, by helping it to come into its own, and against it, reminding it that it is not yet itself.
>
> Adorno, *Hegel: Three Studies*.

An immediate analytic reaction to the ragpickers' negative root-digging of the modern analytic tradition would be to point out that their negation of the analytic tradition dogmatically presupposes the truth of the dialectical tradition. Despite their use of baroque metaphors of ruins, decay, and labyrinths, they implicitly accept that the univocal progress of enlightenment through the progressive dissolution of analytic illusions and prejudices has an end in a pastiched form of Hegelian-Marxism. Progressivism is the Hegelian solution to Nietzschean relativism and perspectivism. Physicalists like David Lewis would judge the historicist claim to have surpassed analytic metaphysics to be unjustified, 'for it does not even settle the prior question of *how* it is to be settled what we refer to.'[1] Those like Lewis would feel that the argument has been so constructed that the cards were stacked against them from the beginning, with dialectics acting as the public prosecutor of analytic prejudice on behalf of an enlightened reason in history. Dialectics, they would mutter, is a part of what Thomas Nagel terms that 'significant strain of idealism in contemporary philosophy, according to which what there is and how things are cannot go beyond what we in principle could think about.'[2]

It would be asked what are the standards, according to which the criticisms of the ontology of analytic philosophy are being made? How are these standards derived? Is there not an implicit teleological notion of progress being presupposed here in order to guarantee the superiority of Hegelian-Marxism over its rivals? Neo-pragmatists would ask: why should we assume that there is dialectical progress, rather than an ebb and flow of a number of different discourses through discussion, dialogue and debate? Postmodernists would add: why not just assume a number of discontinuous language games, rather than the Hegelian assumption that dialecticans stand at the absolute moment when all is revealed?

This is difficult terrain we have stumbled onto, as it involves establishing that our ontologies or metaphysics can be rationally argued about and examined for their plausibility. It involves looking at the way our common philosophical history forestructures the way we go about assessing the adequacy of competing ontologies. The deductive argumentative method we employ in philosophy to rationally establish the plausibility of our metaphysical assumptions leads to difficulties. Argumentation takes the form of a rendering intelligible by way of arguments whereby I state what I am on about. If it is unclear to you about what I am on about, then I provide you with additional premises for clarification. The reasons for my muddied, confusing and unclear sentences are further sentences from within the cultural context of my philosophical tradition. These enable you to understand more easily what I am trying to say. It is the background context which makes my statements intelligible in the form of shaping their sense. So each of us continually refers to his/her different background or philosophical tradition. The going gets more difficult when the metaphysical conflict between the alternative traditions becomes tied up with the problem of incommensurable ontological frameworks. Philosophy now begins to look like the blind speaking to the blind.

The philosophical tradition is actually a number of mutually antagonistic schools, which have their own traditions, modes of justification, problematics, canonical texts, history of debates, forms of rationality and styles to resolve their ongoing problems. Each of us views, describes, interprets and explains problems from the specific point of view of his or her own commitments, and we judge the success or failure of another school from the standards of justification internal to our own. We do not substantially engage with one another, as each tradition largely operates as an inward-looking, self-contained discourse, and so each remains locked up in his/her own prejudices. We are firmly convinced that the conceptual framework of the opposing discourse is deeply flawed; that the opposing tradition has lost its overall direction; that contradictions abound and cannot be resolved from within; and that the failing condition of the tradition indicates its degeneracy and the conceptual richness and resourcefulness of its competitor. Philosophical debate across metaphysical traditions in practice is generally odd remarks at occasional seminar papers and book reviews, which are taken to constitute a basis for the final refutation of the obvious fallacies of the other side. Each school continues to proclaim that they, and only they, possess philosophic truth and that the other school lives in prejudice and error.[3] As in Hegel's day we have 'one party giving out truths only to have them dislodged and brushed aside by truths of just the same sort purveyed by the other parties.'[4] The conversation is fragmentary, full of gaps, silences, repression, dogmatic assertions. There is a continual sidestepping of ontological issues, overlaid by frequent explosions of a repelling of horizons, as the representatives of the different traditions collide into one another. It is difficult to say that one metaphysical tradition is better than another in these circumstances. More often it is silence disrupted by vitriolic polemics.

One response to the ragpickers' root-digging of the analytic tradition is the positivist echo that it is not possible to evaluate rationally our competing implicit ontological assumptions. It is deemed to be a fool's errand, akin to knights on horseback tilting at windmills with lances, for it is an existential or political choice whether we are individualists or holists, analytic or poststructuralist philosophers. There is no neutral ground between our competing social ontologies, as we live in different philosophical or scientific traditions. These are simply different modes of coping with the world under specific historical circumstances. So the best we can do is to recognize that there are different alternatives, accept the cultural provincialism of our own way of thinking, and acknowledge that our descendants will stand to the rationality of most of our beliefs and those of opponents, as we currently stand towards the beliefs of the sixteenth century.[5] This post-analytic turn articulated by Rorty sails close to relativism. But it is the highway we have to cruise, once we reject the Enlightenment assumption that we stand at the pinnacle of a historical process of enlightenment. Superstition and error have been largely overcome. It is only our opponent who still lives in Plato's cave.

The rational justification of our competing metaphysics is not an obtuse problem, posed by a marginalized historicist philosophy in postmodernity, still caught up in playing the old sceptical game. It is a very practical one. Consider this story. Malcolm and Joan have come into the Marriage Guidance Centre for help to resolve some personal problems they have been encountering, and which are currently expressed in the form of sexual difficulties that inhibit their lovemaking because of neurosis. Their relationship is going through a rocky patch as they can no longer genuinely communicate with one another, and live more or less in different worlds mediated by static and stilted conversation. They are anxious about their pregnant adolescent daughter, Ruby Jane, who hangs out on the street with the wrong crowd, mixes with druggies, dealers and car thieves, cuts classes at school, is indifferent to parental punishment and is regularly beaten up by her unemployed boyfriend who has AIDS. She claims to all and sundry around town that she has been sexually abused by her father, and that her mother knew about the rape, but kept quiet about it to punish her for being a bad daughter. Malcolm and Joan cannot agree on what to do about Ruby Jane, even though they agree that their practical rationality ought to aim at striving to do the right thing by each other, so they can live well. They have rejected instrumentally controlling and dominating one another to get their own way. They turn to the clinic because they are attracted by its human face, its social science systems approach, and its emphasis on interpreting and understanding the meaning of their conflicts. They came to the clinic after experiencing a bad time with the behavioural modification programmes of the behavioural psychologists at the private clinic around the corner. These just talked about human beings as a bundle of conditioned responses reacting to stimuli, or as computational machines. They also rejected the natural science approach of the drug-orientated bio-medicine psychiatrists based in a main teaching hospital in Adelaide. They are implicitly aware that the presuppositions of their commonsense discourse is in opposition to those of the behavioural psychologists, and the natural scientific discourse of the psychiatrists. They are also aware that both of them have radically different ways of viewing human nature, social structure, culture and society. Malcolm and Joan each have different approaches to their conflict, which is destroying what they have built in common, and they continually argue about the causal role of individual and structure, going round-and-round in circles, never resolving their conflict. What they want to know is whether one can rationally resolve metaphysical issues without insisting on the unique rationality and truth of one's own metaphysical programme. Caught up in postmodern anxiety they both enrol in philosophy courses at Adelaide and Flinders University. They want to learn how best rationally to tackle the metaphysical conflicts that are blocking their efforts to overcome their lives being pulled asunder. The question they pose to themselves as they enter the portals of philosophy is: can we rationally resolve metaphysical conflicts so that we can say that one metaphysical system is better than another? Answering this question, they reason, will help them to resolve their personal conflicts, and so enable them to live a more enlightened life.

We argue that the negativity of imminent critique in the dialectical tradition can do the job that is required. It allows Malcolm and Joan to critique the metaphysical assumptions underlying a reductive materialism's world picture, whilst remaining within the Enlightenment tradition and its ground rules, for those reasons that we take to be authoritative. It is able to show that the reasons it gives for counting those reasons as authoritative are themselves authoritative reasons.

Encountering the analytic tradition

In studying philosophy, both Malcolm and Joan quickly find that the making intelligible of their isolated claims through appealing to the philosophical background takes the specific form of referring to the analytic tradition. Its dominant tendency is a scientific materialism which holds itself to be the latest form of the modern scientific Enlightenment, and it is science that tells us what really counts as authoritative reasons. Teachers of this school inform first-year students that the task of philosophy is to reconstruct scientifically the pre-scientific or pre-analytic domain of everyday ordinary experience by means of a rigorous metnod. To do so in an excellent fashion, it is added, they need to speak the language of philosophers fluently within the analytic tradition, and be at home with formal logic. As ordinary language is too vague and imprecise, we need to translate the meanings into the precise unambiguous language of the natural sciences. Every sentence must be absolutely true or absolutely false, since it either mirrors the corresponding objects or it does not. Those Hegelians who talk in terms of partially true and partially false talk nonsense.

After a time Malcolm and Joan accept philosophy aligned with natural science as the way things are. It should be the case that philosophy follows the scientific method, the paradigm of which is mathematical physics. They accept that the mode of rationality is formalist, a rigorous formalist method of quasi-mathematical techniques. This enables philosophers to distinguish chatter from philosophy, and put an end to the intrusion of the nonsense of everyday life into the crystal-clear language of philosophy. They adopt a formal account of analysis, which makes the synthesising of beliefs a secondary activity, brackets substantive meaning, places an emphasis on breaking down or taking apart beliefs so as to scrutinize their composition to see if they can be properly trusted, and then regiment these into an ideal language.

By the time Malcolm and Joan are doing honours in philosophy they have become aware that the analytic tradition is often charmed by its own technical facility into thinking that a translation of its opponent's substantive theses into its own discourse is tantamount to a refutation. They feel that the analytic approach dissolves their problem rather than helps them resolve it. They have turned back in the circle from whence they began. Their encounter with David Lewis reinforces this feeling, as he says that the outcome of attempted refutations of philosophical theory is that:

> "the theory survives the refutation—at a price. Our 'intuitions' are simply opinions, our philosophical theories are the same....Once the menu of well-worked out theories is before us, philosophy is a matter of opinion..."[6]

The appearance of analytic philosophy falling back on pre-philosophical opinion as authoritative reason for why we should accept its mechanistic ontology makes them become ill at ease with the systematics of the unification of science programme. It all looks to be a house of cards. The foundations are shaky, as they build on the sand of personal opinion. They begin to find the master builder conception of philosophy unpalatable, and they start entertaining heretical doubts about the influence of Princeton on

Australian philosophy. Is this a sign of American imperialism in philosophy? Opinion as an authoritative reason does not seem to be really authoritative, and the account given of why opinion should be authoritative does not seem to count as an authoritative reason. They become disenchanted with analytic reason.

In their spare moments they begin to hang-out with those academics in politics, sociology and philosophy at Flinders University who have a minimal acquaintance with continental philosophy, and begin to see themselves as free spirits of the future, engaging in conversations without ontological commitment. They discover through chats in cafés over glasses of Chardonnay that one of the limits of a formal method is that knowledge is not limited to knowing the rules, procedures and routines of formal logic. There is, it is propounded, a non-analytical mode of knowing, which centres around synthesising or putting together what is grounded in everyday life, based on particular subjects knowing other subjects. The argument they heard from the café philosophers was this: knowing others in everyday life is a crucial practice in human knowledge and, as we interact and are dependent on others, so in S knows P claims the concrete nature of S needs to be taken into account. As S is marked by gender, class and ethnicity, we are therefore not disinterested and dislocated observers. We are subjects in social relations with others, with these relations often taking the form of domination and submission. So any account of rationality needs to take into account the nature of S as a concrete subject. They discovered that this form of practical rationality was developed by Merleau-Ponty's reworking of Heidegger, and it involves practically knowing your way about, handling things, dealing with things in everyday life. This is a bodily action, and embodied knowing, and so quite different from theoretical rationality. The latter focuses solely on representational states which mirror the world, and computates these representational bits by a disengaged S, who stands over against a world of physical bits of matter.[7] The continental argument claims that there is a need for a synthesizing activity of putting the bits of the jigsaw together, an emphasis on the content as well as the form, and an emphasis on praxis as well as axiomization.

Buoyed by having found a bridge from the rarefied atmosphere of an ivory tower philosophy to the lifeworld, Malcolm and Joan return from the café to the classroom at Adelaide University. In talking about Nietzsche's gay science to their peers, they stumble into the analytic abyss of the incommensurability of discourses. They see that analytic philosophy's formalism effaces our embodiment in the name of objectivity. It defends itself from phenomenology by dismissing the recovery of our hidden subjectivities in social relations by the weapons of 'psychologism', which holds that the phenomenological level can be explained mechanistically on a more basic level. When articulated by Quine, this reductionism holds that epistemology and semantics are a part of psychology, which is a part of physiology:

"Semantics is vitiated by a pernicious mentalism so long as we regard a man's semantics as somehow determinate in his mind beyond what might be implicit in his dispositions to overt behaviour. It is the very facts about meaning, not the entities meant, that must be construed in terms of behaviour."[8]

The general analytic consensus that Malcolm and Joan crash into holds that it is right that rationality is akin to information processing, and is modelled in terms of computer-based models of the mind. This reinforces a disengaged axiomatic rationality, as it builds upon an atomism of neutral input caused by some physical conditions, which are combined by a form of computation in which what the agent finds intelligible is bounded by what can be processed. The unintelligible is what cannot be processed. This is the contextual background of meaning and value of an embodied subjectivity engaged in praxis, and making sense of the anguish and suffering in relationships with other people in our everyday life. Malcolm and Joan are dismayed by the incommensurability of the different philosophical schools. They just talk past each other. Each school finds it difficult to understand what the other is talking about. They become disillusioned. The analytical techniques, formal structures of reasoning in terms of the mathematical spirit and formal logic, and the metaphysics buried in this method and structure do not seem to help them make sense of their lived crisis. It denies the bridge to the everyday world that Heidegger and Merleau Ponty gave them. They wonder whether they should embrace an ethics of tragedy and start reading literature like the café intellectuals.

But they hear about the strategy of reflective equilibrium as a possible solution to the incommensurability of discourses, which involves the mutual comparison and revision of theoretical principles. So they turn to the friendly analytic tutor who plays cricket, is often seen to have a beer or two at the Exeter in Rundle Street, reads *avant garde* poetry, watches French films about the moral decay of bourgeois life, and talks about philosophical nihilism. He offers the view that analysis is certainly an indispensable part of the unity that Malcolm and Joan are seeking, as they struggle to get an overall picture of the way their lives are disintegrating. Joan responds that though it is indeed the case that careful analysis shows that analysis is an integral feature of this picturing, so is the activity of synthesis or making whole. However her central concern is making the torment and suffering of her lived existential crisis intelligible, by using an embodied practical reason that is concerned with the content of their particular life in this particular historical period of economic restructuring and globalization. But this project, she adds, seems to lie outside the boundaries or limits of analytic philosophy. Her position, she adds, recalling the fast tricks philosophers pull in dialogue, has less to do with her dislike of mathematical reasoning, or hostility to formal logic, or her alleged softness for a literary sensibility and metaphor. Metaphor, she quickly concedes, can be a distraction for a philosophical vocabulary that aims to represent an ahistorical reality. Her position has more to do with her realization that the making sense of her postmodern crisis of anxiety and insecurity involves more than the application of a mathematical form or a logical calculus on publicly verifiable observations of linguistic behaviour. It has to do with historically formed meaning, the way language discloses the world, and the interpretation of philosophical pictures.

There is silence. Malcolm, who has recently been skimming feminist texts, steps in and backs her up. He says that they are endeavouring to make sense of their social actions in a co-operative manner. Though these are brought about by desires or intentions, as utilitarians hold, they are distinguished from other events or bodily movements, not by their inner mental background, but by the fact that their actions are directed or aimed to encompass ends or purposes within the particular social relations and culture of Australia. In so acting within a world of public meanings, he says, we become aware of ourselves as we become able to formulate properly what we are on about. So as we become more self-conscious about the purpose of seeking help at the clinic, our social action will be become more guided, coherent and consistent. Such an action is expressive action for it is shared action, and the emphasis is on cultural meaning that expresses our identity.[9]

The young tutor, who loves Quine's metaphor about 'the lore of our fathers as a grey fabric, black with fact and white with convention', struggles to comprehend what initially seems to him to be garbled gibberish, articulated in a vague and fuzzy manner that borders on the ideological. He translates their words into his own precise language. Did they not want to know about convention and reflective equilibrium in foundationalist theory he asks? They nod. The man can cut to the nitty gritty so swiftly. He gently suggests that they read Quine for rigor and toughness. He had found the systematicity of Quine very useful when in a crisis, where he found himself multiplying ontological entities to deal with his emotional bodily side that was causing him so much torment. He adds that the images, metaphors and analogical leaps of the passions are part of our mental or cognitive processes, and they help to make novel connections, thinking up new arguments, and drawing out conclusions from premises. But these should properly be regarded as psychological processes which are irrelevant to the logical reconstruction and evaluation of rational arguments. What is important is not the way the theory is thought up, but the context of justification. Reason consists of those operations tracing out the formal relations amongst words, sentences and propositions. What we want are authoritative reasons that stop the regress of justifications. If scientific philosophy is to succeed in its noble goal of replacing opinion with knowledge, then vague and imprecise speech must be replaced with clear and precise speech. Speech only becomes precise when it is rule-governed, and the rules have to made with precision. That can only come from the philosophical purification of ordinary language.

Malcolm and Joan read Carnap, then Quine yet again. They discover that Carnap does think of language as a formal system. The formal systems that he talks about are not mere rational reconstructions of the language that scientists use, but are forerunners of a future formal language that scientists will eventually employ. Planned language and planned society go together in this modernism, which knows what is good for us. Carnap's vision reminded them of Le Corbusier's architectural programme of machining the world. Both were planning the perfect society as a machine to live in.[10] In re-reading Quine, they find that physicalists like Quine reject the whole notion of meaning, which has become such a central concern for Malcolm and Joan in their disenchanted world. Quine says:

> "there are no meanings, nor likenesses, nor distinctions of meaning, beyond what are implicit in people's disposition to overt behaviour. For naturalism the question whether two expressions are alike or unlike in meaning has no determinate answer, known or unknown, except insofar as the answer is settled in principle by people's speech dispositions, known or unknown."[11]

What we have is the rejection of embodied cultural meaning as understood by Malcolm and Joan. Meaning is reduced to overt behavioural dispositions and speech dispositions, and then further reduced to sensory stimulation of our cognitive mechanism. Mechanisms emit certain sounds which are observed by a neutral observer, who notes the noises they make in what circumstances. The empiricist-behaviourist philosopher then constructs a theory on what knowledge of things it is plausible to attribute to them, through understanding how the sounds are evoked by what surrounds them for the environmental triggers of behaviour. Such a theory is a representation of an independent reality. The aim is on the accuracy of the representation and meaning rehabilitated through the analytic procedures of the natural sciences, based on the tight fit between the sounds of the input/output mechanism and the thing designated. Malcolm and Joan's meanings, associated with their lived crisis, are superfluous entities. These result from their anthropomorphic projections fuelled by their predilection for existentialism, triggered by hanging out in cafés with unsound ideologists with a taste for an out-of-fashion existentialism which talks about human beings accepting their abandonment to freedom.

Malcolm and Joan are somewhat taken by a Kantian existential imperative that provides guidance for free action in concrete situations. By chance they encounter a postmodernist philosopher from Sydney cruising the South Australian vineyards, looking for some bargains to take to her friends for her forthcoming trip to the West Coast of the USA. Over a glass of Chardonnay, after some new Australian cuisine called Goanna and Cumquat Salad, she loosens up. From the perspective of post-Heideggerian hermeneutics, she says, the disengaged stance of analytic mechanism, with its computer models of making intelligible works on the model of bits of input information and rule-following procedures, amounts to a processing of information functioning in abstraction from the cultural background of meaning. Intelligibility or sense is assumed from the start in this model and it does not need a background context to provide it. However hermeneutics shows that in order to make sense of the whole disengaged picture, one requires the cultural background of modernity to be articulated. We can only make sense of it by articulating the metaphysics that underpins this disengaged picture. So we need to give an interpretive account of physicalism and its overcoming of Cartesian dualism metaphysics, within which it was initially enframed. Then the whole issue of the cultural background is out in the open, and we can see that physicalism is only one of the ways of understanding social action and our being-in-the-world, one whose being a such-and-such can only be articulated against its embeddedness in a background of structured interpretative practices of a particular historical culture.

In her paper to the Joint Adelaide/Flinders Philosophy Seminar she adds to these remarks with a gesture to Heidegger. The analytic tradition, she says, has a particular orientation towards reality, as it holds that the world is a sum total of independent existing entities that exist for observing subjects, insofar as those subjects manage to make contact with them. Such a stance, in which we are look disinterestedly at the environment and note the objective characteristics of the objects perceived, is quite different from our practical engagement in our everyday social life in which our skills are guided by our practical interests and concerns. It is this practical engagement in the social world, where we skilfully employ a computer as the most appropriate practical tool to write a thesis, that forms the ground to the theoretical analytic stance. The former is more equiprimordial, as we are first practically engaged with our attention directed at what we are doing and where we are going. Then we adopt the stance of the neutral observer surveying an independent field of objects, focusing on the perceptual characteristics of the computer, and organizing the information in terms of a quasi-mathematical mode of reasoning.[12] Analytic metaphysics is deeply flawed, she held, because it assumes an atomized self with an identity given separately from others, instead of identity being formed in relationship to others. The consequence of this in utilitarian ethics is that the self-present mind governing a white male middle-class body cannot adequately deal with the moral status of sexed female modes of embodiment such as pregnancy.

Joan immediately embraces postmodernism on the grounds of politics, and a future feminist form of life. It philosophically expresses her feelings. She reasons that politics counts as a more authoritative reason than the opinions advanced by Humeans like Lewis. Malcolm, who has been increasingly hanging out with the sociology of knowledge crowd, who hold that medical knowledge is a social construct, gives a paper to the Adelaide Philosophy Club called 'The "Structure" of Authoritative "Reason" in Social "Space": Posting Towards the Future.' He argues that philosophy is increasingly made of oppositional schools, paradigms, and research traditions, which are involved in conflict, and that much time and energy is now spent in smashing the foundations of opposing traditions. Following Laudan, he points out that the success of a research tradition depends on how effective and progressive that tradition is, relative to its competitors.[13] As none can convincingly show this to be the case, we seem to have reached a dead end in terms of the progress and rationality of philosophy, since we are left with different incommensurable worlds. We live in hermetically sealed worlds of competing philosophical schools, without any shared basic ground rules for social agents to justify their beliefs and to guide their actions.

He illustrates his thesis by saying that a physicalist naturalism does not allow us make sense of our lived crisis. This involves the conflict of social meanings involved in the interpretation of the issues over the bust-up of the family. Physicalist naturalism dismisses our intentional contents as a folk psychology. This conceptual framework is marked by explanatory weakness and lack of accuracy, and so should be abandoned for better theories, such as neurology and neurophysiology.[14] It does this according to the requirements of a tough scientific view of knowledge, and it regiments ordinary talk in terms of computer modelling of signs, according to their form. This process sidelines the making intelligible of our engaged actions in actually dealing with our relationship problems. On the other hand, the hermeneutic tradition's concern with meaningful actions within a normative background, can make relationship-shaping actions sense to social actors, given the sort of embodied, engaged agents they are. This background of meaning can only be articulated against a further background of meaning of our engaged agency, care for others and a concern for their particular form of ethical life or ethos (meaning character, dwelling or habitat) which constitutes our embodied place in the world. This replaces the world of universal principles of utilitarianism and contractarianism for one which locates the body as the locus of our ethos. The body is constituted by a dynamic relation between other bodies in a social context of power, desire and knowledge.[15] Truly we live in different worlds. None is better than the other. No philosophical underpinnings are required to justify our metaphysical orientation.

If this be relativism, so be it, says Malcolm; then adds heroically, 'one discourse succeeds in replacing another only as a function of the will to power.' The future belongs to the strong programme of the sociology of knowledge, which provides us with principles of criticism for evaluating the reasons that we do have. Philosophy is a therapeutic, edifying endeavour, as Rorty suggests. It helps us bid farewell to analytic philosophy, then to resist assimilation into its normalizing discourse in the face of the threat of relativism. Philosophy is properly a part of a literary culture based on history, literature and the human sciences, and it aims to foster an awareness of different possibilities of coping with the world, of different life options and new modes of self-description in the form of keeping the conversation going in a liberal culture.[16] Continental philosophy is part of an expressive romantic artistic culture, which ironically grounds social action on aesthetic production, centred around self-respect and recognition, with its romantic ideal of a beautiful ethical life or aesthetic self-making. He concludes with the assertion that the future belongs to a postmodern ethics which rejects universal moral principles of Kantian and utilitarian moral philosophy.

Malcolm's paper did not down well with the serious analytic philosophers working in a scientific culture. It was not a model of clarity. It dealt with vague ill-defined contrasts. It lacked detailed arguments. The students viewed his irony, redescription and embrace of a postmodern literary culture as a losing one's nerve, reason and the world. They dismissed Malcolm as an effete idealist idealogue whose recycling of an aestheticized and historicized form of idealism, indicated a lack of a sufficiently robust sense of reality. An old materialist warrior shouted that in joining the poets, mystics, myth-makers and sociologists, Malcolm was no longer engaged in sound or proper philosophy. He had given up on argument and philosophical rigor, and swapped logic for mysticism and science for poetry. So there was no point in debating him. An expert in the philosophy of science yelled that it was just irrealist bosh and nonsense to say with Latour and Woolgar that scientific operations in the laboratory are not directed towards an independent reality, but are directed towards producing literary inscriptions or texts.[17] Where was his evidence? Malcolm was an unwelcome stranger in the house of philosophy, opined another, speaking from the moral point of view. His 'justice without criteria or universal principles' leaves us in the ethnocentric embrace of a reactionary racist nationalism. Postmodernism suppresses the reality of social oppression, and so the issues of homelessness, poverty, health care, and child abuse, said a modernist sociologist. The dissolving of real living people into the text had been accomplished. The empirical referent has been abandoned. Substance had been replaced by style. The analysts when talking amongst themselves afterwards, agreed that it was the historicist influence of the nihilist Nietzsche that underpinned the perspectivalist relativism being peddled by those in sociology and cultural studies. The sociologists had used Kuhn's concept of paradigm to give their discipline respectability in the university. But as everyone knew the claim failed as sociology continued to languish in the pre-paradigmatic phrase of its development, awaiting its first paradigm.

Working into the problem

We have circled back to our original question: can we rationally resolve the situation of philosophers operating within different ontological frames through which we view the world? Do we live in sealed up worlds? Can we resolve this conflict rationally, and so avoid dogmatism as a way of blocking the infinite regress of justification? Can there be progress in philosophy with respect to metaphysical conflict?

One path into this issue is that cut by Hegel. Though philosophy may indeed suffer from theoretical plurality and internal conflict, Hegel observes, we need to concede that everyone operates with a metaphysics which enframes the way we view the world:

> "Everyone possesses and uses the wholly abstract category of being. The sun *is* in the sky; these grapes *are* ripe, and so on ad-infinitum. Or, in the language of higher education,...we proceed to the relation of cause and effect, force and its manifestation, etc.

All our knowledge and ideas are entwined with metaphysics like this and governed by it; it is the net which holds together all the concrete material which occupies us in our action and endeavour. But this net and its knots are sunk in our ordinary consciousness beneath layers of stuff. This stuff comprises our known interests and the objects that are before our minds, while all the universal threads of the net remain out of sight and are not explicitly made the subject of our reflection."[18]

Hegel is not holding that metaphysics is the commonsense vulgarization of science. Rather, he claims, it is impossible to engage in discourse without employing metaphysical categories, on the grounds that making sense of something is not a matter of pure observing or 'raw-feels'. The empirical material of the matter at hand is apprehended through categorical forms such as self, structure or action. In making sense of the world, we generally use these categories to apprehend the real processes in the social world in an unreflective fashion. We use metaphysical categories—such as mind, nature, community, culture, society, person, social relations, and social change—to unify the manifold particulars of the social world. These are layered in terms of auxiliary theories and assumptions, and that even if we devise simple tests, there is no direct comparison of theory with fact. We describe what we observe through making use of our theoretical assumptions, which are built into our concepts within a network of presupposed theories. The role of philosophy is to question the plausibility of these deep-seated metaphysical assumptions.[19] So we have to dig out our own presuppositions buried beneath piles of beliefs.

Hegel claims that it is very difficult to map our metaphysics rigorously in terms of formal structures, as they are a feature of our social practice, and remain deeply buried amongst piles of stuff, and so out of sight. We can interpret this as meaning that our unconscious metaphysics often surfaces in the form interruption, eruption, silencing, or the rendering of conscious discourse ambiguous. It usually speaks like the Freudian unconscious only as interference, submerged within and subverting the intentions of conscious speech or writing. Often it is all held together by some key category, which underpins and pulls together a mass of phenomena by systematizing it and forming it into a coherent pattern. To unpack it in terms of digging out its presuppositions involves articulating further background beliefs. If we unpack the cultural background of analytic philosophy, for instance, we eventually come up against a whole Enlightenment way of viewing the world. So what do we do once we have unpacked the background beliefs and reconstructed the intelligibility of the analytic Enlightenment and its opponents? Engage in grand systems-building to avoid relativism and to distinguish scientific knowledge from commonsense knowledge?[20]

If we are to remain operating in the philosophy institution, Hegel argues, we soon learn that it is dogmatism to take the systematic metaphysics of the Enlightenment as a foundational given. The Hegelian model aims to overcome the censoring and denial of our metaphysical presuppositions by making our unconscious ontological commitments conscious. A philosophy institution is the very place for reflecting upon the way we use metaphysics, the coherence of metaphysics and their plausibility. The current division of labour in the liberal university means that this metaphysical work is done by philosophers rather than scientists. Social science, for instance, is primarily concerned with social research, and scientists are content to use their social categories relating to human action, social structure and culture in an unreflective manner. It is the role of philosophy to examine our categories, their inter-relationships and their ordering to make the threads of the metaphysical net explicit, and to identify and untie the knots in the threads, so as to make our metaphysics more coherent, plausible and systematic. This pushes Hegel in the same direction of systems-building as Australian materialists; towards an emphasis on the systematic unity of the various knowledge claims, which are ordered into a structure which is internally consistent, coherent, comprehensive and exhibits explanatory power and problem-solving ability. This obtains levels of universality not possessed by commonsense knowledge.

One difference between analytic philosophers and Hegel is that Hegel believes that to understand something is to contrast it with something else. In order to understand 'square' for instance we must contrast it with 'round', as square is also not-round. This indicates that something like a determinate theoretical system or philosophical tradition has boundaries, in the sense that its limits mark the way in which the characteristics of this tradition distinguish it from an alternative one with its own different characteristics and tenets. Hegel states this in his difficult language:

> "Being-for-other and being-in-itself constitute the two moments of something.There are here present *two pairs* of determinations: 1. Something and other, 2. Being-for-another and being-in-itself. The former contain the unrelatedness of their determinateness; something and other fall apart. But the truth is their relation; being-for-another and being-in-itself are, therefore, the above determinations posited as moments of one and the same something, as determinations which are relations and which remain in their unity, in the unity of determinate being."[21]

A tradition is a determinate something, that is a something with particular characteristics. For the analytic tradition to exist, it must have a certain determinate nature, certain principles or conventions that identify as distinct, as against other possible traditions. The analytic tradition has the two aspects of what it is in itself, and what it is in relation to continental philosophy. To understand the characteristics of analytic tradition, we need to understand it in relation to commonsense and postmodernism. The boundary of the analytic tradition is not just a negative relation, on the other side of which is just non-philosophy, as some analytic philosophers are wont to claim. The boundary is the way the analytic tradition distinguishes itself negatively from something else, namely postmodernism. This is not a mere negation, since the boundary is not merely a boundary. It is also a limit, and 'through the limit something is what it is, and in the limit it has its quality.'[22] The limit makes analytic metaphysics a something with specific characteristics. 'A thing is what it is, only in and by reason of its limit. We cannot therefore regard the limit as only external to being which is then and there.'[23] The limit also makes the other, which initially appears as alien, into a something:—say postmodernism, with its specific characteristics of social constructivism, relativism, and concrete ethics. The limit is constitutive of the analytic tradition, as it marks the reality of its scientific metaphysics in terms of its relationship to and negation of postmodernism, which captures that part of everyday reality bracketed out by analytic metaphysics. The limit of an analytic scientific metaphysics can then be transcended, as it is a partial view of reality. To come to grips with what it misses out—embodied existence in everyday life—we turn to postmodernism, as Joan did.

The relation between the two traditions is important, because the characteristics of the determinate analytic tradition is not only defined relatively to postmodernism, but is also defined in part by the type of interactions it enters into with postmodernism or common sense. These interactions help to define the maintenance, alteration or destruction of that tradition. So instead of two hermetically sealed incommensurable worlds, we have analytic and postmodern traditions, with their different characteristics, which are related to one another. The boundary containing each tradition contains what negates each, as well as what essentially constitutes each. What constitutes the limit of the analytic tradition is metaphysical atomism, which is an atomistic individualism in terms of society. The subject in rational choice theory of utilitarianism is a self-contained abstract individual in which the body is the means for the self-identical subject to choose efficient means for pre-given ends of satisfying their desires. Contact with another individual in terms of social relationships does not alter the subject's identity, as the individual is deemed to have a self-contained identity that forms the ground of social relations. What is denied in analytic metaphysics is that the identity of the historical subject is a product and carries with it its relation to what is different—that is, identity is always relational, always the product of an interaction with others, rather than an identity given prior to that interaction.

What lies outside the boundary of analytic metaphysics is a conception of an engaged agency which starts from our practical engagement in our day-to-day practical affairs. This involves a rupture with the core of analytic metaphysics of a fundamental dualism between a detached knower at one remove from the world of material objects in causal interactions, who stands over against the objects, forms representations of them, which are structured by following a set of operational rules so that the formulations are logically consistent and empirically testable. Engaged agency is in the world, as it shapes the world as well as our identities and embodiments being shaped by its discourses and social structure. Our embodied relationships, within cultural discourses and social structure, constitute a way of life in which we have our being as participants. This is an everyday world of hammering away in workshops, turning doorknobs, cooking dinner, driving cars, doing the housework, walking the dog, being pregnant, bringing up children, and talking about our suffering and the pain in our bodies to friends. This is our basic mode of being-in-the-world, which is prior to any split between a theoretical knower and independent objects in causal relations, with the two linked by the correctness of the representations of the world. Praxis is concerned with the task at hand, and such tasks are undertaken within a framework of 'for the sake of' in which I strive to be a good husband or parent, or lover, always aware that our identities are changing in relation to others. Our practical knowledge is bound up with striving to make a better life for ourselves through using theoretical knowledge to transform our current practices and relationships, because we strive to be good human beings, and do the right thing by one another.

Hegel's point is that we cannot understand sameness without the mediation of difference. If we focus on the relation as interaction between these two traditions, with their partial views of reality. we can see that the interaction between the two traditions highlights their mutability, and the way each alters within its own limits. Each maintains itself in competition with the other tradition to prevent itself from going under. Traditions are rooted in contingent circumstances, arise out of problems, perplexities and disagreements in some particular social order, and are articulated in terms of the particularities of the language and culture of that order.[24] Traditions come into existence and pass away, as we can see from the way that the Marxist tradition which flourished in the 1970s has been negated by analytic and postmodern philosophy, and is now in danger of going under as a viable intellectual tradition in our national culture. Marxists thought scientific Marxism to be imperishable, absolute and eternal, rather than finite and transitory; and which necessarily goes under, to be replaced by others. This is the effect of history being bought into philosophy, and history's contingencies help to make us what we. Traditions like finite things alter, and they cease to be. Hegel says:

> "Such changeableness in existence is to the superficial eye a mere possibility, the realization of which is not a consequence of its own nature. But the fact is, mutability lies in the notion of existence, and change is only the manifestation of what implicitly is. The living die, simply because as living they bear in themselves the germ of death."[25]

The dynamic of existence is contradictory, as a philosophical tradition affirms itself in relation to its self-annulment, or negation. In struggling to maintain itself by overcoming its negation, it strives to step beyond its own boundary or limit. Since the limit is also that which defines it, and so constitutes it, its overstepping its limit is its dissolution—or its transformation into something different. The shift from analytic to post-analytic philosophy is a dissolution of the analytic tradition This process of change, in which some traditions become others, which then change, requires us to shift our central point of reference from the particular ephemeral finite tradition to the continuing process—what Hegel calls the infinite—which goes on through the coming to be and passing away.

Hegel offers a dialectical account of this coming to be and passing away. As sketched in *The Phenomenology of Spirit,* this account does not concern itself primarily with how things came about; but with showing how philosophical traditions contained the resources within themselves, to enable them to explain and justify themselves over and against earlier accounts; and to demonstrate and affirm for themselves that their own accounts of themselves are satisfactory or authoritative. This metaphysics of identity and difference has its locus not on any particular finite thing, but the whole culture of limited ephemeral traditions coming into and going out of existence. It is a history of rationality itself, one that claims that latter traditions can be seen in retrospect to have completed the earlier ones, in the sense that they have worked out the insufficiencies of the former ones in such a manner that this latter postmodern tradition has the resources within it to justify that its way of taking things makes up for the insufficiencies of the earlier modern tradition embodied in its form of life.[26] It is a history that is self-grounding.

Is there good reason to shift from one tradition to another, to embrace say a relational account of the subject's identity and difference, and so pass from analytic metaphysics of a collection of self-standing individuals to a postmodern one of embodied changing subjects in relations to others?[27] One reason may well be that a tradition encounters a problem which it needs to resolve, but finds it difficult to do so. Consider the effects of the negation of the Marxist Enlightenment on the old lefties hanging onto the memories of their glorious red wine days of the 1970s, as they sip their cool, rich, unwooded Chardonnay in the University club. The identity of our old lefties has changed in relation to the shift in the national culture. Their Marxist tradition was a part of the national culture. Once recognized by others to be at the cutting edge of philosophical practice, they are now indifferently treated, and their tradition is seen to be in general decay. There is a sadness to their conversation, because they unconsciously feel that their tradition no longer has an affirmative life, as distinct from its ceasing to be, and so becoming nothing. It has been replaced by a trendy postmodernism. Their conversation floats around old memories of the forward march of history to socialism, and cutting fragmentary remarks contemptuously dismissing those postmodernists who claim that there are just a multiplicity of local discourses with their own legitimation and truth They affirm scientific realism, the affirmation of grand narratives of the radical Enlightenment, and the mechanization of the world. These are part of their self-description and identity, which they put forward as an attempt to get things right about their practices; and which they express in certain ways to affirm who they are, in relation to their analytic and postmodern others. They employ these signs to affirm their identity, to establish rapport with others, and as a form of social display.[28] They act as embodied participants engaged in the world they understand within the culturally determined alternative possibilities shaped by our historical form of life.

To make sense of their identity crisis, they have to question the utilitarian metaphysical assumptions about the subject that had implicitly underpinned their theory of social action, and to resolve the problem of identity that they have been posed with. If they can do this in a philosophical manner, then their tradition exhibits rationality. To do this, they may have to dump some things overboard, and take on some new things, if they are to justify to themselves that their own accounts of themselves are satisfactory in relation to their rivals. Not all traditions embody rational inquiry as a constitutive part of themselves, as we can see from some fundamental Christianity sects in the United States. This has to be established by resolving working out the insufficiencies that have been pointed out. So the Marxists need to rework their earlier presupposed utilitarian conception of the subject to incorporate the flux of cultural identity, and then to justify that their new way of taking up things surpasses the earlier utilitarian one they tacitly assumed. Such an account would have to reject a conception of universal transcendent reason or a fixed rational self to provide Marxists with a fixed standard by which they can evaluate all their various contingent claims. They need to shift towards some type of account that understands reason as a form of social practice by embodied subjects, so providing a dialectical-historical narrative that fits their own tradition within the larger narrative that shows how the Australian nation has come to take what it does as authoritative and definitive for itself.

What we can infer from this pastiched exposition of Hegel is that dialectical rationality is an alternative mode of rationality to that of formal logic. It is based on opposition, conflict, difference, relation and negativity, and offers an account of development which places an emphasis on the multiple tendencies of any historical object. This holds that different parts of an entity are activated, repressed or actualized in different and overlapping constellations. It highlights the unavoidable tensions between polar opposites, which constitute a unity, and generate historical change and development. It gives an account of change and development in which one thing follows from another, in such a way that it gives us an account of truth as a historical process, rather than as a fixed criterion for the correctness of propositions. It is grounded on, and takes its bearings from, human affairs rather than mathematical physics. It does not bracket out the objectives or ends of things, as this is seen to be part of the inner drive of the entity. This dialectical conception of rationality is different from the analytic one. In the latter, the end is external to the method, which is indifferent to what is to be formalized for what purpose, as it holds itself to be a neutral and formal instrument. On the other hand, dialectical rationality holds to an internal relationship between its concepts and empirical reality, and so makes explicit the link between the values and purposes of practical activity.

This gives us a diversity of conceptions of rationality embodied in different traditions, which emerge from and are part of our history. So we can recognize that the analytic scientific Enlightenment is one tradition amongst many in modernity. It rejected authority and custom as criteria for deciding conflicting claims in a public realm, in the name of criteria based on standards and methods of rational justification and deciding between alternative courses of social action. Any debate between traditions which hold to different conceptions of rational inquiry in terms of resolving metaphysical conflicts, will have to recognize that there are different modes of rationality and modes of justification. We cannot dogmatically assume the superiority of the rationality of our beliefs within these traditions, nor can we assume in what condition a tradition will emerge from conflicts and dialogue with others. The dialectical account, for instance, cannot be simply assumed as authoritative without question. One of the signs of the decay of the Marxist tradition from the perspective of its rivals is that dialectics is generally held to be an inferior mode of rationality. The dialectical tradition in Australia has been centred around a dialectical materialism in our culture, which was part of a world view associated with a set of codified political beliefs of the Communist Party. This functioned as a radical working-class culture, rather than as part of a critical social science.[29] Though it appeared as a part of the Enlightenment in exposing the false consciousness of an epoch anchored in class institutions, dialectics has been seen to be grounded on faith and dogma rather a self-critical reason, and it became an obscurantism, and a closed system of thought. Its justification in terms of conflicts and difference was primarily in the form of a special pleading based on social relevancy, and it exhibited an inability to recognize that its conceptual resources were inadequate, and an insensitivity to retranslate without distortion what those in the hostile rival traditions were saying. Its internal debates were marked by frequently acrimonious, but unenlightening conceptual strife, often culminating in rival dogmatic claims of orthodoxy among its adepts which did not carry the inquiry forward. It did not consider that there was anything defective with the canon, and it grounded its dogmatic appeal to absolute truth in authority. It failed to develop to the point where its adherents confronted and found a rational way to deal with those encounters with a radically different and incommensurable analytic philosophy that dismissed dialectics in favour of logic.

Given that the dialectical tradition is seen by its analytic rival as being in direct opposition to the critical reason of the Enlightenment, it needs to prove its rationality in terms other than logical form. If it could so it would then undermine the conclusion drawn by analytic philosophers that philosophy should continue in the same analytic way, as dialectics has nothing to offer. To do this, it needs to show that rationality is not ultimately a question of formal relations, with the formal sign system sitting outside the historical world, whipping the vagueness and inconsistencies of ordinary language into the shape of an ideal language within a scientific culture. Instead of retaining the tacit metaphysics of the ideal language presupposed by the traditional mathematical conception of rationality, dialectics can endeavour to explicate the rationality within everyday language grounded on the life content of human experience. The problem that it faces to establish its legitimacy is whether it is able to do this in relation to the problem of showing that we can evaluate rationally our metaphysical conflicts. Can philosophy speak in the language of the vulgar?

Working on the problem

Dialectics, as a form of rationality, is not a mere eclecticism that takes the good bits from one side, and then adds them to the other side to patch something together. The emphasis is on the two-sided and contradictory tendencies of the object. In responding to misinterpretations of dialectic, Hegel says that he does not mean by dialectic a mere sophistry:

> "which takes an object, proposition....given to feeling or, in general to immediate consciousness, and explains it away, confuses it, pursues it this way and that, and has as its sole task the deduction of the contrary of that which it starts...The loftier conception of the dialectic consists not simply in producing the determination as a contrary and a restriction, but in producing and seizing upon the positive content and outcome of the determination because it is this which makes it solely a development and an immanent progress."[30]

The reference to content development and progress indicates that dialectics is not a matter the application of formal techniques to produce a contradiction-free translation of an argument. Hegel goes on to say that:

> "This dialectic is not an activity of subjective thinking applied to some matter externally, but is rather the matter's very soul putting forth its branches and fruit organically....To consider a thing rationally means not to bring reason to bear on the object from the outside and so tamper with it, but to find that the object is rational on its own account."[31]

By 'its rationality' is meant the underlying development of an entity. By the 'matter's very soul putting forth its branches and fruit organically', Hegel means the real nature of an entity, its inner movement, or actualisation of its an inherent tendency. An entity, like a philosophical tradition, is inherently self-moving, and its unity derives from its mediated antagonistic relationships between the different adherents within its boundaries, as they endeavour to resolve its problems. The growth of a particular tradition requires its adherents to confront its problems and paradoxes, recognize its inadequate conceptual resources, frame satisfactorily what others say in rebuttal and criticism, and undertake the necessary transformations. It is the rational movement and transformation within a tradition that is crucial.

The inconsistent nature of ordinary experience—happy and sad, laughing and crying, we say on the one hand this, on the other hand that about the same object—does not lead us to replace life with a consistent formal calculus. We accept that life is full of contradictions. We can then either deny our experience of existential contradictions in our theories in the philosophy institution, cover them up and regress to a pre-dialectical conception of facts, opinions and events and accept the façade uncritically; or we can hold onto the objective dynamics of our philosophical praxis, confront the contradictory object with reason, think the contradictions through, and so represent the motion of process and development in a philosophical culture.[32] We subjects who are grounded in conflicting and dialectical insights can then criticise the lie of those nominalistic cultural representations which are imposed on the object, and which block, deny and reject the two-sided contradictory nature of our philosophical traditions in their specific historical context. We should endeavour to try to get along without formalizing everyday language.

An immediate analytic objection would be that the acceptance of the regional nature of rationality, within a diversity of competing traditions in a philosophical culture, plunges us straight into the incoherence of relativism. All that dialectics has given us is an account of the conflict between rival social ontologies in terms of a narrative, of how the debate as gone so far within a historical context of a conflict between rival ontologies. We seem to have landed in the nightmare of not being able to make objective, scientific assessments or criticisms of forms of life, when we need to confront the eco-destruction of global capitalism. This points to nihilism, in which no authoritative reasons can be offered at all. Alasdair MacIntyre spells out the steps on the relativist path to nihilism, wherein that which is authoritative is only what individuals could personally and idiosyncratically underwrite for themselves out of their beliefs and feelings:

> "there is always the possibility of one tradition of action and inquiry encountering another in such a way that neither can, for some considerable stretch of time at least, exhibit to the justified satisfaction of its adherents, let alone to that of the adherents of its rival, its rational superiority. And this possibility will arise when and if the two traditions, whether embodied in the same language and culture or not, cannot find from the standpoint of either an adequate set of standards or measures to evaluate their relationship rationally."[33]

The timeless and universal mathematical rationality of the analytic tradition, with its arguments for and against certain rival positions based on the ahistorical principles of axioms, deduction and the law of non-contradiction, has been shown to be a specific form of reasoning favoured by the analytic tradition. This rejection of any tradition, independent standards of rationality leaves us with a diversity of traditions, each with their own mode of justification. Though the analytic, postmodern and dialectical traditions share some common ground, an acute problem of how to resolve radical disagreement between these traditions arises. Each are committed to denying the central ontological claims of the other, thereby negating each other.

The situation is one where it seems impossible that we can conclusively refute the central tenets of each tradition, as the defects can be remedied from within. The dialectical tradition, for instance, responds to the reduction of dialectics to logic by reasserting the value of ordinary language, and rejecting the metaphysics of formal logic. MacIntyre states that one can infer:

> "that at any fundamental level no rational debate between, rather than within, traditions can occur. The adherents of conflicting tendencies within traditions may still have enough in the way of fundamental belief to conduct such a debate, but the protagonists of rival traditions will be precluded at any fundamental level, not only from justifying their views to members of a rival tradition, but even from learning from them how to modify their own tradition in a radical way."[34]

The second conclusion that MacIntyre says can be drawn from this situation is that, given the above conclusion, it appears that:

> "each tradition must develop its own scheme in a way that is liable to preclude even translation from one tradition to another. So it may appear that communication between traditions will at certain crucial points be too inadequate for each even to understand the other fully."[35]

So we have a situation in which it each tradition is unable to justify its claims against its rivals.[36] So the rejection of a permanent ahistorical rationality or metalanguage grounded on rock-solid foundations that will withstand historical vicissitudes, has given away to a plurality of different metaphysical traditions that appear to be radically incommensurable.

The inner core of any tradition is its metaphysics, and it is difficult to settle disputes over metaphysical presuppositions, as these cannot be empirically tested in any immediate sense. Take the psychoanalyst at the clinic, who has been counselling Malcolm and Joan, builds upon what Malcolm and Joan tell her. She relates her other cases studies to what they have said about their relationship, and relates both to her knowledge of patriarchal social relations and culture. Malcolm and Joan's case is fairly typical, as this is what she sees everyday in the clinic, so she is quickly able to map out the psycho-dynamics of this family. She then realizes that these cases are entirely different from those centring around repression and the guilt-ridden child of the classical psychoanalytic texts. She concludes that Freud's texts belong to a patriarchal form of bourgeois life grown old, that the psycho-dynamics of the contemporary family have little in common with the oedipal structure of Freud's time, and that his individualist focus on the intraphysic process of the individual can no longer be used to map the terrain of the contemporary pathologies of a dying nineteenth-century capitalist patriarchy. But the underlying metaphysical picture that society is a machine, an organism, a text, or a collection of individuals, commits us to more than what can be ascertained as a matter of fact. It is a metaphysical position, which involves a unified, coherent system of concepts that make the social world intelligible.

Even though our metaphysical categories refer to the entities and processes of the social world, and historical developments in science involve changes in the definition of our metaphysical categories, these metaphysical pictures cannot be empirically tested in any immediate sense, as we would with any scientific hypothesis in a scientific theory about a particular event or phenomenon explaining why Malcolm cannot get an erection. Truth-claims are involved here, as it is a truth-claim when one metaphysics is rejected as inadequate, whilst another is claimed to be just right for the job. In making such claims, an implicit, if not an explicit claim is being made that one knows what one is up to. But though we can revise our metaphysical categories in terms of empirical data, this is difficult to do when the whole metaphysical framework—society is a mechanism, an organism, or text—is being questioned and assessed for its suitability, explanatory adequacy and problem-solving capacity. As everyone can give the same kind of smooth assurance about his or her social ontology, we cannot accept all claims, because various claims contradict one another; and we cannot reject all claims, for this would leave us with nothing to discuss. Hence the popularity of the Rorty's pragmatist solution to treat these vocabularies as pragmatically useful in relation to our coping with the world to get what we want, rather than as some final vocabulary. One should celebrate the mortality of such vocabularies and the value of creating new ones. As a literary culture is able to do this more successfully than a scientific culture, this indicates the superiority of a literary culture over a scientific one.[37]

Looking back to positivism

This postmodern neo-pragmatism is a solution to the mess the positivists landed us in, once analytic philosophers realized that the positivist attempt to eliminate metaphysics from scientific theories was impossible to achieve. Ayer and Carnap eventually acknowledged the metaphysical presuppositions of positivism and the existence of rival metaphysical presuppositions within the natural sciences. But they embraced relativism and took the nihilist alternative as they went on to say that it was not feasible to evaluate these competing metaphysics. Ayer in *Metaphysics and Commonsense,* argued that metaphysical theories are rather like policies, rather than attempts at an objective depiction of the nature of what there is from some Archimedean standpoint. With Ayer there is tolerance of other metaphysics with no objective criteria for assessing them.[38] Policies are neither true nor false. But policies presuppose ends or values; and it was an essential doctrine that the goodness and badness of ends and values is entirely subjective. So the positivist proposal about metaphysics is merely the expression of a subjective preference. Carnap in *Empiricism, Semantics and Ontology*, introduced the concept of a linguistic framework, a way of speaking about entities. He distinguished between the internal questions within the positivist framework—such as the disputes between nominalism and realism, universals, properties, classes, relations, numbers, phenomenalism and materialism—and external questions, by which he meant the questioning of the whole linguistic or metaphysical framework. He then denied that we can make an objective evaluation of the linguistic or metaphysical framework as a whole, as he implied that the questioning of the linguistic framework is not a theoretical question:

> "Those who raise the question of the reality of the thing world itself have perhaps in mind not a theoretical question as their formulation seems to suggest, but rather a practical question, a matter of a practical decision concerning the structure of our language. We have to make the choice whether or not to accept and use the forms of expression in the framework in question."[39]

Though Carnap was prepared to acknowledge that we employ metaphysical frameworks for specific purposes, his case against metaphysics came to the claim that metaphysicians talk nonsense when they try to assess the viability or truthfulness of metaphysical frameworks as a whole. Carnap suggested that we cannot evaluate these conceptual frameworks. All we can do is just make a personal choice of metaphysical frameworks. He suggested that the thing and its properties metaphysics is viable, for it is one we all accept from our early days. However such an acceptance did not imply an ontological commitment, for it is not a theoretical question:

> "If someone decides to accept the thing language, there is no objection against saying that he has accepted the world of things. But this must not be interpreted as if it means his acceptance of a belief in the reality of the thing world; there is no such belief or assertion or assumption, because it is not a theoretical question. To accept the thing world means nothing more than to accept a certain form of language, in other words, to accept rules for forming statements and for testing, accepting or rejecting them."[40]

So disputes between competing metaphysics frameworks are meaningless, since it is merely a personal choice of how one wants to use language. This position has been quite influential in analytic philosophy.[41]

But what counts as a good reason comes to be an acceptance of the loss of intelligibility since the Enlightenment tradition of using science to create a rational form of life becomes a certain language form. Carnap's adherence to this is the expression of a subjective preference for a certain scientific language form. Though the positivist really thinks that dialectics is nonsense, but Carnap can only consistently say that dialectical contradiction is not expressible in the positivist language. But as it is expressible in dialectical language, he has no answer to those who say, 'I do understand your point of

108

view. Positivism is not rational in my system.' The positivist's lack of objective standard means that he ends up a relativist, who has to admit that all philosophical propositions, including his own, have no rational status.[42]

Carnap is right in the sense that it is not a matter of appealing to some higher standard or rationality for choosing the most rational ontology from amongst the competing metaphysical frameworks, as such a self-reflecting reason can only be represented as some sort of historical achievement, and so would be a part of some philosophical tradition. But Carnap's account is flawed, as the levels of methodology and ontology are confused in his account. There is the methodological level of the form of language used to make and test statements—Carnap's rules for forming, testing and accepting or rejecting statements; and there is the ontological level of the world being really structured along the lines of a thing and its properties metaphysic. The confusion is disguised through the reduction of ontology to methodology as part of the logical empiricist foundationalist programme of having a pure epistemology cleansed of ontology.[43] Carnap's conflation of methodological and ontological issues can be separated, and should be, as an assumed ontology needs to be justified independently of which particular methodology to adopt in order to explain the causal processes of the social-historical world. If we do not do this, then we are left with the position that the revision of our social ontology is an internal question to a particular tradition, and the claim that personal choice is the only option we have in choosing between different competing social ontologies. This cannot count as an authoritative reason, because the dialectical and postmodern traditions reject Carnap's thing and properties metaphysics as inadequate.

Carnap's claim that choosing between different metaphysical frameworks can only be based on personal preference is not plausible. It ignores the fact that experience may lead one to reject an atomist metaphysics, because it is an inadequate account of our experiences, or of the objective features of the social world. A distinction can be drawn between what one prefers to believe and what experience forces one to believe. The objective features of the world can, and do force us to revise our ontology. An example would be the conflict between a physical science which tried to explain inanimate nature in terms of the realization of different kinds of entity of their corresponding Form, and a modernist science which explains things in terms of efficient causation mapped by mathematical formulae. Aristotle's natural ontology has been buried by Galileo and Newton, and there is no going back. But grounding convention on personal opinion, with the linguistic shift in positivism, has also to be rejected as untenable. The tacit play of opinion and science here points towards the conventional—as personal preference or human projection—being seen as a relatively superficial thing in scientific ontology. As it is a product of human invention, so it is made up, and so somehow fictitious. Convention requires to be underpinned by the objective, the bedrock in the form of the "furniture of the world." The objective on the "cosmic exile" of metaphysical realism holds that our conceptual scheme is built into nature so to speak, and so is the right way of mirroring the way the world is. So the chair in the room as consisting of particles and fields of certain kinds is the one true theory. It is built into the ready-made furniture of the world, and it is modern natural science alone which describes the world "as it is independent of language."[44] Dialectics contests this thesis that the world divides itself up into objects, independently of our language, which just mirrors nature's joints. It holds that the chair in front of the desk, as held by commonsense realism, partly describes the contents of the room; and that the particles and field description of physics are also a partial description of the contents of the room. Both are perspectival descriptions. It is we who divide up the structured and stratified world, and we do so in a variety of ways. There is not one way based on a fixed reference of object, property and relations which gives us the one determinate metaphysics.

Embracing Pyrrhonian scepticism

Rorty's coping option which treats these vocabularies as pragmatically useful in relation to our coping with the world to get what we want, offers a way through the tangled maze of convention based on personal opinion and projection and talk about some final vocabulary which gives us the one true metaphysics. We should, he says, celebrate the mortality of such vocabularies and the value of creating new ones. The perspective of physics is just one perspective, that of social action another. Rorty's pragmatism links up the conventions of our vocabularies with an institutional form of modern life. In doing so, it takes up the option of self-grounding with the collapse of foundationalism, and involves philosophical reflection on who we are in modern life. It offers an escape route from the difficulties of the post-Galilean scientific world view.

This historicized Kantian option of the self-grounding of different perspectives opens up the possibility of providing good reasons why one metaphysics is rejected in favour of another, along the lines of greater explanatory power of a common subject matter. Each tradition can put forward its thesis in such a way that both its adherents and those of its rival can recognize that it is a common subject matter about which they are making claims, and they can agree, as we have seen, with some standards according to a minimal logic within the tradition of philosophy. But the bog we walk into with this adjudication of disputes between fundamentally different metaphysics or social ontologies, is a difficulty that Kant pointed out in the *Critique of Pure Reason*. This is the problem of the endless chain of justification through argument and counter-argument. Claims are put forward without further grounds. They are usually confronted with an opposite claim advanced in the same way, and therefore with equal right. A problem arises, if we want to avoid stopping the endless chain of justification by dogmatism, question-begging or advocating a stylistic method of persuasion, vying for critical supremacy in the intellectual marketplace, through an interpretative will to power and a rhetoric of persuasion.[45] The ancient sceptic, Sextus Empiricus poses the problem in the following way:

110

"He who prefers one impression to another, or one "circumstance" to another, does so either uncritically and without proof or critically and with proof...(If) he is to pass judgement on the impressions he must certainly judge them by a criterion; this criterion, then, he will declare to be true, or else false. But if false, he will be discredited; whereas, if he shall declare it to be true, he will be stating that the criterion is true either without proof or with proof...the proof always requires a criterion to confirm it, and the criterion also a proof to demonstrate its truth; and neither can a proof be sound without the previous existence of a true criterion nor can the criterion be true without the previous confirmation of proof. So in this way both the criterion and the proof are involved in the circular process of reasoning, and thereby both are found to be untrustworthy."[46]

The Pyrrhonian sceptical solution to Sextus Empiricus's charges of circularity, question-begging and dogmatism for those knowledge claims beyond the appearances of everyday life, is to resist dogmatism and the temptation to philosophize, and to live in a tranquil life in accordance with the appearances of everyday life. It is an acceptance of convention.

Hiley argues that as appearances for the Pyrrhonians mean the laws of one's own country and traditional values, then their moral stance was inherently conservative.[47] This can be seen with Sextus, who says:

"The Sceptic's End is quietude in respect of matters of opinion and moderate feeling in respect of things unavoidable. For the Sceptic, having set out to philosophize...so as to attain quietude thereby, found himself involved in contradictions of equal weight, and being unable to decide between them suspended judgement; as he was thus in suspense there followed, as it happened, the state of quietude in respect of matters of opinion."[48]

The focus is not so much on the possibility of knowledge, but on the desirability of knowledge for virtue. In rejecting the link between knowledge and virtue, Sextus notes that it is the traditional customs and laws that provide the guides for conduct:

"Adhering, then, to appearances we live in accordance with the normal rules of life, undogmatically, seeing that we cannot remain wholly inactive. And it would seem that this regulation of life is fourfold, and that one part of it lies in the guidance of Nature, another in the constraint of the passions, another in the tradition of laws and customs, another in the instruction of the arts...But we make all these statements undogmatically."[49]

111

This eliminates the cosmic exile position of standing outside the appearances of our common life, and of rationally evaluating alternative beliefs and practices in terms of Absolute truth. But it results in the accommodation of oneself to the customary and the traditional.

A recycled Pyrrhonian scepticism with its acceptance of convention is common in contemporary philosophy. It holds to the impossibility of rationally evaluating alternative practices and ontologies, and so encourages us to accommodate ourselves to the existing social order, the customary and the traditional, but to adopt an ironic stance of mitigated scepticism as a way of avoiding dogmatism and questioning-begging. Wittgenstein has been interpreted as holding that the basic opposition of our metaphysics are existential choices that cannot be further grounded, and so cannot be justified, for there is no theory of validation that can offer the justification of one over the other.[50] As it is impossible to see how things are-in-themselves independently of how they appear to us—as God apprehends them—all we can do is to describe our practices as we see them through our own eyes. We describe them within the grid of custom and habit functioning as basic linguistic conventions within a form of life, which is ultimately grounded on our human nature, as determined biology and history. Justification is what we count as justification. This is how late Wittgenstein stood himself on his head, says Gellner. Early Wittgenstein placed the emphasis on a formal language mirroring the inner structure of the world, with culture banished to the doghouse.[51] But the return of culture as language means that we accept the customary in terms of a mitigated acquiescence in traditional custom and beliefs. The philosophical justification comes from an interpretation of Wittgenstein's thesis in *Philosophical Investigations,* that every language game is a self-contained form defined by its internal normativity. The implication is that we cannot open ourselves up to dialogue. Wittgenstein held that the meaning of the words we use gain their significance from the system of signs or from the language to which it belongs, and that the meaning of the word is its use. He argued that there are a multitude of hermetically sealed language games and corresponding life forms, and so does not allow mediation between language games, as this is seen as a return to transcendental rules of a universal language which he outlined in the *Tractatus.* Philosophy, then, is a kind of linguistic therapy, which ends when the philosopher exposes mistaken applications of linguistic rules. Gellner interprets this as Wittgenstein selling:

> "his followers a Closed-Community ethos, though not under that name, but packaged as an alleged revolutionary perception of the true nature of language. This vision also contained, he claimed...a recipe for 'dissolving' all philosophical problems (i.e. all problems concerning validation of the principles we employ in our diverse activities). If it were indeed true that the closed and idiosyncratic community is conceptually sovereign, final, self-sufficient, then indeed such a conclusion would follow.

Return to your custom and totem, for there you will find the only validation that can be given to you. This strange socio-political doctrine...was proposed under the camouflage of a theory of language. So a vision of society is smuggled in on the coat tails of a theory of language. *Gemeinschaft* prevails by default: no trans-communal, universally rational form of thought is possible."[52]

When translated into the language of today this accommodation of oneself to the conventional, as the customary and the traditional with its acceptance of the authority of the tradition, advises us to adopt a form of life centred on tradition and community with their firm sense of the way things are done. It can operate as an opposition to the engineering of society by technocratic liberalism, as it offers a sense of a common project within a common national culture that is under threat from globalization. For the basic or fundamental rules, conventions and values that we follow and accept there is nothing by which we judge something to be a correct application of them. These are taken as a brute given. So what stops the regress is the basic language grounded on a form of life whose conceptual scheme or metaphysics cuts up the world into objects, relations and processes. We then treat those operating in other traditions as foreigners, translating their language into ours. But this bedrock gives no authoritative reason why the good life should involve accepting an ethical life, grounded in tradition and community, for what we should do. This justification is necessary, because the modern project involves freedom as a central norm, and any modern form of *Sittlichkeit* must be intelligible to its participants as a realization of freedom. Wittgenstein offers a deficient form of freedom, as this account does not involve the social subject being self-directing, as distinct from acting in terms of role-given ends. As Pinkard observes, for these common projects:

> "to be ethical ends for *modern* agents, they must be realizations of freedom which requires them to be ends with which the agents as an *individual* and not merely as the placeholder for a social role can identify...For the modern agent these (ethical ends) must be determined internally to the practices that constitute the agent's self-identity...The ethical ends of modern agency must be such that they *can* be understood by reflective agents to be determined by free-standing social practices, to be nonetheless rational, and to be authoritative for what it means for a modern agent in modern "social space" (to be the kind of common projects that they nonetheless take as "their own")."[53]

Wittgenstein's appeal to community takes for granted who we are—what the community's social role says we are—and so undercuts the self-reflection as a form of practical reasoning that is deemed to be constitutive of modernity. Merely to accept any given ends determined by social role would be self-undermining for the agent, as it would conflict with her sense of herself as self-determining and independent.

Rorty's ethnocentric postmodern bourgeois liberalism amounts to a form of mitigated scepticism, to live ironically within the conventions of a postmodern bourgeois liberalism of the American nation state.[54] This accepts the practices and beliefs within the metaphysics of liberal individualism, and it operates as a doctrine of limits, beyond which philosophical criticism of an individualist social and political ontology cannot go. It thereby functions within the legitimacy of the liberal-democratic social order with its division of public and private. Rorty deals with those operating out of a different vocabulary from liberalism by saying that as there are no reasons, only causes for shifting from one vocabulary to another, then the pragmatist has two choices: either to refuse to discuss the issues opened and avoid interaction, or to circumvent the discussion by attempting to shift the ground. If the second alternative is taken, then some explanation for why the ground is shifted must be given. If this takes the form of a rational argument that points out the weakness of one's opponent's viewpoint and the strengths of one's own, then the question about the superiority of one metaphysics over the other has been begged, since one has employed the criteria of strength and weakness found within one's own vocabulary. Rorty's solution is to take the form of a narrative or story of how we got from there to here, and why we might be considering moving beyond this point. The 'method' is one of circumvention combined with recontextualization.

This post-analytic philosophy makes some good points. Politics does intersect with the production of knowledge in the form of gender and class, as knowledge is produced in specific social positions and power relations. Some traditions endeavour to sustain themselves by arrogating to themselves an exclusive title and denying legitimacy to their rivals, by holding that there are mutually exclusive and incompatible ways of understanding the social world with one true and the others false. So one reasons in the mode of refutation by standing in one's own tradition, which is presupposed to be the enlightened truth, and criticises the others for their falsity and irrationalism. Here the truth of the discourse is regarded as a minted coin that can be pocketed ready-made, with the false belonging to the other side. It is assumed that true and false are fixed and isolated from one another, with nothing in common. So whenever two human beings come to opposite decisions about the same matter, one of them must at least certainly be in the wrong.[55] This form of rationality seeks the final authoritative answer that absolutely silences the opposition. Those who have proclaimed that there is one universal, absolute truth, or one right way of representing the world, have usually been the powerful and privileged, who have used their arguments as weapons to dominate the uninfluential, inarticulate, and oppressed.

The scientistic strand in the analytic tradition veers towards this, as it has an adversarial form of philosophy, with its emphasis on winning and losing, as suggested by the following familiar claims: 'your claims are indefensible'; 'he attacked every weak point in my argument'; 'his criticisms were right on target'; 'I demolished her argument'; 'I've never won an argument with him';

'he shot down all my arguments.'[56] No-one wishes to settle disputes through coercion and terror in the philosophy institution, as this would destroy the ethos of philosophy. If it is domination which has made the analytic perspective hegemonic over its rivals, then choosing one over another comes down to politics, for the struggle between perspectives is the struggle between opposing political forces, and so intellectual work is a political intervention, for it is power rather than reason which develops situated knowledges.[57] But if one decides disputes between competing social ontologies by dogmatically claiming that politics is the criteria, then we enter the realm of everyone countering with the equal right of counter-dogmatism.[58] This does not get us very far, since we need to know the plausibility of this background criterion of politics *vis-à-vis* its political rivals. Rorty's strategy of circumvention through recontextualization allows us to avoid this dogmatism, and his narrative is one way of offering an account of plausibility for one's politics. It is one that gives an account of how we have come to be who we are, why the old metaphysics have lost their force for us, and so are essentially part of our self-understanding. It helps to form us into reflective agents within the history of modern life. Its pluralism of different legitimate vocabularies for coping does grant others a place to speak.

But there are several problems with Rorty's recontextualization approach. The first is that Rorty withdraws the categories of true and false. The question of truth loses none of its urgency once we have taken the hermeneutical turn. What we should understand by "truth", relative to philosophy in the humanities, becomes a pressing concern.[59] These discourses do provide different but complimentary perspectives on the social world, situated knowledges that socially inscribed bodies are useful or not useful to the historical and contextual interests they serve. But they are also partial knowledges, partial, but knowledge nevertheless, that do represent some understanding of the nature of the social world. The humanities represent a moral knowledge, that sustains moral character and goodness in the light of human vulnerability in relation to the sheer contingency of human experience. Though social structure is often indifferent to intentions and desires and the vicissitudes of life, it regularly places moral demands on us. In situations of tragic conflicts, our moral character and project, to live the life that is best and most valuable for human beings, is always in danger of coming apart.[60] So we need to evaluate these partial knowledges.

The second problem with Rorty's recontextualization approach, is that his mitigated Pyrrhonian scepticism of ironically living within the values of the traditional liberal American way of life, is not a feasible option for those who want to criticise and change it towards a more democratic, ecologically-sustainable society. In societies akin to American liberal capitalism, economic rationality and commodity exchange are gradually penetrating and restructuring ever broader spheres of civil society and the family. Here inequality induces people to accept work they would not perform of their own freewill, there is an emphasis on acquisitive ethic and instrumental virtues in the public sphere, and a re-vitalisation of the conservative virtues and values

115

associated with an apolitical private life. Ruby Jane realizes through talking to the therapist at the clinic that her problems of depression, despair and anguish are associated with the slow deterioration and destruction of her way of life from child-abuse, social conservatism and unemployment. Things are getting worse, and she realises that her need for help is not as simple as following Rorty's advice to remove some personal suffering by reading more novels or creating new metaphors to live by. She realises that her pain is a feature of the oppression built into the reproduction of social relations and culture, and whose functioning as a system she does not fully understand. In seeking help for the wounds inflicted by the pathologies of modernity, she requires theoretical scientific knowledge, so she can change her practices, do the right thing by others in particular situations, live well and lead a better life. Ruby Jane is not attracted to a Pyrrhonian scepticism which advocates living tranquilly within the common life. She is in opposition to the social processes of domination which Rorty is silent about, or accepts as the price to pay for a liberal democracy. She contests this presupposition of acquiescence by claiming that the destruction of nature and community by unlimited economic growth is not a worthwhile price to pay for liberal democracy. So we are back to square one, with each of us giving different narratives about the process of enlightenment in modernity to justify our position and politics.

Rorty's assumption that we live in different worlds is the third problem with his recontextualization approach. This way of mapping pluralism in late modernity is difficult to accept for three reasons. First, language is also a dialogue between worlds, and there is mediation and translation which results in the transcending of old horizons of given traditions between those engaging in dialogue. The problem of adjudicating metaphysical truth claims, for instance, would be acknowledged by all schools of philosophy to be a philosophical problem. In a dialogue there is a movement from our initial position into what Gadamer calls a fusion of horizons, in which there is a common view of the subject-matter about which there is a dialogue between conversational partners, who participate in exploring common questions on a common subject-matter. This may begin from the collision of alternative traditions, and this makes us aware of the assumptions that would otherwise remain unnoticed. We also aware that our own standpoint and views are not personal idiosyncrasies, as we have inherited certain prejudices from our philosophical tradition which we hold in an unreflective way. We can agree that a serious dialogue seeking rational agreement should bring to light unjustified preconceptions and prejudgments, even though we may not agree that our traditions are grounded in relations of domination. There is common agreement that we do not work to our own rules or our own court of justice when it comes to assessing which social ontology is the most plausible. We recognize that conceptions of philosophical procedure, which are a matter of course to philosophers in one school, tradition or discourse, require explanation and justification for those in others; whilst those that may be considered satisfactory within one tradition may be deemed insufficient for those in another. From here we can see that all schools implicitly assume that not all standpoints about social ontology are of equal value, for theirs, by definition, is better than that of their opponents. None wish to fall foul of Plato's trap for relativists in *The Theatetus,* when universal truth-claims are cashed out as true for me, and so the interesting claims about metaphysics become the uninteresting thesis of only true for me.[61] We also realize that we need to examine the unexamined prejudices, even though we are aware that because of our historicity we can never fully transcend the prejudices of the tradition to which we belong.[62]

The second reason why we do not live in different worlds is that the different philosophical schools are mediated by their relationship to the background conceptions of rationality, which we share, and which need to be made explicit. The other schools are critical of the transformation of the Socratic dialogue by analytic philosophy into winning and losing arguments, philosophy, as distinct from say, literary criticism, with its emphasis on interpretation and rhetorical persuasion involving the devices satire, irony, jokes, ridicule and punning. Despite the critique, there can be agreement that instead of appealing to the facts, as do the empirical sciences, philosophers can agree that philosophy involves argumentation in the form of uncoerced arguments.[63] It is the nature of argumentation that is contested. Perspectival realism presupposes that we do not live in completely different or incommensurable worlds. There is common ground between the different philosophical schools, for instance, about the need for rationality. Despite the antagonism between the different schools of philosophy the different perspectives are within the same philosophical world, since this shared background makes philosophy a distinct type of activity in our culture. Its cultural practices carry a sense of a common mission that unites philosophers who can agree substantively about nothing at all, but still share the view that philosophy is the guardian of rationality, or a special way of arguing a case. It is this that makes it a distinct cultural activity from literature, art criticism, sociology and physics. This philosophical ethos is an:

> "implicit set of presuppositions, sentiments, self images, hopes, and anxieties that together form the collective *raison d'être* about the ultimate significance of the enterprise in the eyes of its practitioners. This ethos relates closely to what the members conceive as the deep cause behind the enterprise—which makes it meaningful to its practitioners. It provides its members with a coherent sense of social identity and mission."[64]

This ethos arises from our place in relation to others within the Humanities building of the university and functions as part of a habitual way of life, which is constituted by the daily repetition of our practices with those who are philosophers and those who are not. Even though we encounter anti-philosophers who call for the end of philosophy, we read them as operating as philosophers, as being part of the history of the group in which there is a continuity between future, present and past generations of practitioners. Even if these grave-diggers subvert the tradition of philosophy by unmasking its formalism, its epistemological bias, academic insulation and absolute truth, we accept that they are part of the ethos of the group of philosophers using the tools of philosophy against it. The interpretive pluralists are still playing philosophy's game, which is one of continually changing the rules. We recognize the pluralism of different schools of philosophy, with their different narratives and conventions within the overall philosophical tradition within modernity. This pluralism is a fundamental aspect of our late modernist culture. It results in the relativization of the logic of argumentation because of the appeals to different criteria, and so points to the importance of dialogue between the schools, in contrast to the emphasis on truth and agreement or consensus. This enables us to distinguish rational inquiry in the form of conversation from mere sophistry, or self-serving myopic illusions, as the commitment to truth still remains.

The third reason why we do not simply live in self-enclosed worlds, is that our philosophical traditions are part of a common national culture, with a shared rationality and language within a broad framework of a scientific conception of nature and society, which has developed out of our bourgeois form of life. In evaluating our social ontologies, we are criticising particular beliefs and values and not the rationality of our beliefs as a whole, for such an evaluation takes place within this modernist metaphysics which makes us view the practices of magic and Dreamtime within our society as quite foreign and irrational. This is our ethnocentricity, a scientific culture which provides the basic standards governing knowledge and criticism in our culture. Though we accept some of the values and practices of our culture as part of being historically-rooted speakers and actors, and so function within its limits, this does not mean that we have to accept the authority of that tradition, or that we have eliminated the possibility of a rationally-grounded critique of the prejudices and untenable assumptions of our scientific traditions. In discussing such issues in our culture, we can reject the duality of an ahistorical objectivity and universality associated with the scientific rationality, exemplified in physics, being the absolute truth; and the embrace of a reckless relativism, that holds any metaphysics is as good as any others. We can hold to a perspectival realism which holds that there is a plurality of perspectives with partial knowledges. We can acknowledge that the difficulties of translation from one tradition to another do not imply unlearnability about the other tradition; and that genuine conversation between traditions is based on a recognition of our fallibility, an openness to the views of others, and a commitment to coming to a shared understanding of the subject-matter at hand. We can acknowledge that dialogue with those in different traditions can result in each modifying their initial position; and that this represents a significant advance over the positions each maintained at the beginning, even though there may be no substantial convergence.

We can therefore, look forward to a better kind of postmodern philosophy than that presented by Rorty. This would be one that would still leave philosophy with the role of untying metaphysical knots that strangle us. There is still the need to overcome the conventional physicalist metaphysics of a scientific culture, which Rorty tacitly assumes. The task is still to continue the metaphysical discussion, for though we ragpickers sense that this materialist position has failed, it is still the only metaphysical picture of modernity that has any contemporary hold. We can reject scientistic materialism claims that physics is a good approximation to a sketch of the one true theory, which gives us a true and complete description of the furniture of the world as false, but still take its picture seriously. When the bare bones of this natural metaphysics are presented to undergraduates in philosophy classes, the picture is remarkably like the metaphysics of the classical Greek Democritus: it is all atoms in the void. It is held that unlike the speculative metaphysics of dialecticans like Hegel, physicalism is science itself. It is then added that as natural science is progressively verifying the one true metaphysics, then everything else is in error. As Putnam observes, physicalist materialism is the dominant form of scientism and, 'since scientism is one of the most dangerous contemporary intellectual tendencies', then a 'critique of its most influential contemporary form is a duty for a philosopher who views his enterprise as more than a purely technical discipline.'[65] But we still take the picture seriously, as it is at the root of all our thinking. So it is to be respected and not treated as superstition.

Resolving infinite regresses

But what we confront in evaluating the competing metaphysics of the different schools is a dogmatism resting in postmodern politics, in physics, linguistic frameworks within forms of life, personal opinion, or narratives. The truth content of dogmatism, says Hegel, is that we put up such self-evident claims in order to avoid being driven into an infinite regress of argumentation noted by Kant. So something as simply first and unproven is posited, and from this self-evident starting point we can build up our metaphysics.

This introduces the question of truth and the problem of the criterion we possess in order to evaluate these knowledge claims in settling metaphysical disputes. Sextus presses this problem by posing the following dilemma:

> "In order to decide the dispute which has arisen about the criterion (of truth), we must possess an accepted criterion by which we shall be able to judge the dispute; and in order to possess an accepted criterion, the dispute about the criterion must first be decided. And when the argument thus reduces itself to a form of circular reasoning the discovery of the criterion becomes impracticable, since we do not allow (those who make knowledge claims) to adopt a criterion by assumption, while if they offer to judge the criterion by a criterion we force then to a regress ad infinitum. And furthermore, since demonstration requires a demonstrated criterion, while the criterion requires an approved demonstration, they are forced into circular reasoning."[66]

This circular reasoning takes the form of the criteria for evaluation of metaphysical assumptions varying from tradition to tradition, and so results in the conflicting bedrock of personal opinions, science, politics or tradition? Dogmatic appeals to one's foundational presuppositions means they are held to be beyond justification. These need to be justified if we are to avoid being dogmatic. But what criteria can we use to evaluate the conflicting bedrocks, if there are no transcendental standards of reasonability and incompatibility?

The problem with just accepting the dogmatic block or foundation is that the mitigated sceptic, who makes strange the taken-for-granted categories of the opposing school, just posits the opposite of that presupposition. Hegel argues that this dogmatic method of assessing truth-claims is problematic as reciprocal recognition is eliminated, since views which share nothing in common come forth with equal right and nullify the other.[67] He claims that to avoid this:

> "the refutation must not come from outside, that is, it must not proceed from the assumptions lying outside the system in question and inconsistent with it. The system need only refuse to recognize those assumptions; the *defect* is a defect only for him who starts from the requirements and demands based on those assumptions."[68]

An external refutation attempts to attain superiority by rejecting the opposing metaphysics through showing it to be defective. The proponent of the defective metaphysics rarely dump their ontology in the face of such external criticism. They more often than not block the criticism through saying it is a misinterpretation, or by showing the errors and defects of the opponent's own theory, or modifying some of the justifying argumentative structure that takes into account some of the criticisms. This gives the impression that metaphysical problems are insolvable, and that it's all a waste of time. Hegel argues that we can avoid this outcome if adopt a different mode of refutation; one which starts from the opponent's own theory, and examines the way it is able to resolve its own problems. He says:

> "The genuine refutation must penetrate into the opponent's stronghold and meet him on his own ground; no advantage is gained by attacking him somewhere else and defeating him where he is not."[69]

This is an immanent critique. It focuses on specific but central problems in a metaphysics, and it examines the attempts to resolve these with an eye on the dilemmas and contradictions which may arise. If these contradictions are not resolved—say the subjectivity/objectivity in the physicalist world-picture— then the metaphysics can be reconstructed by enlarging the categorical framework. If the contradictions are resolved through the categorical framework of the physicalist world-picture being expanded, then the former metaphysical system can be regarded as explanatory inadequate, in comparison to its rival. Immanent critique allows us to take the picture seriously, and to critique it from within, without seeking the cosmic guarantee from outside that metaphysical realism seeks.

On the dialectical model of immanent critique, the criteria of judgement is not externally imposed, as is contained within the theory being evaluated. With physicalist materialism the criteria is based on the ability of the theory to overcome its theoretical problems rationally in terms of the criteria of being true.[70] This procedure assumes that this particular metaphysical theory has the criteria of viewing its internal problems as a defect, in the sense of recognizing that if there is a problem, then it must be resolved through giving a plausible solution. An immanent critique of the rational choice conception of the subject, for instance, would show the self-contradictory nature of the category individual presupposed by the atomist metaphysics of rational choice theory. Though this is a theory about individuals in the social institution of the marketplace, it gives an account of the nature of the individual in terms of biology, thereby making the biological body foundational at the expense of culture. The shortcomings derive from the failure of this model to develop an adequate representation of the individual within social relations and culture in terms of its positivist criteria of truth as correspondence with reality. The attempt is made to show the difficulties—the problematic understanding of identity and difference—and why it has these particular shortcomings. This shows why this individualist ontology is a failed attempt to comprehend the social world, even though it contains some elements of truth which need to be preserved. The negation occurs because attempts to comprehend the social world with inadequate conceptions cannot succeed in giving a truthful account of how human beings operate in the social world.

The advantage of immanent critique is that it breaks with the duality of either Absolute truth or error. The different metaphysics can be regarded as partial accounts of social being, with each having something positive to offer. The theory found wanting is not held to be mistaken in the sense of just being false, but because it also lacks explanatory power. Hegel says:

> "With respect to the refutation of a philosophical system...one must get rid of the erroneous idea of regarding the system as out and out false, as if the true system by contrast were only opposed to the false."[71]

Each metaphysical system will have a truth content and a partial grasp of the situation, and this needs to be recognized.[72] This is a more tenable view than one metaphysics being the truth and the other the error, which is derived from a mathematical account of knowledge. Such a conception of truth does not make much sense of the history of social science, which is one of theories being constructed, superseded and discarded, and so cannot be regarded as one of absolute truth standing in opposition to absolute error.

Another advantage of this conception of dialectics is that it can help us to resolve a problem that has beset those who have followed Foucault in being critical of the way modern mechanisms or technologies of power that operate to constitute subjects around discourses. These, it is claimed, render people increasingly docile and useful for economic and state institutions aiming to maximize control over populations, in order to enhance a productivity and profit within the technocratic capitalist system. The charge that has been laid against Foucault, is that he is unable to tell us why he criticizes some things and not others, why he holds some things are good and others is bad.[73] Thus Charles Taylor refers to Foucault's monolithic relativism and his inability to affirm one set of practices over another.[74] Michael Walzer charges him with 'infantile leftism' and 'anarchism/nihilism.'[75] Richard Wolin accuses him of 'aesthetic decisionism,' within which he is forced to take irrationalist leaps to affirm anything.[76] For all his hostility to dialectics in *The Archaeology of Knowledge*, the latter Foucault can be interpreted as engaging in an immanent critique of the Enlightenment. Immanent critique provides us with a way to uncover the "missing" normative dimension of this critique: it interprets Foucault as working within the ethos of Enlightenment tradition, whilst criticizing it from within, and then reworking the Enlightenment in terms of the conditions of the present. The latter Foucault gestures to this, when he says that he belongs to the ethos of the Enlightenment; but he then redefines it as the 'a philosophical ethos that could be described as a permanent critique of our era!'[77] It is using one's critical capacities to disclose the constraints on creative freedom by knowledges and practices of the present, a task of ceaseless inquiry about that to which we belong: 'a critique and permanent creation of ourselves in our autonomy; that is, a principle that is at the heart of the historical consciousness that the Enlightenment has of itself.'[78] He sidelines the scientistic tradition as it is closely aligned with power and subjugation, and aligns himself with an aesthetic tradition, which he defines as being critically concerned with an ontology of the present, an ontology of ourselves.'[79] He steps beyond the atomistic Kantian conception of autonomy to a conception of autonomy as self-creation or fashioning, which is an effort to creates one's life based on a dialogic intertwining between self and others. So it is concerned with developing those forms of life which would allow the flourishing of human life as works of art. This revaluation of the Enlightenment is a step out of the nihilism of modernity, not the embrace of it, and it is a step towards a new ethics of care.

There are two critical analytic responses to immanent critique. The first is to see it as a form of scepticism, that employs the infinite regress of justification, only to give rise to negative results by being a mere negation of what is. This 'always negating' is an infinitely regressive scepticism. But this has little "bite" as it only shows that the justification must end somewhere. It is a mitigated scepticism derived from Sextus Empiricus and David Hume that has more plausibility. This works from within the physicalist world picture, and it would attempt to show that on the basis of the assumptions of that picture, there are problems with the picture, that some of the claims are untenable, and that some cannot be justified. A successful mitigated scepticism confronts the physicalist metaphysicians with antinomies. However, immanent critique is more than mitigated scepticism, because it incorporates the process of revising our metaphysics. It holds to a determinate negation, in that it gives rise to new ontologies, and so it is positive, rather than simply negative.[80]   Hegel says:

> "In contradistinction to mere Skepticism, however, philosophy does not remain content with the purely negative result of Dialectic. The sceptic mistakes the true value of his result, when he supposes it to be no more than a negation pure and simple. For the negative which emerges as the result of dialectic is, because a result, and the same time the positive: it contains what it results from, absorbed into itself and made part of its own nature."[81]

It does this by indicating what should be retained and what should be discarded, thereby providing a basis upon which we can build the best possible social ontology at this stage of our history for a critical social science. Hegel calls this a sublation which:

> "has a two-fold meaning...on the one hand it means to preserve, to maintain, and equally it also means to cease to exist, to put an end to...Thus what is sublated is at the same time preserved; it has only lost its immediacy but it is not on that account annihilated."[82]

Determinate negation allows us to reject both the traditional Platonic scientific notions of objectivity and rationality as a foundational inquiry in which reason acts as a tribunal. Certainty, foundation and the Archimedean point of view have gone. When cut out of Hegel's system, dialectics as immanent critique does not need to pretend to absoluteness, by aiming at being the one single absolute version of the world. The positive aspect of a "cut down dialectics" is that it is a cultural and human enterprise which works with a historicized rationality in the form of an ongoing dialogue between different traditions.

The second critical analytic responses to immanent critique is to see it as leading to cultural relativism. Dumping metaphysical realism results in embracing cultural relativism. The latter is a far more dangerous cultural tendency than scientistic materialism, according to Putnam, because it denies the possibility of thinking, as opposed to making noises in counterpoint, or in chorus.[83] Putnam equates cultural relativism with being unable to criticize the inherited background tradition, which provides the sense to what we consider to be true and right. Is this right? Consider the non-dialectical form of immanent critique used by Nietzsche in *On The Genealogy of Morals*, where he read and interpreted morality as a system of signs in relation to the body. His genealogy endeavours to give a superior interpretation of ascetic morality in terms of what are perceived to be problems within Christian morality. In doing this, Nietzsche extends the range of immanent critique. Hegel's goal of making the metaphysical system more coherent by introducing new categories to resolve the problems of the system, and so construct a broader and grander system, which incorporates all the other systems, is sidelined, and replaced by a therapeutic text addressed to those who are sick from suffering in our damaged world. Nietzsche's interpretation of morality is that morality is an interpretation of human suffering, and he argues that this suffering is reinforced by a Christian culture or moral discursive formation. This interprets our suffering by bourgeois civilization, as the suffering we endure we deserve, as it makes us responsible for our suffering— we are to blame because our desires and actions are sinful—and so we end up despising ourselves. Christianity is a herd animal morality associated with ascetic priests, who, in endeavouring to make suffering tolerable deepens that suffering by making it ever more inward, poisonous and life-destructive.[84] Though genealogy does not involve a dialectical transition between the earlier and latter interpretations, Nietzsche does claim to offer a better interpretation of morality than that offered by Christianity, and he does so through an immanent critique which aims to provide a more enriched and healthier life. The therapeutic text shows how we have been wounded from the Christian poison, and so become mistrustful and suspicious. It aims to call into question the Christian moral formation, calls for a critique of its moral values and aims to help us undo the damage it has caused, by finding an antidote to its poison.

If anybody can be considered a cultural relativist, it is Nietzsche, whose conception of embodied rationality within everyday life, means that we speak the language of time and place. This is not all bad as we unemployed ragpickers, who are lonely provincials in a dying provincial intellectual culture, can avoid slavishly following our inherited practices and procedures by using reason as immanent critique. After reading Nietzsche we realize that we have been wounded by a scientistic philosophy's slow-acting poisons. These are contained in its formal transcendent rationality, its formal theory of meaning, and the gap between reason and bodily historical existence. As what cannot be included in the system must be excluded, so non-propositional and figuratively elaborated structures of experience have no place in meaning and the drawing of rational inferences. The suffering from the poisons of an oppressive and intolerant scientistic culture on track to achieve Walden 11, provides the impetus for the root-digging. But it is immanent critique within the cultural conventions of Enlightenment discourse that enables we ragpickers to speak in a different voice. We lonely, provincial, ragpickers can be Enlightenment figures, and yet hold to the thesis that scientistic materialism within the Enlightenment tradition represents the domination of reason by hard science, that undercuts the aim of the democratic project to achieve a liberated society. This may be a crude vulgarization of Nietzsche and Heidegger, refracted through Adorno and Foucault; but it is not a cultural relativism singing the siren song of the Enlightenment chorus as the dominant monologue. In resolutely turning against scientific materialism's denigration of the everyday world and human suffering in the name of idealized formal systems of the world, it confronts an Enlightenment culture with itself.

Conclusion

In cruising the dialectical highway, that leads away from the philosophical heritage of logical positivism that still haunts analytic philosophy, we have discovered that Hegel's immanent critique can provide us with a way to resolve our metaphysical disputes rationally. We ragpickers, as particular finite humans, are lonely provincials caught up in the historical moment of our suffering, and beset by doubts about scientistic materialism's philosophical vocabulary and picture of the world. We have been thrown into this tradition, and we feel lonely in our emotional rejection of this entrenched, hegemonic metaphysics. Its adherents treat us historicists with disdain and contempt, whilst the university system provides little infrastructural support for philosophical research as critical intellectual activity. Immanent critique enables us ragpickers to function as anti-systematic philosophers in the philosophy institution, rather than being ejected as failures. It allows us to accept the pain of the loss of the appeal to the transcendent otherness to secure and legitimate ourselves and values, to accept our descriptions of the world as experienced participants and observers, and to live with the increasing solitude flowing from the break-up of collegial relationships within the decaying liberal university.

In cruising on the highway of despair we ragpickers have rebelled against the reams of pseudo-science in academic philosophy. Its style reads like scientific reports and papers, and its practitioners operates with the fiction that they are making step by step advances to a theory that will gives us truth. In our search for a non-scientized philosophy, engaged in the here and now of everyday life, we ragpickers came across the literary philosopher Nietzsche, who operates in the here and now.[85] His use of imminent critique, by a practical philosophy orientated by what is right and good in the historical present, gives us the option to revise our inherited tradition in terms of revaluing all values. Nietzsche forces us to draw a distinction between the utility principles of instrumental action, and the rightness of practical philosophy. This recovery of the normative within the Enlightenment tradition, in the face of its scientistic elimination to the favoured science— physics, biology or historical materialism—provides us with a rationality that enables us to criticise those technocratic discourses which legitimate and reinforce the relations of domination which cause us so much suffering. We ragpickers come into an ethical opposition to the dominant forms of knowledge in the natural sciences and philosophy. In remaining within the modern Enlightenment tradition, we also stand outside it. Nietzsche reaches back to ancient Greek ethics, which aimed to give an account of the best life.[86] In standing on the threshold of post-modernism as a philosophical concept with its incredulity towards master narratives, we have come across a path that could connected us with the ecological concern to lead a better life than that offered by capitalism.

Notes and References

1   David Lewis, 'Putnam's Paradox', in *Australasian Journal of Philosophy*, (1984), p. 221-236, citation p. 226.

2   Thomas Nagel, *The View From Nowhere*, (Oxford University Press, Oxford, 1986), p. 9.

3   Michel Foucault, *Power/Knowledge*, (ed.), Colin Gordon, (Harvester Wheatsheaf, Hertfordshire, 1980).

4   G. W. F. Hegel, *Philosophy of Right*, trs. T. M. Knox, (Oxford University Press, Oxford, 1952), p. 3

5   This the neo-pragmatist position of R. Rorty. *Philosophy and the Mirror of Nature*, (Princeton University Press, Princeton, 1979).

6   David Lewis, *Philosophical Papers*, Vol. 1. (Oxford, 1983), pp. x-xi.

7   Maurice Merleau-Ponty, *The Phenomenology of Perception*, trs., Colin Smith, (Routledge and Kegan Paul, London, 1981).

8   W. V. O. Quine, *Ontological Relativity*, (Columbia University Press, New York, 1969), p. 27.

9   C. Taylor, "Hegel's Philosophy of Mind", in C. Taylor *Human Agency and Language: Philosophical Papers Vol. 1*, (Cambridge University Press, Cambridge, 1985), pp. 77-96.

10 These links are suggested by Hilary Putnam, "Convention: A Theme in Philosophy", in his *Realism and Reason. Philosophical Papers Volume 3*, (Cambridge University Press, Cambridge, 1983),pp. 170-183.

11 Quine, *Ontological Relativity*, op. cit., p. 29.

12 Heidegger, *Being and Time*, op. cit., pp. 105-6.

13 L. Laudan, *Progress and Its Problems: Towards a Theory of Scientific Growth*, (Routledge and Kegan Paul, London, 1977), p. 120.

14 P. M. Churchland, *Matter and Consciousness*, (MIT Press, Cambridge, Massachusetts, 1984), p. 43.

15 R. Diprose, *The Bodies of Women: Ethics, embodiment, and sexual difference*, (Routledge, London, 1994), p. 19.

16 R. Rorty, "Philosophy as a Kind of Writing", in Rorty, *Consequences of Pragmatism: Essays 1972-1980*, (The Harvester Press, Brighton, 1982), pp. 96-97.

17 B. Latour & S. Woolgar, *Laboratory Life: The Social Construction of Scientific Facts*, (Sage, California, 1979), p. 237.

18 G. W. F. Hegel, *Introduction to the Lectures on the History of Philosophy*, trs. by E. S. Haldane and F. H. Simpson, 3 vols, (Humanities Press, London, 1892-6), pp. 27-8.

19 This has affinities with the post-empiricist philosophies of science such as, T. Kuhn, *The Structure of Scientific Revolutions*, 2nd edition, (University of Chicago Press, Chicago, 1970; I. Lakatos, *The Methodology of Scientific Research Programmes*, (Cambridge University Press, Cambridge, 1978); M. Hesse, *Revolutions and Reconstructions in the Philosophy of Science*, (University of Indiana Press, Bloomington, 1980).

20 The supersystems option was advocated by Joseph Wayne Smith in *Reductionism and Cultural Being*, (Martinus Nijhoff, The Hague, 1984).

21 G. W. F. Hegel, *Science of Logic*, trs. A. V. Miller, (Allen and Unwin, London, 1969), p. 119.

22 Ibid, p. 126.

23 G. W. F. Hegel, *Encyclopedia Logic*, trs, William Wallace, (Clarendon Press, Oxford, 1975), section 92, Addition. p. 136.

24 A. MacIntyre, *Whose Justice? Which Rationality?*, (Duckworth, London, 1988), p. 327.

25   Hegel, *Encyclopedia Logic*, op. cit., p. 137. Also, Hegel, *Science of Logic*, op. cit. p. 129.

26   For an account of the dialectical history in Hegel's *Phenomenology* see, T. Pinkard, *Hegel's Phenomenology. The Sociality of Reason,* (Cambridge University Press, Cambridge 1994).

27   This is the central argument of the differences betweeen the two given by Roz Diprose, *The Bodies of Women*, op. cit., ch, 1.

28   Charles Taylor, "Theories of Meaning," in C. Taylor, *Human Agency and Language: Philosophical Papers vol.1*, op. cit. pp. 248-292.

29   For a personal description of this see, Boris Frankel, *From The Prophets Deserts Come,* (Arena Publishing, Victoria, 1993).

30   Hegel, *Philosophy of Right*, trs. T. M. Knox, (Oxford University Press, London, 1967), para. 31, p. 34.

31   Ibid, pp. 34-35.

32   Existential contradiction is taken from Stanley Rosen, "Logic and Dialectic", in S. Rosen, *The Ancients and the Moderns. Rethinking Modernity,* (Yale University Press, New Haven, 1989), pp. 118-159.

33   MacIntyre, *Whose Justice? Which Rationality?* , op. cit.p. 328.

34   Ibid, p. 348.

35   Ibid, p. 349.

36   This conflict between objectivism and relativism is regarded as the central contemporary problem in our culture by R. Bernstein, *Beyond Objectivism and Relativism: Science, Hermeneutics and Praxis,* (Blackwell, Oxford, 1983).

37   Richard Rorty, *The Consequences of Pragmatism*, op. cit., pp. xli, & 149.

38   A. J. Ayer, *Metaphysics and Commonsense*, (MacMillian, London, 1969).

39   R. Carnap, "Empiricism, Semantics, and Ontology" in *Meaning and Necessity: A Study in Semantics and Modal Logic,* (University of Chicago Press, Chicago, 1947), p. 207.

40   Ibid p. 208.

41   Thus Paul Roth finishes his book with the following flourish that Carnap is surely right, for "to insist otherwise is perhaps the most dangerous of all the confusions engendered by the pseudo-problems in the social sciences." Paul A. Roth, *Meaning and Method in the Social Sciences,* (Cornell University Press, Ithaca, 1987), p. 245. Nelson Goodman in the *Structure of Appearance* limits himself to an investigation of what can be formulated within particular systems and neither makes nor recognizes any claims concerning the metaphysical adequacy of competing metaphysical frameworks. Nelson Goodman, *The Structure of Appearance,* (Bobb-Merrill, Indianapolis, 1966), pp. 101-107.

42   See Hilary Putnam, "Beyond Historicism", in his *Realism and Reason. Philosophical Papers Volume 3,* op. cit.,pp. 287-303.

43   Bridgeman, the American philosopher of science and physicist, is a classic example of this confusion of levels. He writes that the atom was only 'a construct' and its existence entirely referential and then goes on to maintain "we are as convinced of its physical reality as of our two hands and feet." P. W. Bridgeman, *The Logic of Modern Physics,* (Macmillian Publishing Company, London, 1927), p. 59.

44   The strong metphysical realist way of talking about what exists in the natural world and the projections of morality, consciousness and mathematics can be found in Simon Blackburn,*Spreading the Word,* (Clarendon Press, Oxford, 1984).

45   Style, rhetoric and interpretation are advocated by Frederic Jameson, *The Political Unconscious,* (Cornell University Press, Ithaca, 1981). Marxism, Jameson argues, is a superior form of interpretation, for its power of intepretation is so great that it incorporates and transcends all others. It is also advocated by Terry Eagleton, *Literary Theory: An Introduction,* (Blackwell, Oxford, 1983); Frank Lentricchia, *Criticism and Social Change,* (University of Chicago Press, Chicago, 1983).

46   Sextus Empiricus, *Outlines of Pyrrhonism*, trs. R. G. Bury, (William Heinneman, London, 1933), Bk.1, para 116-117, pp. 67-69.

47   David R. Hiley, *Philosophy in Question*, (University of Chicago Press, Chicago, 1983). (footnote 21), pp. 16-17.

48   Sextus Empiricus, *Outlines of Pyrrhonism*, op. cit., p. 19.

49   Sextus, *Outlines*, op. cit, p. 17.

50   Wittgenstein, *Zettel*, (eds.) G. E. M. Anscombe and G. H. von Wright, trs. G. E. M. Anscombe, (Basil Blackwell, Oxford, 1967), pp. 121-126; G. H. von Wright, *Explanation and Understanding*, (Cornell University Press, Ithaca, 1971), p. 32.

51   Ernest Gellner, *Reason and Culture*, (Blackwell, Oxford, 1992), pp. 116-123.

52   Ibid, pp. 121-22.

53   Terry Pinkard, *Hegel's Phenomenology*, op. cit, pp. 272-273.

54   R. Rorty, "Postmodernist Bourgeois Liberalism", in R. Rorty, *Objectivity, Relativism and Truth*, (Cambridge University Press, Cambridge, 1991), pp. 197-202.

55   See C. Romano, "The Illegality of Philosophy," in A. Cohen and M. Dascal, (eds.), *The Institution of Philosophy: A Discipline in Crisis?*, (Open Court, Illinois, 1989), p. 212.

56   Mark Johnson and George Lakoff, *Metaphors We Live By*, (University of Chicago Press, Chicago, 1980), p. 59.

57   Liz Grosz, "Bodies and Knowledges: Feminism and the Crisis of Reason", in L. Alcoff and E. Potter, (eds.), *Feminist Epistemologies*, (Routledge, London, 1993), pp. 197-216.

58   Hegel, *Encl. Logic*, op. cit., para. 10, p. 14.

59   One attempt to explore this can be found in Brice R. Wachterhauser, (ed.), *Hermeneutics and Truth*, (Northwestern University Press, Evanston, 1994).

60   These themes are fully explored in Martha Nussbaum, *The Fragility of Goodness: Luck and Ethics in Greek Tragedy*, (Cambridge University Press, Cambridge, 1986).

61   Plato, *Theatetus*, (Clarendon Press, Oxford, 1973), 152a-179a-especially 170e-171c, pp. 16–58.

62   Hans Georg Gadamer, *Truth and Method*, (Sheed and Ward, London, 1975).

63   Janice Moulton, "A Paradigm of Philosophy: The Adversary Method," in S. Harding and M. Hintikka, (ed.). *Discovering Reality*, (D. Reidel, Dordrecht, 1983), pp. 149–64.

64   A. Cohen, "The 'End-of-Philosophy': An Anatomy of a Cross Purpose Debate", in A. Cohen and M. Dascal, (ed.), *The Institution of Philosophy: A Discipline in Crisis?*, op. cit. p. 117.

65   Hilary Putnam, "Why There Isn't a Ready-made World", in *Realism and Reason*, op. cit., pp. 205-228, citation, p. 211.

66   Sextus Empiricus, *Outlines of Pyrrhonism*, op. cit., Bk. 2, para. 20, p. 163.

67   For an exploration of this, refer to, Michael N. Foster, *Hegel and Skepticism*, (Harvard University Press, Cambridge, Massachusetts, 1989).

68   G. W. F. Hegel, *Science of Logic*, op. cit., p. 580.

69   Ibid, p. 581.

70   Hegel, "Introduction", *Phenomenology of Spirit*, op. cit., para. 81., p. 54.

71   Hegel, *Science of Logic*, op. cit., p. 580.

72   For an idealist defence of the relative truth and error thesis refer F. H. Bradley, *Essays on Truth and Reality*, (Clarendon, Press, Oxford, 1914); for a materialist defence, S. Sayers, *Reality and Reason*, (Blackwell, Oxford, 1985). Also, S. Sayers, "F. H. Bradley and the Concept of Relative Truth," *Radical Philosophy*, No. 59, (Autumn, 1991), pp. 15-20.

73   N. Fraser, "Foucault on Modern Power: Empirical Insights and Normative Confusions", in N. Frazer, *Unruly Practices. Power, Discourse and Gender in Contemporary Social Theory*, (Polity Press, Cambridge, 1989), pp. 17-34.

74 Charles Taylor, Foucault on Freedom and Truth", in David Cousins Hoy, (ed.), *Foucault: A Critical Reader*, (Blackwell, Oxford, 1986), pp. 69-102.

75 Michael Walzer, "The Politics of Michael Foucault", in ibid, pp. 51-60.

76 Richard Wolin, "Foucault's Aesthetic Decisionism", *Telos*, no. 67, (1986), pp. 71-86.

77 M. Foucault, "What is Enlightenment?", in P. Rabinow, (ed.), *The Foucault Reader*, (Penguin, London, 1984), pp. 31-50, citation p. 42.

78 Ibid, p. 44.

79 M. Foucault, "Kant on Enlightenment and Revolution", *Economy and Society*, vol. 15, no.1, (1986), pp. 88-96, citation, p. 96.

80 Hegel, *Phenomenology of Spirit*, op. cit., para. 79, p. 51.

81 Hegel, *Enc. Logic*, op. cit., para. 81, Add. p. 119.

82 Hegel, *Science of Logic*, op. cit. p. 107.

83 Hilary Putnam, "Why Reason Can't Be Naturalized", in *Realism and Reason*, op. cit., pp. 229-247, especially p. 235.

84 Friedrich Nietzsche, *On the Genealogy of Morals*, trs. Walter Kaufmann, (Vintage Books, New York, 1989), Bk. 111, section 15, pp. 15-28, & section 28, pp. 162-3.

85 For a different voice of rebellion to a scientized academic philosophy see Roger Scruton, *An Intelligent Persons Guide to Philosophy*, (Duckworth, London, 1996).

86 For an ethical reading of Nietzsche see, Peter Berkowitz, *Nietzsche: The Ethics of an Immoralist*, (Harvard University Press, Cambridge, Massachusetts, 1995).

4 Nietzsche contra scientism

The history of philosophy is a secret raging against the preconditions of life, against the value feelings of life, against partisanship in favour of life. Philosophers have never hesitated to affirm a world provided it contradicted this world and furnished them with a pretext for speaking ill of this world. It has been hitherto the grand school of slander; and it has imposed itself to such an extent that today our science, which proclaims itself the advocate of life, has accepted the basic slanderous position and treated this world as apparent, this chain of causes as merely phenomenal. What is it really that hates here?

Nietzsche, *The Will to Power.*

(The) distinction between knowledge and values...was a momentous event in the intellectual history of the West, leading as it did to the emancipation of specialized scientific disciplines from the body of natural philosophy. But it was a perilous event, too, in that it led to in the long run to a conception of the universe as a clock-like mechanism and to the gradual elimination of such elements of our knowledge as disagreed with that mechanistic view-including intrinsic values, which were replaced by instrumental values.

Henryk Skolimowski, *Eco-Philosophy.*

Nietzsche's new kind of philosophy of the future is concerned with overthrowing idols, the revaluing of all values, and recovering what has been devalued and misinterpreted within the culture of modernity. Nietzsche is timely, as what has been devalued in late modernity are the critical voices that have been raised against the evolutionist optimism of the liberal scientific Enlightenment's project. This aimed to use reason to emancipate human beings from the despotism of myth, to control and dominate nature through science and technology, and to eliminate social ills to create a more rational society. We now stand in the present cultural situation with an incredulity towards the Enlightenment tradition. We recoil from it and gnash our teeth at its destructiveness in the form of economic rationalism of the technocratic New Right. We seek revenge for the victims, whose suffering deserves to remembered. Our anger drives our political critique of this social engineering, as we seek to unlearn philosophy's appeasing stamp of the eternal.

A brief narrative sketch of this disenchanted philosophical discourse of the optimism of modernity would include Rousseau's critical counterblasts, which represented a significant ethical corrective to the uncritical positivism of the political economists. It would also include Marx's perspective on the new interaction of science and technology under the exploitative rule of capital, and the way an uncritical Comtean positivism had become a common frame of reference for a multiplicity of ideologies. After the positivist burial of Hegelian philosophy as an 'unscientific metaphysics', we come across the artist-philosopher Nietzsche, who noted that of all 'the interpretations of the world attempted hitherto, the mechanistic one seems today to stand victorious in the foreground. It evidently has a good conscience on its side; and no science believes it can achieve progress and success except with the aid of mechanistic procedures.'[1] By the end of the nineteenth century mechanism provided the interpretive horizon of our suffering in late modernity. It was integrated with science, which was the basic foundation of our values, and was coupled to a neo-positivist ideology of value-free science. Science became the idol of modernity, scientists became the paradigmatic reasoners, and reason became a brilliant strategy for the legitimation of oppression. Philosophers made science an idol. They defended it, initially with logical positivism in the 1930s, then in response to the general devaluation of positivism in the 1960s, as a broadly realist enterprise that progressively attains truth. Realism holds that 'scientists find out things about a world that is independent of human cognition; they advance true statements, use concepts that conform to natural division, develop schemata that capture objective dependencies.'[2] Philosophy is largely identified with philosophy of science. The problem that many have with science cannot be fully articulated within analytic philosophy of science.

What creates a rupture with the late nineteenth century of Marx and Nietzsche is less the shift from positivism to realism, than the integration and instrumentalization of science and technology within industry and the military. This has led to a new configuration of capitalist society, in which technical and scientific knowledge, automation, computers and advanced technology have given rise to techno-capitalism. Douglas Kellner defines this as meaning that under techno-capitalism:

> "as machines, automation of production, new technologies and computerization replace human labour power, both manual and mental, the source of surplus value shifts from extraction from humans to extraction from machines, and accumulation is fuelled by technological development and automation, and not just by more efficient organization of human labour power, as during the era of scientific management and Taylorism."[3]

New technologies, electronics and computerization come to displace machines and mechanization, as information and knowledge come to play increasingly important roles in the production process. The dominant form of culture becomes a technoculture, representing a configuration of mass culture, a consumer society of consumer goods, film, television and mass images, and computerized information. In this new form of culture, commodity aesthetics colonises everyday life, and so transforms politics, economic and social relations. Techno-capitalism remains a form of capitalism because knowledge, information, computerization and automation are introduced into the exploitative and oppressive social relations of the production process, in order to enhance capitalist profitability, power and social control, and to enhance falling rates of profit.[4] In the increasingly cyborg culture of techno-capitalism the model of cybernetic organism has been conceived as a way to shape people into perfectly flexible 'human components' of a control system, to realize capitalism's long-standing dream of an orderly, consensual, profitably productive society.[5] This model creates an ideal world of a closed society, defines the enemy as inefficiency, disorder and dysfunction, and imposes its order on the real world. Political value commitments are presented with claims to neutrality and objectivity by appealing to the authority of science.

The concern here is less to do with science-bashing, or a failure of science to live up to its ideals of truth and rationality, than a critical exploration of the machine/human interface in a hegemonic scientific culture, in relation to the broad role that the science institution plays in our lives. This is not the concern of analytic scientific philosophy, which aims to offer an accurate picture of science, its goals and its achievements. Scientific realism is held to provide the best way to achieve this. Science provides us with understanding of phenomena to the extent that science is able to explain the causal structure of the natural and social world. Scientific realism presupposes that the things or processes in the world to which our laws and theories refer, and of which they are true or false, are to be understood as referring to real existents with genuine objective properties and tendencies. It holds that the current scientific view of the nature of reality is the best guide to what there is, and the way we classify kinds of things is defined by a common possession of some general or essential property which makes that thing a member of a particular kind. Scientific realism assumes the conventional Enlightenment position that science provides a new basis for knowledge and value, and that it does so by bringing triumphant human progress towards real knowledge of the real world. If science does not yet represent truth, science is well on to the way to no other goal. Truth is the central concern.

If we accept scientific realism as an accurate picture of science for the time being, and so put to one side engaging in debates over anti-realism between pragmatists and realists, then we can note that the picture drawn by analytic philosophy of science does not substantially deal with science as a social institution in techno-capitalism. The two discourses of analytic philosophy of science and Critical Theory do not come together. They jar and collide, even as they intermesh around the thesis that social forces constrain scientific practice, and that consensus practice in the scientific institution is socially determined by the social structure within the scientific community. Critical Theory's offer of a historical and critical perspective on science as an institution—as distinct from a relativist one—is generally lost in the spectre of relativism that haunts analytic discussion of philosophy of science since Kuhn and Feyerabend. What we have are qualified realist accounts which do accept a limited 'relativism' to save the appearances of the process-orientated character of a historically and culturally changing science.[6] The ethos of scientism, with its paternalism and intellectual autocracy of a mandarin culture, inhibits a critique directed at the social value of science. Any such critique of science that is ventured is inevitably dismissed with the denigrating charge of being "anti-science." Critique undertaken by the philosophical labourers within philosophy of science is rather narrow, as they work within a scientific critique that is concerned with the theoretical accounts of science as a form of knowledge that will give us truth. Relating science to the best life for humans is outside their concern.

Putting Nietzsche into play offers us the possibility of shifting the analytic ground of the current debates. Nietzsche is untimely in relation to the science, as he sets himself against the stream of modernist and historicist progress. He opened up a whole matrix of questions, which stand as the philosophical groundwork for a critical appraisal of the dominance that science plays in our life, its attempts at self-legitimation, and its use to lessen our suffering through providing knowledge which enlightens us about the causes of our suffering. Nietzsche can be read as advocating that we wrench ourselves from this established scientific perspective, and confront this idol by reviewing its metaphysical system with new eyes. Nietzsche is currently dismissed in analytic philosophical culture. He is seen as not being scientifically inclined, as not engaging in a serious philosophical discussion of science and scientific culture, and as being an anti-scientific poetic thinker. So, it is concluded, one should not take Nietzsche seriously on the matter of science. Now, it is true that Nietzsche as a poet-philosopher undercuts the affirmation of the modernist world-view based on mathematical physics, which provides the main system of signs for interpreting our suffering in the world. But in doing so, he asks a different question: does this metaphysical discourse further our suffering or does it lessen it? This is not incompetence.

It signifies a shift in terrain, as it introduces an ethical perspective that enables us to ask whether Australian materialism's commitment to science and a physicalist metaphysics helps us to increase or lessen our suffering? The drift of these general questions opens up a philosophical critique of science that challenges the ruling role of science in philosophy and our national culture.

We can begin to walk onto this new terrain by re-reading Nietzsche's argument in *The Birth of Tragedy*, that Apollonian Hellenism, which stands for law, order, form and rationality, which have their historical origins in Dionysian sexuality, energy, irrationality, and formless passion. We can re-read this in terms of contemporary social theory's critique of instrumental reason. If Western civilization is the oscillation of the two contradictory principles of reason versus desire, as Nietzsche holds, then within a scientific culture with its celebration of universal reason, lurks the darker and more irrational forms of passion and desire.[7] We ragpickers can appropriate this in relation to the almost religious affirmation of a reductive scientific materialism culture by Australian materialists, and so see this metaphysics as a rigid system corresponding to a rigid modernist ego. Science is an attempt to control the irrational passions caused by the contradictions of progress, the pathologies of modernity, and the storm of capitalist progress piling up debris and ruins at our feet. Desire and passion are repressed by a rigid authoritarian ego, which veils the negative with the optimism of a civilized scientific reason.[8] The affirmative image of reason derived from the paradigm of mathematical physics can be contrasted to the negative world of late modernity, in which living things die to make way for dead things—the achievement of modernity is the growth of dead things in the form of the destruction of natural world.

This offers us the possibility to probe the scientific Enlightenment's system of interpretation with fresh eyes by using Nietzsche's writings on science. In doing so, we do not try to peer beneath the tangled system of Nietzsche's writings to dig out his systematic structured position on science. Nietzsche's work on science is a series of quick dives into problems, followed by quick exits, and is a dialogue of many voices which invite different interpretations. As his observations on science are one mask he wore, the aim here is to read his perspective on a scientistic Enlightenment from an aesthetic culture, to make strange the scientific idol in our culture as part of a rendering problematic the ideals of our Enlightenment culture. Nietzsche calls into question the Enlightenment as a self-grounding form of life, given the loss of the intelligibility resulting from modern science's junking a natural hierarchy of ends for belief and action. Nietzsche's criticisms of science as the most recent expression of the nihilism of Western culture opens up the whole question of the ethical ends of science, and highlights the Weber thesis that though science has increased control over modern life, it has failed to provide us with values to guide our lives. The result is the gradual privatization of meaning and value in modernity. This is exemplified in the instrumental rationality of modern economics, which identifies wellbeing with the satisfaction of preferences, and so all that can be said is that it is a morally good thing to satisfy a person's preferences within techno-capitalism. It is in the sense that we can be said to have arrived at the afterglow of European civilization, at some sort of epochal twilight, decline, or exhaustion, to use some of Nietzsche's words. With the "death of God" virtually forgotten after scientific materialism, it is the contemporary debate around the postmodern thesis of the "death of the Enlightenment" that engages us.

Science as the best guide to what there is?

The arguments by analytic naturalist philosophers in favour of science are based on their value judgement that our best science, rather than philosophy or art, is our best guide to what there is. Brian Ellis in *Truth and Objectivity*, for instance, argues that it is up to scientists, using a naturalistic epistemology, to decide what the best explanations are, whilst philosophers argue about the ontological implications of the explanations scientists accept. Ellis justifies the value judgement that science is the best guide to what there is by arguing that:

> "Scientific inquiry is the most rational, and epistemically the most objective, of any inquiry about the nature of things. The scientific view of man and the world is therefore the most rational view to take on these matters. "[9]

He goes on to argue that there is no other:

> "body of knowledge which is as well supported or attested, as thoroughly checked, as precise and detailed in its predictions, as comprehensive and systematic in its explanations, or as satisfying intellectually. Moreover, the practice of science, and the body of knowledge it has yielded, are the products of a long history of inquiry by many thousands of dedicated men and women, operating with a code of honesty and objectivity, or reporting designed precisely to yield objective knowledge of the world, i.e. knowledge that which is independent of creed, political interest and authority. One would have to have very good reasons indeed, or be very arrogant, not to accept the scientific viewpoint on questions of ontology as the best there is."[10]

We discover problems in life and science solves them. The big ambition in scientific culture is to create a theory of everything in the form of a set of equations which would provide a mathematical model of the entire history of the universe.[11] Science provides us with a way of knowing everything, and what is unknown is only a matter of detail.

If science is the best guide to what there is, then it follows that the social and natural ontology of science must be one that is adequate for a realist science. The scientific realist tradition in Australian philosophy presupposes that physicalism is the most adequate ontology for science. Naturalistic philosophers who derive their ontology from science, Ellis argues, should turn to fundamental physics to accept what sort of things there are; what basic categories of things we need to postulate to explain their existence, and what kinds of things in each category exist most fundamentally. On the scientific realist assumption that the currently accepted scientific accounts of the nature of reality are the best theories available, we should, concludes Ellis, hold that the implied ontology of scientific realism is physicalism and that an atomistic physicalist ontology is the one most adequate for science. He identifies the scientific point of view with physics and considers it a small uncontroversial step to reduce all matter to fundamental particles, all properties to the few primitive properties of fundamental particles and some spatio-temporal relations and all causal connections to a few primitive kinds of causal interactions.[12] Ellis says that a physicalist ontology:

> "is the kind of theory of reality one would expect a scientific realist to hold, for it is constructed on the assumption that currently accepted scientific accounts of the nature of reality are the best theories available. It admits no more entities than appear to be necessary for these accounts to be viable."[13]

Papineau concurs with this when he says:

> "Like many other contemporary philosophers, I have strong physicalist intuitions. I am inclined to think that chemical phenomena, for example, are all at bottom physical, even though chemists do not describe those phenomena in physical terms. What is more, I am inclined to think the same about the phenomena studied by meteorology, biology, psychology, sociology and the other so called 'special sciences.'"[14]

Papineau's intuitions are those of most materialist philosophers. To be a materialist in philosophy is to be a physicalist, and a philosophical physicalist naturalism assumes that the smooth process of reduction, which results in the wholesale replacement of the social ontology of the everyday world to a new physicalist ontology can be achieved without explanatory or predictive loss. Paul Churchland says: 'This smoothness (of reduction) permits the comfortable assimilation of the old ontology within the new and thus allows the old theory to retain all of most of its integrity.'[15]

A scientific culture flows from the traditional process of inter-theoretic reduction in physicalism within physics. There is the research programme of a naturalised epistemology of cognitive science, experimental psychology and neuroscience, whose hopes lie in connectionism or neuro-computing, where the attempt being made to design circuits that emulate neural networks leads to working machine-systems. This research is connected to computer technologies like artificial intelligence, whose goals are increasingly given in military terms of battle management, rather than machine translation from ordinary human language to computer programmes. A more comprehensive physicalist ontology containing explanatory resources and capabilities that are equal to or greater than those of everyday life is deeply implicated within, and a spin-off from the American military dream of computerized battle management systems and autonomous machines in battlefields.[16] Enlightenment rationality within this culture has increasingly taken a scientistic turn to a goal of an automated or cybernetic society in which the Enlightenment ideals of freedom and progress become appropriated as technocratic expression of cybernetics rooted in nature.[17] This model, which holds that the brain is like a computer, human beings are like machines and society like a cybernetic feedback system, tells us little about the relation of science to catastrophe, ecological crisis, the collapse of tradition, and the emergence of an uncertain and destructive present.[18] There is little in scientific culture which addresses the questions: what is the moral purpose of this form of scientific inquiry? What is the meaning and purpose of this system of signs in terms of our life? The response would be that these questions are irrelevant. The universe is bleak, cold and empty. So what? It is science that makes us human, and our society will truly be enlightened when it is in harmony with the principles of science.[19] Yet we are still left with the institution of science rolling on, sustaining and subservient to a techno-capitalism, whose imperatives of expansion impose the overall research orientation upon science.

The current situation in the scientific culture in the philosophy institution then, is one where dogmatic physicalists square off against dogmatic anti-physicalists. The friends of physicalism start with their physicalist intuitions and treat physicalism as beyond debate, since natural science is neutral, value-free and gives us timeless, ahistorical truth. The debate about the social relevance of science is added on as the social responsibility of scientists with individual consciences, who raise questions about the social responsibility of science. The debate is within the physicalist paradigm, and on its terms, with its distinctions between pure and applied science, and the objectivity and neutrality of the natural sciences, in contrast to the more socially involved and compromised character of the social sciences. It's a crude debate. All those who resist physicalist reductionism are deemed to reject science, embrace an explicit anti-realism, belong to the relativist camp, and are ideologues or mystics. Those who oppose the identity of philosophical naturalism with physicalism dismiss those physicalist intuitions as symptoms of an overblown admiration for science—a case of physics worship and envy by those who remain starry-eyed by physics and neuroscience—which results in a scientism with authoritarian tendencies. Dogma confronts dogma. Such is the state of academic philosophy in Australia in late modernity.

If we use Nietzsche to open this dogmatic circle, we become involved in the new project of overcoming Western metaphysics, making a space for a new kind of philosophy to combat European nihilism, and seeing this as a prelude to a philosophy of the future. Nietzsche held that the project of the Enlightenment had long failed to live up to its promise, and he highlighted the continuing relevance of the Platonic search for unity and permanence of the hidden essence of things behind the multiplicity of appearances of the everyday world. Nietzsche is seen as the primordial, postmodern philosopher by Heidegger, Derrida and Foucault, all of whom follow Nietzsche's path of philosophy, debunking science in the name of demystifying rhetoric aligned with an aesthetic reason. This is commonly seen to be bidding a bold farewell, or saying goodbye, to the self-grounding Enlightenment project in modernity, and the introduction of a post-Enlightenment philosophy.

Starting with Nietzsche means that we become caught up in the divide between continental and analytic articulations of philosophy, and the common interpretation made by analytic philosophers of the postmodern debunking of reason. This interpretation holds that scientific realists do not need to bother with the continental critique of science. Why shift the problem of science to art, and then beyond art to life? Scientific inquiry provides the most credible source of knowledge; Nietzsche is seen to make claims that there are no objective truths, whilst continental philosophers like Heidegger and Adorno, in spending too much time with the poets, have become drunk on romantic subjectivity and mythology. They are seen to recycle a romantic critique of reason which holds that science falsifies reality, and are expressly hostile to science. Contemporary Nietzschean-inspired postmodernists are held to embrace extreme forms of relativism, scepticism, historicism and nihilism, and hold that science is nothing more than a series of sublimated metaphors. On this interpretation Nietzsche is saying goodbye to science, and leaving it behind. The conclusion drawn by analytic philosophers is that scientific realism does not need to be defended against the unmasking critique of the latter day neo-Romantics, who like Nietzsche, are caught up in nihilism. This is deemed not to be a rational alternative, as it holds that there are no authoritative reasons at all.

Nietzsche contra reason?

There is some justification for this consensual interpretation amongst the scientific realists committed to a physicalist metaphysics. Nietzsche did call himself untimely, and he declared his philosophy to be an attack on the optimistic temper of modernity and its Platonic-Christian culture. He was deeply mistrustful of epistemology, and guarded against settling down into any dogma by looking out of different windows.[20] His critique of the superstitions of philosophy included an attack on the metaphysics of physics as a bad interpretation of reality, and that knowing absolute truth was an illusion, and impossible ideal. He held that science self-destructively affirmed its own limits as an ascetic ideal. He saw traditional philosophy as an attempt to slander and bespatter the everyday world by inventing a real world behind the apparent one, and sustaining the tyranny of the latter over the former. As a free spirit he aimed both to break the tyranny of this set of values sustained by the scholarly beaver and ant-like spirit, and to revalue our moral values, so that we have a picture of the world in which our most powerful desires are free to function.[21]

What are we to make of these hammerings on the scientific idol of modernity from an artist-philosopher who celebrates an aristocratic politics with its heroic virtues of nobility and strength? Habermas makes sense of Nietzsche's farewell to scientific philosophy, and his unmasking critique of scientific reason by arguing that it is undertaken from a standpoint that is outside the horizon of reason. He says that 'Nietzsche had no choice but to submit subject-centred reason yet again to an immanent critique—or to give up the program entirely. Nietzsche opts for the second alternative: he renounces a renewed revision of the concept of reason and *bids farewell* to the dialectic of enlightenment.'[22] Habermas argues that Nietzsche embraces myth as the other of reason, and that he does so by using the ladder of historical reason in order to cast it away. He leaps out of the dialectic of Enlightenment into the salvation of art and an aesthetically renewed mythology, which entails the valorisation of the archaic. Nietzsche, Habermas writes, confronts reason with its absolute other of non-reason, as he:

"enthrones taste, 'the Yes and No of the palate,' as the organ of knowledge beyond true and false, beyond good and evil. But he cannot legitimate the criteria of aesthetic judgment that he holds on to because he transposes aesthetic experience into the archaic, because he does recognize as a moment of reason the critical capacity for assessing value that was sharpened through dealing with modern art—a moment that is still at least procedurally connected with objectifying knowledge and moral insight in the processes of providing argumentative grounds. The aesthetic domain...is hypostatized instead into the other of reason."[23]

So he opens a path up to Heidegger, Derrida and nihilism. Habermas opposes this irrationalism in the name of a universally valid communicative reason as part of a reconstructed social science, and the affirmation of modernity as an uncompleted project.

Habermas offers a powerful and plausible interpretation of Nietzsche's hammerings on the idols of modernity. It can be re-contextualized as part of the general view that Nietzsche's perspectivism has given rise to an alternative aesthetic picture of the world to the world-picture of scientific materialism. The alternative holds that language is a historical artefact that reflects the particular historical perspective, as well as the inflection imposed on that perspective by individual thinkers. The world has no determinate structure. Being is becoming, and becoming is innocent, as it is the accummulation and discharge of force. It is intrinsically self-modifying chaos. We can impose on its random motions whatever value or perspectives we will. Human beings are shaped by chaos, through which the will to power flows from chaos into the shape of a form of life. But human beings are producers who overcome the play of forces by making order. What is valued from a human perspective is a healthy life rather than a sick one. The general analytic interpretation of Nietzsche's epistemology is that our concepts do not correspond to this chaotic world because it has no structure; our theories are mere interpretations that reflect our needs; and no perspective can enjoy epistemic privilege over any other, as there is no epistemically privileged mode of access to the characterless world.[24] His politics of modernity is concerned to remove the decadent, sickly order of late-modern European civilization imposed on chaos, and to replace it with a new, vital and healthy one. This requires that Nietzsche enlighten his contemporaries by accelerating the dissolution of their way of life, return to chaos as origin, help to create/produce the birth of a new race of human beings as warrior artists. So begins a new cycle in the eternal return.

There is no doubt that Nietzsche is a troubling writer. He denigrates democracy, glorifies war, is hostile to feminism and socialism, and affirms a healthy aristocracy whose noble individuals are ready to subordinate and sacrifice others. He is a dangerous public philosopher in a liberal polity, as Rorty recognizes.[25] He does debunk science by looking at science from 'the perspective of the artist', as 'the problem of science cannot be recognized in the context of science.'[26] He explicitly rejects an Alexandrian culture of science, which he characterised as Socratic:

> "Socrates is the prototype of the theoretical optimist who, with his faith that the nature of things can be fathomed, ascribes to knowledge and insight the power of panacea....To fathom the depths and to separate true knowledge from appearance and error, seemed to the Socratic man the noblest, even the only true human vocation."[27]

This is replaced by a Dionysian artistic culture in *The Birth of Tragedy*. As part of developing a metaphysics of art dealing with appearances, he reworks Schelling's romantic programme of replacing the unifying cultural role, previously formed by a now-disintegrating Christianity, with a revived culture through art as a public institution. This romantic programme would heal the pathologies and wounds of modernity and regenerate the ethical totality of the bourgeois nation through restoring a lost solidarity. Nietzsche also embraces myth as the other of reason. This is a necessary fiction, without which we cannot live, as it can harness potentially destructive forces of life, so that we can live with the primordial forces and chaos, and so affirm life as sublime, beautiful and joyous, in spite of all suffering and cruelty. The purpose of culture is to enable the formation of sovereign human beings.[28] There is also Nietzsche's anti-science tenor of devaluing truths accessible through a systematic scientific knowledge, and establishing the cognitive superiority of art in *The Birth of Tragedy*. This is reinforced by the devaluing of truth in an early essay, in which there is an explicit denial of truth as representation. Nietzsche says:

> "What, then, is truth? A mobile army of metaphors, metonyms and anthropomorphisms—in short, a sum of human relations, which have been enhanced, transposed and embellished

poetically and rhetorically and which after long use seem firm, canonical and obligatory to a people."[29]

The denial of truth in the early Nietzsche sustains the radical interpretation of Nietzsche's perspectivism, which goes beyond a rejection of Cartesian foundationalism to a position that human knowledge, especially science, distorts or falsifies reality. The progress of knowledge becomes the train of metaphors and tropes, whilst truth becomes worn out metaphors that have lost their sensuous force.

The broad position analytic interpretation of Nietzsche, is that he is engaged in the traditional philosophical enterprise of laying out basic truths about the world. This enterprise is then held to fail because Nietzsche's position that all knowledge is perspectival, perspectives always distort or falsify, truths are illusions, and science is a useful and necessary fiction, collapses into relativism.[30] Relativism is self-refuting. If truth is dumped, and there is an infinity of perspectives, then we have no grounds for rejecting perspectives. So Nietzsche, whilst maintaining the impossibility of knowledge as knowledge, holds that there is no knowledge. Nietzsche is mistaken or confused. If there is no determinate structure to the world that constrains us in interpreting it as genealogy, then, as this is just another perspective, so we can only talk in terms of the political effects of discourses.[31] This seems to confirm the thesis of Habermas, which holds that Nietzsche says farewell to reason.

One way of tackling this irrationality thesis is to make a distinction between science and its interpretation. As Horkheimer contended, these are two different things.[32] It has been the interpretation of science that is the issue in the continental tradition, especially the positivist interpretation of science, with its implicit physicalist metaphysical foundations and claim that science has a disinterested, value-neutral objectivity that gives us absolute truth. Nietzsche, struggling against the dominance of science, observes that 'it is not the victory of science that distinguishes our nineteenth century, but the victory of scientific method over science.'[33] The victory of scientific method is identified with Comtean positivism, and Nietzsche can be read as engaging in a critique of a particular positivist interpretation of scientific reason in modernity. He argues against positivism through foregrounding the question of the social and political aspects of science in terms of the will to power. He draws out the implications of science as a human practice serving identifiable human social and political goals of the mastery of nature, and argues that a science, merely concerned with the truth or the adequacy relation in terms of the correspondence of interpretation and reality, falls well short of offering us an adequate comprehension of life. This is an immanent critique, because Nietzsche holds that we are enclosed within a horizon of the interpretation of positivism, for it is this in which we live and move, and from which we cannot escape, since we are in our webs.[34] But within this imprisonment within our perspectives, we seekers of knowledge can move beyond narrow and conventional perspectives.

The project of overcoming metaphysics associated with Nietzsche can be located within the tradition of Hegel's critique of foundationalism, and the metaphysical atomistic presuppositions of modern science. Nietzsche replays Hegel's argument in *The Phenomenology of Spirit* against Kant's instrument metaphor, and the whole modernist foundationalist epistemological project, with its emphasis on method inherited from Descartes.[35] Hegel found a bundle of dubious, unexamined and arbitrary presuppositions of the tradition of knowledge as an instrument to know the Absolute as it really is, in opposition to that which is untrue, phenomenal and normal. He then argued that the whole foundationalist approach to knowledge needed to be rejected, because these foundations rested on presuppositions as to the nature of the knowledge and the subject. The ground is important because to answer the question, "What is knowledge", we needed to have knowledge of what knowledge is. The problem of the ground of knowledge is the core of the problem. Nietzsche writes within this tradition. He says that with foundationalism:

> "One would have to know what Being is...what certainty and knowledge are, and so forth. But as we do not know these things, a criticism of the faculty of knowledge is nonsensical: how is it possible for an instrument to criticize itself, when it is itself that exercises the critical faculty. It cannot even define itself!"[36]

Nietzsche's overcoming of the metaphysics is a process of undermining the dogmatic appeals to foundations, and so is a furthering of modernity's attempt to view everything as the product of autonomous self-legislation. He criticises the foundationalist assumption that the structure of the world can be read as logic, or language or science, and that this representation is held to be an eternal and unchanging truth. The object of critique is a modernist reason in the form of Platonic reason:

> "The aberrations of philosophy are the outcome of the fact that, instead of recognizing in logic and the categories of reason merely a means to the adjustment of the world for utilitarian ends (basically, toward an expedient falsification), one believed one possessed in them the criteria of truth and *reality*.....And behold, suddenly the world fell apart into a "true" world and an "apparent" world...Instead of employing the forms as a tool for making the world manageable and calculable, the madness of philosophers divined that in these categories is presented the concept of that world to which the one in which man lives does not correspond—The means were misunderstood as measures of value and even as a condemnation of their real intention."[37]

Nietzsche, like Hegel, rejects any secure resting place in method or concept, in favour of our current revisable standards of rational acceptability and the fallibility of knowledge. Platonic reason is not the whole of reason, nor is anti-foundationalism identical to a bidding farewell to reason. Anti-foundationalism does not necessarily imply the falsification thesis that all our beliefs are illusions or fictions. Anti-foundationalism is concerned with the certainty and justification of knowledge, and not the truth or falsity of our beliefs. Anti-foundationalism can take up the option of perspectivism, that knowledge is social and historical, that knowledge involves interpretation, an acceptance of different situated knowledges, and their fallibility and revisability—a turn to hermeneutics. What is retained after the denial of absolute truth is an aesthetic reason, which is critical of the scientific Enlightenment and relies on style, taste and judgement. Aesthetics and morality are combined and are concerned with the meaning of life in a nihilistic culture.[38] This does not necessarily involve a standpoint that is outside the horizon of reason, so bidding farewell to the dialectic of enlightenment. Nietzsche could be operating within a dialectic of art and the Enlightenment that links science to the problem of nihilism and the problem of meaning. Reason lives on after the dumping of Platonic reason as an aesthetic reason. As articulated by Nietzsche, it assumes that art is a separate sphere of society, and it takes back the self-dissolution of art, proposed by Hegel in terms of Nietzsche's dream of the rebirth of tragedy from the spirit of Wagner's music.

One can therefore agree with Habermas that Nietzsche does engage in an unmasking critique of scientific reason. But the dualist position of being either for or against science, in terms of the Enlightenment science versus a romantic anti-Enlightenment, is too simple. There is another voice to be heard in Nietzsche, that of Nietzsche as the flag-bearer of science. Though Nietzsche is a critic of science and philosophy, his critique of positivist science does not involve a rejection of science, a wallowing in nihilism, or an "anything goes" in terms of interpretation. Nietzsche defends science:

> "On the whole, scientific methods are at least as important as any other result of research: for it is on the insight into method that the scientific spirit depends: and if these methods were lost, then all the results of science could not prevent a renewed triumph of superstition and nonsense."[39]

Science is better than superstition, nonsense or an opinion which is fanaticised, and pressed to one's heart as a conviction of grabbing anything that comes into our heads that looks like an explanation. To truly engage in self-creation requires knowledge, as we need to avoid mistaking the effect for the cause, or a conditioned reflexive response for a freely chosen deed. In *The Twilight of the Idols,* in defending Heraclitus against Platonists who rejected the testimony of their senses in the name of the true world behind the apparent one, he says:

> "And what magnificent instruments of observation we possess in our sense!...Today we possess science precisely to the extent to which we have decided to *accept* the testimony of the senses—to

the extent to which we sharpen them further, arm them, and learn to think them through."[40]

He says that now that we have destroyed morality, we have become completely obscure to ourselves. In this situation 'physics proves to be a boon for the heart'. Science, as a way to knowledge, acquires a new charm after morality has been eliminated. It is here alone that we find consistency, we have to construct if we are to engage in the creation of new values. This yields a sort of practical reflection on the conditions of our existence as men of knowledge.[41] Science is not just another perspective, equally valuable as any other; it is an interpretative practice to be understood in terms of a background of culture and the mastery of nature. Creativity depends upon what is lawful and necessary in the world.[42] With right value-making depending on right-knowing, Nietzsche is prepared to carry the banner of Enlightenment science forward, after the suitable corrections have been made. His revision of science holds that science should 'descend to a modesty of hypotheses and a provisional experimental point of view' and so have a certain value in the realm of knowledge; but that it should always be supervised by the police of mistrust.[43] The problem with positivist science is that it forgot that it was a particular perspective on the world founded on specific interests and proclaimed itself a God's-Eye-view of reality that gave us Absolute truth. So a positivist science, with its suspicion of any metaphysics outside science, its principle of clarity, and the use of logical techniques to achieve that clarity, needs to be regulated by a new ethics of self-creativity based on freedom.

A more modest science is linked to his emphasis on interpretation. This highlights his opposition to the positivist assumption that an unmediated access to the world was possible. He rejects the positivist claim that science is a pure theory which is an accurate picture of the way things really are in the name of interpretation:

"In opposition to Positivism, which halts at phenomena and says, "here are only *facts* and nothing more,"—I would say: No, facts are precisely what is lacking, all that exists consists of *interpretations.* We cannot establish any fact "in itself": it may be even nonsense to desire to do such a thing."[44]

Read on its own, this passage can be interpreted to mean that there are only interpretations, on the grounds that once human mediation enters the picture, the world is well lost, and we never compare an image, word or sign with an object, but only with other signs. But as Nietzsche still holds that the evidence of the truth comes from the senses, he can be interpreted as criticising the myth of the given in positivism. The empiricist picture of scientific knowledge is rejected, because its emphasis on bare facts is at the expense of interpretation and perspectival knowledge, in which there are facts within the context of interpretations. Nietzsche is holding that facts are always mediated by particular interpretations, a position which has affinities to the issue of theory/observation raised by Russell, Hanson and Wilfred

Sellars in contemporary analytic philosophy. Positivism is rejected, because to designate something as a fact involves the imposition of value; it is an interpretation from a particular perspective, since it is to group together in relative isolation a state of affairs taken from the flux of becoming. Absolute truth is displaced in favour of a perspective on the world, an interpretation that is more or less adequate or comprehensive than its rivals. As a mediated access to the facts it is a particular point of view, that will bring some things into the foreground and leave some in the background. Hence positivism as a philosophy of science is explicitly rejected, as we have cultural knowledge of an interpreted world, and not a mirror of the world of naked facts. It is human knowledge which is historically informed.

Far from this ethically orientated historicism bidding farewell to science as Habermas implies, Nietzsche, in *The Gay Science,* can be interpreted to be pointing beyond positivism, to a different post-positivist science:

> "So many things have to come together for scientific thinking to originate; and all these necessary strengths had to be invented, practised and cultivated separately. As long as they were still separate, however, they frequently had an altogether different effect than they do now that they are integrated into scientific thinking and hold each other in check. Their effect was that of poisons: for example, that of the impulse to doubt, to negate, to wait, to collect, to dissolve. Many hecatombs of human beings were sacrificed before these impulses learned to comprehend their coexistence and to feel that they were all functions of one organizing force within one human being. And even now the time seems remote when artistic energies and the practical wisdom of life will join with scientific thinking to form a higher organic system..."[45]

He identifies himself in the preface to the *Genealogy of Morals* as 'we men of knowledge' who need to free ourselves from naive and commonplace ways of thinking. They do so in order to show us that there are different ways of thinking that allow us to comprehend what we are, and that we can become creators of laws and our selves.[46] But he does not carry this any further. He initially held in *The Gay Science* that we need to become physicists so that we 'become the best learners and discoverers of everything that is lawful and necessary in the world' in order to realize this possibility of being creators.[47] But he changes his mind in *The Genealogy of Morals,* as his concern increasingly shifts to the meaninglessness of the world, resulting in the disappearance of valuations. The emphasis is on the renewal of ethical value rather than the value of truth, and the need to introduce meaning, to posit a goal, and to shape the world according to the goal of self-creation.[48] This active interpretation aims to humanize the world, so that we ourselves are more and more masters within it.[49] The value of the world lies in our interpretation, and, from this perspective, our previous perspectival interpretations have been concerned with our survival in life, with the will to power, and self-formation.[50] We need to overcome narrow interpretations like Christianity that assume an external moral order that is independent of human will; or those interpretations which have lead philosophy astray. We need to face up to the moral and political implications of the decay of Christianity for the good life. Every strengthening and increase in power opens up new perspectives and horizons.[51] The way for those free spirits who set out to sail on the stormy, uncharted seas to make a new morality is through art. Freedom is the most comprehensive form of creation, as it involves making the world in which live, by becoming masters of the world.

This reading Nietzsche as contra scientism is meditated through the texts of the early Frankfurt School. The early Frankfurt School in the 1930s made a sustained attempt to step beyond the inadequacies of positivist science and philosophy articulated by a resurgent scientific philosophy of the Vienna Circle.[52] This overcoming was done in relation to the inadequacies of an orthodox Marxism to explain the crisis in capitalist society, and in opposition to a metaphysical materialism which attempted to capture the totality of being in a universal philosophical system.[53] It took the form of constructing a historical materialist social theory, uniting philosophy and the sciences, that focused on human needs and suffering, the ways in which economic conditions produced suffering and the changes necessary to eliminate human suffering and increase human well-being.[54] Looking back from this perspective, Nietzsche can be interpreted as a radical hermeneutist articulating an early view of the crisis in bourgeois culture. This fractures into a formal reason in positivist science that gives us truth, and an artistic metaphysics whose fundamental drive is a search for meaning and value of human existence. The positivist Enlightenment which is grounded on the natural sciences then devalues and marginalizes a metaphysical need that makes sense out of human suffering. Nietzsche is then read as the dark or counter side of the Enlightenment, which operates with a negative, pessimistic view of history. This contests the myths of scientific culture around the absolutism of science, which holds that there can be no knowledge outside the empirical sciences, which take a transcendent stance. In returning philosophy to the world of appearances, Nietzsche highlights the lack of ethical identity for concrete human praxis in an increasingly nihilistic European culture. Nietzsche opposes the hegemony of positivism in scientific culture by shifting the grounds of critique to an aesthetic/ethical rationality, which operates as a form of cultural criticism with an emphasis on the art of self-creation. Nietzsche represents the dawning of self-understanding of 'we modern men of knowledge' in European culture that its project of a self-grounding form of life is beginning to decay. He is proposing an interpretation of this decay, what it may mean for us in terms of a free human social life, and a critique of philosophy's attempt to provide authoritative reasons for a destructive modern form of life.

This reading of Nietzsche highlights the consequences of the hegemonic role of science in Enlightenment culture within the crisis of modernity. A dogmatic positivist science with its formal analytic logic, which denies the role of interpretation, is cut down from its pedestal of knowledge so as to allow for a plurality of different interpretive perspectives of the empirical world. Nietzsche provides us with something more than the sounding of the idol of science by Feyerabend's "anything goes", or Kuhn's institutional emphasis on the historicity of science, that caused such intellectual ferment in the 1960s and 1970s. These critiques of science enabled the newly establishing social sciences like sociology to wear the garb of science, and so become academically respectable. But this re-thinking of positivist science avoided the whole issue of nihilism and the revaluation of new values in relation to the good life. In contrast, Nietzsche opens up a new pathway with his insight that philosophy and then science affirm a picture of the world in itself, and in doing so they speak ill of, and rage against, our everyday world, which they dismiss as being merely an apparent one.[55] The significance of Nietzsche's interpretive perspectives, based on different capacities and interests, is that philosophy leaves its cosmic exile on the mountain top, and returns to living in the everyday world of appearances. Nietzsche's multi-valued perspectivalism is the precursor of the postmodern conception of situated knowledges of historical human beings operating within ordinary language in everyday life. In *Beyond Good and Evil*, Nietzsche then undertakes a critique of modernity from the perspective of the good life, and he critiques different cultural forms of interpretation to understand their moral significance or its value for life. In opening the world of meanings he takes outside the language of a science that steps beyond the observable to the unobservable to describe and explain the mechanisms of a reality remote from the meanings of human experience.

Undermining science and metaphysics

Nietzsche's critique of science also involves criticism of the metaphysics of science, as well as the epistemology of positivism. Hegel's argument that metaphysical assumptions are built into our scientific vocabulary, and that we cannot use language without presupposing them, is accepted. Nietzsche makes the familiar Hegelian claim that there can be no science without presuppositions and, as it is faith in these metaphysical presuppositions that science rests upon, so it is these which require justification.[56] His reflections on scientific metaphysics relates metaphysics, to the affirmation of human life in the face of human suffering, within the drift into European nihilism.

Nietzsche's perspectivism makes physics a partial interpretation of reality that requires justification, rather than a being a mirror which captures the law like nature of the world as it really is. Physics has a limited metaphysical interpretation of the world, because it is an explanation of an essentially mechanistic world functioning as a clock or a system of levers and pulleys, as a mechanism of isolated parts that impinge on each other only as an effect of external forces, and so is a meaningless world.[57] Nietzsche says that to:

> "comprehend the world, we have to be able to calculate it; to be able to calculate it, we have to have constant cause; because we

147

find no such constant causes in actuality, we invent them for ourselves—the atoms. This is the origin of atomism."[58]

He goes on to say that:

> "Physicists believe in a "true world" in their own fashion: a firm systematization of atoms in necessary motion, the same for all beings—so for them the "apparent world" is reduced to the side of the universal and universally necessary being which is accessible to every being in its own way (and also already adapted—made "subjective"). But they are in error. The atom they posit is inferred according to the logic of perspectivism of consciousness—and therefore itself a subjective fiction. This world picture that they sketch differs in no essential way from the subjective world picture: it is only construed with more extended sense, but with *our* senses nevertheless.[59]

Nietzsche's overcoming of metaphysics through immanent critique splits method from ontology, and it can be seen as breaking away from the epistemic fallacy in contemporary philosophy, which is most commonly associated with the positivist project.   Roy Bhaskar defines the epistemic fallacy in the following terms:

> "The chief metaphilosophical error in prevailing accounts of science is the analysis, definition or explication of statements of being in terms of statements about our knowledge of being, the reduction of ontology to epistemology which I have termed the 'epistemic fallacy.' As ontology is in fact irreducible to epistemology, this functions to merely cover the generation of an implicit ontology...[60]

Bhaskar's claims that 'Nietzsche deconstructed knowledge but left Humean ontology intact' is misleading.[61]   Humean empiricism within positivism presupposes an atomist metaphysics which places an epistemological emphasis on impressions of sense, or sense data, as the fundamental building blocks of knowledge; and it assumes an ontology of the regularity of the constant conjunction of events, rather than an ontology of persisting things undergoing change.   Nietzsche's metaphysics, in contrast, is the chaos at the heart of things; it is a process philosophy with its chaotic play of forces involving creation and destruction.   That is not Hume.

Another consideration that Bhaskar fails to take into account is that, in contrast to the epistemic fallacy of nineteenth- and twentieth-century positivism, with its repression of its atomistic ontology by an empiricist epistemology, Nietzsche does explore questions of ontology separately from those of epistemology.   He explicitly rejects an obsolete Platonic metaphysics, which holds that true being is the eternal, and that the permanent and the immutable lie behind the world of time and transience.   This attempt is made to identify the eternal unchanging reality that underlies the diversity of moral and political forms of life. Nietzsche affirms the phenomenality of the world of appearances:

> "This apparent world is the world viewed according to values; ordered, selected according to values; ie in this case according to the viewpoint of utility in regard to the preservation and enhancement of the power of a certain species of animal."[62]

He aims to replace the metaphysics of a true world of physics as the sole reality and an apparent world, with a metaphysic of becoming or flux, in which there is only difference and diversity. The old metaphysicians, who saw being as static, tried to impose fixed and static categories onto this flux, and the imposition of a static being metaphysics onto the process of becoming, meant that the character of life was distorted. Nietzsche's artistic metaphysics is an alternative metaphysics to that of mechanistic materialism, as it is one which sees reality as a plethora of forces which constantly move into existence, seek to assert themselves by dominating others, then pass out of existence.

In this early precursor of process metaphysics as a way round modernity, life is held to be a plurality of forces in tension, in which each particular force strives 'to become master of a space, extend its power and thrust back anything that resists it.'[63] Along with Hegel, Nietzsche rejects a thing and its property metaphysic, as he holds that there are 'only dynamic quanta in a relation of tension to all other dynamic quanta: their essence lies in their relation to all other quanta, in their "effect" upon the same.[64] A thing is constituted by its various interrelations and is the sum of its effects:

> "Everything which co-exists in time and space has but a relative existence...Each thing exists through and for another like it, which is to say through and for an equally relative one...The whole nature of reality lies wholly in its acts and...for it there is no other being."[65]

In replaying the old quarrel between poetry and philosophy as to which is better suited to grasping and conveying knowledge about human beings in the world, Nietzsche's artistic metaphysics is a metaphysics of flux centred around will to power. Its substantive claim is that the world consists of quanta of forces, with each centre of force having a tendency to extend its influence and incorporate other centres:

> "And do ye know what "the universe" is to my mind? This universe is a monster of energy, without beginning or end. It is...energy everywhere, the play of forces and force-waves...a sea of forces storming and raging in itself, forever changing, for ever rolling back over incalculable ages to recurrence, with an ebb and flow of its forms...*This world is the Will to Power—and nothing*

else! And even ye yourselves are this will to power—and nothing besides!"[66]

In affirming life by dispensing with the true unchanging world, Nietzsche does not assume an atomist Humean ontology of a constant conjunction of events. He is a later day Heraclitean who is opposed to Platonists, mechanists, atomists, and Hegelian dialecticians who recommend dialectics as the road to virtue.[67] His rejection of the mechanization of the world does not involve a return to the Aristotelian metaphysics of changing and persisting things with real essential natures and teleological tendencies. Nor does it involve a turn to scientific realism with its underlying structure causing appearances. In returning to the world of the senses, Nietzsche dislodges a modernist atomist ontology of the sciences, by placing a process ontology squarely on the table.[68]

This indicates the misleading character of those postmodern interpretations of Nietzsche's dismantling and overcoming of metaphysics which hold that his overcoming of metaphysics is engaged in a total emancipation from all traditional philosophical categories.[69] This is a misleading account of what Nietzsche is with his process view of the world. This is metaphysics. Nietzsche has not developed a schema that is free of all metaphysical commitments, since he is arguing that a process ontology is the right kind of metaphysics for art. The truth of the 'beyond metaphysics' claim, as articulated by Nehamas with its focus on language and interpretation, is that Nietzsche does confront the philosophical tradition as he attempted to overthrow Platonism. But Nietzsche also stands over against that tradition in the sense of constituting a counter movement within the metaphysical tradition, as an inverted Platonism. In failing to see this the 'beyond metaphysics' claim of Nehamas becomes a paradoxical one:

> "Nietzsche wants to show that our linguistic categories are compatible with different versions of the ontological structure of the world. That is he wants to show that the world has no ontological structure. Nietzsche's task is to reinterpret both our language and our world in order to show that just as language makes no ontological commitments regarding the world, so the world imposes no restraints upon language."[70]

This assumes that the world is a piece of malleable clay, that humans are the cookie cutters, for it is language which gives the world its determination, and so there is nothing about the world that constrains us in interpreting it. All interpretation is wilful remaking of the world. Yet Nietzsche holds that the fundamental character of the world is that it is chaotic,: this is what enduring about the world. The implications this has for how human beings should live in relation to human power over the world is what is traced in terms of a rank-ordering of creative activities. Nietzsche, then, is a turning point in metaphysics because in pushing beyond the metaphysical limits of both atomistic modern scientific philosophy and Platonic reason, he also rejects a static thing and its properties ontology. In doing so, he is making an ontological claim that an ontology of becoming should replace the inadequate Platonic and mechanistic metaphysics. He supports his position of overcoming by holding that the world imposes restraints on language, and that the categories of our metaphysics need to account for the process or flux of chaos. If philosophers use static categories like 'thing-in-itself' then they will not be able to account for what the world is, namely a process of conflicting forces. This metaphysics of life is articulated in terms of a metaphysics of art, which sees the conditioned, practical world as becoming, full of change, multiplicity, opposition, and contradiction.[71] This metaphysics of life then involves rank ordering, which evolves into a hierarchy of worlds, that correspond to degrees of power. As Stanley Rosen observes, Nietzsche's will to power 'places a premium on strength, health, vitality, fecundity, continuous self-overcoming, and in general the political and aesthetic values of a spiritual aristocracy that possess the physical strength and courage to flourish and to dominate.'[72] This is the best form of life for self-making.

Nietzsche then is a self-conscious modern who continues the questioning of the presuppositions of the mechanist tradition begun by Hegel. He reads the history of philosophy through a Platonic grid, bids farewell to an early form of what we now call the physicalist/mechanism of a scientific culture, and replaces it with a process philosophy, as part of his attempt to bring philosophy back to its roots of historical human beings living within the city.[73] The radically Platonist nature of Nietzsche's aristocratic politics operates with an evaluative ethical/political philosophy concerned with good and evil, and which functions as a form of cultural critique. Philosophy's entry into the city is a turning against the traditions of the modern city. This aims to overcome the decadent world of the liberal Enlightenment by destroying it, to create new values for the happy, noble few.

Evaluating Nietzsche's critique

Nietzsche does shift the ground as he evaluates science and metaphysics from the ethical perspective of the good life, with its conception of positive freedom as self-creation. This is the case, despite the inadequacy of his attack on scientific culture that centres around the lack of critical reason within a scientific culture alienated from the context of everyday life. Nietzsche concedes to modern science—with its synthesis of classical atomism, experimentalism and mathematical modelling—the monopoly of knowledge, with its dream of the mastery of nature. He criticizes positivism's faith in its presuppositions, on the grounds that the presuppositions of science are grounded on faith rather than a critical reason. Nietzsche undercuts a positivist science's attack on faith as a tissue of superstitions, prejudices and errors, by indicating that such an enlightening science is likewise based on dogmatic presuppositions grounded on faith. In doing so, positivism undermines its own project. Nietzsche's denial of science's capacity for self-reflection can then be interpreted as a positivist science not being able to reflect on its own pre-suppositions, thereby blocking the very possibility of a self-critical science. This thesis was affirmed by Husserl when he argued that, as a consequence of the separation of science and philosophy in the empiricist tradition of science, a naive self-sufficiency in science developed, which resulted in an inability of science to examine its own pre-suppositions. This gave rise to the general crisis of science in the twentieth century, Husserl argued, because its objectivism blocks the view of the origin of scientific analysis in the life-world and allows the reality of the pre-scientific phenomena or life-world to be forgotten.[74]

Clearly Nietzsche's dogmatism thesis in relation to science is inadequate. It ignores the possibility of the self-critique of science, if one distinguishes between dogmatic and critical science. The hegemony of positivism that Nietzsche thundered against has been challenged through the development of a post-positivist science arising from the criticism of logical empiricism by Bachelard, Popper, Adorno, Kuhn, Lakatos, Feyerabend, and Habermas. Science itself has become critical and self-reflective, as the philosophy of science has been one of the most fertile areas in contemporary philosophy, with a vast literature over a very wide field.[75] This explodes any simple attempt to identify contemporary post-positivist science with the nineteenth-century positivism familiar to Nietzsche.[76] A deep process of self-criticism and self-correction has taken place, as the traditional positivist background framework about science—Carnap, Reichenbach, Popper and others—has been radically questioned. Science is now a social practice, embodied in socially situated communities of practitioners, which functions within a set of pre-suppositions or a common paradigm. In the words of Kuhn, science consists of a strong network of theories—conceptual, theoretical, instrumental, methodological, and metaphysical—which are historically informed.[77] The questioning of scientific realism by empiricists who hold the laws and theories of science to be instruments for predictions, and by conventionalists who hold that the laws and theories are mostly conventions, and so can be resolved by definition or stipulation, indicates that science reflects on its own metaphysical presuppositions.[78] Science is a cultural product with conflicting forms, with their different traditions, radically different conceptual schemes, and ways of seeing the world with different mixes of ideology and knowledge. Given our current awareness of the historicity of different forms of science, Nietzsche's dogmatism thesis about the lack of critical self-reflection in a scientific culture must be rejected.

However the conclusion that Nietzsche did not shift the ground of science—symbolized in the early texts by the figure of a Socratic theoreticism which worships daylight and the clarity of reason—would be too quick. The first reason for rejecting this conclusion is that Nietzsche does bring science down to earth, as he holds that we cannot live in the purified air of bright, transparent, pure science existing outside of the everyday world. Science needs to be bought down to the muddy waters of Earth, where it has to swim and wade and get its feet dirty. His argument for this is based on the practical nature of knowledge, and its links to historically specific material interests.[79] For Nietzsche, knowledge works as a tool of power.[80] It is our needs that interpret the world, as we need to grasp a certain amount of reality in order to master it, and press it into service.[81]   We comprehend nature through a categorical framework for the purposes of mastering nature and preserving existence. We interpret the world through our needs, and so the basis of knowledge is human interest:

> "It is our needs that *interpret the world*; our drives and their For and Against. Every drive is a kind of lust to rule; each one has its perspective that it would like to compel all the other drives to accept as a norm."[82]

This will to power expresses the impulse of creation. The categories of reason are just means towards the adjustment of the world for utilitarian ends. Knowledge is power, a tool for coping with reality, and this means that we change our categories so as to fulfil our desires by making things more readily controllable. Nietzsche adds:

> "In order for a particular species to maintain and increase its power, its conception of reality must comprehend enough of the calculable and constant for it to base a scheme of behaviour on it. The utility of preservation—not some abstract or theoretical need not to be deceived—stands as the motive behind the development of the organs of knowledge—they develop in such a way that their observations suffice our preservation. In other words: the measure of the desire for knowledge depends upon the measure to which the will to power grows in a species: a species grasps a certain amount of reality, in order to master it, in order to press it into service."[83]

If we interrogate various forms of reason in history, we find that they are masks of the will to power. Our interpretations are influenced by history, for the individual, by virtue of being situated in a historical process, must adopt a limited and historically circumscribed perspective on the process itself, for only historically limited perspectives are possible.[84] He sees the entire apparatus of knowledge as an apparatus for abstraction and simplification— directed not at knowledge but at taking possession of things for our preservation.[85] Science is the 'transformation of nature into concepts for the purpose of mastering nature.'[86] It is premised on the 'desire to make comprehensible, the desire to make practical, useful, exploitable.'[87]

Nietzsche's power/knowledge claim, in which our knowledge and interests are deeply intertwined, locates him within the Baconian tradition of scientific knowledge as power, which holds that self-assertion is the driving force of modernity.[88] The perspective Nietzsche recovers in his return to the everyday world of appearances is an instrumental conception of science which is practically-orientated to our need to master nature for our self-preservation. The fiction of interest-free knowledge can only be sustained because the moorings of science in social practice, with its dream of the ultimate mastery of nature, remain obscured. As all knowledge necessarily pre-supposes some interests, knowledge can never be disinterested, and so is perspectival. The objectivity of science then is located within a particular system of values, and claims to truth are expressions of claims to power, or are a nexus of need, desires and interests. This is not Marxist baggage imposed on Nietzsche. Richard Miller, the Anglo-American philosopher of science, supports this thesis to the extent that he holds explanatory adequacy in science to be deeply influenced by human interests. He holds that 'explanatory adequacy is essentially pragmatic and field specific. Standard causal patterns change from field to field and time to time, depending on the strategies of investigation and their consequences under the circumstances; and yet they help to determine what is an adequate explanation, not just what is presently acceptable.'[89] He illustrates this with an example of a person driving to the store to seek cigarettes crashing into a drunken motorist careering down the road. Miller observes that there is a rationale for accepting:

"drunkenness and insufficient attention as explanations for car crashes, but not accepting being a smoker, when that was merely the motive for an unlucky errand. This rationale is practical. We can better pursue our practical concern about car crashes, viz., reducing their number, if we know more about the role of drunkenness and inattention in causing them."[90]

This pragmatic thesis that the standard causal pattern of our scientific activity is guided by practical interests results from our scientific theory and inquiry being social practices, in which different people engage in different projects, which are organized by socially acceptable rules within particular forms of life. Hermeneutic philosophy supplements Miller's account by showing how the research process is formed by the scientists having already acquired a pre-understanding about the meaning of their investigation, which is embedded within the horizon of a prior interpretation of meaning.[91]

The second reason for holding that Nietzsche did indeed shift the ground of evaluating science is that Nietzsche links science to ethical considerations of a healthy life worth living. In raising the issue of value perspective in relation to life, Nietzsche poses the body as the suppressed other of scientific reason. He signifies the claim of particularity against universality; a particularity of a body embedded in history, power and suffering. This particularity is given a voice, and its suffering made visible. This ethical standpoint can be illustrated by considering the situation of Malcolm. He eases his provincial aloneness in the polluted modern city by visiting his mother in a country hospital. She is dying of cancer of the throat, and is in great pain. In this situation Malcolm holds that medical science should do more than give us the truth about the invisible causes of the pain in the chest and shoulders, the continual coughing and breathlessness, the increasing unsteadiness of the legs and the terrifying anxiety at night. There is a value perspective here, as medical science should step beyond truth, to be concerned with managing the pain through continual dosages of morphine so that the Malcolm's mother is comfortable. However achieving this quality of life is done in such a heavy-handed way at the country hospital, that the body becomes so drugged that the person is hardly aware of the world around her. She remains bed-ridden and is unable to converse with their family. She is just a drugged body kept alive by being connected up to machines. Malcolm attacks the country doctor for his inhumanity and impoverished mechanical conception of the quality of life— she is happy if there are no sounds of pain coming from the body—and he denounces the way science closes itself to her well-being. He says that the body's discourse should be given respect, as opposed to being treated as raw material in cybernetic technocratic system of the hospital which seeks to eliminate human frailty as a weak link in the system. He moves his mother into a hospice where the goal of truth of medical research is linked to palliative care and a quality of life for the whole person. Malcolm's mother achieves three extra months of quality of care, mobility and well-being in the hospice. The technical problems of pain management are linked to the ethical end of the person being able to live a full human life amongst others in the hospice. Here the value of science lies in its relationship to other human purposes and values. So we value truth on the grounds that one's needs and interests in liberation from suffering or oppression require as much truth about the way society, illness or disease work as possible.

Nietzsche places the question of ethical ends of science at centre stage because a scientific culture has displaced the Platonic-Christian metaphysics as the dominant strand and core component of European culture. We explain ourselves in terms of scientific knowledge and truth, which protects us from chaos, and in this protection from chaos and disorder through escaping from time, truth has a transcendental status. So science needs to be examined in terms of its relationship to life. The question that Nietzsche is asking is: "Does science's concern with the ideal of truth need to be evaluated to see whether it helps us to affirm the value of life?" Nietzsche answers this by saying that a positivist scientific interpretation of the world is one which is the poorest in terms of meaning. An autonomous science pursued for its own sake, with its will to truth, is an interpretation of the world of human valuation, in terms of the calculator and mechanics. Science's truth of this world as a mechanism makes our world an essentially meaningless world.[92] In this sense, science is a closed system of will, goal and interpretation which holds itself to be self-sufficient, and Nietzsche's critique of a positivist science from a value perspective, is along the lines that a positivist science is only an instrument for measuring and arranging mirrors, and that is has no goal beyond truth. A scientific culture with its commitment to absolute truth cannot help us create new forms of life beyond nihilism; it prevents free spirits from engaging in self-transformation, and the revaluation of values in the form of will to power that is necessary with the end of the old Platonic-Christian valuation. Science is unable to engage in a process of self-criticism with respect to its presuppositions around the goal of truth in such a way that helps us to affirm the value of life.

155

Radical implications were drawn by Adorno and Horkheimer about an Enlightenment culture from their reading of Nietzsche's thesis about the interest-based knowledge of science linked to a good life. Nietzsche's claims that science is always relative to a perspective on specific circumstances and is grounded on social interests, was linked it to Lukács' critique of positivist science reflecting the appearances of capitalism and the reification resulting from the capitalist division of labour.[93] They provide a critique of science and technology from a left perspective, as they argued in the *Dialectic of Enlightenment* that a universal Enlightenment rationality is the project of the domination of nature and human beings. Science offers provisional explanations of the regularities and underlying causal patterns of society and nature, yet science is located within contradictory and oppressive social relations of control and domination. The result is that science has become an instrument for the technical control, practical mastery and domination of nature, as with the natural sciences, and the control and administration of human beings in the bourgeois social order, as with the behavioural sciences. Science did not lead to a healthy good life. In becoming an instrument of the state's policy to ensure social order science has helped to ensure an unhealthy life for the majority. Adorno and Horkheimer say:

> "Even the deductive form of science reflects hierarchy and coercion. Just as the first categories represented the organized tribe and its power over the individual, so the whole given logical order, dependency, connection, progression, and union of concepts is grounded in the corresponding conditions of social reality—that is, of the social division of labour. But of course this social character of categories of thought is not, as Durkheim asserts an expression of social solidarity, but evidence of the inscrutable unity of society and domination. Domination lends increased consistency and force to the social whole in which it establishes itself."[94]

To this end the sciences have valorized methods that were most effective and successful in the domination of nature. So criteria of utility, efficiency, and success have guided their endeavour, whilst the modes of calculation, quantification and formalization have been privileged. Enlightenment rationality championed the systems of mathematical physics and formal logic as models of truth, with all other modes of though being deemed to be inferior and ineffective: 'for the Enlightenment whatever does not conform to the rule of computation and utility is suspect...Enlightenment is totalitarian.'[95]

In so shifting the grounds for the criticism of the presuppositions of philosophical and scientific systems as tools for mastering nature Nietzsche can be seen to be an earlier precursor of the crisis of modernity. He understands its implications and confronts its legacy. Standing amidst the dissatisfactions of modernity he endeavours to step outside the institution of philosophy, with its traditional focus on epistemology and metaphysics, and to shift to the broader concern of the problem of value in modernity. As a poet philosopher Nietzsche operates as a public intellectual who sounds out the idols in the city, because he is concerned with the problem of sickness of the culture of modernity. Hence the continuing importance of Socrates for him.[96] His creative concerns with revaluing all values, and the ranking of value as a way out of the bourgeois sickness, involve continuing the destructive process of kicking away the props of absolute grounds, stable identities and unfissured continuities that bourgeois life in modernity depends upon. He confronts the fact that modernity is a world of Christian ruins overgrown by large and small weeds, and so constitutes a dying civilization. Humanity needs to be freed from its illusions, if there is to be the necessary creative transvaluation of values.

In shifting the ground, Nietzsche's gay science, which stands in opposition to system builders, lives dangerously. It is the consummation of the self-assertion of modernity, not its farewell, as Habermas claims, with its reactionary rejection of modernity and a sentimental return to the past. Nietzsche holds that modernity needs to overthrow itself in the name of the self-overcoming of the noble *Ubermensch,* who eternally self-creates and self-develops himself:

> "at the end of this tremendous process, where the tree at last brings forth fruit, where society and the morality of custom at last reveal *what* they have simply been the means to: then we discover the ripest fruit is the *sovereign individual,* like only to himself, liberated again from morality of custom, autonomous and supramoral (for "autonomous" and "moral" are mutually exclusive)."[97]

This is the emancipated individual with the actual right to make promises, is a master of a free will. As a sovereign man he has mastery over himself, over circumstances, over nature and over more short-willed and unreliable creatures. This human being of the future, who is concerned with the overcoming of nihilism, conditioned by the ascetic ideal, is the voice of Zarathustra.[98] This is the modern, spiritually sensitive individual who grapples with nihilism (the contemporary crisis in values in the wake of the collapse of the Christian world-view that assigned humanity a clear place in the world). It is his sense of self-assertion over nature that allows us to read Nietzsche along Heideggerian lines as being the consummation and exhaustion of the technological metaphysics of modernity. Nietzsche's new ethics of self-creation reduces nature to the artefact of a strong will is still dreams the dream of modernity, with its craving for absolute mastery and absolute freedom. The highest goal of the good life in this ethics of creativity is a being who conquers his own world by making his will a law unto itself. In endeavouring to create a higher form of life such a being transcends the world of human beings living within the constraints of ecosystems they are a part of. He becomes god-like as he overcomes his humanity by mastering necessity and seeking reconciliation with eternity. [99]

157

Nietzsche's philosophy of overcoming retreats from this extreme, but in doing so, it lives dangerously in a political sense. The problem that Nietzsche faces is that those living in bourgeois society are not yet prepared to destroy it. This problem is explored in *Thus Spake Zarathustra*. Zarathustra repudiates the citizenry of the town called Motley Cow, as they are not prepared for his message of overcoming. They prefer a lingering death from self-destruction in modernity. He denounces the radical egalitarianism of the mob that is corrupting society. Zarathustra speaks directly to the representatives of the higher men in the belief that they will understand him and enact his teaching.[100] The process of the self-overcoming of nihilism is part of a critique of modernity and involves the critique of philosophy and the proposal of a new direction for philosophy. Values are foregrounded by the noble free spirits or the philosophers of the future, who are concerned to undermine the tyranny of old values, and to create a new order of values in their project of cultural renewal. The future philosophical physician, who is concerned with the health, future, growth, power and life of a people, is to question more deeply, severely, harshly than these have been questioned before, as part of the ongoing process of constantly transforming all that we are.[101] The true philosophers of the future then aim their arrow at the heart of the dogmatists, clear the stage of their prejudices and decayed philosophy by applying a knife to the virtues of their time as part of the process of creating a space for and developing alternatives about the value of life.[102] When the representatives of the higher types visit Zarathustra in his cave for the last supper, it is clear that the doctrines of the revolutionary philosopher, who wears the mask of the religious prophet, are not understood by the representatives. These are useful in overcoming the petty lying mob, since today belongs to the mob.[103]

The aim of his masked rhetoric is to drive the base representatives of the higher types to their destruction by intensifying their evil actions. This helps to prepare the ground for the next generation of supermen who do not yet exist, and to whom he sends his coded message: the corrupt representatives of the higher men—including the conscientious representative of science who seeks security in the mastery of nature—are to be overcome.[104] Zarathustra's guests become the cud-chewers, who forget the will to overcome, and have a festival where they worship the ass, drunk with wine. Zarathustra recommends they have more joyous festivals.[105] This reactive response of the celebration of absurdity is the sign of a dying age, and so marked by the defects of the age and not by the virtues of overcoming. As the beast of burden, this ass represents the mob and the burden of tradition. It is a dangerous time, because the carnival is but one step from the madhouse. Life may be a madhouse for the many, but Nietzsche advocates that the noble few dig their way out through the transvaluation of values to become lords of the earth. This retreat from Zarathustra's perilous ambition to command eternity and become a god, embraces a notion of the good society with aristocratic social institutions, in which the political sphere is made subservient to cultural and ethical ends. Philosophy has entered the public realm in the city.

But Nietzsche does not make Rorty's liberal ironist distinction of the private as the project of self overcoming, self-creation and the pursuit of autonomy, and the public as having to do with the suffering of human beings through the attempt to minimize cruelty and work for social justice.[106] The public and the private is fused for Nietzsche, rather than being Rorty's two irreconcilable language games.[107]

Sounding out the idol of science

If we repudiate Nietzsche's aristocratic politics we need to ask: "What is left of Nietzsche's project of revaluing all values by the philosopher/physicians concerned with cultural renewal in a nihilistic modernity?" "Is there anything here for we ragpickers, who desire to develop a counter-movement to scientistic materialism?" Nietzsche's ethics of knowing directs us to view the relationship between a realist science with a physicalist metaphysics and human life. This metaphysics provide us with security by explaining phenomena in nature with no inherent values. But we should view this with suspicion, as the security of knowledge comes at a cost. This science operates with a movement of reversal in the name of scientific truth. Our encultured human experience of pain and suffering is truncated by this science, as it rejects our commonsense beliefs within everyday life as mere folk beliefs. It recoils from the commonsense image of everyday life to the true world as represented by a mechanistic physics. Its reductionist metaphysics wrenches human beings from their everyday sensuous emotionally-laden world of human suffering into the transcendent, timeless, ahistorical reality of neurophysiology, physics and high-tech cybernetic systems. The realism operating here is a metaphysical realism, which implies a notion of objectivity whose stance or vantage point is external to historical modes of thought and speech. This stood truth on its head, as this truth is explicated from no perspective at all. Truth here is independent of all human interests, rather than a more fallible notion of a cultural bound objectivity. Once truth transcends all human interest, it makes unintelligible the goal or purpose of science as a social practice in relationship to nature. Truth needs to be returned to its feet in common life. The ethics of knowing holds that as human interests and needs condition our knowledge, then knowledge and truth should be linked to freedom and the good life. So philosophers of the future as free spirits need to explore the relationship between knowledge and freedom.

This exploration is beginning to happen amongst those philosophers who are dissatisfied with analytic philosophy. Hilary Putnam's work for instance, represents a shift out of the materialist's conception of the universe as a giant machine, in which we humans are just subsystems in the machine. Putnam describes his step away from this picture of the universe in terms of a shift from the big "R" realism of metaphysical realism with its God's-Eye view to the small "r" realism of perspectival realism grounded on commonsense located in our everyday world. Metaphysical realism understands truth in a

159

certain way, which Putnam characterizes as holding to the view that there is one true theory. Small "r" realism, in contrast, fully acknowledges that there can be more than one truthful perspective on a particular state of affairs. Putnam says that metaphysical realism:

> "presents itself as a powerful transcendental picture: a picture in which there is a fixed set of "language-independent objects (some of which are abstract and others are concrete) and a fixed "relation" between the terms and their extensions...There is nothing wrong at all with holding onto our realism with a small "r" and jettisoning the Big "R" realism of the philosophers."[108]

The content that is packed into the big "R" metaphysical realism is unpacked by Putnam as the position of the cosmic exile which gives us an external perspective on ourselves. He defines this perspective as the thesis that:

> "The world consists of some fixed reality of mind-independent objects. There is exactly one true and complete description of "the way the world is." Truth involves some sort of correspondence relation between words or thought signs and external things and sets of things. I shall call this the *externalist* perspective, because its favourite point of view is a God's Eye view."[109]

Truth is not relational in metaphysical realism, as it talks in terms of the inner structure of the physical world being independent of its appearances, and its true nature being independent of how it can culturally appear. So the truth of the theory does not include in its picture of the world the way the world appears to observers or actors. The conventional appearances of the everyday world that we live in are pushed aside, so that physics gains access to the one determinate structure of the way things are, independent of all human interpretation. The big dream is that a unified science can ultimately gives us the goal of absolute truth of the giant machine that is the universe. So truth corresponds to with a discourse-independent state of affairs. The general deconstructive argument against metaphysical realism made by the more "humanist", revisionist analytic philosophers, such as Wittgenstein, Putnam and Rorty, is a historicist one that follows the path cut by Nietzsche. The general stance of their criticism holds that metaphysical realism's goal of absolute truth can only be obtained by being outside history as it involves a God's-Eye view of reality. It is argued that such an Archimedean point is a hopeless confusion, since the only answers we can ever hope to have about the fundamental furniture of the universe comes from ourselves who are inside human history.

Putnam argues that a physicalist ontology is strongly reductionism, as it holds that the secondary qualities of the object are human projections caused by the objects with their primary qualities. A projection is thinking of something having properties it does not have, and so it is not a part of the furniture of the universe as given by physics. In the world according to physics, appearances and values are merely something we project onto the object.[110] Putnam unpacks this with the doctrine of primary and secondary qualities in Descartes' mechanism and Newtonian mechanics.[111] It presupposes both an atomist ontology, which holds that a material object is a collection of particles, and a dualistic picture of the physical world, with its primary or real properties of size shape and location on the one hand, and to be distinguished from secondary colours like colours, mind and "raw feels" on the other. The claim is that the red poster has a power or disposition to affect me in certain ways, to have a sense data or raw feel, or to produce certain sorts of states in our brains and nervous systems, which we then project onto the object. The red poster is not red in itself, as common-sense realism holds. The implication of this, says Putnam, is that our common sense view of the world which we experience ourselves living within, is held to be projection, that is, merely thought. Commonsense representations of nature are held to be one of illusion, and so false, whilst those of science are held to be real, and so true. So reality in the form of a chair is what physics says it is, independently of the false appearances of the manifest image of the chair, which forms Maya's veil over the way things really are. The manifest image, our commonsense picture of the coloured world of tables and chairs, love and fear, meaning, value and freedom, is held to be false, dismissed as a folk psychology and mere poetry, for science only allows spatio-temporally located bodies, whose internal structures and external relations determine and limit the appearance and disappearance of everything that happens.[112]

Jack Smart's physicalist picture of our place in nature illustrates the steps a metaphysical realist needs to take to hold the cosmic thesis of science seeing the physical world as a gigantic machine being independent of its appearances. Its picture of the universe must exclude the experience of humans as expressed in their cultural traditions. Smart steps beyond the apparent world of everyday life by reducing our commonsense representations in ordinary language to the scientific language of neurophysiology and information theory. Consequently:

> "We avoid colour words and words for tastes, smells and sounds, because this vocabulary is too closely bound up with the particular circumstances of the human sense organs and nervous system to be of cosmic interest...this helps us to see the world in a way which is not too anthropocentric or too dependent on a particular perspective in space-time."[113]

This cashes out into our moral discourse containing words like 'synapse' and 'binary digit', but not 'belief' or 'desire'. To get to the God's-Eye view of Newtonian physics, metaphysical realism devalues the humble tarnished coming-to-be and passing-away of everyday human life. The ontological core of this physicalism is that the world and all its parts is nothing but a complicated physical mechanism, made up of lots of elementary particles buzzing around. So Smart's utilitarian moral philosophy, which links knowledge to morality, assigns the human world only derivative value, starts from the axiom that we are sophisticated utility machines in a timeless world under the sign of eternity. Social meanings and values about the good life are like colours in that they are a projection by us onto the world. Value and meaning become personal preferences of the naturalized body that lead to mechanistic action. The dream of a description of physical reality, as it is apart from observers, means that reference to non-physical things like historical meanings and cultural values is almost impossible, as these are not part of the furniture of the world. It is impossible for this physicalist scientism to give a historical account of itself as a cultural tradition within the form of life of modernity, since truth is independent of observers and social actors altogether. Smart explicitly rejects the historicist thesis that scientific and metaphysical theories impose an important core of cultural tradition and values onto the world. This is to walk on the slippery slope of idealism, and to avoid it, interpretation must be naturalized.[114] This does not understand itself as a description of the world as experienced by those living in capitalist society with an Enlightenment culture. It denies that this naturalist metaphysics is of a particular time and place, and so it is a cultural tradition constructed by analytic philosophers in the late twentieth century who use their reason as a capacity to systematize and justify their speculative metaphysics. The human way of talking about colour, tradition and value has to be rejected, says Smart as it 'would not be suitable for conversation with an extra-terrestrial rational being (a denizen of some planet of a distant state, for example) who might have a very different visual system.'[115] Although Smart acknowledges that concepts in ordinary practical life are highly contextual and dependent on particular human interests, he holds that they can be relegated to second-grade discourse. They are not suitable for science or metaphysics.

Resolving an incoherence

The incoherence within this physicalist metaphysics lies within the tension between formal reason as formal logic and a realist science that is empirically grounded. Formalism assumes method to be a neutral, formal set of rules and procedures which speaks in the voice of no particular social individuals. It pre-supposes the observer standing outside all language, translating from an everyday language into a formal language. Knowledge and truth are disembodied, abstracted and separated from the everyday world. These are impersonal, and so the God's Eye view reappears. Yet the empiricism within scientific realism implies that empiricists develop a general knowledge of the world out of particular experiences that humans have through sensory stimulations. A philosophical translation manual is then used to re-work these sensations, embodied in the indeterminate and vague signs of everyday language, into the clear signs of the formal language of hard science. But why one model? Why not several? Presumably because the ideal system of science would contain everything that could be justified as true or false from the transcendental standpoint of a total science. What underpins scientism's metaphysics is a conception of reference that holds that science reflects the built-in structures of the world. Science has direct access to this structure, as it singles out the one correspondence between signs and their objects, and gives us the one single absolute version of the world. However the reference between sign and object here is a feature of the organism-cum-environment, and what we count as referring depends on our background knowledge, social interests, and the process of interpretation. The denial of the historical, means that reference is a physical relation somehow built into the causal structure of the world. To read the social into the natural, to call the latter the true ready-made world, and to call that a total explanation, is a scientized philosophy gone made. It ignores the subject in the everyday world, who lives within a commonsense historically formed world, as well as operating as a scientific philosopher within a scientific discourse. Incoherence arises at this point, since the suffering, historical, philosophical subject is hardly a projection upon the furniture of the world. As Roger Scruton says, though we are a part of nature obedient to natural laws, a smile of another human being is more than human flesh moving in obedience to impulses in the nerves. We also understand a smile in terms of making it intelligible in terms of cultural meaning. So a smile is always more than flesh for us, even if it is only flesh.[116] As we have many different ways of talking about the world we live in, so we need to take into account the way that reference is relative to the discourses and social relations we culturally work within.

Smart's omniscient observer assumption is metaphysics gone mad. It is wild ontological extravagance which is a dressed-up prejudice of modernity, a pious pose on behalf of disinterested reason still inflected with religiosity. To put it simply, the sentences of the ideal language live in a Platonic heaven of the one true theory. We haven't got there yet, but the one true theory resides there whether we know it or not. If physicalist metaphysics is to be consistent, it needs to naturalize interpretation and reason. Hooker advocates the biological embedding of reason as a way of stepping beyond the tensions inherent in physicalist materialism. He sees formal reason as being bogged down in paradox and impotence:

> "Briefly the critique of empiricism comes to this: formal reason (logic) lacks the resources to construct the edifice of scientific theory from any plausible observational foundation, and it also lacks the resources to critically determine membership in the foundation, so science cannot be understood as a product of empiricist reason. Empiricism has a radically incomplete characterization of scientific rationality which illustrates the difficulties generated from pursuing a formal conception of reason."[117]

He regards this as a degenerating research programme that needs to be replaced with another more positive programme; one where 'cognition is theorized as the information face of biological self-organization, at sufficient regulatory sophistication, with judgements as the basic units of organization.'[118]. He holds that naturalized reason is a natural feature of living systems, evolving as part of intelligence; intelligent systems are best characterized in terms of regulation or control processes, not logico-symbolic ones. Living systems are modelled as part of a dynamic self-organizing adaptive process which sees people as strategic adaptive systems pursuing complex goals. A functional system, or naturalized servo-mechanisms which interact with their environment, is one where the adaptive processes include 'both adaptation and adaptability, that is, (respectively) alteration of specific traits so as to increase fitness in their environment and alteration of these alteration processes.'[119]

The problem with Hooker's revision of formal reason in physicalist naturalism is that in naturalizing reason he assumes that these self-organizing adaptive systems have a body which is pre-social and biological. This reduces the complexities of social relationships, social purpose or meaning in a nation state to self-survival in a meaningless, valueless universal world of nature. Even though Hooker takes seriously the idea that human bodies provide a basis and contribute to knowledge, his reductionism results in a devaluation of our particular life in historical time. There is no conception of the humble, tarnished coming-to-be and passing-away of historical everyday life, in which there are marked gender and ethnic differences which alter the characteristics of bodies. Hooker fails to see that the biological body, as a functional system, is an unfinished body, as the materiality of the body requires us to see the body as a social entity. Acts of labour are required to develop and hold the physical shape of bodies to learn how to present the body skilfully through styles of walking, talking and dressing. The body of the strategic adaptive systems pursuing complex goals, bears the imprint of an individual's gender and social class, as it learns to adapt socially to the social environment of the university bureaucracy, so that it can engage in the complex behaviour of philosophical research of revising a theoretical system. The brain processes of the social animal interpenetrate in complex ways with its social interests, cultural traditions with their normative values, and the material conditions of social life. Philosophy is a form of writing, and so it is a culturally bound reflection and argument within the economics of research and publishing in a capitalist economy. Hooker's naturalized reason needs to offer an account of reason within the *Lebenswelt* in which we daily live and work before it is reasonable. Philosophy, after all, is one of the humanities and not a natural science.

Smart talks in terms of the historical and interest-based concepts of ordinary practical life being a second-order discourse that is highly convenient for practical activities and social intercourse, but not suitable for metaphysics. But there is a metaphysics in the everyday, which is highlighted by Nietzsche's emphasis on the suffering of the historical human body. This undercuts the utilitarian conception of the rational individual as a utility machine increasing his fitness in their environment by efficiently satisfying his desires. Nietzsche's emphasis is on the frailty of individual beings, who are buffeted about by the winds of history, and moved by the pressure of all manner of contradictory threats, expectations, and rewards of others within an already-formed ethical life in which we commonly dwell. This challenges the utilitarian assumption that we are free-sailing architects of our destiny in the marketplace, by holding that we are raw and incomplete at birth, and so require finishing through education, therapy and disciplining through a process of working on oneself—of giving style to oneself, of creating oneself, of shaping and transforming oneself. This process of valuation is concerned with questions about the rationality of ends of the health-giving, and self-creating growth of social human beings. So scientistic materialism does secrete a metaphysics of the social, which oozes out of the social ontology buried in its utilitarianism.

Consider the way the egoism of isolated and self-sufficient utility machines as bundles of elementary particles buzzing around forms the core content of a metaphysical morality locked into a reductive materialist world view. A socio-biological science gives a scientific explanation of the egoistic foundation of desire as little atomic impulses of self-seeking, which provide us with our way of valuation as utility machines. A utilitarian morality is primarily concerned with the internal completeness and consistency of an individual's preference, and the connection between preference and choice. Value is placed on natural human desire as preference-satisfaction. Given the difficulty of making interpersonal comparisons of the well-being of different individuals, and the identification of preference-satisfaction with welfare, the underlying logic of utilitarianism is to construct a system of morality to ensure that life is not solely nasty, brutish and short. This is structured around what a life without morality would be, given the logic of a self-interested utility machine seeking to maximize its utility. As self-interest functions as a foundational given in utilitarianism, the system of morality performs the vital function of preventing the world from being a Hobbesian one of a raw, cruel and blood-soaked place through pursuing our best interests to maximize our advantage. The problem of order is resolved by economic science through a welfarism, which is based on aggregating individual welfare through perfect competition. So perfectly competitive equilbria are morally desirable, and imperfections that interfere with the achievement of competitive equilbria are deemed morally undesirable. But this form of welfarism does not help with those states of affairs that improve the preference-satisfaction of some people, while harming others. Unemployment of some, as the price for economic growth for the many, is a classic example. This, coupled with well-being as the satisfaction of preferences, means it has a problem with the dissatisfactions of the minority who are harmed. This edges utilitarianism towards an authoritarian system of morality as a set of rules that have to obeyed, in response to an undesirable state of affairs caused by our desires. It is simply a matter of what changes produce the most welfare, given the mechanical levers that are available to the state to manage the economic machine.

The moral stance of metaphysical realism—the impersonal and impartial one of the ideal observer—then functions as a counter to the fundamentally egoistic stance in a nihilistic everyday world. Bernard Williams describes the Ideal Observer theory as postulating either 'one omniscient, impartial and benevolent observer—he might be called the world agent—who acquires everybody's preferences and puts them together', or the 'omniscient, disinterested, dispassionate, but otherwise normal' observer who surveys the world from the outside in a dispassionate spirit.[120] The observer's motivation is to bring about the most welfare or utility, and this should be done in the most efficient manner. The Ideal Observer becomes the Ideal Legislator in the well-ordered society, who benevolently makes the trade-offs between different objectives. In the well-ordered society of 'cosmic' utilitarianism, in which society mirrors nature, individual bodies in the social machine are like the parts of the watch. These cyborg bodies can be sacrificed to achieve total happiness, by a rationality dedicated to efficient system maintenance of society conceptualized as the smooth functioning machine, to which bodies adapt.[121] This undermines the modern stress on individual freedom, in which each machine is the best judge of its happiness. The liberal stress on the autonomy of the individual is liquidated by the smoothly functioning machine.

From a Nietzschean perspective the Platonic moral stance of metaphysical realism, in the form of the impersonal and impartial stance of the ideal observer, functions to counter the anxiety of subjective decisions within the egoistic stance. It is the coherent solution to the decisionism inherent in utilitarian moral philosophy. This materialist ethics reduces interest to emotional disposition, which is then coded as natural. Reason is an instrument to satisfy desire as instinctual impulses, which are not susceptible to rational argument. Hence the metaphysical need for the Ideal Legislator to step into the breach where the force of argument cannot reach. This signifies the return of myth to sustain the Enlightenment progress of reason. Universal reason requires myth and the projection of harmonistic illusion to unify the splintering of reason and desire, reason and action that flow from the destructive consequences of the Enlightenment project itself. Utilitarian reason, as instrumental reason in its pure form of pragmatic calculation, endeavours to deflect the consequences of the Enlightenment of rationality reduced to self-preservation with harmonistic doctrines. Reason rules the world in the form of the Ideal Legislator, who controls the irrationality of the world of desire deriving from the different subjective objectives of bourgeois individuality. This is politics appearing in the guise of morality, which functions as a pseudo-ethical façade on an egoistic background to avoid the lapse into irrationality and the chaos of capitalism. It is necessary to sustain the fiction that bourgeois life is the embodiment of reason.

The myth of the capitalist state as a benevolent Ideal Legislator is that it mystifies the way the state has historically sustained the domination of human beings by other human beings in capitalism. Here in late modernity the objective necessity of the social order as an economic machine, as disclosed by social scientists and bureaucratic experts, comes to predominate over the decisions made by politicians in a cybernetically self-regulating society.[122] The politicians function as managers of the system, who are guided by Treasury economists, with their own political and social engineering agenda. Habermas describes this process as follows:

"The dependence of the professional on the politician appears to have reversed itself. The latter becomes a mere agent of a scientific intelligentsia which, in concrete circumstances, elaborates the objective implications and requirements of available techniques and resources as well as of optimal strategies and rules of control....The politician would then be at best something like a stopgap in a still imperfect rationalisation of power, in which the initiative has in any case passed to scientific analysis and technical planning."[123]

Rational administration, guided by scientific insight into what is objectively necessary for stability, growth and adaptability of the economic machine means the end of Enlightenment for the majority. What is necessary are public relations and promotion to secure for the enlightened bourgeoisie the loyalty of a depoliticized public. Weber's thesis of rationalisation—the subjection of increasing domains of action and interaction to formal, abstract, uniform and predictable rules and regulations in the form of the hierarchal bureaucracies—has proceeded to the extent of making economic science an instrument of those in power seeking to sustain their domination.

The forgotten history of this scientistic Enlightenment, covered up by the Platonic myth of the Ideal Legislator, was excavated by Foucault's history of the birth of modern prisons, and the extension of the carceral system to other bureaucratic institutions. This suggests that the spread of this system through the social world is accompanied by a corresponding shaping of people into normal, as opposed to abnormal, delinquent and deviant. This develops hand in hand with the social sciences, which are implicated in the normalisation process. The process of normalisation is an imposition of a model of well-ordered activity on all aspects of social life; a process of inculcating discipline into individuals through technologies developed in prisons, armies, and schools. Social sciences, like economics and psychology, are concerned with the control of human behaviour, and the crisis management role of adapting human behaviour to a bad reality. Here citizens are seen as objects or moving bodies, whose behaviour in terms of observable events is able to be controlled and manipulated within a given set of social relations which are naturalised. Scientific criteria are then appealed to, in order to claim that the whole functioning mechanism of society, and the steering decisions made by social administrators, are rationally ordered. This means of controlling people makes the person into a personnel sub-system—a cybernetic organism—in a complex machine system, by training them to adapt rationally to the predefined and pre-programmed purposes and goals of the social institution of the market. A scientized philosophy, concerned with the underlying mechanisms in a reality behind appearances, tacitly functions within the historical world of appearances as the purveyor of myth of the Ideal Legislator. It is myth as mass deception, put about by the philosopher priests, whose cultural meaning is that we should accept that our destructive form of life produced by a capitalist Enlightenment is the best of all possible worlds. Enlightenment has turned into its other.

Conclusion

Nietzsche, as Habermas rightly notes, does pose a real challenge to the philosophical Enlightenment discourse on modernity. His location within this discourse shifts the argument, as he endeavours to explode modernity's husk of unreason residing in the Enlightenment tradition. But contrary to the irrational thesis of Habermas, Nietzsche does not leap out of the dialectic of Enlightenment, bidding it farewell, only to embrace myth as the other of Platonic reason. Nietzsche embodies reason in his Dionysian programme of cultural renewal, based on his process metaphysics for artists. The critical capacity for assessing value is located in the lived experience of the socialized human body, which gives central place to the embodied structures of understanding by which we grasp the world. Nietzsche returns to the everyday world from the mountain top, and his success in finding his way back to the everyday world makes his philosophy a counter discourse to the God's-Eye-view of metaphysical realism of universal scientific and moral reason. He forged a link between self and the everyday world around the suffering of the human body, and his turn towards an ethics that affirms the life of the healthy social animal, is in opposition to the diseased suffering in a nihilistic modernity. Nietzschean embodiment is the uninvited guest in the analytic tradition who offers the basis for a different account of how meaning occurs. This provides a starting point for an oppositional criticism that takes the problem of ethical, suffering and valuation seriously. It prises us out of the peculiar moral institution, with its stripped down conception of ethics, that distorts our everyday embodied moral experience.

It also prises open the implicit politics in the physicalist naturalism tradition which holds that human beings as complex mechanisms, are component parts of the social body of the state. The abstract model is based on the relation of the individual to the state being the same as the relation of any physical system to its material components. The individual mechanism is abstracted out of the historical social relationships of individuals, with the state emerging out of the consequences of the actions of egoistic individuals. As a social body in motion, the society's harmony is undermined by the chaotic conflict caused by the changes of movement in its own egoistic parts. This requires the subordination of individual desires, emotion and self-fulfilment by the state using instrumental rationality to ensure system maintenance of the social body. This system-maintenance arises of necessity from the intrinsic character of the individual parts of the machinery, with the state as enlightened legislator holding at bay the horror and anarchy within an enlightened modernity. It repairs the breakdown in the components of the internal conflict in the machine, since the gears between the different machine components do not function smoothly. Since this malfunctioning is capable of threatening the peace and security of the social machine, the subordination of the individual to the smooth functioning of the social system is implicit in the logic of mechanism.

Notes and References

1   Friedrich Nietzsche, *The Will to Power,* trs. Walter Kaufmann, (Vintage, New York, 1968), Bk. 11, section 618, p. 332.

2   See P. Kitchner, *The Advancement of Science,* (Oxford University Press, Oxford, 1993).

3   Douglas Kellner, *Critical Theory, Marxism, and Modernity,* (Polity Press, Oxford, 1989), p. 179.

4   For some of the connections between industrial and scientific research and the military-industrial complex in the U.S refer to, David Noble, *Forces of Production: A Social History of Industrial Automation,* (Alfred A. Knopf, New York, 1984).

5   For the way the cyborg world is structured by military paradigms, refer to, Les Levidow & Kevin Roberts, *Cyborg Worlds. The Military Information Society,* (Free Association Books, London, 1989).

6   The hegemony of a sophisticated analytic philosophy of science is so pervasive and subtle that in an earlier work we collapsed perspectivism into relativism. See Joseph Wayne Smith, Graham Lyons, & Gary Sauer-Thompson, *Healing a Wounded World,* (Praeger, Wesport, 1997), p. 81. Not all perspectives are of equal value in the situated knowledges of perspectivism. They are ranked. This is not so with relativism.

7   For one attempt to read Nietzsche in relation to Weber's thesis of the rationalization process and critical theory, see G. Strauth and B. S. Turner, *Nietzsche's Dance: Resentment, Reciprocity and Resistance in Social Life,* (Blackwell Oxford, 1988).

8   This works from Freud's reading of modernity, in which the demands of bourgeois civilization requires the repression of sexual desire and the formation of neurosis. It is reading that is refracted through Adorno.

9   Brian Ellis, *Truth and Objectivity,* (Basil Blackwell, Oxford, 1990), p. 264.

10   Ibid, p. 19.

11   This modernist dream is stated in Stephen Hawking, *A Brief History of Time: From the Big Bang to Black Holes,* (Bantam, New York,1988).

12   Brian Ellis, *Truth and Objectivity,* op. cit., p. 20.

13   Ibid, p. 2.

14   Papineau, *Philosopical Naturalism,* (Blackwell, Oxford, 1993), p. 9.

15   Paul Churchland, "Reduction, Qualia and the Direct Introspection of Brain States", *The Journal of Philosophy,* Vol. LXXXII, (Jan-Dec. 1985), pp. 8-28, citation p. 11.

16   For the connection between the mechanistic world view, systems language, computer science, artifical intelligence, and the blinkered strategic thinking of the Vietnam war refer to James B Gibson, *The Perfect War: TechnoWar in Vietnam,* (Atlantic Monthly Press, New York, 1987).

17   For an early insight into this, refer to, Richard Wolin, "Modernism vs. Postmodernism", *Telos,* vol. 62, (1984/5), pp. 9-29. For a statement of modeling society as a system rooted in nature, refer to, James Beniger, *The Control Revolution: Technological and Economic Origins of the Information Society,* (Harvard University Press, Cambridge, Massachusetts, 1986).

18   For one expession of this, refer to, John Ralston Saul, *Voltaire's Bastards: The Dictatorship of Reason in the West,* (Penguin, London, 1993).

19   This neo-positivist scientism is stated by Raymond Aaron who says: 'A society is not truly industrialized until the actions of men and the operation of institutions are in harmony with the spirit of industry. Provisionally, we have called the spirit of modern economy scientific. Fundamentally, industrialized societies may be called scientific, in

that both mechanization and productivity are the fruit of the scientific spirit and are the ultimate causes of both industralization and the progressive nature of the economy.' Raymond Aron, *The Industrial Society: Three Essays on Ideology and Development*, trs. T. Bottomore, (Weidenfield and Nicolson, London, 1967), p. 57.

20   Friedrich Nietzsche, *The Will to Power*, op.cit., Bk. 2, Section 410, p. 221.

21   Ibid, Bk. 2, section 418, pp. 224-5; 7 section 464, p. 256.

22   Jurgen Harbermas, *The Philosophical Discourse of Modernity: Twelve Lectures*, trs. Frederick Lawrence, (MIT Press, Cambridge. Massachusetts, 1987), p. 86.

23   Ibid, p. 96.

24   This is the received view of Nietzsche in the secondary literature. For a questoning of the plausibility of this interpretation, refer to Brian Leiter, "Perspectivism in Nietzsche's Genealogy of Morals", in Richard Schacht, (ed.), *Nietzsche, Genealogy, Morality*, (University of California Press, Berkeley, 1994), pp. 334-357.

25   Rorty defends liberalism from Nietzsche's affirmation of cruelty and denigration of liberal democracy by invoking the public/private distinction. He suggests that we split ourselves into private and public persons in order to maintain liberal values, and that we proceed differently in our public and private lives, in that we are free to constantly redefine our private identity, but refrain from continually redefining society's aims. Society remains a liberal polity which allows maximum personal liberty whilst minimizing cruelty. R. Rorty, *Contingency, Irony, Solidarity*, (Cambridge University Press, Cambridge, 1989).

26   F. Nietzsche, "Attempt at Self Criticism", in Nietzsche, *The Birth of Tragedy or: Hellenism and Pessimism*, trs. Walter Kaufmann, (Vintage Books, New York, 1967), pp. 18-19.

27   F. Nietzsche, *The Birth of Tragedy*, ibid, section 15, p. 97.

28   F. Nietzsche, "Schopenhauer as Educator", in *Untimely Mediations*, trs. R. J. Hollingdale, (Cambridge University Press, Cambridge, 1983). pp. 125-194

29   F. Nietzsche, "On Truth and Lie in an Extra-Moral Sense", in *The Portable Nietzsche*, (ed.), Walter Kaufman, (Penguin, Harmondsworth, 1976), pp. 46-47.

30   Arthur Danto, *Nietzsche as Philosopher*, (Macmillian, New York,1965); Alexander Nehamas, Nietzsche: *Life as Literature*, (Harvard University Press, Cambridge Massachusetts, 1985); Alan Schrift, *Nietzsche and the Question of Interpretation*, (Routledge, New York, 1990).

31   F. Nietzsche, *The Gay Science*, trs. Walter Kaufmann, (Vintage, New York, 1974), Bk. 5, para. 374, pp. 336-7.

32   M. Horkheimer, "The Latest Attack on Metaphysics," in Horkheimer, *Critical Theory. Selected Essays*, trs. by M. J. O'Connell et el, (Continum, New York, 1986), pp. 183-4.

33   Nietzsche, *Will to Power, An Attempted Transvaluation of All Values*, trs. Walter Kaufman and R. J. Hollindale (Vintage, New York, 1968), Bk. 3, section 466, p. 261.

34   Nietzsche, *Daybreak*, trs. R. J. Hollingdale, (Cambridge University Press, Cambridge, 1982), section 45.

35   Hegel, *The Phenomenology of Spirit*, trs. A. V. Miller, (Oxford University Press, London, 1977), para, 73, p. 46.

36   Nietzsche, quoted in Habermas, *Knowledge and Human Interests*, (Beacon Press, Boston, 1971), p. 298.

37   Nietzsche, *The Will To Power*, op. cit., Bk 111, "Principles of a New Evaluation", section 584, pp. 314-15; also section 516, pp. 279-80.

38   For the aesthetic turn refer to, James J. Winchester, *Nietzsche's Aesthetic Turn: Reading Nietzsche after Heidegger, Deleuze and Derrida*, (State Univesity of New York Press, Albany, 1994).

39   Nietzsche, *Human, All-Too-Human* , in *Collected Works*,(ed.) Oscar Levy, (Russell and Russell, N.Y. 1964), vol.6, section 635.

40   Nietzsche, "'Reason' in Philosophy", in *The Twilight of the Idols*, Section 3, in Kaufman, (ed.) *The Portable Nietzsche*, op. cit., p. 481.

41   Nietzsche, *The Will To Power*, op. cit., Bk. 111, section 594, p. 324.

42   Nietzsche, *The Gay Science*, op. cit., Bk. 4, section 335, p. 266.

43   Ibid, Bk. 5, section 344, p. 280.

44   Nietzsche, *Will To Power*, op. cit., vol. 11, Bk. 3, section 481, p. 12.

45   Nietzsche, *The Gay Science*, op. cit., Bk 3, para 113, p. 173

46   Nietzsche, "Preface", to *Genealogy of Morals*, trs. W. Kaufmann, (Vintage Books, New York, 1989), Section 1, p. 15.

47   Nietzsche, *The Gay Science*, Bk. 4., section 335, p. 266.

48   Nietzsche, *The Will to Power*, op. cit., Bk. 111, section 605, p. 327.

49   Ibid, section 615, p. 329.

50   For what this would look like in terms of a Nietzschean philosophy of science, refer to Babette E. Babich, *Nietzsche's Philosophy of Science*, (State University of New York Press, Albany, 1994).

51   Nietzsche, *The Will to Power*, op. cit., section, 616, p. 330.

52   M. Horkheimer, "Notes on Science and the Crisis", in M. Horkheimer, *Critical Theory*, op, cit, pp. 3-9.

53   M. Horkheimer, "Materialism and Metaphysics", ibid, pp. 10-46.

54   M. Horkheimer, "Traditional and Critical Theory", ibid, pp. 188-243.

55   Nietzsche, *Will To Power*, op. cit., section 461, pp. 253-4.

56   Nietzsche, *The Gay Science*, op. cit., Book V, para 344, pp. 281-283;*The Genealogy of Morals*, op. cit., Third Essay, Section 24, p. 152.

57   Nietzsche, *The Gay Science*, op. cit., Bk. 5., section 373, p. 335.

58   Nietzsche, *The Will to Power*, op. cit., Bk. 111, section 624, p. 334.

59   Ibid, Bk. 111, section 636, p. 339.

60   Roy Bhaskar, *Dialectic the Pulse of Freedom*, (Verso, London, 1993), p. 4. The argument is also made in Bhaskar *A Realist Theory of Science*, (Harvester Press, Sussex, 1978), pp. 36ff.

61   Bhaskar, *Dialectic The Pulse of Freedom*, op. cit. p. 359.

62   Nietzsche, *The Will To Power*, op. cit., Bk. 111, section 567, p. 305.

63   Ibid,Bk. 3, Section 689, pp. 164-165; section 636, pp. 120-121.

64   Ibid, Bk. 3, section 635, p. 339.

65   F. Nietszche, *Philosophy in the Tragic Age of the Greeks*, trs. Marianne Cowan, (Henry Regnery, Chicago, 1962), p. 5.

66   F. Nietzsche, *The Will to Power*, op. cit, Bk Four, section 1067, pp. 549-550. 431-32. See Gilles Deleuze, *Nietzsche and Philosophy*, (Columbia University Press, New York, 1983).

67   Nietzsche's criticism of the dialecticians is found in *Will To Power*, section 430-431, pp. 235-236.

68   For an argument that a process metaphysics offers a way around modernist philosophy refer to, Robert Cummings Neville, *The Highroad Around Modernism*, (State University of New York Press, Albany, 1992). Neville is concerned with recovering the American tradition of process metaphysics, especially Whitehead, and fails to recognize the steps taken by Nietzsche towards a process philosophy.

69   Michael Haar, "Nietzsche and Metaphysical Language", in David Allison, (ed.), *The New Nietzsche*, (Dell, New York, 1977), p 6. Walter Kaufmann, *Nietzsche: Philosopher, Psychologist Antichrist*, (Princeton University Press, Princeton, 1974), held that Nietzsche's metaphysical claims were presented as empirical truths.

70   Alexander Nehamas, *Nietzsche Life as Literature*, op. cit., p. 96-97.

71   Nietzsche, *The Will to Power,* op. cit. Bk. 11, section 579, pp. 310-311 & section 584, pp. 314-315.

72   The distinctions between the few and the many is central to Nietzsche. Postmodernists follow G. Deleuze's *Nietzsche and Philosophy,* , which sidesteps the rank-ordering in favour of the multiplicity of perspectives. S. Rosen, *The Mask of Enlightenment. Nietzsche's Zarathustra,* (Cambridge University Press, Cambridge, 1995), p. 144.

73   For postmoderrn steps towards elaborating a process metaphysics refer to, Arran E. Gare, *Postmodernism and the Environmental Crisis,* (Routledge, London, 1995).

74   Edmund Husserl, *The Crisis of the European Sciences and Transcendental Phenomenology,* trs. David Carr, (Northwestern University Press, Evanston, 1970).

75   See, for instance, the symposium on Thomas Kuhn, in *Radical Philosophy,* vol. 82, (March/April 1997); Steve Fuller, *Being There with Thomas Kuhn: A Philosophical History of Our Times,* (University of Chicago Press, Chicago, 1997).

76   This identity is assumed by D. W. Conway in a critique of the feminist standpoint theory of S. Harding, in "Das Weib an sich, The slave revolt in epistemology," in P. Patton, (ed.), *Nietzsche Feminism and Political Theory,* (Allen and Unwin, Sydney, 1993), p. 110.

77   Thomas Kuhn, *The Structure of Scientifc Revolutions,* 2nd edition, (University of Chicago Press, Chicago, 1970) pp. 41-42. Kuhn draws upon and significantly reworks the earlier views of Alexandre Koyre, *Metaphysics and Measurement,* (Cambridge Mass., 1968); Herbert Butterfield, *Origins of Modern Science,* (New York, 1965), Michael Polanyi, *Personal Knowledge,* (New York, 1958).

78   As for instance in the work of John Dupre, *The Disorder of Things: Metaphysical Foundations of the Disunity of Science,* (Harvard University Press, Cambridge, Massachusetts, 1993).

79   Nietzsche, *The Gay Science,* op. cit., Bk. 4., Section 293, p. 236.

80   Nietzsche, *The Will to Power,* Bk. 111, section 480, p. 266.

81   Ibid, sections 480 & 481, pp. 266-267.

82   Nietzsche, *The Will To Power , op. cit.,* Bk 111, sec. 481 p. 267.

83   Ibid, section 480, p. 267.

84   Nietzsche, *The Gay Science,* op. cit., Bk 5, section 354, pp. 297-300.

85   Ibid, section 503, p. 274.

86   Ibid, Bk.111, section 610, p. 328.

87   Ibid, Bk.111, section 677, p. 359.

88   The Baconian as well as the Cartesian strand of modernity is explored in Hans Blumenberg, *The Legitimacy of the Modern Age,* (MIT Press, Cambridge, Massachusetts, 1976).

89   Richard W. Miller, *Fact and Method, Explanation, Confirmation and Reality in the Natural and Social Sciences,* (Princeton University Press, Princeton, 1987), p. 95.

90   Ibid, p. 93-94.

91   J. Habermas, *On the Logic of the Social Sciences,* trs. S. W. Nicolson and J. A. Stark, (Polity Press, Cambridge, 1988).

92   Nietzsche, *The Gay Science,* Bk 5, section 373, p.335.

93   G. Lukacs, *History and Class Consciousness,* trs. R. Livingston, (Merlin Press, London, 1971).

94   M. Horkheimer and T. Adorno, *Dialectic of Enlightenment,* trs. J. Cumming, (Verso, London, 1979). p. 21.

95   Ibid, p. 6.

96   The complexities of Nietzsche's relationship to Socrates are explored Paul R. Harrison, *The Disenchantment of Reason. The Problem of Socrates in Modernity,* (State University of New York Press, Albany, 1994).

97   Nietzsche, *Genealogy of Morals*, op. cit., Second Essay, Section 2, pp. 59-60.

98   Ibid, Second Essay, Section 24 & 25, p. 96.

99   Nietzsche, *Thus Spake Zarathustra*, trs. R. J. Hollingdale, (Penguin, Harmondsworth, 1961), Part Three, "The Seven Seals", subsection, 1 & 2, pp. 244-245.

100   Ibid, Part 4, "Of the Higher Men", subsection 1 & 2, pp. 296-297.

101   Nietzsche, "Preface for the Second Edition", in *The Gay Science*, op. cit., section 2, pp. 33-35; also Bk 1, section 2, p. 77.

102   Nietzsche, *Beyond Good and Evil Prelude to a Philosophy of the Future*, trs. Walter Kaufmann, (Vintage, New York, 1966), sections 43 & 44, pp. 53-54. Also refer to section 214, p. 137.

103   Nietzsche, *Thus Spake Zarathustra*, op. cit., Part 4, "Of the Higher Men", subsection 8 8 & 9, pp. 300-301.

104   Ibid, Part 4, "Of Science," pp. 311-313.

105   Ibid, Part 4, "The Ass Festival", subsection 2 & 3, pp. 325-326. This follows the reading by Stanley Rosen, *The Mask of Enlightenment. Nietzsche's Zarathustra*, op. cit.

106   The liberal private/public distinction is made in Richard Rorty, *Contingency, Irony, and Solidarity*, (Cambridge University Press, Cambridge, 1989).

107   For a recent discussion of Rorty's liberal ironist politics, refer to, Chantel Mouffe, (ed.), *Deconstruction and Pragmatism*, (Routledge, London, and New York, 1996).

108   Hilary Putnam, *Realism with a Human Face*, (ed.), James Conant, (Harvard University Press, Cambridge, Massachusetts, 1990), pp. 27-28.

109   Hilary Putnam, "Two Philosophical Perspectives," in Putnam, *Reason, Truth and History*, (Cambridge University Press, Cambridge, 1981), p. 49.

110   Hilary Putnam, *The Many Faces of Realism*, (Open Court, La Salle, 1987).

111   He is following the path of E. Husserl in *The Crisis of the European Sciences*.

112   Hilary Putnam, "Two Philosophical Perspectives,"in *Reason, Truth and History*, Cambridge University Press, Cambridge, 1981, pp. 49-50.

113   J. C. C. Smart, "Under the Sign of Eternity", in J. Smart, *Essays: Metaphysical and Moral*, (Blackwell, Oxford, 1987), citation p. 131.

114   J. C. C. Smart, "A Form of Metaphysical Realism", *The Philosophical Quarterly*, vol. 45, no.180, (July 1995), pp. 301-315.

115   Ibid, pp. 305-306.

116   R. Scruton, *An Intelligent Person's Guide to Philosophy*, (Duckworth, London, 1996), pp. 22-23.

117   C. A. Hooker, *Reason, Regulation and Realism*, (State University of New Press, Albany, 1995), pp. 294-5.

118   Ibid, p. 335

119   Ibid, p. 14

120   Bernard Williams, *Ethics and The Limits of Philosophy*, (Fontana, London, 1985), pp. 83- 84.

121   The sacrifice of individuals by the moral system of utilitarianism is explored in the section by Williams in J. C. C. Smart and B. Williams, *Utilitarianism for and Against*, (Cambridge University Press Cambridge, 1973).

122   M. Pusey, *Economic Rationalism in Canberra*, (Cambridge University Press, Cambridge, 1991).

123   J. Habermas, "The Scientisation of Politics and Public Opinion", in Habermas, *Toward a Rational Society*, (Beacon Press, Boston, 1970), pp. 63-64.

5 Nihilism, value in a disenchanted modernity

Nihilism stands at the door: whence comes this uncanniest of all guests?

Nietzsche, *The Will to Power.*

A nihilist is a man who judges of the world as it is that it ought not to be, and of the world as it ought to be that it does not exist. According to this view, our existence (action, suffering, willing, feeling) has no meaning: the pathos of "in vain" is the nihilist pathos—at the same time, as pathos, an inconsistency on the part of the nihilists.

Nietzsche, *The Will to Power.*

Reason can only realize its rationality through reflection on the sickness of the world, as it is produced and reproduced by people; in such a self-critique reason will at the same time remain true to itself by clinging to the principle of truth, which we owe to reason alone, and by not turning to any other theme.

Horkheimer, *Critique of Instrumental Reason.*

Nietzsche's critique of a universal enlightening science in modernity is two-pronged. It holds that a scientific interpretation of the world is one which is the poorest in terms of meaning. An autonomous science pursued for its own sake, with its will to truth, is an interpretation of the world of human valuation in terms of the calculator and mechanics. The truth of this mechanistic world makes our world an essentially meaningless world.[1] This makes human suffering senseless. Nietzsche's other prong of attack claims that a scientific culture is grounded on the ascetic ideal directed against life. This means that it destroys all our dreams and hopes for a better human life. Hence overcoming the ascetic ideal in terms of science's will to absolute truth means overcoming this value-commitment to absolute truth at any price, as science cannot help us create new forms of life beyond a scientistic nihilism.

This critique of the ascetic ideal involves the destruction of the ascetic ideal and the creation of a counter-ideal. It retains a commitment to the value of truth, but in the service of another more life-enhancing ideal than the life-destroying ascetic one. But our situation is one in which we have no cultural ideal that could function as an alternative to the ascetic ideal; no alternative which is life-enhancing and life-affirming. Nietzsche claims that in the face of this condition of nihilism, it is art that can provide the basis for the revaluation of all value. Art is a means of enhancing life, both in setting new conditions for life, and as that which supports, furthers and awakens the self-making of noble individuals through the reworking of their character and developing their powers and capacities. Art is fundamentally opposed to the ascetic ideal, and it is an artistic culture that will develop a new alternative ideal to replace the now empty ascetic ideal.[2] Culture emphasizes meaning, and so is self-reflection, and it is art which affirms life and culture. The affirmation of life is the realm of reason, freedom and the self-making of the individual. Culture admits the tragic aspects of modernity, but it does not sacrifice a critical reason. Though a critical humanist culture denies that knowledge, virtue and happiness are a unity, it is able and willing to avail itself of the visions and myths of art. A humanist culture affirms life, in that it emphasises the formation of human beings as the true end of culture. This formation is the realization of the overman, which is scanned in terms of a poetic self-making or shaping, in which the focus is on one's relationship to oneself within an aristocratic politics. Aesthetic self-fashioning of the philosopher-artist beyond good and evil, is a process of *Bildung*, and is the self-overcoming of one's basic physical nature through a stylishly acquired self-mastery and acquisition of a nobility of character.

This chapter introduces Nietzsche's argument about universal science being the latest expression of the ascetic ideal, which results in truth being valued at the expense of all other values, including those of the good life. It does so in order to evaluate a scientific realism with a reductive materialist metaphysics, from a moral point of view. This science, it is maintained, is caught up in, and reproduces the ascetic ideal, and this reinforces the Enlightenment's nihilistic consequences. It shows the incoherence of the subjectivism of value in mechanistic materialism, in terms of the way this undermines its own rational justification of its Enlightenment project in modernity; and its inability to evaluate different conceptions of the good life rationally. This results in a social physics like neo-classical economics serving pre-existing political ends of the technocratic control of nature and society. It then advocates a turn to a practical ethical humanism in order to confront the rationality of an instrumental science ensnared in the ascetic ideal.

Nietzsche on science and the ascetic ideal

Nietzsche's probing of the edifice of ethics and morality in bourgeois culture is similar to how psychoanalysis probes the confusions of the unconscious. His diagnosis of the ethical problem is that it is the advent of European nihilism. He saw this in the signs and symptoms of life in modernity losing all meaning—the whole system of values of Christianity collapsing, belief crumbling everywhere, and the world becoming devoid of sense. He interpreted these signs to mean that everything which had value is worth nothing. It is the problematic of the contradictory logic within the European culture of nihilism as the emptying-out or devaluing of our highest values, that engaged Nietzsche, rather than the sceptical thesis that, as nothing is true or moral, so everything is justified.

It is the latter thesis that analytic philosophers generally work with. They see nihilism as the thesis that there are no moral facts, no moral truths, and no moral knowledge. Gilbert Harman, for instance, says:

"An extreme version of nihilism holds that morality is simply an illusion: nothing is ever right or wrong, just or unjust, good or bad. In this version we should abandon morality, just as an atheist abandons religion after he has decided that religious facts cannot help explain observations. Some extreme nihilists have even suggested it is merely a superstitious remnant of religion. Such extreme nihilism is hard to accept. It implies that there are no moral constraints—that everything is permitted."[3]

On this reading of nihilism, Nietzsche is seen as an immoralist who is beyond good and evil. He sees morality as a bad thing, and so holds that it should be rejected. He is read as a kind of aristocratic thug, who lords it over others, practises a callous indifference to the suffering others, and takes pleasure in displays of violence and cruelty.[4] This interpretation of Nietzsche as proto-Nazi also points to a despair in the face of the senselessness and incessant suffering of human life. This leads to the grim interpretation that life is not worth living. In the absence of guiding values and ideals that the human animal currently needs, we can but live amidst the disorder of chaos.

However, Nietzsche is a philosopher/physician who is concerned with the problematic of nihilism in which our highest values have emptied out. He offers a diagnosis of a diseased culture in modernity which makes us sick and increases our suffering. Life as it exists in this world is no good. In the face of this decay and our sickness, we need to affirm life. This encounter with nihilism leads to self-affirmation in the face of our sickness, which is due to the time into which we have been thrown. This time is the result of a long historical process, and it is a time:

> "of extensive inner decay and disintegration, a time that with all its weaknesses, and even with its best strength, opposes the spirit of youth. Disintegration characterizes this time, and thus uncertainty: nothing stands firmly in its feet or on a hard faith in itself; one lives for tomorrow, as the day after tomorrow is dubious. Everything on our way is slippery and dangerous, and the ice that still supports has become thin; all us feel the warm, uncanny breath of the thawing wind; where we still walk, soon no one will be able to walk."[5]

The deeper one looks, the more meaninglessness approaches and our valuations disappear. Nihilism is held to be imminent, and it cannot be averted.[6] Everywhere are the sounds of doubt, melancholy, weariness of life and resistance to life. His diagnosis of this condition is that there is a hollowing-out of the public moral culture of bourgeois society, as our highest values have lost their worth, the point of existence is missing, and we have no sense of where we are going. We live within a numbing sense of nothingness and pathos. We are lost for a while, as life has lost all meaning, the world has become devoid of sense; and we have become pessimistic because the world does not have the value we thought it once had.[7] This tragic situation, which makes nihilists of all of us, represents a crisis of modernity. It is our present historical situation, and it is the consciousness of our suffering in this state which separates us from those in early modernity.

Nietzsche then evaluates this situation from the realm of value of self-creation, nobility and good, strong character—a classical virtue ethics returning through the backdoor, in the guise of the artist/philosopher who creates by destroying. As a philosopher-physician he offers a remedy for our sickness, rather than just advocating that we passively wallow in it. Though the world seems meaningless, this is only a pathological transition stage, Nietzsche argues, as what is required is that we revalue our values, by finding the pathos that impels us to seek new values.[8] We are the creators of our values. The will to the negation of life crosses over into its opposite. We can say yes to life, and affirm our creative power as the legislator of new values. He does this by returning to the Stoical ethical tradition; with its concern with self-command toward and within oneself, self-sufficiency and completeness, as a way of achieving *eudemonia* or a flourishing life. Here the virtuous person is truly complete in himself or herself, whatever the world is doing.[9] Such a person shapes chaos, creates new values out of his or her affirmation of life, and sculptors a new kind of human being.[10]

Nietzsche's problematic of nihilism links science to the ascetic ideal. It holds that the critical Socratic spirit, allied with the radically experimental methodology of science, has undermined and displaced all transcendent faiths. Science has displaced the Platonic-Christian metaphysics or centre of gravity by virtue of which we lived. It is no longer the dominant strand and core component of European culture. Nietzsche then links nihilism, as the emptying out of our highest values, to a scientific culture by way of arguing that a scientific culture makes us unhappy, just like Christianity did. His first argument for this claim holds that science has been influenced by the ascetic ideal. An ascetic ideal is the belief that the best human life is one of self-denial, a life based on a hatred of the human, the animal, the senses, the body in such a way that there is a negative valuation of human existence. A form of life based on the ascetic ideal is an unhappy life:

> "Read from a distant star, the majuscule script of our earthly existence would perhaps lead to the conclusion that the earth was the distinctly ascetic planet, a nook of disgruntled, arrogant, and offensive creatures filled with a profound disgust at themselves, at the earth, at all life, who inflict as much pain on themselves as they possible can out of pleasure in inflicting pain—which is probably their only pleasure."[11]

This life-denying tendency of the ascetic ideal is reinforced by unpacking the way that an ascetic ideal is absolutist. Nietzsche says:

> "That which *constrains* these men, however this unconditional will to truth, is *faith in the ascetic ideal itself,* even as an unconscious imperative—don't be deceived about that—it is the faith in a *metaphysical* value, the absolute value of *truth,* sanctioned and guaranteed by this ideal alone (it stands or falls with this ideal)."[12]

The consequence of this is that an absolutist ascetic ideal allows no other ideals legitimate existence. It:

> "permits no other interpretation, no other goal, it rejects, denies, affirms, and sanctions solely from the point of view of *its* interpretation...it submits to no power, it believes in its own dominance over every other power, in its absolute *superiority of rank* over every other power—it believes that no power exists on earth that does not first have to receive a meaning, a right to exist, a value, as a tool of the ascetic ideal, as a way and means to *its* goal, to *one* goal."[13]

The classic example of the ascetic ideal is Christianity, which explained human suffering as punishment for sin, and provided the goal of overcoming one's attachment to life at the cost of the devaluation of human life. It means, he concludes in the *Genealogy of Morals,* that apart from the ascetic ideal, human beings have no meaning and no goal:

> "*This* is precisely what the ascetic ideal means: that something was *lacking,* that man was surrounded by a fearful *void*—he did

not know how to justify, to account for, to affirm himself; he *suffered* from the problem of his meaning...The meaninglessness of suffering, *not* suffering itself, was the curse that lay over mankind so far—*and the ascetic ideal offered man meaning!*.. man was *saved* thereby, he possessed meaning, he was henceforth no longer like a leaf in the wind, he could now will something...We can no longer conceal from ourselves what is expressed by all that willing which has taken its direction from the ascetic ideal: this hatred of the human...a *will to nothingness,* an aversion to life."[14]

The ascetic ideal deprived human life of intrinsic value because it treated it as valuable only as a means to its own negation—going to heaven—thereby making the outbreak of European nihilism inevitable. Human life is now without a goal, and it appears in danger of appearing to be devoid of value.[15]

Nietzsche argues that, with the demise of Christian culture and the rise of scientific culture, it appears that modern science is a counter-ideal to the ascetic ideal. Science is what is prescriptive in our culture, as it is the supremely authoritative source of human knowledge. However, he says, science's faith in truth means that is the latest expression of the ascetic ideal.[16] The ascetic ideal of science is what it has in common with Platonic/Christian metaphysics: namely its will to truth, which is the ideal of science. This will to truth requires a critique in the name of the transvaluation of all values:

"No! Don't come to me with science when I ask for the natural antagonist of the ascetic idea, when I demand: "where is the opposing will expressing the *opposing ideal?*" Science is not nearly self-reliant enough to be that; it first requires in every respect an ideal of value, a value-creating power, in the *service* of which it could believe in itself—it never creates values. Its relation to the ascetic ideal is by no means essentially antagonistic; it might even be said to represent the driving force of the latter's inner development. This pair, science and ascetic ideal, both rest on the same foundation on the same belief that truth is inestimable and cannot be criticised. Therefore they are necessarily *allies,* so that if they have to be fought they can only be fought and called into question together. A depreciation of the ascetic ideal unavoidably involves a depreciation of science."[17]

Science's commitment to the absolute value of truth, its unquestioning faith in truth as a self-sufficient foundation that cannot be criticized, means that the value of truth is more important than other values, such as *eudemonia* or a flourishing life. This commitment leads science, Nietzsche says in *The Gay Science,* to affirm the real world of science in terms of the fundamental furniture of the world, as distinct from the apparent or phenomenal everyday world that we commonly live in. This reductionist picture holds that, apart from natural objects which extend in space, there is no reality, other than the world as a complicated mechanism made up of lots of elementary particles buzzing around. Human beings just are a part of this machine. True knowledge always refers to natural reality, conceived as a functioning machine, which is subject to the necessity of natural law. Nietzsche says:

> "Thus the question "Why Science? leads back to the moral problem: *Why have morality at all* when life, nature and history are not moral"? No doubt, those who are truthful in that audacious and ultimate sense that is presupposed by the faith in science *thus affirm another world* than the world of life, nature and history; and insofar as they affirm this "other world"—look, must they not by the same token negate its counterpart, this world, *our* world? But you will have gathered what I am driving at, namely, that it is still a metaphysical faith upon which our faith in science rests."[18]

From this perspective of an ethics of knowing, science is driven by a will to truth. With metaphysical realists like Smart, the will to truth is a drive to the one true theory, which is to be distinguished from warranted assertability even in the Peircean limit, as the latter might be false.[19] Such a science shelters an acknowledged faith in the redemptive capacity of truth. This faith is complicit with the gloomy ascetic ideal in a world grown old and sick, and so science is not life-enhancing.

The second strand of Nietzsche's argument about science making us unhappy in a nihilist modernity, holds that it is self-defeating to take science to be normative for all spheres of thought. This argument centres on the valuation that the ascetic philosopher or scientist places on our life. It holds that the modern scientific truth-seekers are implicated in nihilism, because their negation of Christianity's true world leaves us with just scientific truth and its metaphysical comforts, based on the absolute point of view. This metaphysical faith leaves the moral questions—how does one want to be? what does one want to become? what is the good life?—unanswered. Nor can this be answered by the truth discovered by physics, in terms of its universal elementary laws, its unified view of nature based on elementary particles and their mutual interactions. This makes our everyday world an essentially meaningless world that has no value.[20] Science's faith in truth as the ultimate value, Nietzsche argues, is the latest manifestation of an ascetic ideal that devalues everyday life in the name of the true world. It gives us mechanistic materialism's world picture of nature as a mechanism. Therefore a scientific culture, grounded on the ascetic ideal of absolute truth directed against life, destroys all our dreams and hopes for a better life. The crisis in modernity inheres in the obliteration of the horizon of meaning that gives the sense of rootedness and sense of purpose that enables us to flourish as human beings. Science destroys values but it cannot create new ones. The belief that truth could fulfill this function is an illusion.

Hence, overcoming the ascetic ideal in terms of science's will to absolute truth, means overcoming this commitment to absolute truth as part of a general critique of our highest values. This revaluation of our values is necessary, because science represents a force against ordinary living, and its world picture is such that the agonies of living have no meaning at all. It means that in the transitional stage of nihilism we need to say 'no' to its whole approach to life which is driving us towards to nihilism, and say 'yes' to this world of appearances or everyday life. The revaluation of values as a way out of the labyrinth of nihilism requires that we go beyond truth to pose the moral questions about our self-command and self-forming or development as human beings. We become a certain kind of moral person with the virtues of hardness, like that of the disciplined dancer. This involves a turn to art, as artists, unlike philosophers, have not:

> "lost the scent of life, they have loved the things of "this world"—they have loved their senses. To strive for "desensualization": that seems to me a misunderstanding or an illness or a cure, where it is not merely hypocrisy or self-deception. I desire for myself and for all who live, *may* live without being tormented by a puritanical conscience, an ever-greater spiritualization and multiplication of the senses...We no longer need these (priestly and metaphysical) calumnies: it is a sign that one has turned out well when, like Goethe, one clings with ever greater pleasure and warmth to the "things of this world":—for in this way he holds firmly to the greater conception of man that man becomes the transfigurer of existence when he learns to transfigure himself."[21]

It is the value of life and not truth that is ultimately decisive. So we downplay truth as the ultimate ideal by questioning the truth imperative, as this is what has lead us into nihilism and holds us captive. Though the collapse of the old certainties is a catastrophe, it provides new opportunities for the revaluation of values.

Nietzsche's critique of the ascetic ideal in philosophy and science, with their commitment to the value of metaphysical truth, is a part of his diagnosis of the nihilistic problematic of European Enlightenment culture. The destruction of this decayed culture is made in the service of another more life-enhancing ideal, which makes art the counter-force. This critique—involving the destruction of the ascetic ideal, the creation of a counter-ideal, and the revaluation of all values—is difficult to pull off. The condition of nihilism means that we have no cultural ideal that could function as an alternative to the ascetic ideal, an alternative ideal which is life-enhancing and life-affirming. We are not sheltered from pessimism and nihilism, since the ascetic ideal is not limited to saints and priests. With the massive shrinkage of space occupied by religion in modernity scientists, doctors and nurses, and men and women can become caught up in ascetic regimes.[22] An instance of this is the way that asceticism has returned with economic rationalism. Here it functions as a harsh Protestant ethic of self-denial and hard work, with its rational ordering of the body in the interests of capitalist production.[23] Nietzsche's remedy is that art can provide the basis for the revaluation of all values, and so be a means of enhancing life.[24] It can do so both in setting new conditions for life, and as that which supports, furthers and awakens the self-making of individuals through the reworking of their character and developing their powers and capacities. An artistic, aristocratic culture can develop a new ideal to replace the now empty ascetic ideal, because art realizes that delusion and error are conditions of human knowledge. 'Art as the good will to appearances' provides us with eyes, hands and above all, the good conscience to be able to be exuberant, floating, dreaming, mocking and childish—to wear the fool's cap in opposition to the will to truth which animates the ascetic ideal.[25] Art is the way out of the chaos of nihilism, as creation is the great redemption from suffering, by giving it meaning. It is art that is the superior counterforce to the denial of life. Nietzsche says:

> "Art...is much more fundamentally opposed to the ascetic ideal than is science: This was instinctively sensed by Plato, the greatest enemy of art that Europe has yet produced....To place himself in the service of the ascetic ideal is therefore the most distinctive *corruption* of an artist that is at all possible; unhappily, also one of the most common forms of corruption, for nothing is more easily corruptible than an artist."[26]

The dangers for art are illustrated by the old, diseased, decadent Wagner at Bayreuth when he put chastity to music in *Parsifal* and so espoused the ascetic point of view, thereby signing his death warrant as an artist and musician.[27] Still, it is art which affirms life and culture, and the remedy it offers is the affirmation of life and the self-making of the individual. It enables us to flourish in the world, as it admits the tragic aspects of modernity whilst affirming the formation of human beings as the true end of culture.

This is not the return to a simple conservatism, with its unswerving adherence to tradition providing the horizons of meaning that scientific reason cannot find. Nietzsche's diagnosis is that the venerable traditions that once preserved the canopy of meaning are dead. There is no point in reviving them, as stultifying conventionalism is repressive of life. The remedy for nihilism is to destroy tradition, create new values, and engage in the process of *Bildung*. Nietzsche scans this in terms of a poetic self-making or shaping. Here the focus is on one's relationship to oneself: it is the self-overcoming of one's basic physical nature through a stylishly acquired self-mastery, and the acquisition of a nobility of character. We become poets of our life. But it is only the rarest of noble individuals who can create new values, as it is only they who have creative energy inherent to give them the self-propulsion necessary to achieve the high level of this new culture. It is the elite humanity of creators as legislators and commanders who are able to create the true culture out of chaos. The labouring backs of the many provide the material and political conditions to ensure that this elite can overcome the past and create a new culture from the chaos of nihilism.[28] The genuine philosopher, as opposed to the journeymen and scientific labourers who underlabour to ensure the untroubled transmission of tradition, has the task of understanding the problem of value, positing new values, and determining the order of rank among values. The genuine philosophers are the commanders and legislators, and as artists of the new humanity, they have a prominent world-shaping function that is of the utmost public significance.[29] They are the physicians of culture, now that Christianity has decayed, and science has led us to the abyss of a disenchanted world. Here the classical unity of truth, virtue and happiness, whereby the pursuit of knowledge is linked to the pursuit of virtue and the good life, has been ruptured. Scientific knowledge is deemed by a scientific culture to be more valuable than anything else within a self-reproducing capitalism. Virtue and the good life have dropped away. It is the sum of qualities like industriousness and efficiency, associated with successful money-making in the market, that are deemed desirable and respectable. Happiness is just being rich and successful.

Sketch of a genealogy of reason

The question that needs to be asked is: does the recycling of Nietzsche's critique of European Enlightenment culture bite in relation to a reductionist materialist philosophy, that is locked up in the closed professional ethos of the liberal academy? Do the serious analytic philosophers wear the mask of the ascetic ideal, and rage against the sensuousness of life? Are they against life when they defend the truth represented by hard science? Does science block the path of revaluation out of nihilism? Are analytic philosophers the secular equivalent of ascetic priests? Do we need to turn away from science to art, as Nietzsche suggested, if we desire to find our way out of the labyrinth of nihilism? Is science now the heart of the problem in relation to nihilism, after the decay of Christianity?

One view is that Nietzsche's attack was on a positivist science, and as this has been replaced by scientific realism in a scientific culture, we do not need to pay any more attention to Nietzsche's thesis about science, nihilism and the ascetic ideal. Those in scientific culture see the path opened by Nietzsche to lead to a defence of religion, the turn to a new spirituality leading to New Ageism, and the pseudo-science of a non-expert constituency audaciously proclaiming its own authority as culture. It is the return of the Dark Ages.[30] However Byran Appleyard argues that science does deepen nihilism, and that we should take this seriously. He says that:

> "we have paid a high imaginative price for the success of science. Hard scientific truth denies us our place in the world, an ultimate significance and a sense of worth of our own actions, it subverts values insisting upon the contingency of all that we do and are. Nobody who has read the history and philosophy of the last four hundred years—indeed nobody who has read the great scientists—can reasonably deny this and, I note, many pro-science

writers celebrate the way science frees us to live without 'illusions'. In other words, science does transform the human imagination, it does impose values, it does not just sit happily and objectively in its laboratories."[31]

Appelyard works the ground in a very Nietzschean manner. He says that the ebbing of religious faith has left a vacuum of a cold, meaningless universe— Nietzsche's nihilism—and this represents the failure of the entire Enlightenment project of making a better human world. This poses two questions: can we live with that vacuum and can or must we fill it? Like Nietzsche his answers are no and yes.

Do we have a nihilist vacuum in our culture? One way of getting at this is in terms of narrative. Science is authoritative in our culture, and the cultural narrative of modernity in a scientific culture is one in which the cultural neutral operation that is employed is reason. Here the transformation to modernity is explained in terms of the operation for rational thought, in the sense that any culture could, under suitable conditions, undergo a scientization of its world view. It considers modernity to unfold as a result of a 'coming to see' the truth of the scientific world-view, the differentiation of fact-value, and the efficiency of instrumental rational action. These truths are waiting there to be seen when the right conditions obtain. A culture becomes modern when the obstacles to these conditions obtaining are removed. Ideology needs to be is swept away, as all previously held beliefs that stand in opposition to modern science are grounded in deception or error. This then implies that any culture which does not converge with the scientific world-picture of Western capitalist modernity can be dismissed as lacking in rationality. Its notion of critique is centred on establishing the limits of reason or demarcating natural science from other human forms of knowledge, and criticizing illusory, inadequate or false beliefs about the natural world, such as the creationist theories of fundamentalist Christians. The narrative is one of progress from the barbarity of magic, superstition and religious dogma to Enlightenment through natural science; a process which illuminates the darkness of irrationality which still casts a shadow over us. Reason remains forever the same and we are able, here and now, to get close to grasping the truth for all time. So the meaning, value and comfort provided by religion and folk beliefs are gone. We stand naked in a nihilistic world pictured by reason. Philosophers then sustain themselves in their cosmic loneliness by devoting their energies to seeking solace in mathematical logic, logical analysis and the scientific method. They seek a perfect philosophical science, isolated from the past and, untouched by myth, grief or love.

This narrative is too crude as it stands. It identifies natural science with reason, makes logic and love two worlds that do not connect, and fails to take into account reason in ethics and aesthetics within the historical development of the rationalization process in modernity. Habermas refines this narrative so as to integrate logic with everyday human life. He argues that the project of a universal reason modernity, as formulated by the philosophers of the Enlightenment, consisted in their:

> "efforts to develop objective science, universal morality and law, and autonomous art, according to their own inner logic. At the same time, this project intended to release the cognitive potentials of each of these domains to set them free from their esoteric forms. The Enlightenment philosophers wanted to utilize this accumulation of socialized culture for the enrichment of everyday life, that is to say, for the rational organization of everyday social life."[32]

This project was centrally concerned with providing universal standards by which to justify particular courses of action in every sphere of life. He argues that at the level of culture, the logic of the process of rationalization in modernity has resulted in progressive differentiation of reason into the autonomous value-related spheres of science, ethics and aesthetics. In

> "Kant's concept of a formal and internally differentiated reason there is sketched a theory of modernity. This is characterized by, on the one hand, its renunciation of the substantial rationality of inherited religious and metaphysical world views and, on the other hand, by its reliance upon a procedural rationality, from which our justifiable interpretations, be they pertinent to the field of objective knowledge, moral-practical insight, or aesthetic judgement, borrow their claim to validity."[33]

We can avoid the implicit neo-Kantianism by giving this narrative a more Hegelian twist. What is being articulated by the narrative of Habermas is the transition to modernity in terms of the intrinsically compelling characteristics of the emergent culture of modernity. In the naturalist Enlightenment discourse, the emphasis of reductive materialism is on universal reason of natural sciences, with a universal reason in utilitarian ethics subordinated to the truth of science. There is a complete ignoring of aesthetic reason. The value conflict between the sphere of science and ethics is resolved by value orientation, which subordinates ethics to the truth of a realist, value-free, natural science.

What Habermas is offering is a modernist account of the differentiation of reason by way of a Weberian narrative about the disenchantment of the world, characterized by rationalization, which has a built-in implicit normative appeal that this differentiation of reason is a good thing.[34] Disenchanting the world of mythical, religious and animist beliefs about nature is part of the more general process of rationalization of our practices and beliefs. So we see the world in terms of rational calculation and technical control. The list of phenomena that Weber subsumed under rationalization is diverse, as it included all three spheres of reason. But its interpretation of the historic process of change as the disintegration of the knowledge of totality and rise of the hegemony of formal reason results in as bleak a perspective on a nihilistic capitalist modernity as that of Marx. Weber says:

> "The Puritan wanted to work in a calling; we are forced to do so...when asceticism was carried out of monastic cells into everyday life, and began to dominate worldly morality, it did its part in building the tremendous cosmos of the modern economic order. This order is now bound to the technical and economic conditions of machine production which today determines the lives of all the individuals who are born into this mechanism, not only those directly concerned with economic acquisition, with irresistible force. Perhaps it will so determine them until the last ton of fossilized coal is burnt."[35]

The compulsion here within rationalization is part of the normalizing authority of the social institutions which engage in social engineering. But Weber took a dialectical view of rationalization in capitalist modernity. He regarded the normative dimension of rationalization as the heightening in the level of reason, and he held that this provided the value orientation for institutions and individuals.[36] But he accepted that value conflict as an irreconcilable expression of our cultural fate in modernity, that the judgement of the validity of values is a matter of fate, and that faith has withdrawn from a disenchanted world. The hegemony of formal rationality in science goes hand in hand with the irrationality of morality and art. This suggests that bourgeois culture has difficulty in legitimating itself from itself.[37]

The way that it has politically endeavoured to do so in a nihilistic culture is by the scientific value sphere asserting itself against its rivals in terms of a secular scientism that delivers the goods. This was initially articulated within an Enlightenment framework which held that science will bring benefit by mastering the physical world, and that economic growth will remove the dirt, death and darkness, increase material comfort by overcoming starvation and disease. So science will provide security and comfort. This framework had its roots in Francis Bacon's *New Atlantis,* a popular Renaissance utopian tract, whose depiction of Solomon's House is an influential expression of seventeenth-century scientism linked to a resounding call for the public support of scientific research in the service of human well-being. Bacon states that the 'end of our Foundation is the knowledge of causes and secret motions of things, and the enlarging of the bounds of Human empire' through an organized, universally valid, and testable body of knowledge.[38] This scientific basis for material progress at Solomon's House was still within a Christian and authoritarian society, but this was slowly discarded during the history of modernity, as was the humane humanism of the Renaissance. With the decay of the Enlightenment as the arbiter of value and meaning, science as world interpretation has developed into the anti-humanist and amoral scientism of today. The meaning system of this technoculture holds that the progress of humanity depends upon the domination over nature by a value-free science, unlimited economic growth to increase utility, and the power of science used to minimize other areas of culture.[39] With the fading of the Enlightenment it is the techno-scientific ideal that is central as the social arbiter of value in a cultural crisis. Scientific technology promises us salvation from the abyss of nothingness, and so permits us to remain where we are, because it can heal the cultural crisis.

The ebbing away of religious faith and philosophical idealism, and their replacement by science in Western culture, meant that after 1945 science was the counter-movement to nihilism. It was the saving power of science that was emphasised. Science was packaged by ideologues to provide the basis for the growth and character of democratic and republican government within industrial capitalism. Growth in consumer goods and political freedom stood as the meaning system in opposition to totalitarian and nationalist states like the Soviet Union. With the collapse of the Soviet Union in the late 1980s, science and technology are now seen as playing dominant roles in political and economic policy decisions. Science and technology dictate, with all the promised benefits resulting from advanced technology being used by capitalists. Neo-classical economics promises long-term pleasure over short-term pain, with the opening out of a closed national economy to a global capitalist market through deregulation, tariff reduction and low inflation. The use of scientific knowledge to intervene in the natural and social world to further human emancipation from the oppressive social relations of capitalism has been quietly dropped. Capitalism is all there is. So we must adapt to it or go under. Freedom is economic choice in the market. If we get the economic fundamentals right, the economic experts say, then the high-tech firms will invest in Australia, and there will be jobs for all. The authority of economic truth holds that the Fortress Australia needs dismantling and that efficiency and productivity in the free market economy is all that matters. This truth is independent of all other values, such as an efficient and productive economy being run by the state for the benefit of the citizens so they can live the good life. There is little in the way of a sense of worth of our own actions that can be derived from economic rationalism's truths about the mechanism of the free market delivering economic growth based on the domination of nature. There is also little that this science offers as an interpretation of the positive value of human suffering caused by the policies of globalization.

Despite this, economics has become our touchstone with the decay of values. It increasingly provides us with our frame of reference, and with the basis for our values in terms of the secular ethics of utilitarianism. The notion here is that the ultimate objective of mankind is happiness defined in terms of the utility principle. The key is the individual's pleasure or pain or preferences within a world that appears to be regular and calculable. This provides us with our confidence to know what is good and bad, right and wrong in a chaotic world. This underpins our faith in universal reason to comprehend and ameliorate the human condition. It provides us with a reasoned skepticism that enables us to walk a middle course between hopeless despair and baseless commitment flowing from the lack of jobs, the steady destruction of rural Australia, the general decline in living standards, and the slow erosion and decay of the social order. There are limits to this, as the means/end instrumental rationality of neo-classical economics marginalizes all other modes of cognition, even though society and the economy are on a collision course. Its scientism effectively thwarts the hoped-for rational reorganization of everyday social life for the benefit of citizens. Economic scientism works within the horizon of the existing social order, and is seen to be the defender and guardian of this order, which has traditionally exploited the oppressed, such as the working class, women and aborigines.[40]

Economics can be construed as a moral phenomenon from the perspective of Nietzsche's ethics of knowing. Economic science as a world interpretation operates in terms of the meaning systems of consumer pleasure created by capitalism, that destroys nature to sustain the ticking over of the economic machine. The efficacy of science in producing technological goods to provide consumer pleasure means that science outdoes religion. But the consoling illusion of the noble lie of progress is seen to be at the expense of human life. There is a moral emptiness behind the narcissism of consumer culture, as the application of the policies recommended by the economic scientific experts breeds increasing resentment, anxiety, fear and suffering. It produces an intellectual culture of the technician, manager or business type, and it is one which human beings become resource material for capital—human capital as self-preservation, without the self. In the wake of nihilism this culture is the mechanization of contentment in the face of nothing, with its loss of ends about the good life. We have a cultural crisis here, because we have a mediocre culture that is a sick culture, which preserves its degeneration through a regimen of restrictions. So long as the economy continues to work, nothing really matters. Lifestyle through fashion and body sculpture through plastic surgery are the therapeutic solution to the cultural crisis that is nihilism. We consequently find it difficult to interpret the meaning of suffering resulting from the loss of autonomy and freedom.

The subjectivity of value

We are then left with the following questions. "Does the Enlightenment project, in the form of scientific realism with its reductive materialist metaphysics, reinforce and deepen nihilism?" "Or does it help us find our way out of it?" "How plausible is physicalist materialism as a proposal for alleviating the cultural crisis?" "Can this cultural crisis be conceptually understood and overcome with the help of physicalist materialism?" The quick answer is that this metaphysics deepens nihilism, due to its general anti-realism with respect to ethical value. In exploring this, we can begin to see the process of the self-destruction of universal reason in modernity.

The retreat from a thorough-going universal realism results from a physicalist reductionism assuming its world-picture to be approximately correct and approximately complete. If moral values are unsuited to the task of describing the furniture of the world, then they need to be displaced. It draws a difference between the way the world appears to commonsense—the manifest image—and the way it is in itself as represented by natural science. The tendency has been to see commonsense representations of nature to be ones of illusion and so false, whilst those of science are held to be real and so true. Reality in the form of a chair is what physics says it is, independently of the false appearances of our commonsense manifest image of the chair. This keeps the sphere of science and positive knowledge authoritative, whilst the manifest picture—a coloured world of tables and chairs, love and fear, meaning, value and freedom—is dismissed as a folk psychology. The grounds are that physics sees spatio-temporally located bodies in terms of the distinction between primary and secondary qualities. Primary qualities are held to be in the object, whilst secondary qualities are those properties of the object that arise only in our experience of them. It is our experience of objects as human beings that endows objects with colour, and Alpha Centaurians may well experience the objects differently. The light that objects give off would be of a certain wave length, and there could well be no such thing as what humans call colour. Values are like secondary qualities in that they are not ontologically placed in things, but in our sensibility or in our individual experience of things, and so they are subjective and so projected onto the world. The subjectivity of value is an inherent part of physicalism's world-picture inherited from the seventeenth century, and analytic moral philosophy can be seen as working out a conception of morality that would make it compatible with a physicalist metaphysics.

The narrative of modernity within the value-sphere of ethics can be quickly highlighted by positivism's sharp distinction between fact and value. Truth was relevant to the scientific realm, but not in the realm of value. The emotivism of the positivist held that normative and evaluative claims fall outside the realm of reasonable discussion and evaluation altogether. Such ethical claims are cognitively meaningless, and lack cognitive content, as they are the expression of personal emotion.[41] The consequence is that the classic concern of evaluating questions about the good and proper life are excluded. All that can be rationally said is that these are personal emotions or preferences. Liberal humanism's project of cultivating higher qualities to bring about the self-realized individual is undercut. As James Buchanan says:

> "'The making of higher-quality men'—this familiar high-sounding objective has an appealing and persuasive ring. But we sense the emptiness once we think at all critically about definitions of quality. Who is to judge? By whose criteria are qualities to be determined?"[42]

For Buchanan no authoritative standards exist, for unlike the sciences there are no authoritative criteria of goodness. Individuals have their own standards of evaluation, and their own preferences. Such value subjectivism in ethical and subjective matters is the standard position in both neo-classical and Austrian economics. It leaves us with making heroic decisions *ex nihilo*.

Nihilism operates here, as our highest ethical values are devalued by the truncating of the moral evaluation of the human experience of pain and suffering from the cruelties of exploitation and oppression in capitalism, as expressing a personal emotion or preference with no cognitive impact. Authoritativeness has no place, because ultimately values are a matter of subjective choice, or a matter of sovereign, consumer preference. Since the world does not contain the corresponding features or properties, the anti-realism in ethics is a form of Humean projection of an inner emotion onto the outer world. As ethical properties are literally made by our ethical sensibilities, then all that is wrong with cruelty to humans and the non-human world is that I don't approve or prefer it. The reasoned skepticism of scientific materialism is nihilistic in its very core.

Nietzsche's nihilism bites at this point. All we sovereign consumers can say about the purposeful creation of long-term unemployment resulting from the jobs disappearing through systematic retrenchment, de-industrialization, globalization, and computerization of middle management, is that I don't approve of it. Social justice has no cognitive bite against an economic scientific discourse, which holds that "technological unemployment" results from rapid technological change and global economic forces creating a new kind of post-industrial society based on information and computation. The Humean projectivism of an instrumental economic reason displaces an ethically-informed critique that points to radical social alternatives based on changing social power relations. So we are left with seeing the world from the standpoint of capital. This is one of future shock from the uncontrollable self-propelled mechanism of scientific discoveries and technological developments, with technological fixes being offered for the increasing tensions arising from unemployment. We are beyond good and evil in this scientistic configuration. The novel combination of science with an ever-expanding productive technology, coupled with a powerful mechanism of feedback operating through the competitive determinations of the market, means that science and technology no longer function in the service of human ends of a flourishing life within a more egalitarian, more open, diverse and democratic society. Hence our appalled reaction to the nihilistic perversion of ethics in scientism, as it strikes us ragpickers as a shocking affront to the future of the eight hundred thousand unemployed. The jobs that were there, just aren't there any more. They won't be back. We unemployed are left on the scrap heap, as ascetic politicians committed to authoritarian populism talk about the need for compulsory labour and involuntarily voluntary work. They are able to harness popular discontent now that the social democratic politics of redistributing wealth from within the limits of the existing economic cake no longer do the trick, and the middle class takes a sharp drop in living standards. Humean projectivism in ethics does not allow us to ethically criticise the reactionary character of the social project of Howardite populism (it is socially and sexually regressive, patriarchal and racist) because it is objectively harmful, causes sickness, and increases our suffering. Scientism leaves us naked to contest the way authoritarian populism is remaking and becoming the commonsense of the age, with its defence of the small business, lower middle-class respectability, self-reliance and self-discipline. Utility, as the greatest happiness of the greatest number is cashed out as an efficient free market economy providing economic growth.

One path out of this nihilism is offered by Hooker's naturalized turn away from a formal universal reason to our biological history, which lies underneath human history, and so is shared by all ages and cultures. Hooker's naturalized reason is a development out of Quine's naturalised epistemology, in which science studies the way physical human bodies construct their picture of the world in terms of the stimulation of their sensory receptors. Reason is an instrumental capacity which is part of a self-correcting regulatory system whose judgements are functional behavioural responses to external environmental stimuli. Rationality is a strategic process of using certain tools to transcend our imperfections, operating within our finitude, and under the constraints of limited resources, with the process being directed towards the ideals. This biological system 'makes progress by transcending limitations and imperfections through moving toward realizing the principle regulatory ideals: truth, goodness, beauty and reason.'[43] The regulatory ideal is judged valuable for finite imperfect creatures that are self-reproducing, self-organizing systems. Hooker explicitly denies that the ideal of goodness can be reduced to being simply derived from the requirements for a negotiated stable society along Hobbesian lines, or that the ideal functions as a non-natural transcendental entity.[44] The ideal is to be located within the self-organizing, self-correcting system, where it functions as a theoretical term in the concept of cognition, which is 'theorized as the information face of biological self-organization, at sufficient regulatory justification, with judgements the basic unity of organization'.[45] Hooker, in making the move to naturalized reason, has yet to generate an ethical theory which gives some substantive content to the regulatory ideal of goodness in the face of variant rival theories of what freedom and happiness mean in a disenchanted nihilistic modernity. As it currently stands, this naturalized instrumental reason offers adaptation within the given history of late capitalist modernity. This is naturalized as nature, and Hooker has yet to recognize substantially that human cognizers are also socially embedded cognitive agents, within the cultural and historical divergences within a disenchanted culture in late modernity. He has yet to link the cultural ideals and values of the Enlightenment, such as freedom, equality and justice, to the material conditions of society, which do not correspond to them. The question to be posed is: Do these ideals and values retain their actuality, or have they lost their substantive content by being emptied out in reality?

It is a crucial question. The central tendency in physicalist materialism is to collapse value into the subjectivity of experience. These analytic philosophers continue to treat the moral values of the Enlightenment, embodied in everyday moral language, as a projection or invention. Thus Mackie says that the implicit assumption of everyday moral talk that values are objective is false, because they are not part of the furniture of the world. He adds that if there were 'objective values, then they would be entities or qualities or relations of a very queer sort, utterly different from anything else in the universe.'[46] They are action-guiding rather than world-guiding, as the evaluative content of ethics—we ought to do x—makes them incapable of depicting the world as it really is. Mackie goes on to say that:

"On a subjectivist view, the supposedly objective values will be based in fact upon attitudes which the person has who takes himself to be recognizing and responding to those values. If we admit what Hume calls 'the mind's propensity to spread itself on external objects', we can understand the supposed objectivity of moral qualities as arising from what we can call the projection of objectification of moral attitudes. This would be analogous to what is called the 'pathetic fallacy', the tendency to read our feelings into objects. If a fungus, say, fills us with disgust, we may be inclined to ascribe to the fungus itself a non-natural quality of foulness."[47]

To claim otherwise is to be in error and so speak the untrue. So the naturalist philosopher wraps himself in the cloak of the ascetic priest as he withdraws from everyday life by spurning or denying it in the name of the truth.

But reasoned scepticism intervenes at this point in Mackie's error theory, because Mackie does not dump the error that he highlights in everyday moral talk. This should be rigorously dumped and replaced by non-error according to the authoritative conventions of scientific culture. But Mackie's rigorous analytic reason fails at this point. And it has to, because without the world of values, we would not have a human world. So in the same book Mackie merrily goes on his way to express straightforward moral views about such topics as whether it is permissible to commit suicide or abortion in the old error-ridden language.[48] Aware of the problem, he advises that what is left for moral philosophy to do, is to decide 'what moral views to adopt, what moral stands to take.'[49] But why should we continue in error? Does this not go against, and undermine, the whole the ethos of the scientific Enlightenment? Error should be replaced by truth. To wallow in error is to live in Plato's cave. Should we not give up error by purging the metaphysical nasties of everyday discourse and embrace truth, however uncongenial? Should not the ascetic naturalist philosopher be less fuzzy and confused, and be more thorough-going? Should he not replace moral terms and concepts by different non-moral ones? Why continue doing philosophy wearing the mask of the ascetic ideal and living off commonsense morality? Should he not eliminate the normative instead of engaging in incoherence? Should he not say that we just live in a world of swirling particles, DNA molecules, and machines that compute? The objective world of the universal cultural values of the Enlightenment does not exist. It is a fiction. There are just desires, values are just feelings, and the universe is an indifferent, uncaring energy machine.

Nietzsche's ascetic ideal argument cuts in at this point, as this picture of modernity is an ethical, sceptical one. Nietzsche observes: 'Skepticism regarding morality is what is decisive. The end of the moral interpretation of the world, which no longer has any sanction after it tried to escape into some beyond, leads to nihilism'[50]. The sceptic neither affirms nor negates in a disenchanted world. He stares at the abyss of the crisis of modernity opening up, and searches for guiding principles to order his life. Mackie finds them in the tradition of everyday morality. We can interpret Mackie's valuation of juxtaposing an inferior everyday life to the true world of natural science, as an ascetic philosopher posing to save us from our sickness. Mackie operates with a view of morality that functions as constraints on the conduct of egoist individuals. The problem that morality is meant to solve is the Hobbesian problem of order in a nation state: Mackie says a plurality of interacting rational egoists does not constitute a rational society as 'limited resources and limited sympathies together generate both competition leading to conflict, and an absence of what would be mutually beneficial cooperation.'[51] Morality is designed to guarantee a life less nasty, less brutish and considerably longer, by restraining the presumptuous, overbearing and greedy seeking their own advantage on the one hand, and safeguarding and protecting the weak, disadvantaged, weak and frail on the other. The presumption of the universality of a unitary and clearly individuated self, naturally motivated by egoism, leads to a firm or authoritarian moral law. This ascetic philosopher seeks to save us by alleviating our suffering and furthering our happiness by placing egoism on the one side and morality on the other, and then turning them into a fundamental opposition. Tradition as the convention of the everyday holds the incoherence of instrumental reason together.

A physicalist philosophical naturalism remains within the boundaries of realism with respect to the world of science, and an anti-realism with respect to the world of ethics. These ascetic philosophers endeavour to step away from the implausibility of humans responding to a value-free world by continuing to hold that projectivism is an explanatory theory that maintains that moral values are projections of sentiment. Pettit puts the idea in terms of response-dependent concepts. This, he says, is 'the claim that the concepts in question, objective though they may seem, are really response-dependent notions: they conform in relevant respects to the general image of secondary quality concepts.'[52] Simon Blackburn's quasi-realism seeks to protect a projectivist account of moral judgment on the lines that moralising is a matter of having attitudes and projecting them onto the world.[53] Blackburn's neo-Humean projectivism revises Mackie's error theory by acknowledging that the institution of morality is something 'sufficiently external to us to act as a constraint or bond on our other sentiments and desires. The chains and shackles must come to us from the outside.'[54] Blackburn's quasi-realism endeavours to justify the projectivist's commitment to valuing as an expression of our subjective sentiment, that values are just feelings. But he also seeks to go beyond the fact—value dichotomy that he inherits from positivism, by affirming what he sees as the most important and characteristic part of the phenomena of everyday morality. This is its obligatory nature or its cultural way of reinforcing feelings of respect, honour and duty which regulate and oppose immediate desire in those sections of the population that are in particular need of them.[55] Here morality functions in terms of authority and discipline that constrain the unruly mass. Morality as a social institution is rule-following, which socially functions to minimize conflict, with its consequences of violence and social disintegration. Values are not just a mythology. Without them we would not have a human world. The social world of human flourishing has to be acknowledged, if we are to talk sense. So we have science and rule-following tradition.

The problem with Blackburn's quasi-realism is that it undercuts liberal democracy by feeding directly into a conservative law and order regime, where a liberal society battens down to go through a period of iron times with more than usual order and more than usual law. Liberal freedom as autonomy or independence of the individual person, derived from freedom from constraint, is pushed to one side by the ascetic philosopher, in tune with the general drift into tougher social discipline associated with the general turn to the right in civil and social life. This holds that the egoism of the unemployed must be harnessed and contained by ensuring that the welfare layabouts and scroungers follow the rules that have been put in place by the state to deal with a crisis. The state has the right say, the ascetic politicians, to move swiftly to stamp hard and fast on the dole-bludgers who break the rules. Resorting to a rational assessment of self-interest to pursue their best interest turns the unemployed into free-riders who dump their responsibilities. If we are to reach the light at the end of the tunnel promised by the logic of capital accumulation, there is a need to keep society on the straight and narrow. The unemployed should follow the moral rules. Morality as rule-following can even be justified as being advantageous on evolutionary grounds, in the sense that the role of social morality can be engineered to produce the right motivational states for the kind of people required to make a utilitarian society function as a well-ordered society. Blackburn's practical rationality is the practical rationality that has come to prevail in our society: namely an instrumental rationality concerned with extending our mastery over the natural and social worlds, a rationality of technique and calculation, of regulation and administration, concerned with finding ever more effective forms of domination in the name of human utility.

This indicates the way that the ethical scepticism of scientistic materialism is compatible with nihilism. Its tacit appeal to the institutions of morality as being what mechanisms desire or prefer within the crisis of modernity, does not offer us much. Right and wrong, as embodied in the institution of morality, does not allow us to talk about substantive values and conceptions of the good life within ecologically sustainable development as being objectively better than the happy life in liberal capitalism. In order to say that as a judgement of reason, we need to step outside of, and be critical of the institution of morality that conditions our feelings and desires. But why should one go against this institution? Only because I desire to do so. If instrumental reason cannot dictate ends, then there is no reason why I should go against tradition, except for another desire. Nor does the turn to rule-bound tradition as the solution to the nihilistic crisis of modernity give us a consistent set of answers in the ordering of chaos. There is a multiplicity of traditions in common life, as the arguments over abortion illustrate, each with their different conceptions of what constitutes the good life. This plurality can be overcome by public definitions of the public interest by a morality that provides the legitimation for political power which resolves the practical problems of everyday life into technical problems associated with the steerage of society by scientific experts. Blackburn's defence of quasi-realism in the ethical sphere provides no grasp of what freedom from domination could mean in a scientific/technological, liberal capitalist society. It leaves us with instrumental reason's conception of rationalization as our increasing subjection to the formal, abstract, uniform and predictable rules and regulations within hierarchical and bureaucratic structures, occupied by functionaries and experts trained to obey. Good Benthamites follow the rule of the greatest happiness of the greatest number, and punish the unemployed for their failure to get a job, by withdrawing welfare to increase the general satisfaction of those in the market in the long run. As Putnam observes, 'the inability of the super-Benthamites to get the way the human world is right is a direct result of their sick conception of human flourishing.'[56]

Enlightenment becomes deeply intertwined with the myth of progress to cover up the sickness inherent in its cultural moral tradition. In its naive form, it is this myth of progress that needs to be unmasked.[57] So we become critical of the metaphysical picture of reality that dumps ethics into the junk heap of appearances, and wraps itself in the mantle of science progressing towards the single truth given by its explanatory picture of a perspective independent reality. We can adopt the position that ethical discourse, with its talk of justice, goodness and virtue, is not reducible to the discourse of physics, and that it is not for that reason illegitimate. It is a non-scientific discourse that is firmly grounded in the human world that we ordinarily inhabit, and that we cannot get along in this world without engaging in some kind of moral discourse. Such a moral discourse works with some kind of knowledge about the ethical situations of the suffering and injuries caused to individuals that we ordinarily relate to. We use this knowledge to relate this suffering to some conception of the content of their well-being, and to what is deemed good in terms of their flourishing as human beings.

The moral crisis of the Enlightenment

The conclusion that we can draw from reflecting on this incoherence within the physicalist picture of the relationship between science and ethics, is that the conception of individuals as mere machines is not an entirely appropriate starting point for understanding who were are. Consider Malcolm, who is sitting in the hospice listening to his mother Pat struggling for breath, as she copes with the continual pain in her chest. The nurse has just made her comfortable so as to ease her pain. He tries to imagine Pat's struggles for breath as the sounds and movement of the gears of a mechanism, which can move in such and such a way. When alone in his study reading Daniel Dennett he can, like Wittgenstein, imagine the nurses and volunteers around him as automata. But he cannot keep hold of this idea in the midst of ordinary discourse with Pat and the nurses in the hospice. He did try when he was celebrating Pat's 82nd birthday with the others. But he found that he could not say to himself that the person laughing over there, sipping champagne with her daughter, telling her stories and listening to jokes is mere automata, and that all her liveliness and talk about her quality of life is mere automatism. As Wittgenstein says, in such situations 'you will either find these words become meaningless, or you will produce in yourself some kind of uncanny feeling, or something of the sort.'[58]

The uncanny queer feeling produced in Malcolm was that the Enlightenment project had collapsed. His mother was no mere utility machine seeking to satisfy her preferences in competition with others. His queer thought was that he was living amidst the broken pieces of the Enlightenment's picture of the world. Canberra is filled with the economically trained, who are in the grip of its picture. The picture was still there in the universities. It remains almost invisible to those, like the neo-classical economists, who live their life modelling the world according to the picture; or those like the philosophers who spend their philosophical lives laboriously filling in the metaphysical details of the picture. Malcolm realized that though the picture should be taken seriously, as it still informs our lives, it no longer makes sense. Its sense now lies far in the background. The application of the picture is no longer easy to survey, even though we easily see the disastrous effects of its economic modelling in everyday life. Malcolm now realizes that he no longer understands its application when he tries to see through the lens of the way it informs our practice as utility machines. He sees that this picture both held him captive—it once held him in its grip—and that it lies in the philosophical/scientific language of the university, which endlessly repeats the picture to him inexorably. He could not get outside it when inside the philosophical world, and he realizes that to give up thinking and talking in terms of the picture, he has to give up the form of life in which the picture has its basis.[59]

Malcolm's queer idea that the Enlightenment project has collapsed can be given some substance in terms of a moral crisis of the Enlightenment tradition. This flows from the nihilistic developments in the ethical sphere which undermine the viability of the scientific Enlightenment project in late modernity. The separation of values from knowledge, the attachment of supreme importance to scientific knowledge, and the subjectivity of value makes the Enlightenment project internally incoherent. The denial of the reality of objective values in the world undermines the valuation placed on the categorical framework of science mirroring the structure of the natural world by cutting reality at the joints. In his valuation of science as a good thing, the naturalist philosopher tacitly endorses his own thinking as coherent, valid, well-founded. Since science is successfully arriving at the truth about the world in itself, the naturalist philosopher sees himself as engaged in operations which have a point and a meaning. He sets himself a goal of knowing truth, and he implicitly judges his success or failure in achieving that goal. He evaluates his own thinking, plus that of others whom he considers in relation to his own, and so he is applying standards of valuation in these evaluations of his own and that of others. In doing so, he brings values into the world. But as the content of his theory is that there are really no such intrinsic values and objective value standards in the world, therefore his own cognitive operations can only be valued as the expression of his non-cognitive feelings. Consequently, according to the content of his theory, the values of his own theory is pretty well worthless, as it is a mere projection, and so a distortion of the real activity of science. But he also holds that science is a valuable activity in itself. It is good and has intrinsic value, and this goodness of science is deemed to be the appropriate attitude to take towards it. It is saying that there is a specific form of value, which arises from human activity, and is something in which we ought to engage in. This value is deemed to be objective in some way, as it the best that we think we have, over and above merely what the culture of our society approves.

This account is incoherent. To describe science as a human activity that gives us truth about the world, cannot be so described solely in non-evaluative terms referring to merely its physical attributes of molecules in motion. On the emotivist account, the attributing of value to science is merely saying "I desire or dislike science", and so the reductive materialist is utterly mistaken with his own efforts to defend science as a valuable a human activity in a world that has collapsed into relativism and nihilism. All such materialists then are deluded about the existence of the value of science, and can never be guided by such things in engaging in philosophy, as objective values do not exist. These are just projections that express our feelings, and the most that can be said about this valuation of science is that it is good in relation to my preferences. If this is too subjectivist, then we can say that in commending science as good, we are saying that it is good for something because it has utility value—the price for which it can be sold or the monetary return it can yield for the investment dollar. Science is valuable because of its exchange value: it is an efficient instrument for producing truth about explaining how things work in themselves, which we can then use to further our desires to make more money and satisfy the desires of shareholders. This means that science is valueless in itself. Its value depends upon its utility, but any content can be pumped into utility. Yet the reductive materialist stands firm in his claim that science is valuable in itself. The analytic form of the Enlightenment project—including that of neo-classical economics, whose philosophical ancestry is a logical empiricism that assumes the dichotomy of fact and value—is incoherent and self-defeating. In writing as if the old positivist fact/value dichotomy is beyond challenge, they are caught up in a moral crisis flowing from their attempt to divide the human world neatly into fact and value in opposition to the deep entanglement of fact and value in our world.[60]

It is Alasdair MacIntyre who has dug deeply on this ground of a moral crisis within Enlightenment culture.[61] He says that though emotivism is dead, we live in an emotivist culture—in the sense that 'in moral argument the apparent assertion of principles functions as a mask for expressions of moral preference.' He adds that emotivism gives expression to this characteristic of an Enlightenment culture by saying 'that there are and can be no valid rational justifications, for any claims that objective and impersonal moral standards exist, and hence that there are no such standards.'[62] Hence the oft-noted way in which emotivism's attempted reduction of morality to personal preference continually recurs in the writings of those analytic philosophers who do not think of themselves as emotivists. The unrecognized philosophical power of emotivism is one clue to its cultural power, which presupposes the obliteration of any genuine distinction between instrumental and non-instrumental social relations. Evaluative utterances have no point, but the expression of my own feelings or attitudes and the transformation of the feelings and attitudes of others. The sole reality of a distinctively moral discourse is the attempt of one will to align the attitudes, feelings and preferences of another with its own. Others are always means, never ends.[63] A world looking through emotivist eyes is a form of life of the competitive struggle in an unregulated market, and the bureaucratic structures of the state and large corporations, where rationality is matching means to ends economically and efficiently. The end that is implicitly appealed to is successful power, whilst the character or masks worn by analytic moral philosophers are an emotivist self, which provides our culture with its moral definitions and beliefs that command universal assent.

MacIntyre holds that the problems of modern moral theory emerge as the product of the failure of the Enlightenment project. He reads Nietzsche as the last word in the Enlightenment project, in that Nietzsche expresses the problem of the rational secular foundation for morality in an entirely new way by constructing a table of what is good. Nietzsche's central thesis, says MacIntyre, is that all rational valuations of morality manifestly fail: if there is nothing to morality but expressions of will, then my morality can only be what my will creates. He states the problem this way:

> "On the one hand the individual moral agent, freed from hierarchy and teleology, conceives of himself and is conceived by moral philosophers as sovereign in his moral authority. On the other hand the inherited, if partially transformed rules of morality have to be found some new status, deprived as they have been of their older teleological character and their even more ancient categorical character as expressions of an ultimately divine law. If such rules cannot be found a new status which will make appeal to them rational, appeal to them will indeed appear as a mere instrument of individual desire and will."[64]

MacIntyre's narrative of the ethical institution in an enlightened culture is that the Enlightenment project has failed to provide moral agents with a secular rational justification for their moral allegiances, even though this ethical discourse assumes that this project has succeeded. The significance of Nietzsche's problematic of nihilism in our culture, says MacIntyre, is that Nietzsche saw the failure which represents the culmination and self-overthrow of the Enlightenment: the purported appeal to objectivity is an expression of subjective will.

MacIntyre says that the moral Enlightenment's project of an independent rational justification of morality on universal tradition-independent rational principles, is now historically and politically embodied in liberalism, and that it is chiefly the project of a modern liberal society rather than simply that of the philosophers.[65] He argues that the transformation of liberalism into a tradition signifies the collapse of liberalism's moral enlightenment's project of developing an independent rational justification of morality on universal tradition-independent rational principles:

> "The starting points of liberal theorizing are never neutral between conceptions of the human good; they are always liberal starting points. And the inconclusiveness of the debates within liberalism as to the fundamental principles of liberal justice...reinforces the view that liberal theory is best understood, not at all as an attempt to find a rationality independent of tradition, but as itself an articulation of an historically developed and developing set of social institutions and forms of activity, that is, the voice of a tradition."[66]

The failure comes from its own self-undermining because its core beliefs were internally incoherent. He says that we if contrast the various Enlightenment's strong conceptions of rationality, in which the point of rational debate was to establish truths, and those methods were acceptable which led to the conclusive refutation of error and the vindication of truth with current academic practice, then we see that the outcomes of rational debate on fundamental issues are systematically inconclusive. What is required for a conclusive termination of rational debate he says:

> "would be an appeal to a standard or set of standards such that no adequately rational person could fail to acknowledge its authority. But such a standard or standard, since it would have to provide criteria for the rational acceptability of any theoretical or conceptual scheme, would itself have to be formulable and defensible independently of any such scheme. But—and it is here that contemporary academic practice breaks radically with its Enlightenment predecessors—there can be no such standard; any standard adequate to discharge such functions will itself be embedded in, supported by, and articulated in terms of some set of theoretical and conceptual schemes...each rival theoretical standpoint provides from within itself and in its own terms the standards by which, so its adherents claim, it should be

evaluated, rivalry between such contending standpoints includes rivalry over standards."[67]

What is concluded is that when such large-scale theoretical standpoints are at odds with one another, there can be no way of rationally settling the difference between them: there is just this plurality of individual conceptions of the good life with the state remaining neutral between them.

There is a moral crisis in a scientific liberal tradition like that of neo-classical economics, which endeavours to employ the principle of utility to provide autonomous moral agents with an objective and impersonal criteria to replace the hollowed out Christian moral system of signs based on resentment. This formal system of ethics, based on the moral character implicit in emotivism, the impartial moral standpoint, and the basic separateness of persons, constitutes and sees itself as a system which is globally exhaustive in its determinations. It presents itself, like its competing rights discourse, as a consistent system which tells us what we ought to do and how we should live. Yet if the world is as reductionist materialism says it is— molecules in motion, energy and mass and so devoid of meaning and value—then it is difficult to see how utility machines can be moral beings with moral agency in the world concerned to bring about a happier life, based on the liberal values of autonomy. There are just these deterministic physical processes, devoid of interests, purposes and meaning, and all we have are machines with fixed natures causally interacting with one another. Though utilitarianism shudders at pain and suffering in order to fashion a morality independent of history, it conflates all desire or individual preference into a single system of desire to establish the principle of utility. Rather than allowing the subject to reproduce the variability of desires, and thereby render the merely abstract diversity of subjective desire concrete, utilitarianism tends to efface the difference between subjects. We are all just utility machines in the market place, responding to the price signals of interest rates in order to achieve what we desire. The whole thrust of utilitarianism, Charles Taylor argues, is to do away with qualitative distinctions of worth:

> "on the grounds that they represent confused perceptions of the real basis of our preferences which are quantitative. The hope has been that once we have done away with strong evaluation we will be able to calculate."[68]

The principle of utility is a moral fiction which provides the semblance of rationality for the modern liberal polity. Since the objects of educated human desire are irreducible and heterogeneous, the notion of summing the preferences up in terms of the greatest happiness for the greatest number is the mask of morality which conceals what are, in fact, the preferences of arbitrary will and desires of utility machines.

What has value for the economic utilitarian is the satisfaction of the individual's interest—where interest means what people desire or prefer—but

200

not the individual who has that interest. This is seen as a caricature of morality by Kantian rights-based liberal humanism, on the grounds that it allows for harming of some individual, purely to produce an aggregate balance of pleasure over pain, as in executing an innocent person for a crime they were believed to have committed, so as to act as a deterrent to would-be criminals or give satisfaction to the law and order moral majority.[69] The denial of qualitative distinctions, by reducing them to the quantitative, means that utilitarianism provides an impoverished conception of justice. Justice as welfare involves more than the fair distribution of material goods, for even if the conflicts over our economic interests were justly adjudicated, our society is normatively defective, to the extent that it systematically denies groups and classes the recognition they deserve.[70] Members of marginalized and subaltern groups like the Aborigines have been systematically denied recognition for the worth of their culture or way of life, the dignity of their status as persons, and recognition of their integrity.

The crisis of Enlightenment politics

The moral crisis is linked to a crisis in the politics of the Enlightenment project. Rawls indicates this with respect to the utilitarian strand. He says that the attempts by classical utilitarians—Bentham, Edgeworth and Sidgwick—to construct a morality based on the subjective desires of machines concerned with their own self-interest, result in the efficient administration of resources to maximize the satisfactions of the system of desire. This is constructed by the impartial spectator from the many individual systems of desire which are accepted as an *a priori* given. Something is right when an ideally rational and impartial spectator would approve of it from a general point of view, should he possess all the relevant knowledge of the circumstances. The conceptual device of the impartial spectator is conceived as carrying the required organization of the desires of all egoistic persons into one coherent system of desire. Morality becomes a system of norms, which keep social order well-ordered, and we obey these norms insofar as it is in our interest to do so. As Rawls observes 'it is by this construction that many persons are fused into one.'[71] Rawls says that the impartial spectator in this discourse is endowed with 'ideal powers of sympathy and imagination', and is 'the perfectly rational individual who identifies with and experiences the desires of others as if they were his own'.[72] This masculine spectator operates with instrumental rationality, concerned with the efficient means for attaining pregiven ends. The politics here, as we have previously seen, begins with the ideal, impartial spectator as the state; a state which seeks to maintain the bourgeois social order, which is continually undermined by the disturbances to the self-regulating system by the consequences of its exploitative and oppressive nature. The state, as ideal spectator, helps to reproduce this social order in which it is a subsystem, and if it is to remain sufficiently detached, then concrete personal desires about our suffering must be ignored. The political crisis arises when the ideal spectator, as the legislating state, orders all desires if as they were his own, and so organises society along the command-obedience model in the name of the 'natural.' This connection between legislative moral reason and an enlightened state in the scientistic Enlightenment, undermines liberal politics, because it gives rise to the behavioural social engineering of an enlightened state that has its roots in Government House utilitarianism. This sanctions a form of practical reason, which succumbs to the demand for expert administrators, teachers, and scientists to align themselves with the rational control of the state; an enlightened state which moulds and cultivates our human psyche and body, and does so by appealing to the secular faith in progress. We enter the super-Benthamite world of the economic rationalist state whose:

> "free market policies are killing the Australian economy and causing hardship and financial ruin for millions of Australians. the economy has been bought to its knees by financial and economic deregulation, the elimination of tariffs, unsuccessful structural reform in industry, free trade in agriculture, open slather for imports, privatization, repressive monetary policies...The public sector capital stock—the economic infrastructure on which industries depend and the social infrastructure which determines the quality of life—is in a state of chronic decay. The economy has plunged into a recession we were told we had to have, but which is so deepseated that it can be reasonably be regarded as full-scale depression. Homelessness, poverty, and despair have become common place..."[73]

The political crisis is that the free market policies of the neo-classical economic Benthamites have placed Australia on the "Mexican road" towards a "fish and chips" economy in a "banana" republic. The model of politics within this scientistic materialist tradition suggests that domination can be located within the utopian model being imposed on society against the will of the majority.

The thesis that domination is inherent in Enlightenment reason's project of re-ordering society through the legislating state, can be explored if we turn to Helvetius and Bentham, two of the patron philosophers of reductive mechanistic philosophy. Baron Paul d'Holbach sketches a general metaphysics in which nature, including human beings, was a lawfully ordered mechanism. It was seen as a giant piece of clockwork, that, with appropriate direction and guidance from the outside by those who understood its laws, could run very well indeed.[74] It is Helvetius who develops the implicit anthropological conception of Locke's epistemological conception of the mind as a clean slate or *tabula rasa*, with its dimension of malleability of human beings who can be 'moulded and fashioned as one pleases' into a politics.[75] In Helvetius, the Lockean metaphors of waxen minds and blank slates become transformed into the human puppet. He says that 'To guide the motions of the human puppet it is necessary to know the wires by which it is moved.'[76] Elsewhere he says that 'Man is a machine, which, being put into motion by corporeal sensibility, ought to perform all that it executes.'[77] In expelling the ghost of mind in Cartesian dualism, he leaves us with human beings as automata. These have the passive capacity to register sense impressions, and to respond positively or negatively to those they find pleasurable or painful. The susceptibility of human beings to being modified from the outside opens the prospects of the artificially designed improvement of all mankind. Helvetius, who is aware of this, says:

> "If I can demonstrate that man is in fact nothing more than the product of his education, I shall doubtless reveal an important truth to mankind. They will learn that they have in their own hands an instrument of their own greatness and their felicity, and that to be happy and powerful nothing more is requisite than to perfect the science of education."[78]

This Enlightenment optimism operates in terms of man educating himself, fails to spell out who is the "they" who hold the instrument to educate the others. Who are the "others"? As Marx said: who will educate the educators? Who is the knower, and who is the known? Who controls and who is controlled? Who is the subject and who is the object here? Who floats above nature discerning the truth about the laws of nature, so they can, from the Archimedean point of their Olympian detachment use their objective knowledge to leverage the world? Who are determined by passivity, manipulability and blind determination in the realm of necessity? Who are leveraged by those pulling the mechanical levers?

The technocratic answer is that those doing the leveraging are the enlightened experts, who have the clear and definite knowledge of all the motions of nature, including the motions of human beings as parts of the gigantic machine that is nature. They look down and see it all, in the words of Bentham, from the 'elevated point from which the whole map of human interest and situation lies extended to his view.'[79] Thus returns the *deus ex machina* of the rational and systematic ideal Legislator who has the knowledge of the wires that move the human puppet. He has the knowledge of the pleasure and pain mechanisms, which can be fashioned on behalf of public utility, so the greatest number can be happy. Thomas Spragens sums up the early modernist technocratic conception of politics:

> "Society should be rationalized by the strategic application of scientific knowledge. From his elevated perspective the scientist is to observe the motions of mankind and infer from these observations the laws of human nature. Legitimated by his positive knowledge and by his moral disinterest, he can become a true 'doctor of morality' who compels men to be virtuous through an experimental physics of the soul. His primary tools are legislation and education, both of which involve controlling the environment in order to attach pleasure to socially usefully acts and pains to socially mischievous acts. He need not be inhibited in his work by fear of infringing liberty or natural rights. And his ultimate goal is to achieve a smoothly

functioning society that maximizes the pleasures of the human artefacts who inhabit it."[80]

The governance of society is a process of control in which the technocrat is the maker of society, who fashions subjects and administers things by imposing order and form on chaos. Technocratic governance signifies the neutrality and objectivity of the efficient means, with the implicit goals within the governance rendered immune to moral challenge. Its politics is that of an efficiently run non-democratic regime. The Enlightened state legislators look down at the masses below, as they legislate a rationally designed order and control chaos. Their gaze is from the central observing tower of the closed high-tech Panopticon—Bentham's Panopticon is the grand metaphor for an orderly, reason-led modernist society in which everyone is happy. A humanized civil society in modernity is a hierarchical world of prisons, workhouses, detention centres, military barracks, lunatic asylums, factories and bureaucracies. Economics, psychology, sociology and psychiatry have formed shifting alliances in their concern to give us knowledge as part of social control. Morality is the affirmation of human-kind's self assertion, and the subordination of the non-human world to human will and valuation (utility to human beings) is underpinned by a progressivist philosophy of history. The greatest good in relation to nature bears an inherent bias to keep the economic machine ticking over, with an ever more efficient management and control of nature based on its value to human beings.

This technocracy arises from an Enlightened liberalism's assumptions of self-seeking machines satisfying their desires leading into the problem of order. First suggested by the early precursor of public choice theory—Hobbes with his theory of sovereignty—it was later incorporated by the early Bentham in his theory of law.[81] Bentham's Constitutional Code, creates a union of duty and interest that would guide political actors towards a consensus around the collective interest; a collective interest of the greatest happiness of the community deemed to be a collection of atomistic individuals. When relocated within the power relations of capitalism, the stance of legislating enlightening reason becomes the self-reproduction of the social order, with its class and gender relations of domination. The paternalist stance in this emotivist culture is seen in one of the central characters, the bureaucratic manager. MacIntyre says this character 'treats ends as given, as outside his scope; his concern is with technique, with effectiveness in transforming raw materials into final product, unskilled labour into skilled labour, investments into profits.'[82] This character, who is also the economic rationalist speaking on behalf of the legislating enlightened state, needs political control to order the world efficiently. He holds that rational economic man operates in the market to maximize his welfare based on utilitarian considerations. Economic agents in market institutions, in capitalist modernity, are characteristically engaged in a competitive struggle for scarce resources to achieve their predetermined ends. Given the failure of the market to deliver desirable social and ecological outcomes—the tragedy of the commons—it is therefore a central responsibility of state expert managerialists to direct and redirect their organization's resources, both human and non-human, as efficiently as possible towards those ends. Instrumental economic rationality in matching means to ends economically and efficiently, appeals to its own effectiveness as a successful power through controlling behaviour and suppressing conflict.

This is an authoritarian stance, as it is willing to destroy regional ways of life and ecological sustainablity to achieve the re-orientation of an economy such as Australia's, so that it provides cheap resources for the northern imperialists. The subtext of economic rationalism is that these sacrifices have to be made to ensure the pursuit of the greater good. It is the price we pay so that capital and labour can be freely moved to where the greatest profits can be made. The economist's mask of neutrality hides his theoretical retreat from everyday practical action, and disguises the way he colludes in the prevailing moral hypocrisy that the good life is the pleasurable life of consuming in the marketplace, with its formal law, manipulation of desire, and contempt for the weak. The mask of neutrality is a nihilistic form of resignation to what is. It is crippled, as it is unwilling to create a world so that we can be humanly at home in it.

Conclusion

Nietzsche charts a way out of the moral and political crisis of technocratic nihilism by asserting the autonomy of the ethical sphere against the imperialism of the scientific/economic sphere. He highlights the worth or intelligibility of the various practices of the revaluation of values outside the scientific sphere in relation to suffering, and so contests the hegemony of a utilitarian form of practical reason.[83] His radical aristocratic path, with its three-tiered social structure, points to a better life for noble human beings, who are more than mere means to utilitarian ends beyond themselves. This involves a determinate conception of flourishing based on healthy human functioning. Science is subordinated to the ends of human action, as it is concerned to promote and help us realize a good, healthy human life, and so become a better kind of human being than that held by utilitarianism.

The conception of a good human life in late capitalist liberal society would include being able to live to the end of a complete life, being in good health, having pleasurable experiences, being able to laugh and play, using our five senses, being able to form a conception of the good life and engage in critical reflection, living for and with others, and living with a concern for and with animals. Such a life is held together through being planned and organized by practical reason, in which we are bound to other human beings by ties of mutual affection and concern. We evaluate our community in terms of how its people are able to function in these centrally human ways, and are able to judge the freedom that is missing from our lives to enable us to continue our self-actualization. In endeavouring to articulate this, in opposition to the technocratic economists, we ragpickers are continuing the process of rupturing from and revaluing the Enlightenment's nihilistic system of values begun by Nietzsche. We continue to confront the emptying out of the highest values of scientific Enlightenment, which scornfully flees from the particular embodied world of actual human suffering with abhorrence. The response is an ethics of resentment that starts from concrete questions of an overwhelming sense of injustice and powerlessness, within an already existing society with its established order of class, gender and race, codes of civility, and measures of strength and weakness.

The process of rupturing and philosophical hammering of the citadel of universal reason can conceived as a dialogue. It is *our* cultural conceptions that are being hammered and reworked by the hermeneutical practices of the phenomenologist as part of defetishizing critique. Our education shows that the cultural given of the Enlightenment tradition is a socially and historically constructed cultural form, which is the result of the building undertaken by modernist subjects. Though it may appear initially alien to us ragpickers, it can be taken into our possession, and transformed to serve human purposes in the present, thereby opening up to the future by transforming and reappropriating the past. This learning process on the sceptical highway of despair is a process where the inadequacy of previous cultural forms are dismantled as part of the process of building new cultural forms within new forms of life. Faced with such a situation, and our awareness that there is no escape from the relations and effects of power, we then engage in a critique of the rational practices we have been trained in, to analyse and defetishize the way we govern ourselves and others. This means a critique of scientific reason, not to argue that there is something inherently wrong with science *per se*, in the sense that there is a logic of domination built into it. It is to draw attention to the need to rethink the nature of scientific rationality because it has too narrow a concept of rationality for digging our way out of a nihilistic modernity.

There has been a sundering of perspective in modernity at this point in terms of dealing with the crisis of modernity. The path taken by liberalism and Marxism has been a concern with science, linked to the problem of justice, arising from domination and exploitation, coupled with an insensitivity to the problem of meaning. This leads to the problems of science and justice being deemed to be the most important problems of modernity. Here we need knowledge derived from an explanation of how the social world ticks behind our backs, in order to be able to set about rationally ordering our society, so that oppressive and exploitative social relations are eliminated. This has given rise a social science that incorporates the ethical dimension in terms of an impoverished utilitarian morality.

The other path within modernity is that of phenomenology and existentialism, which followed the trailmarks of Nietzsche and Heidegger. It is directed to the problem of meaning, but it remains indifferent to the question of justice. This leads to alienation, loss of meaning and demotivation being seen as the troublesome problems of our time, and leads to the emphasis on the creative dimension to human activity, and the problem of ethics in a disenchanted world. A dual perspective can be found in Adorno and Horkheimer, who linked injustice and nihilism in modernity in terms of having a common root in the abstract formalism of an instrumental reason dominating nature. They explored the way an instrumental reason, conceptualizing and mastering a disenchanted nature, leads to its domination by techno-science; and to the domination of human nature by a technoscience integrated into state's crisis management of society. They counterposed to the instrument reason of techno-science an aesthetic reflective reason concerned with particulars. Following the romantics, they defended meaningfulness against its subsumption under the meaning, destroying mechanisms of an Enlightenment science, geared towards the expansion and rationalization of power embodied in the reified economic and political structures of capitalist modernity. Their conclusion was that knowledge, yielding control and mastery of a valueless nature, resulted in the destruction of nature, a social world where human relations were primarily instrumental ones, and an nihilistic capitalist social order, based on the injustice of the domination of the majority of human beings. So ends the Enlightenment project. The task is to dig our way out of the ruins. It is a future task that philosophy can and should contribute to.

Notes and References

1.   F. Nietzsche, *The Gay Science*, trs. W. Kaufmann, (Vintage, New York, 1978), Bk 5, section 373, p. 335.

2.   Ibid, section 25, pp. 153-4.

3.   G. Harman, *The Nature of Morality*, (Oxford University Press, New York, 1977), p. 11.

4.   Philippia Foot, "Nietzsche's Immoralism", in Richard Schacht, (ed.), *Nietzsche, Genealogy, Morality: Essays on Nietzsche's Genealogy of Morals*, (University of California Press, Berkeley, 1994), pp. 3-14.

5.   Friedrich Nietzsche, *The Will to Power*, trs. Walter Kaufmann, (Vintage, New York, 1968), Bk. 1, section 57, p. 40.

6.   Ibid, Bk.1, section 2, p. 9.

7.   Ibid, section 32, p. 22.

8.   Ibid, section 7, p. 11, section 13, p. 14, section. 28, p. 19, section 32, p. 22.

9.   For excellent work on the ancient ethical traditions refer to, Martha Nussbaum, *The Fragility of Goodness: Luck and Ethics in Greek Tragedy and Philosophy*, (Cambridge University Press Cambridge, 1986); & *The Therapy of Desire: Theory and Practice in Hellenistic Ethics*, (Princeton University Press, Princeton, 1994).

10. F. Nietzsche, *Ecce Homo*, trs. Walter Kaufmann, (Vintage, New York, 1989), 'Thus Spake Zarathustra', section 8, p. 309.

11. F. Nietzsche, *Genealogy of Morals*, trs W. Kaufmann, (Vintage, New York, 1989), Third Essay, section 11, p. 117.

12. Ibid, Third Essay, section 24, p. 151.

13. Ibid, Third Essay, section 23, p. 146.

14. Ibid, Third Essay, section 28, pp. 162-163.

15. For an extensive elaboration, refer to, M. Warren, *Nietzsche and Political Thought*, (MIT Press, Cam., Mass., 1991).

16 F. Nietzsche, *Genealogy of Morals*, op. cit.,Third Essay, section 23, p. 147.

17 Ibid, Third Essay, section 25, p. 153.

18 F. Nietzsche, *The Gay Science*, op. cit., Book 5, section 344, pp. 282-283.

19 J. C. C. Smart, "A Form of Metaphysical Realism", *The Philosophical Quarterly*, vol. 45, no. 180, (July, 1995), pp. 301-315, especially p. 310.

20 F. Nietzsche, *The Gay Science*, op. cit., Bk 5, section 373, p. 335.

21 F. Nietzsche, *Will to Power*, op. cit., Book Three, Section 820, p. 434.

22 Women have chastity imposed on them until marriage in a patriarchy which then drives them to hysteria. See Nietzsche, *The Gay Science*, Bk. 2, section 71, pp. 127-8.

23 For the way the body is a problem to be managed by social systems in relation to order, control and sexuality see B. S. Turner, *The Body and Society*, (Blackwell, Oxford, 1986). Turner's emphasis is on the mode of control by which society has sought to control the body in space. He emphasizes the contraints that bodies are placed under, how this affects their capabilities, and illustrates the way bodies break down and become ill as a result of the modes of social control imposed on them. For the way this operates in relation to flight attendants see, A. Hochschild, *The Managed Heart: Commercialization of Human Feeling*, (University of California Press, Berkeley, 1983).

24 F. Nietzsche, *Genealogy of Morals*, op. cit., Third essay section 25, pp. 153-4.

25 F. Nietzsche, *The Gay Science*, op. cit., Bk. 2, section 107, pp. 163-4.

26 F. Nietzsche, *Genealogy of Morals*, op. cit., Third essay, section 25, pp. 153-4.

27 Ibid, Third Essay, sections 2-5, pp. 98-103 & F. Nietzsche, "Wagner as the Apostle of Chastity", in *Nietzsche Contra Wagner*, Section 2, in W. Kaufmann, (ed.), *The Portable Nietzsche*, (Viking, New York, 1954).

28 Contrary to Walter Kaufmann's thesis that Nietzsche is fundamentally anti-political Nietzsche is a very political thinker. The stress on culture as 'self-perfection' or self making as self overcoming is deeply intertwined with politics of this world. The core function of the political order is to promote and sustain the highest human beings who experience their existence as their own justification. See B. Detwiler, *Nietzsche and the Politics of Aristocratic Radicalism*, (The University of Chicago Press, Chicago, 1990).

29 Nietzsche, *Beyond Good and Evil*, trs. Walter Kaufmann, (Vintage, New York, 1989), Part Six, "We Scholars", section 211-212, pp. 135-139.

30 For a more balanced look at New Age culture, refer to Andrew Ross, *Strange Weather: Culture, Science and Technology in the Age of Limits*, (Verso, London, 1991), ch. 1.

31 Bryan Appleyard, *Understanding the Present*, (Pan Books, London, 1992), pp. xii-xiii.

32 J. Habermas, "Modernity versus Postmodernity", *New German Critique*, No. 22, pp. 3-14. Reprinted as "Modernity-an incomplete project", in H. Foster,(ed.), *The Anti-Aesthetic: Essays In Postmodern Culture*, (Bay Press, Washington, 1983), pp. 3-15, citation p. 9.

33 Jurgen Habermas, "Philosophy as Stand-in and Interpreter", in K. Baynes, J. Boham, T. McCarthy, (eds.), *After Philosophy: end or transformation?*, (MIT Press, Cambridge Massachusetts,1987), pp. 296-315, citation, pp. 298-9.

34 The distinction between the two broad types of theories of modernity-aculturalist and culturalist-can be found in Charles Taylor, "Inwardness and the Culture of Modernity", in T. McCarthy et. al. (eds), *Philosophical Interventions in the Unfinished Project of Enlightenment*, (MIT Press, Cambridge Massachusetts, 1992), pp. 88-112, especially p. 88; & "Modernity and the Rise of the Public Sphere", in *The Tanner Lectures on Human Value*, (University of Utah, Salt Lake City, 1993), pp. 205-60, especially p. 205.

35 Max Weber, *The Protestant Ethic and the Spirit of Capitalism*, trs. Talcott Parsons, (Scribners, New York, 1958), p. 181.

36 Weber's own defence of a value free social science is symptomatic of the very rationalization process he so acutely diagnosed. See P. Lassman, I. Velody & H. Martins, (ed.), *Max Weber's 'Science as a Vocation'*, (Unwin Hyman, 1989). This essay along, with his essays in *Methodology of the Socal Sciences*, (ed.) Edward A. Shils &

Harry A. Finch, (The Free Press, New York, 1949), forms the bedrock for the philosophical justifications of twentieth century value-free social science.

37 This thesis was argued by the early Habermas, *Legitimation Crisis*, trs. Thomas McCarthy, (Beacon Press, Boston, 1975), pp. 77-78. The latter Habermas rewrites Weber's dialectics of rationalization so that communicative reason provides the intersubjective foundation for a normative science. J. Habermas, *The Theory of Communicative Action: Reason and the Rationalization of Society*, trs. Thomas McCarthy, (Beacon Press, Boston, 1984). pp. 143-271.

38 Francis Bacon, *The Advancement of Learning and the New Atlantis*, (Oxford University Press, London, 1957), p. 298.

39 For a history of the scientific tradition within western culture up to and including Francis Bacon, refer to, Richard Olsen, *Science Deified & Science Defied*, (University of California Press, Berkeley, 1982).

40 This was explored in relation to positivist science by H. Marcuse, *Reason and Revolution*, (Routledge and Kegan Paul, London, 1967), pp. 340-360.

41 Most notably in A. J. Ayer, *Language Truth and Logic*, (Penguin, Harmondsworth, 1971), pp. 136ff.

42 James Buchanan, "Public Finance and Academic Freedom", in *What Should Economists Do?* (Liberty Press, Indianapolis, 1979), p. 265.

43 C. A. Hooker, *Reason, Regulation and Realism*, (State University of New York, Press, Albany, 1995), pp. 311-313.

44 Ibid, p. 325.

45 Ibid, p. 335.

46 J. L. Mackie, *Ethics Inventing Right and Wrong*, (Penguin, Harmondsworth, 1977), p. 3.

47 Ibid, p. 42.

48 Ibid, pp. 195-197.

49 Ibid, p. 106.

50 F. Nietzsche, *The Will to Power*, op. cit., Book One, Section, 1, p. 7.

51 Ibid, p. 111.

52 Philipp Pettit, "Realism and (response-)dependence", in Peter Menzies, (ed.) *Response Dependent Concepts*, (Working Papers in Philosophy, No.1. Research School of the Social Sciences, Australian National University, 1991), p. 4.

53 Simon Blackburn, *Essays in Quasi-Realism*, (Oxford University Press, Oxford, 1993).

54 Ibid,p. 153.

55 Ibid, pp. 154-5.

56 Hilary Putnam, *Reason, Truth and History*, (Cambridge University Press, Cambridge, 1981), p. 141.

57 As held by the messanic tradition of Walter Benjamin and T. Adorno who inverted the naive progress story of Enlightenment. See W. Benjamin, "Theses on the Philosophy of History", in W. Benjamin, *Illuninations*, (Fontana/Collns, Glasgow, 1973), pp. 255-266.

58 L. Wittgenstein, *Philosophical Investigations*, trs. G. E. M. Anscombe, (Blackwell, Oxford, 1958), para. 420, p. 126.

59 C. Diamond, *The Realistic Spirit*, (MIT Press, Cambridge, Massachusetts, 1991), p. 259.

60 The arguments can be found in Iris Murdock, *The Sovereignty of Good*, (Schocken Books, New York, 1975).

61 Alasdair MacIntyre, *After Virtue: a study in moral theory, 2nd edition*, (Duckworth, London, 1985).

62 Ibid, p. 19.

63 Ibid, p. 24.

64 Ibid, p. 62.

65   Alasdair MacIntyre, *Whose Justice? Whose Rationality*, (University of Notre Dame Press, Indiana, 1988), p. 335.

66   Ibid, p. 145.

67   Alasdair MacIntyre, *Three Rival Versions of Moral Inquiry: Encyclopedia, Genealogy and Tradition*, (Duckworth, London, 1990), pp. 172-3.

68   Charles Taylor, "What is Human Agency?" in C. Taylor, *Human Agency and Language, Philosophical Papers, vol 1*, (Cambridge University Press, Cambridge, 1985), pp. 15-44, citation, p. 17.

69   For J. C. C. Smart's defence, refer to, *An Outline of a System of Utilitarian Ethics*, (The University Press, Cambridge, 1961), pp. 26ff.

70   C. Taylor, "Engaged Agency and Background", in C. B. Guignon, (ed.), *The Cambridge Companion to Heidegger*, (Cambridge University Press, Cambridge, 1993), p. 319.

71   J. Rawls, *A Theory of Justice*, (Harvard University Press, Cambridge, Massachusetts, 1971), p. 27.

72   Ibid, p. 27.

73   Russell Mathews, Is There an Alternative Economic Policy?, *CEDA Public Information Paper*, no. 38, (March, 1992), p. 1.

74   Baron Paul d' Holbach, *The System of Nature*, trs. H. C. Robinson, (Burt Franklin, New York, 1970.)

75   John Locke, *Some Thoughts Concerning Education*, (Cambridge University Press, Cambridge, 1902), pp. 187ff.

76   Claude Helvetius, *A Treatise on Man*, trs. W. Hooper, (Burt Franklin, New York, 1970), Vol. 1. p. 4.

77   Ibid, pp 159-50.

78   Ibid, p. 3.

79   Jeremy Bentham, *Collected Works*, (ed.), John Bowring, (Russell and Russell, New York, 1962), Vol. 1, p. 193.

80   Thomas A. Spragens Jr., *The Irony of Liberal Reason*, (The University of Chicago Press, Chicago. 1981), p. 115

81   Bentham's *Constitutional Code* is usually read a classic text of liberal democracy. For the command obedience interpretation refer L. J. Hume, *Bentham and Bureaucracy*, (Cambridge University Press, Cambridge, 1981). For an analysis of Bentham's arguments that utilitarianism does not justify vested interests, see L. J. Hume, "Bentham as a Social and Political Theoriest", in *Political Science*, Xl, (1988), pp. .11-127

82   Alasdair MacIntyre, *After Virtue*, op. cit., p. 30.

83   F. Nietzsche in *On The Genealogy of Morals* takes aim at the English utilitarians as a way of beginning his analysis of the origins of moral values. The revaluation of all values is also a revaluation of the utilitarian account that all human behaviour can be accounted for in terms of seeking pleasure and avoiding pain. Nietzsche, *On The Genealogy of Morals*, op. cit., Bk. 1, section 1-3, pp. 24-27.

6 Has philosophy come to an end?

There are no more individuals, neither men nor women. These beings—one does not know what to call them—are neither human nor animal, neither liberated nor alienated, neither conscious nor animated by false consciousness. They are perfectly plastic. Their nature is no longer determined by other men but by the perfect machine...These beings no longer speak—they have nothing to say, since they have nothing to think or feel. No more art. No more anything. The electronic machine produces—the word itself has lost all meaning—everything, these beings included.

Samir Amin.

Philosophy turns out to be an endless reflection on its own destruction at the hands of literature.

Paul De Man, *Allegories of Reading.*

Can philosophy help to dig us out of the carnage of a nihilistic crisis within an out-of-control global capitalist system throwing millions out of work? Or has philosophy finished? Can we speak of the end of philosophy in the sense that economic rationalist policies result in philosophy going the way of classics and comparative religion in the globalized world of postmodernity? Has a philosophy, continuous with science, which aims to construct a metaphysical picture of the truth of being in the form of a mechanistic picture of human beings in nature, exhausted its possibilities? Has the physicalist form of philosophical naturalism, which continues to develop the old unity of science programme of the logical positivists, run into a dead end?

The signs of the end of philosophy are manifold. There is a current constriction and stasis in the hegemonic analytic school and there is a disenchantment with the analytic form of an reductionist materialist philosophy. Philosophy, like modernist art, has become increasingly preoccupied with its own existence, ethos and autonomy. It has turned in on itself. Wittgenstein and Rorty have made a therapeutic farewell to an autonomous, systematic philosophy. Rorty has moved on to hermeneutics, and given up expending his energies on transforming philosophy as a way of defending it. The habitual smugness of analytic philosophers about their discipline being unassailable has been questioned by what they see as Rorty's betrayal and attack on the autonomy and integrity of their discipline. Yet this smugness covers up an inner core suspicion that they are in the doldrums, and are left to defend a waning cause, as the world passes them by. The constriction or stasis that now hangs around the philosophy institution, and the increasing calcification of the analytic tradition, can be philosophically expressed as the issue of the end or demise of philosophy.[1]

The end-of-philosophy debate does not really mean very much to those outside the academy. The philosophically unsophisticated have little knowledge of the philosophical tradition, and they see philosophy as part of an academic scholasticism. Those who do read academic philosophy have little empathy with the technical fetish and narrow theoretical concerns of analytic philosophy. Many in the public sphere are puzzled why so much fuss is made over those philosophers who venture outside the canons of tradition to engage with the concerns of a wider intellectual culture. They assume that this is what philosophers do. So why is this seen as being beyond the philosophical pale? Nor does the end-of-philosophy debate have much meaning inside the academy, despite the Marxist challenge to analytic philosophy in the 1970s being a political challenge, with a widespread desire to sweep away a suffocating orthodoxy. That challenge petered out in the confluence of Marxism and analytic philosophy, an affirmation of philosophy being continuous with science, physics worship, and the continuation of the unity of science programme, with the social replacing the natural sciences, as the object of knowledge. It did give us a critical realist science, which Peter Dickens has summarized in terms of the stratification of knowledge:

> "At a general level relatively enduring generative structures are envisaged. These underlie the manifest phenomena of everyday life. Entities, such as humans, other organisms, and those of inorganic nature have latent powers or capacities...But...these structures and tendencies are not observable in an unmediated form. They emerge and combine in complex ways with contingent relations and tendencies. Indeed, the contingent factors may be such that the underlying mechanisms or ways of

acting may not be experienced or observed. Explanation of manifest appearances critically relies, therefore, on *both* abstract laws and theories and on information of a less abstract kind."[2]

The social world is represented by a critical scientific realism as structured, differentiated and changing. Social, as well as natural phenomena, are seen as the product of plurality of structures. Science dissolves ideology whilst philosophy finds its completeness in science. In this sense philosophy is bought to an end. Marxism gained its legitimacy within the academy largely by a critical engagement with a positivist philosophy of science, but at the price of an autonomous philosophy wearing a death mask and having a ghostly significance. Philosophy ensured that the authoritative status of science remained in place in the face of anti-scientistic currents.

Raising the issue about the end of philosophy within Australia is generally seen to be advocating what has been discarded: namely a historicist form of Kantianism, an idealism or an anti-naturalism, which adheres to spooky entities and refuses to acknowledge the supremacy of natural science. It is held that a scientific, analytic philosophy has historically played a progressive role in Australian culture, by furthering the process of Enlightenment. It cleaned out the stables of the nonsense put forth by Christian idealists, who supplied human beings with false comforters and illusions; by romantics who had swallowed too much of Kant's Copernican revolution and set man over against nature; and by wimpy, ordinary language philosophers who had a false conception of science. Philosophy today means physicalist materialism. This sees post-Kantian idealist continental philosophy as a failure, because it makes philosophy into the handmaiden of theology rather than science, and so falls into an anti-naturalism. The consensual interpretation is that idealism either introduces a noumenal metaphysical world beyond the empirical world of science, to make way for God, freedom and immortality like Kant, or its anti-naturalism embraces romanticism which denied that human beings are mere natural creatures. This dualism works with a conception of human beings, nature and society, premised on human beings and society belonging to a different order of things from that pertaining to the structure of the natural world. This cashes out into an anti-naturalism in the form of hermeneutics, which refused to accept the application of natural scientific methods to all areas of knowledge, and holds that the study of the two realms of nature and society require different regulative ideas and different methods. Scientific philosophy, in contrast, retains the Enlightenment's extraordinary confidence in the powers of science to transform human existence to achieve an enlightened society.

But advances in mathematics and the experimental sciences do not yield moral or political progress. On this point, Rousseau was surely right. If philosophy actually is intellectual freedom to think critically, then we require the intellectual freedom to question philosophy's acceptance of what the best natural science says is the one comprehensive truth. If what has traditionally been known as philosophy is but a historical analytic tradition, then the light of one tradition is the continental tradition's darkness. The analytic Enlightenment takes the form of scientific knowledge as mathematical physics, and the frame of reference offered by Rorty's call for the demise of the epistemological tradition with its roots in Descartes, Locke, Kant and Russell, establishes the limits of epistemologically orientated philosophy. Rorty argues that philosophy cannot coherently go on in the manner of trying to determine what can count as knowledge and what cannot, in any domain, by being a cultural overseer who can generally ascertain what is rational and irrational, through providing firm foundations for knowledge. A modernist, foundationalist, transcendent epistemology is finished concludes Rorty. Analytic philosophers have responded with a defence of this tradition by endeavouring to show that, suitably modified, the epistemological tradition is coherent, viable and can make progress.[3] Rorty, however, moves on to a hermeneutical philosophy as a kind of writing, which takes philosophy out of its enclosure by science and pushes it into a hermeneutics of everyday life.[4]

This establishes the limits of a systematic scientific philosophy, in that this attempt at a scientific account of totality has a tendency to collapse into a scientism, whose closure leaves no room for modes of knowledge alternative to those of a reductionist materialist science. There is a general sympathy and popularity for a conversational Rorty in the wider intellectual culture. He is seen as making a critical response to tradition, whilst acknowledging the historicity of understanding within a liberal democratic form of life, structured by interests, concerns and fundamental commitments, which give meaning to our practices. This cheerful, playful, 'can do' postmodern pragmatism pushes the historicizing shift within analytic philosophy to a repudiation of the mathematical scientific Enlightenment and the moral Enlightenment of Kant. It appeals to the classic authors of continental philosophy, yet preserves the values of the Enlightenment as our best hope. As a romantic, liberal postmodernism, which keeps the conversation going by breaking the crust of convention and purifying the Enlightenment, it becomes a pragmatist cosmopolitan liberalism, with its rhetoric of toleration and appeal to the republic of letters. It is the continuation of the Enlightenment as a cheerful nihilism, and is yet another mask of Enlightenment.

Our concern in entering the end-of-philosophy debate is to pick up Rorty's agenda for progress through a pluralistic dialogue, in order to explore the exhaustion of possibilities for philosophy in the broad discourse of a physicalist philosophical naturalism. Our thesis is that the end-of-philosophy thesis can be interpreted as the exhaustion of philosophy within a physicalist naturalism, as this runs itself into hard science. We will argue that the logic of the dynamic in this process of completion is the end of an autonomous philosophy, and will offer the work of the Churchlands as a contemporary example of this trend. We will then argue that the closure of this materialist system has exhausted its possibilities for enabling us to further the goal of realizing the good life, which allows us to be fully human and at home in an ecologically sustainable world. Philosophy survives in the negative mode as an interpretative hermeneutics, which critically evaluates both the presupposed metaphysics of science, and those historical meanings which make sense of, legitimate, and mystify the scientific Enlightenment project.

The cultural background to the end of philosophy

There is some confusion around the end-of-philosophy thesis. Wittgenstein, for instance, is commonly seen to be an end-of-philosophy philosopher, in that the whole idea of his latter philosophy was that philosophy is akin to a neurosis, and that the purpose of his latter work was to enable us to stop doing philosophy. Wittgenstein is generally read as showing us to acquiesce in, rather than chafe against, the limits imposed on knowledge by the logical structure of language, or the contingent nature of our forms of life.[5] Yet we can read Wittgenstein's therapeutic aim as endeavouring to free us from the grip of the picture by changing our point of view—'to show the fly the way out of the flybottle'—with philosophy acting in the form of treating an illness rather than uttering theses.[6] This does not imply doing away with pictures altogether, on the grounds that pictures are bad, and that we should achieve a pictureless view of things. Pictures lie at the root one's thinking and the pictures philosophy constructs enframe us within a form of life and hold us captive. We are in the grip of a realist picture with its reductive materialist metaphysics, and this is deemed to be essential to our lives. From a post-Heideggerian perspective this picture is flawed. In this picture, the world as the object domain of science, is transformed into a representation, over against which we, the subjects of inquiry, stand. We, the subjects, for whom the world is a picture, are left out of the picture, in the sense that the values, commitments, and pre-reflective interpretations which root us in the world, are left out.[7] In doing philosophy we enter into the labyrinths of the picture of metaphysical realism, and we are unable to find our way out. So we forget that it is a but a picture, a misfired attempt at realism. As philosophy runs amok uncovering nonsense, we lose sight of the role the picture plays in our ordinary everyday talk in the philosophy institution. The point of Wittgenstein's therapy is to get philosophers to look at what they do, at the way the picture informs our own practice. The picture carries enormous human weight, as the weight of a form of life may lie in the pictures that form of life uses.[8] If we examine the consequences of reductive materialism's picture of language as making noises in certain observable circumstances of human beings, we see that it gives us a hollowed out public world. It denies human expressive cultural meaning. So the perplexities and problems of philosophy arise from being in the grip of the reductive materialist picture. It is this forgetting that is a picture that continually misleads philosophers, as they go about filling in the picture and making it metaphysically loaded. We do not therefore stop doing philosophy. We begin to do it in a different way, one that takes account of philosophy's social and cultural dimension.

Postmodernists are usually seen as advocates for the end of philosophy. David Hiley, for instance, has argued that the postmodern target is much broader than the regional one of the narrowness of deconstructing analytic philosophy. He says that like

> "the Pyrrhonians, Montaigne and Rousseau...the postmoderns are not merely attacking the current manifestation of the traditional (Platonic) enterprise. They oppose the enterprise itself and its claim for its place in social life, not only because the Platonic-Cartesian-Kantian view of philosophy is problematic on its terms, but primarily because they believe that the end of philosophy, not the practice of philosophy, will return us to ourselves."[9]

Hiley holds that Derrida and Foucault, like Nietzsche and Heidegger, are making a rupture from the Western tradition of philosophy when they call for the end of philosophy. This is a rupture with the whole enterprise of philosophy. There is an apocalyptic tone to the end of philosophy: a death of philosophy, the tearing down of all there is, a despair in the face of a modernistic nihilism, a postmodernism as a historical critique of the present, which is deconstruction without reconstruction. Yet this interpretation is misleading. Take Derrida. He is certainly sympathetic to the apocalyptic tone in philosophy; he is seen to be the very epitome of the anti-philosophy philosopher, and in the case of *Postcard* moves beyond the pale of philosophy. Yet Derrida tries to keep himself at the limit of philosophical discourse.[10] He says 'I say limit and not death, for I do not at all believe in what today is so easily called the death of philosophy.'[11] He adds:

> "I never said a word against philosophy. I insisted on the contrary that philosophy was not dead and that the closure of philosophy was not the death of philosophy...And even if you deconstruct philosophy or if you want to think at the limits of philosophy, or the special kind of limits of philosophy, you have not only to philosophise in a general and a historical way but to be trained in the history of philosophy and to go on learning and teaching philosophy. That's why I am true to philosophy."[12]

Deconstruction, which arose from Derrida's reflections on Nietzsche and Heidegger, is a form of philosophical criticism concerned with the limits of traditional philosophical discourse.[13] It is an attempt to demarcate its range or field of relevance in terms of what is included and excluded. It aims to destablize the discipline of philosophy, by breaking down distinctions such as those between philosophy and literature, which have been essential to philosophy's identity. It involves an opening beyond these limits, and its concern is with what is excluded, with what philosophical discourse leaves unasked, and so remains hidden from view. Those like Gasche see Derrida as very much the philosopher engaged with, and committed to, an ongoing critical dialogue with Kant, Hegel, Nietzsche, Husserl and Heidegger. This 'Derrida' remains squarely within the philosophical tradition. He continues to do philosophy within the Western metaphysical tradition, even though he is engaged in destablizing and overcoming it.[14] He works within the Heideggerian frame of reference of overcoming the tradition, not as a matter of mounting refutations, but as a dialogue with Hegel and Nietzsche to establish limits, and to foreground what is unthought.[15]

The end-of-philosophy debate, then is full of distorting mirrors. Rorty's significance is that he gives us one way into this house of mirrors. He recognizes the orientation of analytic philosophy away from the literary tradition to science in the early twentieth century. This was characterized by the desire to attain the rigor of the natural sciences after 1945, an isolation from the social sciences, the humanities and high-brow cultural criticism, and the way professional philosophy insured the perpetuation of its own disciplinary concerns through its claim to be an adjudicator of the value-conflicts, between kinds of knowledge.[16] The end of philosophy for Rorty, therefore is the end of a kind of systematic analytic philosophy. This is an autonomous foundationalist discipline, which articulates metaphysical, epistemological or ethical foundational claims. It has its roots in taking the Kantian turn, with its split between science, ethics and aesthetics, too seriously.[17] Rorty has argued that getting hung-up on philosophy's professional problems is an intellectual frivolity, and he advocates that philosophy should move beyond what is internal to a professional philosophy discipline.[18] Whoever chooses philosophy today should be concerned with cultural criticism, and less concerned with the narrow professional trends and problems in fashionable philosophy departments in the liberal university. We exit the problems of professional philosophy, step outside its ivory tower, where it looks down upon the world with disdain, onto the rough ground of our common life and into the public culture at large.

This has been an influential thesis. The analytic Marxist philosopher Kai Nielsen agrees with Rorty that there is no profitable return to the ancient regime.[19] Nielsen agrees with Rorty's claim that talk about the nature and function of philosophy is pointless, because meta-philosophy—as something standing before or above philosophy and saying what it properly is or should be—is a pseudo topic. Philosophy, argues Nielsen, is many different things, and there is little point in seeking out something common in this cluster of practices, as there does not 'seem to be any one task or cluster of tasks that is philosophy's to perform. And the same obtains for method, techniques and subject matter.'[20] So where does this leave philosophers today, given the two cultures problem and the 'Science Wars.'?[21] What can they do once they give up trying to be scientists caught up in physics envy? How can they remain academically respectable?

Rorty offers one perspective. He places himself in the line of the twentieth-century liberators from the domination and cultural distortion of systematic philosophy. Traditional philosophy is boring and uninteresting. Though he is generally identified with the postmodern movement, his narrative establishes continuity with what he considers to be the legitimate aims of an enlightened modernity. The preservation of the values of Enlightenment are deemed to be our best hope.[22] He still adheres to scientific materialism in the form of non-reductive physicalism, and is willing to abdicate to the authority of science. He had used postmodernism in the narrow sense of Lyotard as a distrust of Enlightenment meta-narratives, which proclaims that a new age has begun, and is one which though it makes use of the past, has its own self-definition. He now wishes he had not used postmodernism. The term, he says, 'has been so overused that it is causing more trouble than it is worth', so:

> "It seems best to think of Heidegger and Derrida simply as post-Nietzschean philosophers—to assign them places in a conversational sequence which runs from Descartes through Kant and Hegel to Nietzsche and beyond, rather than to view them as initiating or manifesting a radical rupture."[23]

Rorty's way of recontextualising postmodernism holds that Western philosophy follows a single course since Descartes, with some distinct swerves like the postmodern, but with no radical interruption. This is a rejection of postmodernism as a definite end, or overcoming as a radical rupture from the Enlightenment tradition. Yet we have Rorty's consistent rejection of a systematic, foundationalist epistemological philosophy, a consistent shift from theory to narrative, from philosophy aligned with science to a recontextualizing philosophy aligned with art. His narratives go back to the Hegel of *The Phenomenology of Spirit* to justify the emphasis of his edifying philosophy on contextualization, self-perfection, and intersubjective community.[24] His narrative spares no sarcasm in puncturing the illusions of systematic philosophy. It holds that philosophers from Descartes to Kant and Quine have misconceived their own enterprise, and that Heidegger and Derrida are different, in that they do not do serious metaphysical philosophy. Rorty holds that though we cannot make sense of Heidegger and Derrida without the relevant intellectual history, these debates are not of real philosophical interest. He does not offer a radical critique of contemporary culture, nor does he attempt to re-found or re-motivate it. As he says, his attempt to keep the conversation going 'assembles reminders and suggests some interesting possibilities', by bringing together the 'Quine-Putnam-Davidson tradition in analytic philosophy of language and the Heidegger-Derrida traditions of post-Nietzschean thought.'[25] Though Rorty's end-of-philosophy thesis marginalizes the enterprise of analytic philosophy, his neo-pragmatism still bites other philosophers in the service of strong poets, whose task is to sensitize us to pain, and humiliation.

Rorty is still too much of a humanist to be a representative spokesperson for postmodernism. His neo-pragmatist recontextualization aims to avoid or circumvent his being co-opted by an alien left-wing French postmodernism, with its strong critique of a techno-scientific modernist reason, which furthers nihilism and sounds the death knell of modernity.[26] His liberal irony avoids coming to grips with the social problems raised by the Frankfurt School's thesis that the process of European Enlightenment has become caught up in the rationalization in the capitalist economy, the modern bureaucracy, and the disciplining of the body through the integration of science into everyday life. His collapsing of the philosophy/literature distinction is done to develop a poetized culture which is open to the transforming effects of the novel use of language. Liberal ironists, he says, are people who include amongst their 'ungrounded desires their own hope that suffering will be diminished, that the humiliation of human beings by other human beings may cease.'[27] This results in a shift to talking about novels, as it is through novels that it is possible to make the imaginative connections which are the basis for a human solidarity. This has to be consciously made on the basis of an effort to see all others as in some way like me. Rorty's liberal irony as the ethnocentrism of "we liberals", is dedicated to enlarging itself by creating a more and more variegated ethnos by a people socialized to be distrustful of ethnocentrism.[28]

Another perspective on what philosophers can do at the end of tradition is that of the Australian philosopher John Passmore. He has intervened in the end-of-philosophy debate to defend philosophy from its demise, to sort out some of the confusion, and to defend critical thinking, which is drying up in our public national culture. Passmore does this by interpreting the end-of-philosophy thesis as the argument that the current 'busy, fruitful philosophical activity is nothing but the thrashing about of a subject in its death-throes, that its publications are death rattles.'[29] He considers the different forms an argument to this effect might take. The first form is that philosophy once had an intellectual function, but that intellectual function has now been taken over by other forms of inquiry; the second is that all philosophical problems have now been solved or dissolved; the third is that philosophy developed out of what we now recognize to be an erroneous picture of the world or out of an ambition which we now recognize to be incapable of fulfilment. Passmore considers the third to be the most drastic as, in the hands of someone like Heidegger, it explicitly speaks of the end of philosophy, which is seen to have collapsed into the technologizing of the world. It is with Heidegger that we hear the radical anti-Enlightenment voice which sees the Enlightenment as having collapsed into a technocracy that is destroying the earth. Passmore considers that Australians are familiar with the criticisms of a traditional, epistemological philosophy currently made fashionable by Dewey, Rorty and even Heidegger. This is all old news to the students of John Anderson, he says, as they accept John Anderson's rejection of the spectatorial theory; of the division of the world into an internal and external world; of unquestionable foundations, whether in the form of sense data, or analytically true propositions; of the distinction between analytic and synthetic propositions; and of a unified self.[30] Passmore holds that Australian philosophy agrees with Rorty's critique of traditional epistemology, as philosophy should set aside some of its traditional epistemological problems. But, he adds, philosophy should move on to affirm the centrality of argument as the basis for critical thinking. Passmore offers us a picture of the process of defamilarization—breaking the crust of convention—which is little different from Aristotle reworking Plato, Kant reworking Hume, Hegel reworking Kant, and Quine reworking Carnap. There is no need to go hermeneutical, and dump a systematic, modernist scientific philosophy. Those Australian philosophers who followed John Anderson's criticisms of epistemological philosophy, did not consider it necessary to dump philosophy, like Heidegger. These students, such as Armstrong, Passmore and Mackie, continued to do philosophy as a critical thinking in the form of argument that addresses definite philosophical problems by finding definite answers. So Passmore holds that if philosophy is to be a legitimate enterprise, it must do without foundations; but he denies that philosophy without foundations is not a philosophy at all. Analytic philosophy does not need to be abandoned, as Rorty claims.

Rorty shows a deeper understanding of the matter. The high tradition of analytic philosophy as the logical analysis of science is finished, as that tradition becomes increasingly historicized. So we must return to Hegel at the end of tradition, and rethink the grand metaphysical project of working up the reductive post-Darwinian picture of the world into a totality that mirrors the universe-in-itself. This makes us unfit to dwell in the common life as philosophers. This is what Rorty realizes, whilst analytic philosophers continue to conceal this situation with bursts of technical virtuosity within an ethos of professionalism. Passmore offers us little in the way of recognition of a crisis as a form of upheaval that separates us, that cuts us adrift, from the firm and the familiar. There is little sense of the experience of separation that occurs with the movement of upheaval within a delimited space in Passmore. He just reaffirms the firm and the familiar of analytic philosophy; and in giving it this meaning, interprets the crisis, without being shaken by it. In doing so, the authority of the successful analytic philosophers of today tells those who come after them what to do. They are to work on those philosophical problems that have been deemed to constitute the field of philosophy. Passmore does not seriously grapple with Heidegger's challenge to this way of doing philosophy in terms of authority. Heidegger's end-of-philosophy thesis links the epistemological representational approach with a modern mechanistic science, its metaphysical picture of the modern world, and the way this collapses into a technological enframing of the world. Passmore realizes that the latter Heidegger does this, but he then engages in easy dismissals of Heidegger, with quick references to Black Forest primitivism, his association with the Nazi Party, and his making all argument in vain through listening to the call of Being and poetry. The most Heidegger accomplishes, Passmore says, is that he has shown that a certain Germanic tradition of philosophy has reached completion. This pretends to be a serious examination of the work of Heidegger within acceptable standards of scholarship; but it is really crisis management in the form of a carefully constructed polemic designed to defend the authority of analytic philosophy. It indicates that the postmodern gesture of dismantling or deconstructing serious philosophy, and its replacement with philosophy as cultural criticism, stands for the abandonment of rationality. The critics of philosophy are cast into being dogmatists because they don't argue, or they pronounce like Rorty, whereas genuine philosophers like Armstrong, Passmore and Mackie argue, and so defend a critical rationality. So Passmore quickly sidelines Heidegger on the grounds that Heidegger's suggestion that listening to the poets represents the dumping of all critical inquiry, thereby making all argument in vain.[31] Heidegger dumps reason, so he is beyond the pale of philosophy. The critical issues raised by Heidegger's criticisms of philosophy's world-picture of modernity—an ecological critique of a nihilistic, technological enframing of the world—are ignored.

Heidegger does talk about the exhaustion of the modern project, does attempt a radical break with the discourse of Western metaphysics, and does baulk at the scientific technological domination of nature. Heidegger puts the issue squarely on the table. He raises the questions: to what extent has philosophy in the present age entered into its end? What is the task reserved for thinking at the end of philosophy?[32] The end of philosophy, he says:

> "is the place, that place in which the whole of philosophy's history is gathered into its most extreme possibility. End as completion means this gathering."[33]

The end of philosophy is understood as the possibilities of philosophy being exhausted, with the resolution of philosophy into technical science. The first step in this process was the dissolution of traditional philosophy, as a result of the institution of the independence of the sciences. The end of philosophy means that being is no longer understood as subject or object, as it was with Descartes, but as disposable reserve:

> "Philosophy is ending in the present age. It has found its place in the scientific attitude of socially active humanity. But the fundamental characteristic of this scientific attitude is its cybernetic, that is technological character. "Theory" means now supposition of the categories, which are allowed only a cybernetical function, but denied any ontological function. The operational and model character of representational-calculative thinking becomes dominant...The end of philosophy proves to be the triumph of the manipulative arrangement of a scientific-technological world and of the social order proper to this world."[34]

Technologicalized science is that into which philosophy is resolved. This enframes the world as disposable reserve and equates truth with efficiency. Here cybernetic words, such as information, regulation, and feedback, play a leading role in human beings mastering and controlling everything. Though we cannot repudiate the technological world of today, it can destroy itself through the total destruction of the environment. In the history of the coming-to-the-end of philosophy, what remains unhidden is a pondering of what has really come to pass at this end. This requires the dismantling of the Cartesian tradition by dissolving the Cartesian assumptions that have underpinned and dominated modern philosophy.[35] The overcoming of the limits of this metaphysical tradition is not simply a matter of putting it behind us, as suggested by Rorty, but a matter of getting over, in the sense of coming to grips with philosophy's historical past. That which we come to grips with is not simply past and forgotten, since the past means that we deal with it, stay with it, even as we get over it. It stays with us, becomes part of us and determines our own nature.[36] So we need to come to grips with it, and this is the task reserved for thinking at the end of philosophy. Heidegger holds that, as thinking is determined by the basic categories of philosophy, then we must think what is the unthought in the matter of philosophy, as well as its method. The unthought is the opening or clearing, and thinking is a turning to the clearing. Such thinking is a remembering and looking back into the whole history of philosophy, and is a thinking at the limit of Western metaphysics. This is a stepping back out of the philosophical tradition, and a listening to voices other than those of philosophy, which speak differently from the calculative thinking of computer science.

Heidegger's thesis of the end of philosophy is broader than German philosophy. It also has relevance to an analytic philosophy that has become burdened with the weight of its Cartesian/Humean past, and transformed into a reductive materialism, which collapses philosophy into science, and constructs a metaphysical picture of the world as the truth of being. This mechanistic picture of the world divides the world into the furniture of the universe and our projections, holds the universe to be an automaton with a built-in structure, with our signs mapping this structure in terms of the right reference relation that hooks language onto the world. This technological discourse that operates with the calculative thinking of computer science, which sees persons as automata, holds the historical human being to be an inconvenience. It forces us to choose between scientific realism's metaphysical realist conception of "the physical universe with a built-in structure", and a neo-Kantian conception of "a universe with a structure imposed by mind." Heidegger can be recontextualized by suggesting that we who stand at the end of this materialist tradition can continue the Heideggerian project by coming to grips with it, by critically engaging with the technocratic thinking of computer science. Yet Passmore's normalizing discourse nullifies the crisis in the discipline of philosophy that is articulated by revisionist analytic philosophers like Putnam or Rorty and causes its elimination. But why do we need critical thinking if all is well in philosophy? Is not critique without a crisis a sham? Passmore could well argue that it has yet to be established that there is a crisis in philosophy or our culture. But is not the very lack of critical thinking in our culture, that Passmore highlights, a sign of crisis? The question to ask here is: do we have a situation of both critique and crisis, one in which crisis spawns critique, which then actualizes the cut of the crisis, that has yet to be bought to thought? What could interpret the work of Putnam as critique which brings the critical moment of crisis forward, where it can, in the form of a critical discourse, sever ties with the space in which it arose, delimit what is in crisis, and open a space in which thinking can go beyond the entrenched, familiar analytic system.[37]

What is problematic with Passmore's defence is that it leaves one with the impression that it is the superiority of analytic philosophy over its competitors which is the uppermost concern. Let us grant Passmore's case that philosophy is about arguing a case on an issue, that continental literary philosophers do not argue in the way that analytic philosophers do, and that some continental philosophers may not even argue. What then? Is this the end of the matter? What about Heidegger's argument that there is a limit or closure to the tradition of philosophy? Heidegger's overcoming of metaphysics sees the end of philosophy as the limit or the exhaustion of philosophy. Rather than attempting to refute or reject the tradition as just as wrong, the attempt is being made to point out what is inadequate or incomplete in what it fails to think through, and in what it denies. It is not that we philosophers can no longer do metaphysics because it is wrong—the old positivist dogma—but rather because metaphysics has ended in, and been continued by, technology and the natural sciences.

Passmore's crisis management fails to link the narrow disenchantment with established ways of thinking within the philosophy institution, to our disquiet about the transformations in the mode of our social life in modernity. There is a connection here, as increasing globalization involves a sense of a breakup of a stable social order, with its social incoherence, fragmentation, chaos and disorder, and the break of modern modes of social organization in postmodernity. If analytic philosophy is being justified as the defense of critical thinking in the face of the dissolution of our public culture, then we need some account of crisis other than postmodernism as the 'dumping' of critical thinking. There is a need to come to grips with Heidegger's transgressing the limits of the calculative thinking of instrumental reason within a techno-scientific culture. The end of philosophy is also the place where something new can begin. He points to this in terms of an inhabited space as a dwelling place within a community, whose truth is revealed by works of art, opposed to any imposition of techno-scientific rationality upon the world that sees space in the functionalist terms of what le Corbusier called machines for living.

The new form of poetic thinking about space as place is a being-in-the-world, which is a letting-be. In this place, where something new begins as philosophy is embedded in social life, the identification of reason with mathematics is sundered. It is realized that the uniform application of mathematical science to historical human social practices ends up with a formal reason in which content is irrelevant. Analytic rationality is formalist in its core, whilst poetic reason is *phronesis* or judgement, which is a form of reflective moral deliberation that determines right application. Passmore's dismissal of the postmodern critics of the philosophical tradition as the 'dumping' of critical thinking is sheer polemics that functions on the assumption that in the institution of philosophy the pre-analytic tradition is dead. As Stanley Rosen wittily observes, 'the corpses are all dancing the dialectical round dance of life.'[38] The emphasis upon *phronesis* in a post-analytic interpretive philosophy orientated to the humanities lies in the recognition of the limits of analytic rationalism in the face of the ethical inconsistencies and contradictions of everyday life. Here as with Rorty philosophy acts as underlabour to democracy, that criticizes the drift towards reactionary political movements, intolerance and cruelty, and nurtures a gradualist reformist approach to a beautiful liberal society.[39]

Historicism and the end of philosophy thesis

It is the corpses of Nietzsche and Heidegger in the historicist tradition which are currently dancing the dialectical round dance of life. In coming to grips with this tradition Passmore offers a contestable reading of the historicist tradition. He acknowledges that this historicist tradition—which he identifies as Hegel and Collingwood—holds that philosophy is bounded by the culture of a particular time and place.[40] This historicist view holds that philosophy is its own time, apprehended in thought, and social function is to examine the presupposition of the age. Passmore does acknowledge that historicism critiques analytic philosophy's divorce of a universal theory from that of our world of everyday life, with its already interpreted stock of knowledge. Its claim is that this analytic stance is a view from nowhere which is concerned with eternal non-local truth. But historicism for Passmore is a philosophy of reduced ambition, as he holds that, whilst it is true that philosophical problems change, he claims that historicism ends up dissolving philosophical problems. The inference is that in connecting the crisis in philosophy to the crisis in civil society, historicism dissolves philosophy, which functions as the last refuge of critical thinking in a liberal culture. Hence the historicist conception of the end-of-philosophy.

This is a contentious interpretation because it is a reflection of a distorting mirror. For Hegel—surely the historicist philosopher *par excellence*—the completion and the historicity of the system go together. The owl of Minerva—the symbol of theoretical comprehension—flies at dusk, and philosophy's 'grey on grey', as a retrospective reflection on a 'shape of life' grown old, means that its judgement and vantage point is that of the end of system.[41] This limitation of our social knowledge means that we arrive at a conceptual understanding of what has been, which implies that the phenomena has just about run its course. Philosophy reconstructs the actual by examining what has been and what is, so it cannot predict. If it analyzed the potentiality of modernity as a form of life, it would be able to tell us what sort of life is actualized. The end-of-philosophy as a form of theoretical expression, which grasps its own time in thought, would therefore mean that philosophy is no longer adequate to grasp its own time in thought comprehensively. It cannot grasp the totality of what is.

We can illustrate this with Hegel's end-of-art thesis. Hegel's aesthetic theory is explicitly an immanent explanation of art, which holds that art in modernity after the Enlightenment cannot give form or expression to an age, and so is sublated by philosophy. This does not mean that art is no longer produced, but that it can no longer claim or retain our highest interest: 'For us art is no longer the highest form in which truth gains existence.'[42] Art, religion and philosophy are the three forms of absolute spirit as opposed to objective spirit, (history), and Hegel argues that spirit works on objects only as long as they contain something secret and unrevealed. This is the case, as long as the subject matter of art is identical with us, that is one with the spirit of the age. Only as long as the artist is identical with a people, a time, and the specific world-view of the time, can art be the expression of that world-view. This was the case with the Greeks, but the emancipation of subjectivity in modernity represents the loss of substantial oneness with the age, and the dissolution of art. Spirit has moved beyond the limits of art after the Enlightenment, and an autonomous bourgeois art and aesthetic theory are no longer bound by the given contents and forms of a world view. Art stands outside tradition because no form or content is immediately identical with the artist's subjectivity and inwardness. Art can no longer express the totality, as its truth and content have become partial. Art now understands itself as self-production, with the work of art becoming its own self-reflexive theme. Hegel's standpoint to art is in effect a *posthistorie*, a postmortem.[43] Art ends where conceptual thought begins, and art ends when it goes beyond its own limits. The end-of-art thesis gives us a picture of the artist picking up the crumbs of wisdom dropped from the philosopher's table, cooking them up into in exotic stew, thereby giving old spiritual contents the spice of novel, sensuous form.

The thesis that philosophy is at an end in the historicist tradition would then be a reworking of the aesthetic theme of Hegel. It gives a postmortem of philosophy. The judgement would be that though philosophy continues, it can no longer express the totality, as its truth and content have become a partial perspective. Philosophers are then ragpickers who pick up the crumbs dropped from someone else's table. To understand what this might mean, we need to go beyond Hegel. He held that art is subulated by philosophy, which could express the age in thought, and so arrives at its completion of the original project, initiated by the Greeks and radicalized by Descartes. The postmortem thesis would hold that philosophy, contra Hegel, though it continues to be produced, no longer gives expression to the bourgeois world-view, is no longer the expression of an age, and can no longer the express the totality of our place in the world. This was the thesis of Lukács in *History and Class Consciousness*, where he tied philosophy to the crisis of bourgeois tradition. He worked with a fundamental link between self-critique and retrospective knowledge, which he then radicalized in the form of a revolutionary break with bourgeois society by the political *avant garde*, identified as the party of the proletariat. As idealist philosophy is not able to resolve the dialectic of form and content, this leads to the formalization of positivist science, which can no longer grasp its own material content. So it is the historical mission of the proletariat to unite theory and practice, cancel and overcome the antinomies of bourgeois reason caught up in the process of rationalization, understood as the increasing spread of reification. This 'Hegel out-Hegeled' makes the project of the political *avant garde* the historical and theoretical site of the self-critique of bourgeois society, from which the totality of the foregoing development process becomes visible.

So Passmore is right about the historicist tradition dissolving philosophy. The classic Hegelian-Marxist text did indeed dissolve philosophical problems into revolutionary action. All philosophical problems have been solved by political revolution. But this 'Hegel out-Hegeled' is overcome by the transmutations in modernity, which take it beyond the limits of theory that was so carefully constructed. As Adorno observes, philosophy, which once seemed obsolete, lives on because the moment to realize it was missed.'[44] The revolutionary proletariat, as the subject/object of history, failed to deliver the revolutionary goods. Liberal capitalism lives on triumphant, Marxism is on the blink, and Marxists wonder what Marxism adds to socialism, theoretically and practically. Has system and history been sundered? Does this mean that philosophy is in some sense a thing of the past? Does this mean the end of philosophy in that it can no longer grasp the age? Does it mean that philosophy is played-out, and its place has now been taken by science? Does philosophy as a progressive and rational enterprise only function by picking up the crumbs fallen from the table of science, and cooking these up into a world picture for science? Or does it leave open the possibilities for philosophy, as part of a dialectic of enlightenment, to function contra to liberal complacency in the name of a radical democratic politics?

We can begin to answer these questions by probing an assumption about rationality in Passmore's claim that historicism dissolves philosophy. He assumed that though philosophical problems change through history, reason remains the same. He is right about the former, but wrong about the latter, from the perspective of the dialectic of Enlightenment.[45] This historicist thesis is that reason does change in history, and it holds that it is the transformation of reason in modernity which is part of the problem. The logic of the process of rationalization in modernity which aims to make the world predictable, is such that a substantive reason becomes a formal reason. This sunders into formally closed systems—sciences such as economics and physics, the law, and the bureaucratic state—which now function as autonomous, self-validating spheres, unable to grasp their social and material base. This rationality cannot move beyond the antinomy of system and contingency, and at this point it irrationalizes, and reverts to myth.[46] Anglo-American analytic philosophy's system of a transformed epistemologically-centred philosophy, continuing on as a systematic inquiry to produce objective knowledge of truth, is built into most of our scientific and cultural work. This modern form of rationality assumes that the scientific inquiry excludes feelings, desires, social interests, values, political and ethical objectives as far as possible from the professional determination of truth and the acquisition of knowledge; that intellectual problems of inquiry are distinguished sharply from human social problems; that intellectual progress is distinguished from social progress; that there is a rough kind of hierarchy in knowledge with physics at the bottom, followed by chemistry, the earth sciences, biology, ecology, the social sciences and the humanities; that the capacity to reason is to appraise ideas in an impersonal, objective and rational fashion; and that literature and art make no direct contribution to the intellectual inquiry to produce knowledge.[47] Here the logical categories of a systematic formal reason fail to grasp their own material content, and this instrumental reason then reverts to myth, when it holds that philosophy and science stand outside history. A formal reason now circulates endlessly around the closed rational system of a timeless modernity, as exemplified in the formal logic in analytic philosophy and the axiomatic mathematics of rational choice theory in neo-classical economics. This analytic form has given rise to a deep discontent.[48]

This questioning of Passmore's assumption gives us a perspective on the analytic tradition that Passmore works within. It is possible to speak of the death of this tradition, in the sense that analytic philosophy can no longer express the totality, as its truth and content has become partial perspective grounded on the natural sciences. Putnam can be interpreted as expressing this thesis of the end of tradition. He suggests that the current crisis in philosophy is linked to the rejection of scientific materialism that has been dominant since the 1950s. He holds that this scientific materialism asserts the following theses: firstly that everything that is, can be explained and described by a single theory; secondly that we can see in present day science the general outlines of what such a theory would be like; thirdly that the best metaphysics is a unified science, pictured as based and unified by application of the laws of physics; fourthly that this gives us an absolute conception of the world; and fifthly that the task of philosophy is to comment upon and speculate about the progress of science as it seems to bear on the various traditional problems of philosophy.[49] Putnam rejects this analytic metaphysics. He sees it as a mistake, a disaster, a parody of the great metaphysical systems of the past, which...'is merely an attempt to rationalize the ways we think and talk in the light of a scientistic ideology'.[50] He claims that...'analytic philosophy...has come to the end of its project—the dead end, not its completion.'[51] This death of the analytic tradition, with its implicit scientism and physicalist ontology in scientific realism, includes the work of the students of Anderson such as Armstrong and Mackie. What this highlighting of the contrast between philosophy and reality signifies, is that philosophy in living on after science, has become self-aware, as it thematizes itself, considers the problem of how to break through the barriers of formalism in thought in bourgeois society. Putnam's response to the death of the analytic philosophical tradition is the supersession of scientific materialism—not by a pseudo-scepticism or nihilism that there is no world, no truth, no progress—but by sketching a better way in philosophy through a turn to pragmatism. This embraces Dewey's conception of philosophy as a honest reflection on how human beings can resolve the various sorts of problematic situations that they find themselves in. His turn to a pragmatist philosophy dealing with the problems of human beings, is offered as a third way between metaphysical realism and modish forms of anti-realism, or postmodernism. This transformation of philosophy ends with embracing the primacy of practical philosophy committed to the flourishing of diversity and pluralism.[52]

In the philosophical culture in Australia, Joseph Wayne Smith has argued for the death of tradition, in that analytic philosophy no longer expresses the totality of what is, since its truth and content has become a partial perspective. He sees the suicide of analytic philosophy resulting from its undermining of the basis for the critical philosophical examination of the sciences. If philosophy is to become a rational progressive enterprise, he holds, it must revive the tradition of *philosophia perennis* against the failure of analytic philosophy, and the relativist and nihilist implications of Rorty's challenge to analytic philosophy.[53] He identifies Bradley, Bosanquet, Bergson and Croce as adherents of the tradition of *philosophia perennis*. They make a critical philosophical examination of the sciences, rather than merely playing underlabourer or janitor to them, and they argue for a philosophy of wisdom over the philosophy of knowledge. Here philosophy goes beyond reflecting on its own fate and its reflections are only familiar to the initiates familiar with the theory behind it. In *Aids, Philosophy and Beyond*, he argues that the appalling state of contemporary analytic and poststructuralist philosophy is a consequence of its loss of moral direction and contact with what is desirable and of value in human life. Philosophy is no longer concerned with the Socratic questions of: 'what is the good life?' and 'how ought I live?'[54] In this revaluation of philosophy, philosophy begins to be of value as the old ways are up rooted and displaced. To make these questions central, he says, it is necessary to pry philosophy out of its dogmatic and ideological interpretations, and make it part of a radical political, social and cultural critique of late capitalism, and its authoritarian high-tech political tendencies from the standpoint of ecological sustainable development.[55] Such a critique would endeavour to establish the intuition that an affirmative analytic philosophy is inherent in the apparatus of domination in Australia, that we need to cultivate a growing ignorance of the old ways of thinking, and that a critique of the broad analytic scientific discourse would help open up pathways for a new critical relationship to capitalist society. The new way requires a new set of principles, which is a shift to a green perspective. This is not the same content in new forms, as it is a shift in content as philosophy turns the slime of modernity into the philosophical gold of a new interpretation of being, a new metaphysics of a green being-in-the-world. This political commitment places philosophy at the services of the green social movements.[56]

The claims by Putnam and Smith that the crisis in philosophy is a negation of tradition, a playing at the limits of traditional philosophy, and a dislocation of the centre of scientific philosophy in the analytic tradition, can be linked to similar currents in continental philosophy. Husserl, for instance, undercut a scientifically centred philosophy through his reflection on the crisis in this philosophy. The notion of crisis in Husserl is linked around the three themes of the disunity of the sciences, the loss of meaning for ordinary human life, and the decay of secure foundations. The effect of the cutting power of his critique was to carve out a space by bringing the crisis forward, appropriating it, and making the upheaval of the crisis into an opening.[57] Late Heidegger turns away from Husserl's notion of the role of philosophy engaging in crisis management—diagnosing and curing the crisis—to philosophy as critique— examining the structures and limits of crisis without ever pretending to master it.[58] A Heideggerian dismantling of metaphysics aims to complete the death of philosophy by showing how it has reached its completion and end. It has exhausted its possibilities, to the extent that nothing substantially new will be produced. It has collapsed into the sciences and technology.[59]

These themes are being appropriated and put into operation against a reductive materialism which represents the extreme point of techno-science. This analytic metaphysics aims to overcome the disunity and separate paths of the sciences within a unifying physicalist programme, to produce a unified world view through a strict reductionism to a fundamental physics.   This holds that the best metaphysics is that of a unified science, based and unified by the application of the laws of fundamental physics, and that this integrative or reconstruction function is important, given the fragmentation and specialisation of the sciences. It represents the extreme point of a mechanistic metaphysics in high philosophical culture. Heidegger's conception of closure as an end through exhaustion applies here, as all that is left to do is tinker on the details of the system.   But Heidegger's conception of closure as an end through exhaustion is also a transition to a new beginning rather than its nullity, as the end is coupled with a process of loosening up a hardened, closed tradition.   These themes are resonating through an underground oppositional culture in philosophy.[60]   Thus Val Plumwood, the feminist environmental philosopher, holds that a mechanistic metaphysics wears a death mask, because it has exhausted its possibilities. So it needs to be dismantled to make way for a new environmental philosophy.[61]

These Heideggerian themes are being replayed in the discourse of Australian poststructuralist feminism. These philosophers have argued that places like philosophy departments are social institutions and that their traditions have a value-laden character. Moira Gatens, for instance, identifies this as the inbuilt masculine bias within the dualities of mind/body, reason/passion, and nature/culture—that requires an interrogative stance to our philosophical tradition. Gatens argues that to accept the implicit masculine value system in philosophy is to accept the superiority of masculine values and practices and the denigration of women.[62]   Liz Grosz carries this further, by arguing that the crisis in philosophy is wide-ranging, as it has methodological, epistemological, ontological and political dimensions.[63] She locates her work within the dialogue taking place within feminism as to whether feminists undertake a revision of philosophy in light of feminist knowledges, or actively undermine it, or to abandon it.[64]   She analyses the limits of analytic philosophy in terms of the need to overcome male dominance in philosophy and to make a rupture from a feminism working on problems of feminism within the analytic tradition.[65] Unwilling to accept analytic philosophy on its own terms, Grosz challenges and rejects analytic philosophy's underlying sexist, patriarchal and phallocentric assumptions, in which women are taken to embody emotion rather than reason, are bodies rather than minds or consciousness and represent nature rather than culture.[66] She argues that philosophy is unwilling to acknowledge that its categories, such as reason, individuality, mind, body, consciousness are gender-loaded, with women

229

being systematically defined as inferior. Consequently it is necessary to rethink the nature of philosophy, dissolve the old distinction between the internal problems of an autonomous philosophy and the external historical and social relations of civil society, and force philosophy to confront its own limits and the way it represses its roots in gender relations. She concludes that a new kind of philosophy needs to be developed, one that is more amenable to accepting the flaws and limits of philosophy, places an emphasis on the plurality and multiplicity of ways of doing philosophy and represents a particular perspective which openly avows its politics, its grounding in society and its textual history.[67]

The historicist account of the end of philosophy is therefore different from that attributed to it by Passmore, who asserts that it represents the finish of philosophy, because it dissolves philosophical problems. The historicist thesis is that philosophy, after the collapse of the modernist, reductive materialist tradition continues. It has lost its totalizing perspective, has become a partial account, and does not work on problems in the tradition of Russell. But philosophy continues. Like Putnam, the green and feminist voices refuse to remain within the limits of that tradition, as they search for a breakthrough from its metaphysical closure. They step outside that tradition, by negating it through countering what Husserl called the sedimented dimension of a tradition—those aspects which have been settled or consolidated.[68] The point of the critique is to recover the past in relation to the crisis of the present by re-activating the founding presuppositions from which the tradition began, and on which it depends for its identity. A critical historicist philosophy does this in order to awaken a sense of crisis in the face of the denials of the existence of crisis by restorationist philosophers like Passmore. The old is not just dismissed or dissolved, as Passmore claims. Tradition is something made and produced through a critical engagement with those aspects of the analytic tradition that analytic philosophers hand down without question. If there is no outside to the philosophical tradition from which to critique what is inside, then there is also no inside to the tradition from which one can speak without contamination by the outside. There is space to move around within the philosophical tradition, as philosophical traditions in modernity are hybrid ensembles with distinct counter cultures—historically Oxford linguistic philosophy, then Marxism and now postmodernism. When one is confronted with a unified and pure conception of tradition, as in Australian materialism, then Derrida's deconstruction strategy is to show how such a conception is premised on certain exclusions—philosophy fails to think through the way it represses its differences with science—and then to argue that these exclusions cannot be excluded.[69]

Contrary to Passmore then, the issue raised by the historicist end of philosophy thesis is not the end of philosophy as such; but a concern to get philosophers to face the crisis of the present in such a way that the analytic tradition is forced to acknowledge the limits of its jurisdiction, and the failure of its demand for exclusivity. After the collapse of tradition, a historicist hermeneutical philosophy looks back retrospectively, in an attempt to point out what is inadequate or incomplete in what the calcified tradition fails to think through, and in what it denies. Philosophy, to the extent that it fails to do this, and to see the way that it is also part of the humanities, runs into the danger of endless chatter that becomes totally incomprehensible to all those who are not insiders speaking the special coded language. A technocratic scientific philosophy has become an esoteric activity performed by professional experts for other experts. This narrowing and emptying out is the death of naturalist philosophy. It has exhausted its possibilities, as it is limited to picking up the crumbs from the table of science. It is now science which aims to give a unified knowledge of all that exists.

The first cut: the disappearance of autonomous philosophy

Has Australian materialism exhausted its possibilities as the historicist thesis in its Heideggerian form claims? It could be argued by Australian materialists that, if philosophy is aligned to natural science, then Australian materialism can continue to construct the broad world-view of the naturalist picture of the place of human beings place in the universe, as outlined by Jack Smart.[70] It is being continued by those in the analytic tradition, who see the state of philosophy as normal and not in crisis, and do not see any need for a post-historical closing of accounts. There is a quiet confidence in this physicalism, which holds that the world contains nothing more than those entities with properties and relations designated by physics.[71] This physicalist naturalist metaphysics is a vital research programme which is extending into the project of artificial intelligence.[72] The underlabouring role of philosophy is a modest one, but nevertheless a role, and it has been the basis for philosophy's acceptance as a legitimate discipline in the liberal university. Systematic analytic philosophers become the custodians of a particular discourse about science. They see their task to preserve, extend and elaborate it, when necessary, to defend it from the incursions of other discourses, and to sterilise the contamination of the categories of scientific discourse by the metaphorical concepts of everyday language in the public culture. The talk is about what the best science tells us, and where philosophy does not concern itself with the clarification of scientific concepts and the organization of the sciences into a system, it is concerned with concepts that are related to scientific ones but are more basic and general.[73] The task of philosophy is to elaborate the implicit concepts of science and eliminate commonsense anthropocentric notions, as philosophy, under its systematic aspect, is the conceptual unravelling of the implicit ideas in the assumptions of the sciences. This conceptual unravelling is, as David Papineau states:

> "a part and parcel of the construction of scientific theories. Even if there is no direct involvement with empirical evidence, the task of philosophers is to bring coherence and order to the total set of assumptions we use to explain the empirical world."[74]

This underlabouring conception of philosophy means that philosophical problems emerge from science, and philosophy, as a second-order reflection on these problems, sorts out and clears up conceptual confusions through technical rigor, clarity and the logical precision in the form of deductive argumentation. Philosophy works on problems about things such as universals and abstract entities like the mathematical entities required by physics, which threaten the internal incoherence within physicalism. The Platonist assumptions about abstract entities like mathematics, propositions and principles such as Occam's Razor do not sit comfortably with a thorough-going reductive materialism, and these constitute a problem. Scientific philosophy's role as the caretaker, advocate, watchdog and underlabourer of the established conceptual system of science, generally engages in a rational reconstruction of our scientific modes of cognition along reductionist lines, as it holds that it is only a physical science which gives us the true account of the real structure of things.

All of this represents a narrowing of the role of philosophy. On the one side philosophy has become wedded to the point of view of science, and has become scientistic, as natural science is held to be the sole mode of knowledge and understanding. There is no distinctive activity of philosophy apart from science. On the other side there has been a continual displacement of alternative kinds of philosophy. So the Ryle and Strawson linguistic view of philosophy as a second-order activity, reflecting on ordinary folk talk about the world in terms of a pure and careful interpretative linguistic description, has faded into the background. Few practise the Passmore/Berlin/Oxford version of the neo-Kantian conception of philosophy as categorical analysis, in which our historical but semi-permanent governing presupposed categories, in which experience is conceived and classified, are elucidated, systematised, analysed and criticized. The transformative view of philosophy has also been lost. This, as Austin puts it, holds that:

> "In the history of human inquiry, philosophy has the place of the initial central sun, seminal and tumultuous: from time to time it throws of some portion of itself to take station as a science, a planet, cool and well regulated, progressing toward some distant final state."[75]

The perplexities and puzzles thrown up by the life-world and science are transformed through careful logical, linguistic or conceptual analysis into genuine questions of either the formal or empirical sciences. In so paving the way for real knowledge, philosophy performs a useful function. There is also the denial of legitimacy to a hermeneutic philosophy, a revised version of Rorty's notion of philosophy as a kind of writing, since it takes philosophy out of its enclosure by science into everyday life, where it operates as a cultural criticism. The consequences of this narrowing of philosophy are that philosophy has lost contact with the problems of ordinary people in our everyday common life. This is what Passmore identifies as the socio-political kind of philosophy, advocated by Dewey, which deals with 'the great social defects and troubles from which humanity suffers.'[76] Passmore identifies this as a transformation of philosophy that is so considerable that it is a revolution rather than a reform. He implies that it is the death of philosophy.

These severe limits on what philosophy legitimately is in late modernity can be interpreted, from a Hegelian perspective of looking back on the scientific Enlightenment, as a process of the sublation of philosophy into science. Philosophy becomes a part of science, and depends more and more upon science for its existence as philosophy. So Passmore's defence of philosophy as a form of critical reasoning, taking the form of arguments, now becomes limited by tradition. His universal 'philosophy' is actually identical to the actual particular philosophical practices of the Smart/Quinean notion of scientific philosophy, which is now held to be the paradigmatic philosophical practice. What it means to be a naturalist is that philosophy can say little about science except what science itself can discover about science. Science is physics. The crisis of the analytic tradition then is both the collapse of the progressive development of an autonomous philosophy, and philosophy no longer functioning as the critical appraisal and dismantling of a closed mechanistic ontology worked up from the natural sciences. This is deemed by naturalists to be the one determinate ontology, which to all intents and purposes, reflects the true nature of things. There is very little left for philosophy to do.

One could shrug here and say that the proper end of philosophy is in the natural or social sciences, with philosophy functioning in the broader public culture as critical reason defending science. But the danger of philosophy being continuous with science, rather than being demarcated and autonomous from science, is that the autonomous role of philosophy can collapse into scientism. We end up in a situation where scientism pushes for the elimination of philosophy. As Putnam observes:

> "Analytic philosophy has become increasingly dominated by the idea that science, and only science, describes the world as it is in itself, independent of perspective...the idea that science leaves no room for an independent philosophical enterprise has reached the point at which leading practitioners sometimes suggest that all that is left for philosophy is to try and anticipate what the presumed scientific solutions to all metaphysical problems will eventually look like."[77]

If science is its own justification and everything else is something akin to dabbling in the occult, then we are being asked to take the current physicalist theories on trust, because that is all there is.[78] This represents the death of autonomous philosophy, as it is science that becomes critical thinking. It is true that Passmore does not accept this, as he highlights the lack of critical thinking in science. But to defend philosophy as critical thinking, he needs to become more critical of the analytic tradition, and negate its inherent scientism, which undermines the very foundation required for critical thinking in a public culture. Scientism leaves us with formal reasoning in an expert, academic discourse in the ivory tower.

This raises the following question: does the death of philosophy mean that philosophy ceases to be plausible, and no longer needs to done? Philosophy is a bit like theology, in that it becomes irrelevant, now that we have science. This thesis of philsophy having exhausted its possibilities can be dug out from its sedimentation in the movement in analytic philosophy from Quine to the Churchlands. Quine's scientific philosophy was concerned with knowledge and nature of the world as part of the scientific system of the world, and it rejects the strong foundationalist conception of a first philosophy providing a firm basis on which to build science. With Quine, the old questions are replaced by new ones within psychology and neuroscience. Quine's renovation of the theory of knowledge does not declare the traditional central problems of epistemology to be obsolete, but keeps them in view.[79] But the tendency in Quine towards there being no distinctive activity for philosophy apart from science is reinforced in the movement from Quine to the Churchlands. This movement is one from a naturalised epistemology which abandons the traditional problems in the theory of knowledge, to the Churchlands' abandonment of traditional problems in the theory of mind, in which an empirical neuroscience supersedes philosophy.[80] If philosophy has a role in the Churchlands' scientism it is to demonstrate the reducibility of psychology, the viability of neuroscience and the synoptic role of helping neuroscience orient itself in the scheme of the sciences as a whole. Once the case for neuroscience is made, philosophy is made redundant.[81] That represents the end or death of philosophy.

It is this death of philosophy in the analytic tradition that Passmore fails to consider, in his survey of the end-of-philosophy debate. He had assumed that it was the continentals like Derrida, Rorty, or Heidegger who destroyed philosophy, whilst the analytic philosophers defended philosophy. That simple narrative with its good guys and bad guys is an enchanting view, but it looks like a fairy tale spun in the review columns of the media. One needs to walk more carefully amidst the distorting mirrors of the end-of-philosophy debate. The end of philosophy thesis in Australian philosophical culture is the way that a philosophical physicalist naturalism destroys philosophy as a viable autonomous enterprise. The story told by the ragpicker's narrative holds that Smart's original conception of philosophy as underlabouring for science, located philosophy within a scientific culture, placed science at the pinnacle of culture, and made philosophy a servant of science. Philosophy was grateful for an after-life picking up the crumbs that fell off the table of science, after its death at the hands of positivism. But the scientistic logic within physicalist naturalism has eliminated this subservient role for all intents and purposes. The thorough-going scientism of the Churchlands means that the autonomous role of philosophy, as a subject or discipline, is eliminated by an empirical neuroscience. It is the analytic philosophers who have destroyed philosophy, whilst it is the postmodern historicists who want to renew it, and who point to a different kind of philosophy. Rorty's post-philosophical ethical reconstruction of liberalism does risk repeating the exhausted abstractions of classical liberalism, but philosophy circumvents the analytic tradition to function in the public sphere as the underlabourer of democracy.

Saving philosophy

If we turn our attention to Patricia Churchland, we note that the reasons for her abandoning philosophy are geared to her reasons for doing away with folk psychology. Since philosophical work in the philosophy of mind is linked to philosophical work geared to folk psychology, Churchland's argument for eliminative materialism centres around the claim that folk psychology needs revision, and that its concepts of belief, perception and consciousness do not provide the most useful taxonomy of psychological states and processes for the purposes of predicting behaviour. She defines folk psychology as:

> "that rough-hewn set of concepts, generalisations, and rules of thumb we all standardly use in explaining and predicting human behaviour. Folk psychology is common sense psychology—the psychological lore in virtue of which we explain behaviour as the outcome of beliefs, desires, perceptions, goals, sensations and so forth. It is a theory whose generalisations connect mental states to other mental states, to perceptions, and to actions. These homey generalisations are what provide the characterisation of the mental states and processes referred to; they are what delimit the 'facts' of mental life and define the explananda. Folk psychology is 'intuitive psychology', and it shapes our conception of ourselves."[82]

Once folk psychology as a commonsense framework for understanding mental states and processes is held at arm's length and evaluated in the way that any theory is evaluated, it comes across as inadequate. So it requires first revision, then ultimately elimination in favour of the conceptual framework of a matured neuroscience.

The problem with the argument is that the useful revision of folk psychology does not imply the necessity of scrapping folk psychology. We still have the option of a philosophy that is part of the Humanities which can help deal with our commonsense pictures of the everyday world we live in. But this option is closed off with scientism. It holds our commonsense picture to be shot through with Cartesian metaphysics of the 'inner' as a self-standing private realm completely independent of the 'outer' public realm. Realism about the 'inner' thus seems to imply a commitment to private mental entities accessible to only one person. So naturalist materialists throw away a picture of the inner world altogether, look upon commonsense as experiences of metaphysical confusion, and subtract the subjective side from the Cartesian dualist picture. We are then left with noises and marks impinging on the nerve ends of the biological body. As these noises and marks are no longer expressive of anything inner, then the arts such as dance and music, which are modes of knowledge that give expression to our-being-in-the-word, are eliminated. What a scientistic physicalist naturalism reacts against in its push towards scientism is the presumption of *a priori* investigation of questions by philosophy. This is pushed to one side, for what is relevant is the empirical evidence that has a close bearing to the causal workings of the brain, as explained by neuro-science. Patricia Churchland says:

> "Since it is the nervous system that achieves these things (representing reality) the fundamental epistemological question can be reformulated thus: *How does the brain work?* Once we understand what reasoning is, then we can begin to figure out what reasoning well is."[83]

Neural science replaces folk psychology, and philosophy disappears with the reduction from the mental to the physical, the philosophical to the scientific and the rational to the causal. All we need talk about is transient states of neuronal networks. All philosophical problems have been eliminated, and philosophy has no status distinct from that of science. Science stands alone. Dennett expresses this scientistic standpoint when he says:

> "I will try to explain every puzzling feature of human consciousness within the framework of contemporary physical science: at no point will I make an appeal to inexplicable or unknown force, substances or organic powers."[84]

The Enlightenment project of modern science, as unprejudiced reason explaining the causal processes of an independent nature, gives us the end-game of physical science versus sorcery, witchcraft and miracles as the options. It is an end-game as all rational people would take the option of physical science. But in doing so, what we are committed to is to the ordinary standards of physical science, science being its own justification, and rationality as just neuronal events in the brain. So all questions of justification are reduced to questions about how the brain functions. Everything else just wallows in mystery, mysticism and witchcraft. The reductionist tendencies within a scientistic physicalism have gone so far that philosophy self-dissolves into the vanishing point of neuroscience.

Scientistic philosophers shrug at this point. We are pro-science, they say, and that is a good thing. But there is a tension here. If science is shot through with metaphysical assumptions as scientific realists hold then there is a philosophical issue of the plausibility of the scientistic form of philosophical naturalism. Churchland is engaged in justifying her physicalist interpretation of philosophical naturalism, and her justification takes the form of a reduction which refuses to allow philosophy a role distinct from that of science. In arguing for eliminative materialism, Churchland is making an appeal to authoritative reasons for her position, as part of an overall attempt to justify physicalism. The justification in the form of reductionism, is quite different from the scientific theory which attempts to explain how the brain works. It is a philosophical justification she is engaged in, and in doing philosophy in the guise of science she raises the whole question about the plausibility of the method of reduction in relation to a naturalist metaphysics.

The justifications for science, the physicalist reduction of the practical social world to the natural, and the elimination of the subject to chemical events in the brain, cannot be adequately accounted for from within neuroscience. Since science is a product of human beings in society, it presupposes a background metaphysics that frames what it is that science is trying to explain. This background is the scientific Enlightenment in our culture. But this holds that an enlightening self-legislating reason must question the metaphysical foundations of science, rather than take them on trust or faith. What has gone wrong with Churchland is that a certain metaphysics, suggested by a fundamental physics and neuroscience and interpreted by naturalist philosophers, has been confused with science itself. It is the standard dodge of naturalist philosophers. The dodge is quickly followed by another which holds that the truth of this metaphysical picture is endorsed and confirmed by science, which mirrors the fundamental furniture of the world. But what if the metaphysical presuppositions of our best natural and social science are suspect? In raising this question, philosophy is informed by science, but it is not a part of science. So the problem and preoccupation with the plausibility of metaphysics within the limits of science does not take us beyond science, since the metaphysical issues can be raised and explored without refusing to take scientific findings seriously. This constitutes a concern that prevents philosophy's outright assimilation to the natural sciences by the Churchland-style scientism so prevalent in analytic philosophy.

The Churchland's thesis that philosophical problems, which initially arose from science for conceptual analysis, should be treated as being nothing but scientific problems which can be resolved by neuroscience, is a problematical one. This account makes rationality, and the philosophical justification for the metaphysical theory of physicalism, just a multiple of physical processes, which science explains in causal terms, with science being taken on unargued trust. Neuroscience dissolves the ragpickers, as social subjects of reason who make rational assessments about the metaphysical foundations of science and its relation to the good life, into a myriad of brain processes conceived as information processing systems. If the workings of the brain are all there is, then the very idea of rationality has been reduced to multiple physical processes, as discovered for us by science. Science becomes the master subject. This means that the major metaphysical claims of science, as articulated by physicalists like Dennett and Churchland, cannot be assessed in terms of rational judgement on their account. The social subject becomes a random bucketful of energy scattered in space and time. If the workings of the brain is all there is, then the very idea of rationality has been reduced to multiple physical processes as represented to us by neuro-science. The scientistic strand of analytic philosophy eliminates the very ground that Passmore, as a social subject, stands on to defend philosophy as critical thinking. It indicates that any viable form of a renewed philosophy as critical thinking must be willing to engage in an immanent critique of its own tradition. Philosophy must turn on itself, if it is to have any credibility as critical reasoning.

If epistemology and metaphysic are reduced to the causal workings of the brain, as explained by neuroscience, then the Churchlands' claim is not one which simply advocates a materialist theory of the mind, in the form of eliminativism. It is a claim that the old philosophical mind/body problem, flowing from Cartesian metaphysics, has been resolved. Science has shown us what is what, and so no philosophical issues remain. If philosophy has a role in Churchland's scientism, it is to demonstrate the reducibility of psychology, the viability of neuroscience and the synoptic role of helping neuroscience orient itself in the scheme of the sciences as a whole. Once the case for neuroscience is made, an autonomous philosophy is made redundant in the name of science, and so superseded. The result is philosophy's outright assimilation by the natural sciences, and philosophy's acquiescence to the natural sciences. It is then difficult to see how a critical perspective on this philosophical picture can be derived from within, given that the reduction of folk psychology to neuroscience means the dissolution of the social subject of reason, like the ragpickers, who make critical rational judgements in a particular historical culture.

So the end of philosophy is no longer Rorty's debunking of a systematic analytic philosophy, or his dismissal of the traditional philosophical approach of putting forward arguments to solve a philosophical problem as uninteresting. Nor is the end of philosophy just the post-Nietzschean turn to poetic reason as a postmodern literary criticism which scorns philosophical controversy. The end of philosophy is also the scientistic dissolution of autonomous philosophy as critical reasoning in the analytic tradition by a physicalist materialism. So philosophy, if it is to have an afterlife as a critical reason, must overcome this metaphysics. In overcoming this particular kind of metaphysics there will still be philosophers continuing the metaphysical discussion in a search for better ways of thinking about ourselves in post-modernity. We ragpickers can agree with Passmore that a critical thinking, which overflows the boundaries of dogmatic scientific or literary culture, is a good thing. And we can accept the need to criticize those postmodernists who really dump critical thinking *per se,* as distinct from merely doing away with a particular style of critical thinking. But critical thinking in the public sphere requires an enlightened social subject as the bearer of critical reason—as opposed to computers or calculators within cybernetic systems. To sustain the plausibility of Passmore's project of nurturing critical thinking in the public sphere of a liberal culture, we need to confront the materialist analytic tradition, keep it within its limits, deconstruct its scientism, and critically take apart its historically informed concepts, which have been handed down to us with the authority of science. We need to stake out the positive possibilities within this tradition, if we are to underpin Passmore's useful conception of philosophy as historical subjects engaging in the probing criticism of the free and public use of critical reason.

So Passmore needs to tackle the scaffolding of the metaphysics of reductive materialism propounded by scientific realists, as this has the logical consequence of philosophical nihilism, which undercuts the very ground that Passmore stands on with respect to the encultured meanings of what it is to reason critically. If physics and neuroscience provide the metaphysical underpinnings of our civilization, then we should conform to our highest values of science and the scientific method, as this gives us the true picture of being. This scientific point of view—and it is a point of view, as it repudiates religion providing the authoritative ground for our practices—is what gives value and meaning to our lives in a scientific culture. The cultural formation of the Enlightenment is a complex of values and meanings, and this is accepted as long as it continues to perform effectively the task of providing justification and legitimation for our practices. But physics and neuroscience cannot provide any justification for human value, meaning or worth of a human life—its ontology holds there are just these sounds impinging on the nervous system, which is a physical process. Consequently physicalism's ontology cannot give any account of the meaning and value of the theoretical system of physicalism as a cultural formation within modernity, nor what it means to reason critically. If what exists is truly described by the entities of a perfected physics, then physics makes no provision for normative concepts such as a reason for acting, for what is desirable, rational, good, or what accords with a rule or convention. Physics simply tells us what follows from what, not what justifies what. It explains the occurrence of certain events, given certain other events, and the initial state in no way justifies the outcome in terms of rational or irrational, desirable our undesirable, sensible or stupid. These normative concepts are seen as anthropocentric, and as projected onto the natural world of physics. Physics makes no provision for agency, for the notion of the agent as an independent being thinking for herself is logically tied to our normative concepts.

Any attempt to abandon all concepts other than those of physics is self-defeating. If we were to justify our decision to use only the language of physics by appealing to philosophical reasons, the decision would be self-defeating, because the notion of a reason for a decision is not part of the language of physics. If we stop using normative concepts altogether, we have no way of expressing what we have done and why we have done it. The very existence of an argument about the status of physics presupposes a common culture and language in which to speak. But as physics and neuroscience deny the very existence of this common culture in their ontology, they can offer us no account of what it means to reason critically as philosophers in a public culture. These sciences offer no account of philosophical questions in the form in which they generally impose themselves on us, as questions not admitting of satisfactory answers; nor do they have anything to say about the philosophical activity of searching for directions, ways to think, in response to these questions. As Rorty observes it is high time to 'peel apart

Enlightenment liberalism from Enlightenment rationalism.'[85] Enlightenment rationalism constitutes an obstacle to the deepening of the democratic project based on a diversity of contextual practices and discourses.

In a scientific culture where scientism is hegemonic, it is the physical sciences that set the standards of truth. The public arena is held to be the preserve of science where truth can be objectively established, and all else is swept into the category of the subjective. The whole notion of moral judgement in practical deliberation, with some reasons being recognized as being better than others, is collapsed into subjective opinion and feeling. Questions about the aim or purposes of science in relation to the democratic project are meaningless—equivalent to those about the end or purpose of human life. A fundamental science like physics cannot assess its own objectives, purposes to which it is employed by human beings with social interests, or the worth of its own activities for human wellbeing. We cannot assess the social mission of the Enlightenment to subjugate the natural and social world to the power of science, so that human beings can master the earth. If these objectives, purposes and interests are characterised as irrational, then scientific realists, in holding to the values of objectivity and value freedom by favouring reason over unreason, science over non-science, adopt a particular value stance to the exclusion of others. However their ontological presuppositions do not allow them to resolve the contradiction in their position since, in spite of all its emphasis on the intelligibility of the world, it holds that the choice of a form of life is a value, and values are not part of the furniture of the universe. Facts are distinct from values, values are personal preferences, projections, or errors, and they are clearly beyond the scope of science, not open to rational investigation and so the value commitment to science can only be justified by opinion, decision or faith.[86] If science is the truth, philosophy is a part of science and all else is feeling, then it is no longer rational to raise the question of whether science serves life, or whether our form of a liberal democratic capitalism is the best form of the good life in terms of being human within an ecologically sustainable society.

We stand at the end of tradition because philosophy as critical thinking is practised less and less in late modernity. In the end philosophy has destroyed itself. The finality of the scientific Enlightenment is its own undoing. The terrible legacy of scientism is that, if rationality is equivalent to mathematical reasoning, then ethical and political reasoning deteriorates into a calculative thinking, which is only of use if it exists to further the unfettered pursuit of profit and consumption. This, as economic rationalism is currently showing us, is implicitly an interpretation of freedom, as its social engineering furthers the drift to domination, and the under cutting of the democratic project. The ragpickers see the stresses and strains in reductive materialism, and seek to drive wedges into the cracks of the contemporary dogmas that we have inherited. This acts to shape, rather than merely conform to the prevailing intellectual agenda of the time, and so enables philosophy to speak in a different voice. The ragpickers turn on the analytic philosophical tradition, not because they are just being blown by the winds of overseas fashion. They realize that something has gone terribly wrong with the philosophical underpinnings of the political and ethical side of the Enlightenment's universal reason.

Philosophy and politics

The problem with Passmore's defence of the analytic philosophy as a form of critical thinking is that Passmore does not spell to the ends such critical thinking is being used for. Critical thinking is an instrument and it all depends on whether that instrument is used to further or undermine the democratic side of the Enlightenment project of building a better society. Passmore assumes that the ends critical reasoning will be worthy ones. One presumes that these ends are implicit in his defence of critical thinking, as he belongs to the liberal Enlightenment tradition. Here critical thinking, since Kant, is deemed to be a necessary part of the defence of democracy, with its ideals of liberty, equality and democratic citizenship. Though individual analytic philosophers may be disenchanted with economic rationalism, and favour progressive democratic politics this personal stance is undercut by reductive materialism's conception of the individual as a utility maximizing machine. As the individual is abstracted from social and power relations, language, culture, that is the whole set of practices that make agency possible, so the crucial question of how is democratic agency possible is precluded. Into this vacuum flows a historical concern with the technical design and utilitarian political blueprints for a well-ordered modernist society. Here human action, as a succession of impulses and responses to stimuli, needs to be well ordered, so that we can efficiently and mechanically function in the computerized Panopticon, controlled by those experts with access to natural and behavioural sciences. This 'Platonic' stance has been one of applying knowledge by social engineers in the name of social utility, to control the environment within the imperatives of survival. The scientist or economist supplies the knowledge needed for running, steering and managing the nation state. The tacit acceptance of the fact/value dichotomy means that normative inquiry is barred, and the technocrat accepts the values and goals of the bourgeois social order. The heavenly city of reductive materialism is one in which those who run the city in the name of truth reduce human beings to the level of a conditioned and behaviouring animal, and submerge human praxis into biology. There is no purposive behaviour here, as we merely have reactive, causally-induced behaviour and so a form of passivity, a predictable object and sheer biological existence, to which no cultural meaning is attached. It is the passive endurance of the dull habit of the everyday, punctuated by blind impulse within the economic machine, which the politicians keep ticking over to ensure economic growth. Harmony is achieved with the individual's goals tacitly coinciding with conventional habits within established cultural values and social role patterns, continual economic growth and the development of more tolerant attitudes. Since philosophy becomes the enemy of liberal democracy, and critical reasoning is used to enforce an undemocratic social order, Passmore needs to spell out the ethical/political ends of philosophy as critical thinking in relation to the real issues of politics, if he is to enhance the democratic citizenship inherent in the Enlightenment legacy.

In the debates about the legacy of the Enlightenment's collapse and ruination arise we need to learn to re-read the analytic tradition politically. We ragpickers read the analytic tradition politically. We have fought our way through the ranks from our roots in the working class to the inner heart of high bourgeois culture, and we still desire to further democratic socialism, after Marxism. We see serious analytic philosophers as having retreated from the everyday world to a world of the mathematical natural sciences, and so becoming segregated from the domain of the social and the political. Analytic theory has become divorced from practice, to the extent that it sees that our common everyday world akin to Plato's shadowy cave, whilst the sunlit exterior is the world of natural science, and that the rays of the sun do not penetrate the shadowy cave of human practice, which remains a place of dark shadows. The emphasis is on the spectator perspective, which looks at the closed system of the universe from the outside. Philosophy is the concern of the few against the many, and so becomes an esoteric philosophy cultivated behind closed doors, leaving the many to the prejudiced opinions on which an unenlightened society rests. The social domain becomes the preserve of the ignorant, robbed of insight, truth, and so social and political life becomes an uninteresting and ultimately meaningless venture. If the analytic philosopher is a pure spectator looking down on the city from above, then such a philosopher is the stranger in the chaos of everyday life. He is the stranger as cyborg who has split the reflective part of ourselves from the ordinary and the practical. As a form of scientific paternalism a legislating scientific philosophy results in the tyranny of form, presence, structure, rules and universality within a technocracy committed to cybernetics and genetic engineering. Those academics now acting in the hollowed-out role of a legislating modern philosophy bear the uneradicable traces of their situation and interests as organic intellectuals. They function as a nihilistic technocratic cadre who empower the dominion over the earth, subordinate the university to the market, operate according to procedures in management manuals, and accept the enforced internalization of managerial control mechanisms.

Analytic reason's collapse into a scientism entangled with power and interest, operates with a fundamental contradiction between a mathematical science on the one hand, and the desire for individual and political freedom on the other. The coercive managerial control mechanisms are being brought to bear on universities, because in order to train technocrats, academics must be made to conform to technocratic procedures through behavioural conditioning. This technocratic discourse, which provides tacit support for the hierarchical socio-economic system of late capitalism, is an esoteric discourse which distinguishes between those favoured few 'inside the know' and the great unwashed 'out of the know.' Its elitist scientific values and mode of existence, which have been codified into a formalized and institutionalized academicism, preserve the political and social order of class and rank. What it keeps hidden behind a meritocratic ethos, whose standards are continually broken in practice but rarely admitted, is the way the academic system is structured to sort and weed out the undesirables from entering the upper ranks of the social hierarchy, and to ensure the steady supply of underlabourers needed to support the noble master class of technocrats, and the weeding out of resentful, ragpicking socialists.

The transmission of the 'order of rank' is done subtly. The technocrats claim interest in the affairs of science, disinterest in the affairs of the state, and they endeavour to convince the unwashed masses that they have a voice in determining power—which they do have to a limited extent. But we unwashed do not have real power—and never will, if the technocratic elite can help it. That is the political education given to us by those 'disinterested' Enlightenment, mathematical technocrats, who believe they are opposing tyranny, when in promoting the wordly interest of technocratic elites, they are supporting the conceptual undergirding of the economic system. The rhetoric of freedom that is traditionally associated with science, loses its force once the subterranean link between science and domination is spotted and grasped. Given that philosophy was born in and through the polis, and was part of the same movement that brought about Greek democracy, then the end of philosophy means the end of freedom. It is the end of critical thinking on behalf of the democratic project for a substantive democratic citizenship.

We ragpickers make the death of philosophy an occasion for renewal of philosophy furthering democracy. From our post-Heideggerian perspective, the renewal of philosophy involves clinging to and sifting through the wreckage of the Enlightenment in the late twentieth century. It is a renewal which is grounded in a deep, socialized experience of our damaged life in the iron cage of late modernity, and the extreme difficulty of engaging in critical philosophical research as public intellectuals. Those who are still committed to a critical philosophy in a wrecked world, are faced with working in the negative mode: sorting through the wreckage, seeking to understand the past, and trying to figure out what went wrong. We are left with the mainly negative goal of salvaging something genuine and true from the wreckage of a broken-backed Enlightenment tradition, reduced to the pathos of instrumental reason economizing the world through its technocratic domination of nature. What is left of a critical philosophy as a critical self-reflective activity committed to human freedom, is located in the marginalized and stagnant backwaters of the devastated humanities. These, after their linguistic turn, have collapsed into dealing with an aesthetic mode of experience allied to literary texts. The postmodern humanities countered the turn to subjectivity, which accompanied the complex and contradictory changes of modernity, by subverting the dominance of the subject, through identifying the ways we are already located in a public language. However this turn has given rise to a one-dimensional view of subjectivity, as the effect of discourses or texts, we are located within. This trend in the literary institution corresponds to the exclusion of subjectivity by mathematical science and bureaucratic rationalization in the name of 'objectivity' to ensure increased control over nature.

The sources for renewal is that this objectivity and language depend upon the social subject's sensuous relationship to the world, namely those aspects of life that are identified as belonging particularly to historical human beings; rather than human beings conceived as simply natural objects, as servo-mechanisms, or as the effects of texts. A critical philosophy within the humanities opens up a space for the social, through recalling the way the whole range of bodily attributes and abilities (styles of walking, bike riding, cricket, swimming, dancing, sleeping, and spitting) are acquired through the direct inculcation and imitation of body techniques. These are neither rationally controlled by the mind, nor presented to it in the form of unconscious representations. These techniques fall within the sphere of social existence—the training of the young—not governed by those practices called epistemology or representing the world as knowledge. This social construction of the subject is the outcome of our training in routines of calculation, which are the outcome of the subject's habitus or mode of life, not subject to the procedures we call knowing.[87] Being a subject in the brute existence of the social institution of the market place means having mastered a particular conduct of life with a particular ethical self-cultivation. If, by human agency we mean different capacities for thought and action, then technologies of existence and conducts of life are going to be different for cricket and philosophy, even though both are the products of social institutions peculiar to the West. This opens up to a world of entities like families, households, clubs, universities, societies, states, nations, markets that are not included in the entities offered to us by physics and neuroscience, but which do seem to be necessary to inform human actions.

This returns philosophy to the city, from whence it banished itself for a modernist sojourn on the mountain top looking down on the world. Whilst there, it forgot about the historical relativity of its concepts , and thought that it could picture the world without any historical grounding in the social relations that characterized late modernity, as a specific moment in history. But the history was there, sedimented into its concepts, as analytic philosophy functioned as a defender of the existing social order, with philosophers acting as the agents of repression and censorship to ensure that this social order subsisted as though it were the only possible order. Philosophy's ideological illusions meant that it provided us with little to help us understand modernity and its discontents. By contrast Rorty's liberal distinction, between the private ironist desire for self-creation and autonomy and the public concern with minimizing cruelty, encouraging tolerance and community, works with a conception of the postmodern humanities which is explicitly concerned with human beings as political beings. It may well be that Rorty's underlabouring for a liberal democracy results in the banality of democracy as people becoming nicer to one another, and behaving in more tolerant ways. But it is no small achievement to have reconnected the humanities to human beings as political beings, who are able to conduct their practical life in terms of practical ethical reason linked to furthering democratic politics, with its insistence on dialogue and conversation.

The end of philosophy as the realization of freedom

We can make sense of the ambiguity of the death of philosophy in scientism, and its persistent after-life as a historicist practical reflexivity, by turning back to Hegel's link of philosophy with freedom. The end of philosophy in history for Hegel is the self-actualization of human freedom in modernity. This happens when a free people, whose individuality is fully developed and acknowledged by right, choose to devote themselves to a universal or collective end which they acknowledge as the foundation of their individual worth. This recovers the Greek solidarity of philosophy with democracy. Here both are, in the words of Castoriadas, 'expressions, and central embodiments, of the project of autonomy.'[88] Philosophy is self-reflective activity at the level of thought, whilst democracy is self-reflective activity at the level of self-government. This gives rise to a conception of the philosopher-citizen embodied in Socrates. With the fall of democracy in Greece, the philosopher, with Plato, ceases to be a citizen. Here the philosopher gets out of, or above the polis, and tells the people what to do, deriving it from his own episteme. He searches for a unitary ontology and tries to derive from this fundamental ontology the ideal polity. It is this Platonism which has dominated the mainstream history of philosophy.[89]

A marginalized critical philosophy, concerned with human freedom and aligned with the humanities rather than the natural sciences, does look seedy and threadbare. But this is because the abstract character of philosophical work is rooted in social conditions of existence in capitalism. Despite its crippled condition, there is still a rational and critical potential in philosophy, as Passmore is so right to highlight. It can use this potential to cast a critical ironic eye over the way technocratic capitalism denies the conditions for human self-actualization. There is nothing *necessarily* democratic about the economic liberal state. Australia is still a repressive class society riven by contradictions, and its utopian potential is denied by the existence of increasing poverty, because of the unequal class-based distribution of wealth and productive forces, which the liberal state is concerned to uphold. This requires the bourgeoisie to use and to tolerate repression to ensure their self-preservation as a class. But the increased use of overt repression by the state only exacerbates its legitimation crisis, because the values of the Enlightenment—universal freedom, universal self-determination and the linking of utopia to universal reason—do not give the bourgeoisie's domination reliable service. They continually turn against this domination and repression. Given the emancipatory potential which still exists in capitalism, the bourgeoisie need to find a way to legitimate their objectively obsolete rule. They do so both through science, making the social relations of domination natural, sovereign, and acceptable, and also through a culture industry, that manipulates whatever desires, bonds and obligations prove appropriate to us, putting up with what is offered.

A renewed philosophy orientated to the postmodern humanities opens up the possibilities for philosophy to defend the necessity to criticise the way things are. Though this is a very minimal after-life, it does provide a space for a retrospective reflection on the way that a modernist analytic philosophy has retreated into itself to protect its purity, and also to affirm a bad reality which denies human freedom as democratic self-determination. Philosophy as a self-reflective activity reflects on the way a reified analytic philosophy, concerned with order, system, universality, technical questions and a formal language, has failed to come to grips with the loss of freedom, meaning and respect for human life and non-human life. It recalls analytic philosophy's historical refusal to interpret the genuine expressions of our suffering in society gone badly wrong, its capitulation to reified economic forces outside our control, and its failure to face the contradictions and disintegration of society in modernity. Philosophy's after-life is sustained by the need to criticize its complicity with the bourgeois social order, so as to realize a more substantive freedom than the one available for the unemployed and the impoverished working class. As their future is bleak, since economic growth will not improve their material conditions of life by much before the year 2000, we can, contra Rorty, work the rich vein of Nietzsche, Heidegger and Foucault, to counter the liberal conception of possessive individualism, its conception of freedom as negative liberty, and its slippery slope into a behaviouristic disciplining of the subject.

Criticism of philosophy, Adorno argues, 'is not a plea for disappearance of philosophy as such, or even for its replacement by a single discipline, social science, for instance.'[90] Philosophy's survival, after its failure to redeem the promise of the Enlightenment, mirrors the premature death of those victims of history who carried civilization on their backs. We must face up to the fact that analytic philosophy colluded in these very deaths, through its own failure to engage in a critique of the bourgeois social order. We ragpickers feel in our bones that Rorty's postmodern philosophy has misread its cure to ask why the world, which could have been paradise on Earth, has become a global supermarket with citizens sunk in unhappiness, nihilism and anxiety. Though a conservative analytic philosophy has failed to engage in a critique of the present, and though its distorted reified analytic form does reconcile us to the unfreedom of the bourgeois social order, the kernel of critical thinking residing inside this reified form means that philosophy remains the crippled carrier of the broken promise of a deformed Enlightenment. In the face of this affirmation, philosophy can only eke out its existence by virtue of the injustice of the world. Insofar as an authentic culture grounded on critical thinking can exist in the administered world of capitalism, it can only be one of protest.[91] This involves a coming to terms with the past through working through it, as one does in psychoanalysis, because the past has a latent hold on our ways of being and acting in the absence of a viable public intellectual culture, because of the hollowing out of critical thinking.

The situation today is a tragic one for philosopher-citizens, as our relation to the past is poisoned. The decisive gesture is that the past is no longer acceptable, and must be dismantled. It stands in the way of the political emancipation of the oppressed. This poison is mediated by our being educated as philosophers in the analytic tradition. We must bear the weight of the ugly history of reason's relapse, even as we refuse to reconcile ourselves with what is, and as we remember those victims who have picked up the tab for the progress of bourgeois civilisation.[92] We need to bear the full force and pressure of this history, to remind ourselves constantly that we are not outside the boundaries of analytic philosophy. So we need to make explicit the overall picture of physicalism, interpret its social meaning, decipher its social text, identify its desire to appropriate and conquer, subject it to rational critique and think through the real political meaning of confronting our philosophical past. Analytic philosophy's failure to engage with the suffering and pain of unfreedom suggests we need to cultivate a systematic distrust of this philosophy, rather than go limp under its weight. We need to prise open the door it has closed on what was to have been the future for generations now dead or silenced, rather than accept that the accounts have been closed. We need to rethink the future, rather than accept analytic philosophy's claim that a physicalist form of philosophical naturalism is the final word on the nature of things.

A melancholy green philosophy reflects on the Enlightenment having seen better days. Though effectively shunted aside by analytic philosophy as romantic nonsense, it functions to recover what has lapsed in our culture, and so represents the unthought within Western philosophy. It can expose the illusory shadows an affirmative philosophy casts, identify the worthwhile from the regressive features in our heritage, recover what has been lost and forgotten by instrumental reason, and link these traces to human suffering and the promise of a better world. Philosophy is concerned with the truth content of philosophical categories and these, as Marcuse argues, point beyond and transcend existing society, and thus cannot be reduced to it.[93] A humanist eco-philosophy functioning as cultural criticism, sorting through the wreckage of the analytic tradition, is like a ragpicker who is in revolt against society, and who lives a precarious existence.[94] Like the ragpicker facing the sewer, it looks for the bits that can be salvaged from the havoc unleashed by the mechanist economic Enlightenment. As a rebellion against a reductionist materialist philosophy, it escapes the latter's shadow by transforming itself by taking a socio-historical turn. In doing so it becomes different forms of socio-historical analysis carried out with the practical intent of gaining critical distance from those traditions that inform our lives.

This romantically informed overcoming of metaphysics counters the growing dogmatism of a scientific Enlightenment that has wandered into nihilism, only to remain there. Nihilism, understood in Nietzsche's sense as the devaluation of our highest values, and in Heidegger's sense of being at the end in which there is nothing left, once stood at the door of modernity. It now lies deep within it. The physicalist philosophical naturalism defended by Smart and Quine, with its naturalist reduction of objective value to individual desire, means that if physics and neuroscience cannot value human life, then clinging to the true world of natural science gives us an incomplete or partial nihilism, which effectively undermines or devalues the realm of authority of the highest values associated with an enlightening natural science. This metaphysics underpins the scientism that reduces the social sciences to a neo-classical economics, which posits the structure of value as the will to power of utility machines to master nature, to further their subjective desire. Here in this discourse the previous goals and values of society have been dissolved, as all that exists is raw material for the unfettered pursuit of profit or consumption. Things are valuable only in so far as they are posited as being of use to utility machines in market terms. There are just these objects, which are law-governed, and subject to manipulation and control by consumers, who conduct themselves rationally by following the norms and rules of the cultural sphere of the market to further their desires. Growth becomes a self-referential process with all obstacles to growth needing to be removed. More growth is positive, lack of growth is negative, with growth being infinite and without end. The machine just keeps ticking over.

The ragpickers construe romanticism as a defensive form of opposition, which emphasizes the web of meaning or significance against a meaning depleting scientific Enlightenment. It asks: growth for what purpose? Growth for what end? It places a democratic political project on the table which imagines the future very differently from the technocratic one inherent in reductive materialism. Such a critical theory of the present asks Rousseau's question about the goodness or badness of civilization in modernity. If the proper end of philosophy is the realization of human freedom, and philosophy functions in our public culture as a form of critical thinking to realize that freedom, then the ragpickers post-analytic philosophy has its critical purchase based on its reference to substantive values of the good life that transcends capitalism. If the end of philosophy is the actualization of concrete freedom as self-actualization of human beings, then the aim of a greened philosophy is to replace current social arrangements with those that are more ecologically sustainable. As the voice of a critical Socratic reason it is concerned to help those suffering human beings who aim to live a human life well, and who have a sense of identity as citizens in a nation state concerned to bring about the ecological good life. From this perspective, as things now stand, analytic philosophy represents the bourgeoisie's triumph over its victims, and is a part of the discourse of an analytic reason that speaks as an appeasing tradition, which is an officially sanctioned reconciliation with what is. At the end of analytic philosophy, a romantic philosophy searches for ways to articulate what cannot be said within the discourse of analytic reason. It critically looks at the ethical and political basis of the newly forming postmodern humanities opened up by Rorty or Derrida.[95] It explores the possibilities opened up for philosophers to act as public intellectuals in everyday life.

Notes and References

1   The debate is canvassed in K. Baynes, J. Boyman, & T. McCarthy, (ed.), *After Philosophy End or Transformation?* (MIT Press, Cambridge, Massachusetts, 1993).

2   Peter Dickens, *Society and Nature: Towards a Green Social Theory*, (Harvester Wheatsheaf, Hemel Hempstead, 1992), p. xv.

3   We have in mind Alvin Goldman, *Epistemology and Cognition*, (Harvard University Press, Cambridge, Massachusetts, 1986).

4   For an account of Rorty, refer to, David L. Hall, *Richard Rorty: Prophet and Poet of the New Pragmatism*, (State University of New York Press, Albany, 1994).

5   A challenge to this interpretation in the secondary literature on Wittgenstein is made by Hilary Putnam, *Words and Things*, (Harvard University Press, Cambridge, Massachusetts, 1994); & *Pragmatism: An Open Question*, (Blackwell, Oxford, 1995).

6   Ludwig Wittgenstein, *Philosophical Investigations*, trs. G. E. M. Anscombe, (Blackwell, Oxford, 1958), para. 255, p. 91, & para. 309, p. 93.

7   M. Heidegger, "The Age of the World Picture", in Heidegger, *The Question Concerning Technology amd Other Essays*, trs. William Lovitt, (Harper and Row, New York, 1977).

8   Hilary Putnam, *Renewing Philosophy*, (Harvard University Press, Cambridge, Massachusetts, 1992), p. 156.

9   D. Hiley, *Philosophy in Question: Essays on a Pyrrhonian Theme*, (Chicago University Press, Chicago, 1988), p. 2.

10   J. Derrida, "Of an Apocalyptical Tone Recently Adopted in Philosophy", in *Semeia*, XX111, (1982), pp. 63-97.

11   J. Derrida, *Positions*, trs. Alan Bass, (University of Chicago Press, Chicago, 1981), p. 6.

12   J. Derrida with Geoff Bennington, "On Colleges and philosophy," in *ICA Documents*, 4 & 5, (1986), pp. 66-71.

13   R. Rorty, "Deconstruction and Circumvention," in R. Rorty, *Essays on Heidegger and Others, Philosophical Papers*, vol. 2, (Cambridge University Press, Cambridge, 1991), pp. 85-106, gives an account of two forms of deconstruction-philosophical and literary.

14   R. Gasché, *The Tain of the Mirror: Derrida and the Philosophy of Reflection*, (Harvard University Press, Cambridge, Massachusetts, 1986).

15   Heidegger remarks: 'Refutation belongs among those petty intellectual entertainments which the public needs for its amusement.' M. Heidegger, *Nietzsche*, vol. 2, trs. D. F. Krell, (Harper, San Fransisco, 1984), p. 229.

16   R. Rorty, "Professionalized Philosophy and Transcendentalist Culture", in Richard Rorty, *The Consequences of Pragmatism: Essays 1972-1980*, (University of Minnesota Press, Minneapolis 1982), pp. 60-71.

17   Richard Rorty, "Habermas and Lyotard, on Postmodernity", in *Essays on Heidegger and Others*, op. cit, pp. 164-176, especially p. 170.

18   Richard Rorty, "Philosophy in America Today", in *The Consequences of Pragmatism*, op. cit., pp. 211-230.

19   Kai Nielsen, *After the Demise of the Tradition: Rorty, Critical Theory and the Fate of Philosophy*, (Westview Press, Boulder, 1991).

20   J. Couture and K. Nielsen, "On Construing Philosophy", in *Canadian Journal of Philosophy*, Supplementary Volume, *Metaphilosophy: Reconstructing Philosophy?*, (ed.), Couture and Nielsen, 1993, pp. 1-55, citation pp. 52-53.

21   See P. Gross & N. Levitt, *The Higher Superstition: The Academic Left and Its Quarrel with Science*, (John Hopkins UniversityPress, Baltimore, 1994); & Andrew Ross, (ed.), *Science Wars*, (Duke University Press, Durham, NC, 1996).

22   This view is judged to be entirely justified. R. Rorty, *Philosophy and the Mirror of Nature*, (Princeton University Press, Princeton, 1979), pp. 335ff.

23   Richard Rorty, "Introduction", in *Essays of Heidegger and Others*, op. cit., pp. 1-2.

24   Richard Rorty, "Nineteenth Century Idealism and Twentieth Century Textualism", in *The Consequences of Pragmatism*, op. cit., pp. 139-159.

25   Richard Rorty, "Introduction", in *Essays of Heidegger and Others*, op. cit., pp. 5-6.

26   For an alternative postmodernism which emphases nihilism, refer to, Gianno Vattimo, *The End of Modernity: Nihilism and Hermeneutics in Postmodern Culture*, trs. J. R. Synder, (John Hopkins, University Press, Baltimore, 1988).

27   R. Rorty, *Contingency, Irony, and Solidarity*, (Cambridge University Press, Cambridge, 1989), p. xv.

28   Ibid, p. 198.

29   John Passmore, "The End of Philosophy?", *Australasian Journal of Philosophy*, vol. 74, no. 1, (March 1996), pp. 1-19, citation p. 3.

30   Ibid, p. 19.

31   Ibid, p. 14.

32   M. Heidegger, "The End of Philosophy and the Task of Thinking", in *Basic Writings*, trs. David Farrell Krell, (Routledge and Kegan Paul, London, 1978), pp. 373-392

33   Ibid, p. 375.

34   Ibid, pp. 376-7.

35   See H. L. Dreyfus, *Being-in-the-World: A Commentary on Heidegger's Being and Time*, (MIT Press, Cambridge, Massachusetts, 1991).

36   Hans-Georg Gadamer, "Hegel and Heidegger," in *Hegel's Dialectic Five Hermeneutical Studies*, trs. P. Christopher Smith, (Yale University Press, New Haven, 1976), p. 100.

37   See for instance, Hilary Putnam, *Representation and Reality,*, (Harvard University Press, Cambridge, Massachusetts, 1989); & *Realism with a Human Face*, (ed.) James Conant, (Harvard University Press, Cambridge, Massachusetts, 1990).

38   S. Rosen, *The Ancients and the Moderns. Rethinking Modernity*, (Yale University Press, New Haven 1989), pp. 118-159, citation p. 159.

39   One could of course dismiss Rorty's *Contingency. Irony and Solidarity* as belonging to the genre of literary criticism and so is not philosophy. But this pre-judges the whole issue.

40   John Passmore, "The End of Philosophy?", op. cit, p. 10.

41   G. W. F. Hegel, "Preface", *The Philosophy of Right*, trs. T. M. Knox, (Oxford University Press, Oxford, 1952), pp. 11-13.

42   G. W. F. Hegel, "The Position of Art Relatively to Finite Reality, Religion and Philosophy", in Hegel, *Aesthetics*, trs. T. M. Knox, (Oxford University Press, Oxford, 1975), vol. 1. pp. 125-44.

43   For a fuller development of this refer to David Roberts, *Art and Enlightenment. Aesthetic Theory after Adorno*, (University of Nebraska Press, Lincoln, 1991).

44   T. Adorno, *Negative Dialectics*, trs. H. B. Ashton, (Continuum, New York, 1987), p. 3.

45   Max Horkheimer's argument in *The Eclipse of Reason*, (Seabury Press, New York, 1974) held that there was a transformation of reason concerned with the ends of humanity to an instrumental reason in modernity concerned with efficient means to pre-given ends.

46   Lukács reads Hegel as ending up in the mystified form of a world spirit and so Hegel's philosophy is driven inexorably into the arms of mythology. G. Lukács, *History and Class Consciousness: Studies in Marxist Dialectics*, trs. R. Livingston, (Merlin Press, London, 1971), p. 147.

47   The characteristics of the philosophy of knowledge are fully described in Nicholas Maxwell, *From Knowledge to Wisdom: A Revolution in the Aims and Methods of Science*, (Blackwell, Oxford, 1987), pp. 10-46.

48   For the discontent in economics, refer to, Donald McCloskey, *Knowledge and Persuasion in Economics*, (Cambridge University Press, Cambridge, 1994).

49   Hilary Putnam, *Renewing Philosophy*, (Harvard University Press, Cambridge, Massachusetts, 1992), p. 2.

50   Ibid, pp. 141 & 197.

51   Hilary Putnam, *Realism with a Human Face*, op. cit., p. 51.

52   Hilary Putnam, *Pragmatism*, op. cit.

53   Joseph Wayne Smith, *Reason, Science and Paradox: Against Received Opinion in Science and Philosophy*, (Croom Helm, London, 1986), pp. 2-3.

54   J. Wayne Smith, *Aids, Philosophy and Beyond*, (Averbury, Aldershot, 1991), pp. 53-65.

55   Joseph Wayne Smith, *The High Tech Fix*, (Averbury, Aldershot, 1991).

56   Graham Lyons, Evonne Moore, Joseph Wayne Smith, *Is the End Nigh? Internationalism, global chaos, and the destruction of the earth*, (Avebury, Aldershot, 1995).

57   For a late statement of the crisis, refer to, Edmund Husserl, *The Crisis of European Sciences and Transcendental Phenomenology*, trs. David Carr, (NorthWestern University Press, Evanston, 1970). Early Heidegger follows Husserl very closely here. Refer Heidegger, *History of the Concept of Time: Prolegomena*, trs. T. Keisel, (University of Indiana Press, Bloomington, 1985), pp. 1-2; Heidegger, *Being and Time*, op. cit., pp. 20-30.

58   Heidegger's critique of Husserl has to do with the latter's subjective turn to overcome objectivism. Heidegger holds that this results in phenomenology becoming entangled in the crisis rather than resolving it by seeking a more primordial ground.

59   For a discussion of the problem of closure, refer to, Simon Critchley, *The Ethics of Deconstruction*, (Blackwell, Oxford, 1992), pp. 59-106.

60   The end of tradition and the new beginning can be seen in Gary Sauer-Thompson and Joseph Wayne Smith, *Beyond Economics*, (Avebury, Aldershot, 1996).

61   Val Plumwood, *Feminism and the Mastery of Nature*, (Routledge, London, 1993).

62   M. Gatens, *Feminism and Philosophy: Perspectives on Difference and Equality*, (Polity Press, Oxford, 1991), p. 2.

63   E. Grosz, "Bodies and Knowledges: Feminism and the Crisis of Reason", in L. Alcoff and E. Potter, (eds.), *Feminist Epistemologies*, (Routledge, London, 1994), pp. 187-216.

64   The different positions in the debate include Carol Gould and Marx Wartofsky, *Women and Philosophy: Towards a Theory of Liberation*, (G. P. Putnam, New York, 1976); Mary Daley, *Pure Lust: elemental feminist philosophy*, (Beacon Press, Boston, 1984); Rosi Braidotti, *Patterns of Dissonance*, (Polity Press, Cambridge, 1991).

65   A women philosopher working within the analytic tradition on the problems of feminism is Janet Radcliffe Richards, *The Sceptical Feminist: A Philosophical Inquiry*, (Penguin, Harmondsworth, 1982).

66   This is explored in Genevieve Lloyd, *The Man of Reason: 'Male' and 'Female' in Western Philosophy*, (Metheun, London, 1984); Moira Gatens, *Feminism and Philosophy*, op. cit.

67   Liz Grosz, "Philosophy," in Sneja Gunew, (ed.), *Feminist Knowledge Critique and Construct*, (Routledge, London, 1990), pp. 147-174.

68   For sedimentation, refer to, E. Husserl, *The Crisis of European Sciences and Transcendental Phenomenology*, op. cit., p. 52; T. Adorno, *Hegel: Three Studies*, trs., S. H. Weber, (MIT Press, Cambridge, Massachusetts, 1993).

69   See for example his response to Heidegger's reading of Nietzsche in and Foucault's reading of Descartes in "Cogito and the History of Madness", in Derrida, *Writing and Difference*, trs. Alan Bass, (Routledge, London,1978).

70   J. C. C. Smart, *Between Science and Philosophy*, (Random House, New York, 1968).

71   J. C. C. Smart, "The Content of Physicalism", *Philosophical Quarterly*, vol. 28, (1978), pp. 339-341.

251

72   For the background to this, refer to Justin Webb, *Mechanism, Materialism, and Metamathematics*, (D. Reidel, Dordrecht, 1980).
73   W. O. V. Quine, "Has Philosophy Lost Contact with the People?", in *Theories and Things*, (Harvard University Press, Cambridge Massacusetts, 1981), p. 191. Also *Word and Object*, (MIT Press, Cambridge Massachussetts, 1960), pp. 3 & 275-6.
74   D. Papineau, *Philosophical Naturalism*, (Blackwell, Oxford, 1993), p. 3.
75   J. Austin, *Philosophical Papers*, (Clarendon Press, Oxford, 1961), p. 180.
76   John Dewey, *Reconstruction in Philosophy*, 2nd edition, (Beacon Press, Boston, 1948), pp. 124-126.
77   Hilary Putnam, *Renewing Philosophy*, op. cit., p. x.
78   Taking science on trust is held by B. Fine, *The Shakey Game*, (University of Chicago Press, Chicago, 1986), p. 171.
79   For the debate about philosophy with repect to epistemology naturalized, refer to H. Kornblith, *Naturalizing Epistemology*, (MIT Press, Camb.,Mass. 1985); A. Shimony and D. Nails, (eds.), *Naturalised Epistemology*, (Reidel, Doerdrecht, 1987); T. Sorrell, *Scientism: Philosophy and the Infatuation with Science*, (Routledge, London, 1991).
80   W. O. V. Quine, "Epistemology Naturalized", in *Ontological Relativity and Other Essays*, (Columbia University Press, New York, 1969), pp. 69-90.
81   P. Churchland, *Neurophilosophy*, (MIT Press, Cambridge, Massachusetts, 1986); & "Epistemology in the Age of Neuroscience", *Journal of Philosophy*, No. 84, (1987), pp. 553-5.
82   P. Churchland, *Neurophilosophy*, op. cit., p. 299.
83   Patricia Churchland, "Epistemology in the Age of Neuroscience", op. cit., p. 546.
84   Daniel Dennett, *Consciousness Explained*, (Little, Brown and Co, Boston, 1991), p. 40.
85   Richard Rorty quoted by Chantal Mouffe, "Deconstruction, Pragmatism, and the Politics of Democracy", in C. Mouffe, (ed.), *Deconstruction and Pragmatism*, (Routledge, London, 1996), pp.1-12, citation, p. 5.
86   Max Horkheimer, *The Eclipse of Reason*, (Seabury Press, New York, 1974).
87   Marcel Mauss, "Techniques of the body", *Economy and Society*, No. 2, (1973), pp. 70-87.
88   Cornelius Castoriadis, "The "End of Philosophy", in *Philosophy, Politics, Autonomy*, (ed.), D. M. Curtis, (Oxford University Press, Oxford, 1991), pp. 13-32, citation p. 21.
89   Ibid, pp. 22-3.
90   Theodore Adorno, "Why Philosophy?', in *Critical Theory: The Essential Eeadings*, (ed.) David Ingram & Julia Simon- Ingram, (Paragon House, New York, 1992), p. 20.
91   Theodore Adorno, "Cultural Criticism and Society", in *Prisms*, trs. Samuel and Shierry Weber, (MIT Press, Camb,. Mass., 1982), pp. 17-34.
92   Adorno, *Aesthetic Theory*, (Routledge and Kegan Paul, London, 1984), p. 72.
93   Herbert Marcuse, "Philosophy and Critical theory" in *Critical Theory: The Essential Eeadings*, op. cit, p. 13.
94   For the ragpicker, refer to Walter Benjamin, *Charles Baudelaire: A Lyric Poet In The Era of High Capitalism*, (Verso, London, 1973), p. 20; and "The Destructive Character", in *Reflections: Essays, Aphorisms, Autobiographical Writings*, (ed.), Peter Demetz, trs, Edmund Jephcott, (Harcourt Brace Jovanovich, 1978), pp. 300-1.
95   The thesis that deconstruction is marginal to politics is held by R. Rorty "Is Derrida a Transcendental Philosopher?", in Richard Rorty, *Essays on Heidegger and Others. Philosophical Papers Volume 2*, op. cit; & T. McCarthy, *Ideals and Illusions*, (MIT Press, Cambridge, Massachusetts, 1991).

Index